LIBRARY IN A BOOK

ANIMAL RIGHTS

Lisa Yount

Ⓜ®
Facts On File, Inc.

ANIMAL RIGHTS

Facts On File, Inc.
132 West 31st Street
New York NY 10001

Library of Congress Cataloging-in-Publication Data
Yount, Lisa.
    Animal rights / Lisa Yount.
    p. cm.—(Library in a book)
Includes bibliographical references and index.
    ISBN 0-8160-5027-9
    1. Animal rights. I. Title. II. Series.
HV4708.Y84 2004
179′.3—dc22   2003017507

Facts On File books are available at special discounts when purchased in bulk quantities for businesses, associations, institutions, or sales promotions. Please call our Special Sales Department in New York at (212) 967-8800 or (800) 322-8755.

You can find Facts On File on the World Wide Web at http://www.factsonfile.com

Text design by Ron Monteleone
Graphs by Patricia Meschino

Printed in the United States of America

MP Hermitage 10 9 8 7 6 5 4 3 2 1

This book is printed on acid-free paper.

To Frodo, Leo, Bertha, Midnight Louise, and Mira
and in memory of Mary, Frodo I, Panzer, Richard,
and King Kong, beloved companions all

CONTENTS

PART III
APPENDICES

PART I

OVERVIEW OF THE TOPIC

CHAPTER 1

ISSUES IN ANIMAL WELFARE AND ANIMAL RIGHTS

It has been hailed as "the civil rights movement of the twenty-first century."[1] It has been criticized as the domain of sentimental cranks, wild-eyed terrorists, or simply spoiled city people with no real understanding of nature. Whether praised or damned, the quest for better treatment of animals—even perhaps extending to granting them some form of legal rights—has already made significant changes in Western society and law, and it may well make more profound ones in the decades to come.

Humans have always had a close but complex, even what animal rightist attorney Gary Francione calls "schizophrenic," relationship with other species. On one hand, the myths of most cultures show ancestors, spirits, or even gods in animal form and describe animals as worthy of respect and sometimes awe. People have valued domesticated animals as working partners and companions for thousands of years. At the same time, humans throughout history have killed animals to obtain food and clothing, bought and sold them as property, and exterminated them as vermin.

Although theologians and philosophers occasionally discussed human responsibilities to the "brute creation," systematic attempts to change or legislate people's treatment of animals arose only in the 19th century. Ironically, and perhaps tellingly, as several historians of the animal protection movement have pointed out, these efforts came mainly from the group whom the Industrial Revolution had separated most completely from daily contact with animals (except pets and some working animals): the upper classes in the cities of Europe and America. These early crusades, which focused on cruelty to horses and other working animals and on the use of animals in scientific experiments, produced the first organizations and the first laws aimed at protecting animals from mistreatment.

By the end of the century, however, social concern for animals was waning. It remained in the background until shortly after World War II, when

3

an upsurge in the use of animals, particularly in farming and medical research, raised new issues and spurred the formation of new organizations. Then, in 1975, Australian philosopher Peter Singer published a book called *Animal Liberation*, which inspired some members of the ongoing crusade for animal welfare to spawn a new social movement with different goals: the movement for animal liberation (as Singer called it) or animal rights. Most animal welfarists had focused on caring for homeless animals and trying to prevent "unnecessary" cruelty, leaving unquestioned the morality of confining or killing animals for socially accepted purposes such as the production of meat. Singer and his followers, however, boldly asked whether humans had a right to hurt or kill animals for any reason.

During the rest of the 20th century, the animal rights movement, along with the broader-based and more moderate animal welfare movement from which it sprang, used a variety of attention-getting and frequently controversial methods to produce major changes in public (and, to a lesser extent, legislative and judicial) thinking about the treatment of companion animals, wildlife, and animals in agriculture, science, and entertainment. It made many people examine, often for the first time, the morality of their relationship to animals as a whole.

THE PHILOSOPHY OF ANIMAL RIGHTS

In the King James Version, Genesis, the first book of the Bible, states that God told the first humans, "Be fruitful, and multiply, and replenish the earth, and subdue it: and have dominion over the fish of the sea, and over the fowl of the air, and over every living thing that moveth upon the earth."[2] In general, the Judeo-Christian tradition taught that, although "brute beasts" should be treated gently and respected as part of God's creation, they were made for humans to use.

Thirteenth-century theologian and philosopher Thomas Aquinas, echoing ideas found in ancient Greek and Roman writings, stated that animals deserve no consideration in themselves because they lack reason. The Bible prohibited cruelty to animals, Aquinas said, only "lest through being cruel to other animals one becomes cruel to human beings."[3] French philosopher René Descartes expanded on Aquinas's view in the early 1600s by saying that animals were essentially living machines. He maintained that they could not really suffer because they did not possess reason, soul, or feeling. The cries they made when scientists operated on them, he said, had no more significance than the squealing of ungreased machine parts. Some thinkers in the second half of the 18th century began to question this picture of animals, however. In 1789, British philosopher Jeremy Bentham wrote, "The question is not, Can [animals] *reason?* nor, Can they *talk?* but, Can they *suffer?*[4] He even speculated that "the day may come when the rest of the animal creation may acquire those rights which never could have been withholden from them but by the hand of tyranny."[5]

Philosophical consideration of the nature, purpose, and value of animals, as well as of the nature of rights and their possessors, is at the heart of the modern animal rights movement. Indeed, Richard Ryder, a philosopher himself, has written that "animal liberation is possibly unique among liberation movements in the extent to which it has been led and inspired by professional philosophers."[6] Many of these philosophers' (and their opponents') discussions center on abstract, often dauntingly abstruse, questions such as "What are rights?," "What are the requirements for having rights?," and "If two rights conflict, how does one decide which is the more important?" No one has answered these questions definitively in regard to human beings, so it is certainly no surprise that they provoke disagreement when applied to animals.

PETER SINGER

Peter Singer's 1975 book, *Animal Liberation*, has been repeatedly called "the Bible of the animal rights movement." Nonetheless, Singer did not use the term *animal rights* in the book except, as he puts it, as a "convenient political shorthand," and he felt that "in the argument for a radical change in our attitude to animals, [this term] is in no way necessary."[7] Furthermore, unlike Tom Regan and some later writers in the movement, Singer does not demand (or at least does not expect) that all human uses of animals be abolished. His book chiefly urges people to expand their range of moral concerns to include animals. He says that humans should stop discriminating against animals simply because animals are not members of the human species.

Singer is a utilitarian, a follower of Jeremy Bentham and other philosophers who hold that the goal of all sentient beings—those who can feel pleasure and pain—is to maximize pleasure and minimize pain. Because animals (mammals, at least) can feel pleasure and pain, Singer says, they are sentient beings and therefore have an interest in avoiding pain and achieving pleasure that humans should respect. "Pain is pain," he writes, "and the importance of preventing unnecessary pain and suffering does not diminish because the being that suffers is not a member of our own species."[8]

As a utilitarian, Singer calculates value in terms of the total amount of pleasure and pain resulting from an action. This way of thinking permits causing pain to a few if it brings pleasure or cessation of pain to a far greater number. Singer therefore grants that using animals in medical research can be considered moral if the research can be done in no other way and is likely to save many human lives, because the good that will probably result from the research outweighs the harm done to the animals. Using animals for meat or to test cosmetics, on the other hand, is not moral because the good resulting from those uses is relatively slight and can be achieved in other ways.

Singer sees animals as having inherent value, or value in themselves, not merely as means to human ends. Nonetheless, he does not say that all animals should have the same rights or that any animals should have all the rights granted to humans. A living thing's level of inherent value depends on its level of sentience, he believes, and he admits that normal adult humans can suffer in ways that animals cannot—by imagining future pain, for example. Such humans therefore have a greater value than other animals. He maintains, however, that animals should be treated the same as humans who have a capacity for suffering similar to their own, such as people with severe brain damage or human babies. He has said that no experiment is right to perform on an animal that would be wrong to perform on a three-year-old human child.

Valuing humans more highly than other creatures simply because they are human is what Singer calls speciesism. (Richard Ryder coined this term in 1970, but Singer adopted it, and it is often associated with him.) He equates speciesism with racism and sexism, saying that neither race, gender, nor species is a justifiable reason for discrimination. He compares human use of animals to slavery and the animal liberation movement, as he terms it, to 19th-century crusades to free African slaves.

TOM REGAN

Another philosopher, Tom Regan of North Carolina State University, went beyond Singer's ideas in a 1984 book, *The Case for Animal Rights*. This book defines many beliefs of the animal rights movement's more radical wing.

Unlike Singer, Regan explicitly uses the term *rights* in connection with animals. Furthermore, eschewing Singer's pragmatic or utilitarian notions, Regan states that all human uses of animals that cause suffering are morally wrong and should be abolished, no matter how much benefit they might bring to humans. He writes, "It is not larger, cleaner cages that justice demands in the case of animals used in science, but empty cages; not traditional animal agriculture, but a complete end to all commerce in the flesh of dead animals."[9]

Regan sees animals—mammals, at least—as "subjects of a life," meaning that they are conscious beings with some concept of self-identity and of goals that they wish to pursue. He goes further than Singer by stating that animals' inherent value, and, therefore, their moral standing, is the same as that of humans. Because animals and humans have the same inherent value, Regan believes that they are entitled to the same basic rights, including rights to life, bodily integrity, and respectful treatment. Unlike many philosophers, he does not feel that they need to be able to understand these rights in order to possess them. Some animal rights activists have carried Regan's line of thinking to striking—some would say shocking—extremes, as when Michael Fox, currently a senior scholar in bioethics with the Humane Society of the United States, said, "The life of an ant and the life of my child should be granted equal consideration."[10]

EVALUATING ANIMALS

One area of major disagreement between animal rights philosophers such as Singer and Regan and their critics concerns the criteria for having rights and the evaluation of whether any animals—and, if so, which ones—meet those criteria. Interpretation of scientific data as well as philosophical terminology is involved in these discussions. Common criteria for having rights include the ability to reason and understand abstract concepts, the ability to distinguish between right and wrong, the ability to use language, and possession of some concept of self.

Whatever Descartes may have thought, few modern observers would deny that birds and mammals, at least, and possibly all animals with a central nervous system, can feel physical pain. When treated in ways that humans would call painful, they show the same behaviors that people in pain do: they cry out, writhe and make facial contortions, avoid the painful stimulus if they can, and so on. Thus, they are clearly sentient beings in the sense that Singer used the term. Whether they can also "suffer" in the way that humans do is more debatable. Most people familiar with mammals, such as cats, dogs, and horses, have observed behavior suggesting that these animals experience emotions that go beyond immediate physical needs and that they can remember, predict, and learn. However, critics such as Michael P. T. Leahy, senior lecturer in philosophy at the University of Kent in Britain, say that people's own emotions often lead them to anthropomorphize, or ascribe human mental processes to, animals and that there is no real way to know what mental experiences animals have.

The intellectual powers of animals, especially of great apes (chimpanzees, bonobos, gorillas, and orangutans), relative to those of humans are just as hard to evaluate. Animal rights supporters point to behavioral studies that appear to break down most, if not all, of the distinctions usually made between the intellects of humans and apes. For instance, primatologist Jane Goodall observed chimpanzees in Africa not only using but making tools. Other researchers have taught chimpanzees, gorillas, and bonobos

to communicate with humans through sign language or computer key-
boards. Some of these scientists report that the animals produced novel
signs, such as combining the signs for *water* and *bird* to indicate a swan, and
that they demonstrated some understanding of syntax (grammar and word
order). Chimpanzees have also demonstrated the ability to recognize themselves in a mirror, which has been held to indicate that these apes have some
concept of themselves as unique beings. Animal behaviorist Frans de Waal,
for one, claims that apes can transmit cultural knowledge. Because apes
seem to have intellectual capacities that overlap those of humans so closely,
animal rightists say, they should be allowed a similar overlap of rights.

Critics such as Clive D. L. Wynne, senior lecturer in the Department of
Psychology at the University of Western Australia, dispute some of the conclusions of the ape scientists and their followers. Wynne says it is by no
means clear whether chimpanzees who use signing or computers are really
thinking linguistically or have merely learned elaborate tricks to please their
human testers and obtain rewards. Similarly, he believes that apes' ability to
recognize themselves in mirrors does not necessarily indicate self-awareness.

In any case, critics say, none of the ape experiments shows the capacity for
abstract thought or the ability to understand such concepts as right and
wrong, which many philosophers require for possession of rights. British
philosopher Roger Scruton, for instance, has written that "the notion of a
right . . . is an expression of the sovereignty that human beings claim over
their own lives, and is only doubtfully applied to creatures who do not understand moral ideas, and who have no conception of their duties."[11] Similarly, another British philosopher, David S. Oderberg, claims that even if
animal rights supporters are correct in saying that some animals possess consciousness, self-concept, memories, desires, and even the ability to use language—which he is by no means convinced is the case—these characteristics
do not entitle them to rights. "A right holder must, first, know that he is pursuing a good, and secondly, he must be free to do so," he writes in *Human
Life Review*. Neither of these things applies to animals: "No animal knows
why it lives the way it does; no animal is free to live in one way or another."[12]

Philosophers who deny that animals are entitled to rights frequently emphasize that they are not thereby saying that treating animals cruelly is
morally acceptable. Conservative Christian Matthew Scully writes, for instance, that "we are called on to treat [animals] with kindness, not because
they have rights or power or some claim to equality, but in a sense because
they don't; because they all stand unequal and powerless before us."[13]

In addition to questioning whether animals can have rights, some
philosophers and scientists disagree with Peter Singer's classification of
speciesism as an evil equal to racism and sexism. For instance, Lewis Petrinovich, an emeritus professor of psychology at the University of California,

Riverside, claims that there is no biological basis for discrimination on the basis of race or gender, but a desire to help members of one's own species—the pool of potential partners for reproduction—is built into humans (and all other animals) by evolution. He believes that humans incapable of abstract thought, such as babies and severely brain-damaged people, can justifiably be given more rights than animals because they are part of the social community that nature drives morally active humans to value.

THE LAW OF ANIMAL RIGHTS

Because so much disagreement and confusion exists about philosophical, moral, and ethical definitions of rights, some commentators say that the term should be used only in the context of law. In *Animals and the Law: A Sourcebook*, St. Cloud State University professor Jordan Curnutt defines legal rights as benefits that the law protects and defines as being owed to the holders of those rights.

Focusing on animal rights as defined by law certainly simplifies the issue in one way. Commentators such as Curnutt say that Western laws, from ancient Babylonia to the present day, present a clear and unanimous view of the rights of animals: They have none. In the eye of the courts, animals are things, or property—period. As such, they have no legal standing, or value in their own right. Laws have protected animals only in order to benefit humans, for instance by safeguarding economic interests or guaranteeing that meat is fresh and therefore likely to be safe to eat. Curnutt writes that judges have almost unanimously interpreted even laws against cruelty to animals as being intended "not really to protect animals . . . [but] to protect humans from harm and prevent the decay of their moral character."[14]

STANDING TO SUE

Because animals have no legal standing, attorneys cannot file suits on their behalf, even when the animals are treated in ways that appear to violate existing laws. Organizations attempting to use lawsuits to compel government agencies to enforce animal protection laws therefore must use human plaintiffs, and finding plaintiffs that courts will accept has proved extremely difficult. This is because "standing to sue," as opposed to legal standing as a whole, refers to a person's relationship to a particular legal situation, and the rules governing it are extremely complex. *Black's Law Dictionary* explains that, in order to be acceptable plaintiffs in a lawsuit, individuals or groups must show that the actions of the defendant(s) "invade a private substantive legally protected interest" belonging to them.[15] In several landmark court

9

cases, the Supreme Court has spelled out further requirements that animal protection groups, like the environmental groups involved in the cases, have found extremely hard to meet.

In *Sierra Club v. Morton* (1972), the first of these cases, that well-known environmental organization filed suit against Rogers Morton, secretary of the interior and head of the U.S. Forest Service, in an attempt to force the Forest Service to stop a development in a California wilderness area that the group claimed would violate several laws governing the preservation of national forests. A district court granted a preliminary injunction against the development, but the Ninth Circuit Court of Appeals removed it, saying that the Sierra Club had not proved that the project would violate any of its members' legally protected interests. Reviewing the case, the Supreme Court upheld the ruling of the appeals court. It granted that "esthetic and environmental well-being are important ingredients of the quality of life in our society, . . . deserving of legal protection through the judicial process." Nonetheless, it held that the Sierra Club's lawyers had not demonstrated that the development would violate club members' esthetic and environmental interests because the lawyers had not shown that the members visited that particular area.[16] The group therefore lacked standing to sue.

In a 1992 case, *Lujan v. Defenders of Wildlife*, the Supreme Court, in a majority opinion written by Justice Antonin Scalia, defined the requirements for standing more precisely. In order to obtain standing to sue, Scalia wrote, a plaintiff's lawyers must prove three things:

1. that a "concrete and particularized" injury (invasion of legally protected interests) to the person or to one or more members of the group has occurred "in fact"—in a manner "actual or imminent, not conjectural or hypothetical";
2. that the injury is "fairly traceable" to (clearly caused by) the actions of the defendant (not those of some third party) that are alleged to be illegal; and
3. that a legal decision in favor of the plaintiff is likely to stop the injury or prevent further injury of the same kind.

Scalia concluded that the Defenders of Wildlife, like the Sierra Club in the previous case, lacked standing to sue because the group had not shown exactly how and when the development it wanted to stop would cause "actual or imminent" injury to its members. Courts threw out several animal rights groups' suits for alleged violations of the Animal Welfare Act (AWA) for the same reason.

In a key 1998 case, *Animal Legal Defense Fund v. Glickman*, however, the District of Columbia Circuit Court of Appeals granted Animal Legal Defense Fund (ALDF) member Marc Jurnove standing to sue Agriculture Secretary Dan Glickman, who, as head of the U.S. Department of Agriculture (USDA), was responsible for enforcing the Animal Welfare Act. Among other things, the AWA governs the treatment of animals by zoos or other exhibitors, and Jurnove claimed to have suffered aesthetic injury when he repeatedly saw conditions at a Long Island (New York) zoo that, he alleged, violated the AWA's requirements for treatment of primates.

In the court's majority opinion, Judge Patricia Wald ruled that Jurnove had established that he had been injured "in a personal and individual way . . . by seeing with his own eyes the particular animals whose condition caused him aesthetic injury."[17] He had also shown that the vagueness of the USDA's AWA regulations permitted the conditions that caused the injury. Finally, she wrote, it was reasonable to believe that more specific rules would prevent future injury because Jurnove had testified that he planned to revisit the zoo frequently to monitor the animals.

ALDF v. Glickman was the first AWA case in which standing to sue was granted. Rob Roy Smith, a student at the Northwestern School of Law of Lewis and Clark College, wrote soon after the appeals court decision that it "la[id] a foundation for animal welfare litigation to follow" and potentially would "spark a legal and political revolution in animal law."[18] The appeals court later rejected Jurnove's case on its merits, however, showing that standing to sue is far from the only obstacle that animal rights attorneys must overcome.

ANIMALS AS LEGAL PERSONS

Some animal rights activists in the legal profession, most notably Gary Francione, who teaches law at Rutgers University, and Steven Wise, who teaches law at Harvard University, hope to progress well beyond ALDF's qualified victory. It seems unjust to them that cruelty to animals can be redressed only through reference to the emotional distress of human beings observing it. They maintain that the intellectual and emotional capacities of chimpanzees and bonobos should entitle these animals, at least, to some of the legal rights of humans—enough to end most medical experimentation on them and prohibit their being kept in zoos, for instance. Wise calls the present rigid legal distinction between humans and animals "arbitrary, unfair, and irrational."[19]

Wise and the Great Ape Project, a group of scientists, scholars, and activists working for great ape rights, believe that apes should be granted legal personhood, which would allow human representatives to bring suits on their behalf, just as a suit can now be filed on behalf of a small child or an incompetent adult. They note that categories of legal persons that are not persons in the usual sense, such as corporations and ships, already exist and that the definition of legal persons has been broadened in the past, when Africans and their descendants in the United States were reclassified as persons rather than property. Thus, they believe, there is no fundamental reason why animals could not be defined as legal persons.

Not surprisingly, the proposal that apes and perhaps other animals be made legal persons has aroused considerable criticism, even ridicule. "Would even bacteria have rights?" queries University of Chicago law professor Richard A. Epstein, who terms the concept of animal rights "intellectually dangerous."[20] Even some supporters of animal rights think that establishment of legal personhood may not be necessary to protect apes. Eric Glitzenstein, part of a husband-and-wife legal team in Washington, D.C., which has represented many animal rights and environmental protection groups, feels that "you can take existing law and accomplish much of the same thing."[21] Gary Francione, however, says that "we have had 'humane' laws for 200 years now; yet we use more animals, in more horrific ways, than ever before." Such laws, Francione claims, "may make us feel better, but they do little for animals."[22]

At the very least, books by Francione and Wise have attracted considerable attention both within and outside the legal community to the subject of animal law, which includes all laws relating to human activities that affect animals, not just those supported or envisioned by the animal rights movement. The law schools of Harvard University and of Georgetown University in Washington, D.C., began offering courses in animal law in 1999. Jordan Curnutt wrote that by 2000 at least 20 books and one journal were devoted wholly to animal law, a dozen or more law schools offered courses in the subject, and hundreds of attorneys had made it their specialty.

THE ANIMAL RIGHTS MOVEMENT, ITS OPPONENTS, AND THEIR TACTICS

Peter Singer's *Animal Liberation* was a call to action, as well as a philosophy treatise, and action resulted, partly because his ideas fell on fertile ground already plowed by other social movements, such as the African-American Civil Rights movement and the feminist movement, and drew on a common distrust of capitalism, large industries, and science. By the end of the 1980s, through a series of memorable and often controversial campaigns, what came to be called the animal rights movement had branded itself on the consciousness of the public—not to mention that of its opponents in agriculture, research, and other fields—as a mainstream grassroots movement. Targeted industries began to form their own advocacy and lobbying groups to counter the animal groups' actions.

The animal rights movement declined in strength and visibility during the 1990s, but it by no means disappeared. In 2001, Lyle Munro, a sociologist at Monash University in Australia (where Peter Singer also formerly taught), estimated that 10 to 15 million people worldwide belonged to the "animal movement," although it is not clear whether he meant just the animal rights movement or all animal protection movements combined. The United States and Britain each have several hundred organizations devoted to one aspect or another of animal protectionism (which includes both animal rights and animal welfare). People for the Ethical Treatment of Animals (PETA), perhaps the best-known animal rights organization in the United States and one of the largest, alone claims to have 700,000 members.

MEMBERS OF THE ANIMAL RIGHTS MOVEMENT

Even more than most social movements of the late 20th century, the animal rights movement in both the United States and Europe has been characterized by grassroots activity, with many campaigns and demonstrations planned independently by local groups and small organizations. Most animal rights groups consist of a handful of professional leaders, backed by far larger numbers of volunteer activists. "Professionals keep the movement organized," says animal rights activist Stephen Fox. "Amateurs keep it honest."[23]

Several surveys conducted in the 1990s painted a statistical portrait of the typical animal rights activist. In one such survey, done in the United States in 1990, 97 percent of the activists interviewed were white, 78 percent were women, 57 percent were between ages 30 and 49, 33 percent had higher education degrees (as compared to 7.6 percent of U.S. citizens as a whole at the time), and 39 percent had incomes of $50,000 or more (when only 5 percent of the U.S. population had incomes at this level). About 70 percent had no living children, and 90 percent shared their homes with at least one animal (the national figure was about 40 percent).

Lyle Munro extensively interviewed about 350 animal rights activists and supporters in Australia, Britain, and the United States in the mid-1990s. Most of the interviewees told him that they had joined the movement because of close relationships with individual animals or a powerful emotional encounter with animals—what sociologist James Jasper calls a "moral shock." An Australian named Roger, for example, said he had become an activist after treating ducks injured in a wildfire.

I can remember the heartbeat. I can remember the calming effect of covering the bird's head. . . . I felt I had done something constructive, something positive to relieve the terror and the horror that bird was experiencing.[24]

Supporters, critics, and animal rightists themselves agree that most people in the movement feel a powerful emotional attachment to their cause. Lawrence and Susan Finsen, who wrote about the animal rights movement in America in the mid-1990s, said that the moral foundation of the movement is compassion. Hunting supporter Ward M. Clark, an opponent of the movement, describes this compassion as "misplaced" and accompanied by "intellectual laziness," but animal rights activists see their emotions, which include anger as well as compassion, as literally the heart of their crusade.[25] Tom Regan, the quintessential animal rights philosopher, wrote that "philosophy can lead the mind to water but only emotion can make it drink."[26]

For most animal rights activists, Lyle Munro found, "animal protection had become a way of life."[27] They generally ate a vegan diet, excluding animal products such as milk and eggs as well as meat, and tried to avoid all other uses of animal products. They felt an extremely strong moral commitment to their cause and belief in its rightness. This conviction—Ward Clark calls it "arrogance"—helped them endure disapproval from family and friends, but it also sometimes made them impatient with slow, incremental changes in laws and public opinion. On occasion, it led them to criticize more moderate animal protectionists who, for example, still ate meat.

TACTICS OF THE ANIMAL RIGHTS MOVEMENT

Both traditional animal welfare groups such as the American Society for the Prevention of Cruelty to Animals (ASPCA) and more aggressive animal rights groups such as PETA employ the standard tactics used by virtually every social or political advocacy group: fund-raising and member recruitment, education (including programs aimed at children), direct mail and letter writing campaigns, and, in recent years, web sites and e-mail contact lists. Animal rights groups, like other organizations working vigorously for social change, also use high-profile media campaigns, boycotts, lobbying of legislators, sponsorship of ballot initiatives, and lawsuits (usually aimed at pressuring government agencies to enforce animal protection laws). A few extremist animal rights organizations resort to threats, vandalism, arson, and occasionally physical assault against those they consider to be abusers of animals.

Animal rightists' tactics have worked better in some areas than others. Most commentators probably would agree with Andrew N. Rowan of the Humane Society of the United States (HSUS), who wrote in 2000 that "the movement has enjoyed greater success in reshaping cultural attitudes than in securing laws."[28] Difficulty in meeting legal requirements such as those for standing to sue has often caused animal rights groups' lawsuits to be thrown out, and powerful opponents in Congress with ties to agriculture or other industries that the groups attack usually block their efforts to have new laws passed or gain more funding to enforce existing ones. Animal rights publicity campaigns, on the other hand, have frequently been highly effective in gaining attention and, sometimes, in changing public opinion and persuading businesses to adopt more animal-friendly policies. At the same time, some of these campaigns have created considerable controversy.

Ranging from appearances by supermodels clad only in banners proclaiming that they would rather go naked than wear fur to distribution of "Unhappy Meals" featuring pictures of dead cattle and toys in the shape of wounded farm animals, the campaigns launched by PETA have become particularly famous—or infamous—for their flamboyance. "Probably everything we do is a publicity stunt," PETA's cofounder, Ingrid Newkirk, said in a 1991 interview. "We are not here to gather members, to please, to placate, to make friends. We're here to hold the radical line."[29] Even PETA's numerous critics admit that they have done so very successfully. "Think what you want, but PETA's approach is working," Betsy Cummings, executive editor of *Sales and Marketing Management*, wrote in 2001, calling the group's tactics "forceful, persistent, pointed, and attention-getting."[30]

Some of PETA's nervy broadsides have produced strong complaint. College students may have liked PETA's 2000 "Got Beer?" campaign, which claimed that beer was more healthful than milk, but Mothers Against Drunk Driving was not amused. A second PETA anti-milk campaign launched at about the same time, which focused on an alleged link between diets high in meat and milk and an increased risk of developing prostate cancer, was also widely criticized because it featured a picture of New York mayor Rudolph Giuliani, who had just been diagnosed with the disease. Commentators faulted PETA for making capital out of Giuliani's illness, and the group finally withdrew the Giuliani material and sent the mayor (who had threatened to sue them) an apology. A 2001 billboard advertisement reading "Eat the Whales," intended to point out what PETA saw as the hypocrisy of environmentalists who protested whaling but still ate meat, alienated groups who might have become PETA's allies.

PETA and some other animal rights groups have become famous for using language and pictures to make their audience feel intense emotions. "We have to shock and mesmerise and entice, and tell powerful stories about the suffering of animals," Andrew Tyler of Britain's Animal Aid has said.[31] PETA's Newkirk has compared the killing of chickens for meat to the murder of Jews in Nazi concentration camps. Other groups have used pictures of animals that the public finds attractive or "cute," such as tigers, pandas, and big-eyed baby seals, to elicit sympathy. Videotapes of alleged animal abuse create shock.

However, as Lyle Munro points out, "the politics of emotion . . . have to be carefully managed if they are to avoid alienating potential supporters."[32]

The Jewish Defense League has objected to the Holocaust comparison, and opponents within the movement say that the sympathy campaigns ignore animals that are just as endangered or abused as the featured ones but are less appealing. Researchers and meat industry spokespeople have claimed that "abuse" photos and tapes are often used out of context (photographs may not have been taken at the places mentioned in accompanying text, for instance, or may be decades old) or are altered to create a false impression.

The greatest debate has arisen over the tiny number of animal rights groups who employ threats and violence, particularly the shadowy organization called the Animal Liberation Front (ALF), which began in Britain in the 1970s but now also has representatives in the United States, Canada, Australia, New Zealand, and several European countries. Both Scotland Yard in Britain and the Federal Bureau of Investigation (FBI) in the United States have classified the ALF as a domestic terrorist group, and concern about the activities of this and other violent animal rights groups prompted the U.S. Congress to pass the Animal Enterprise Protection Act in 1992, which makes physical disruption of animal production and research facilities a violation of federal law. However, according to physician Edward J. Walsh, whose experiments on cats have been criticized by animal rightists, as of early 2000 no one had actually been charged under this law.

Most of the ALF's activities, such as firebombing cars, "liberating" experimental animals, and smashing equipment in laboratories, have caused only property damage, but that damage has often been extensive. The ALF and a related environmental group, the Earth Liberation Front (ELF), have claimed responsibility for more than 600 acts of arson and vandalism in the United States alone since 1996, producing damages totaling more than $43 million, according to FBI Domestic Terrorism section chief James Jarboe. The ALF has repeatedly insisted that it takes "all necessary precautions against hurting any animal, human and nonhuman,"[33] and Jarboe admitted in March 2002 that "so far—knock on wood—they haven't [actually harmed anyone in the United States]." Jarboe feared, however, that "that may not last."[34] Certainly the ALF and related groups have at least threatened to cause injury, as when a group calling itself the Justice Department mailed razor blades and threats to 87 American scientists who did research on primates in 1999. In 2003, a group calling itself Revolutionary Cells set off bombs at Chiron and Shaklee, two corporations indirectly involved in animal testing, and threatened to do the same to similar firms. No one was injured in the blasts, but the group warned similar businesses that employees and their homes might be targeted next.

The ALF and a few other groups in Britain have gone beyond threats to actual violence. The British ALF kidnapped documentary filmmaker Graham Hall, who had made an exposé film of the group, and burned the organization's initials into his back in 1999. In February 2001, animal rightists armed with baseball bats attacked Brian Cass, the managing director of Huntingdon Life Sciences, the world's second-largest commercial animal testing facility, producing a broken rib and a head injury that required 10 stitches. Although so far Cass has been the only person physically attacked, his beating was part of an extensive campaign of threats, property damage, and harassment that a group called Stop Huntingdon Animal Cruelty (SHAC) directed, not only at Huntingdon, but at banks, investment companies, suppliers, customers, and other businesses connected to the company. Revolutionary Cells said that Chiron and Shaklee were targeted because they subcontracted animal testing to Huntingdon, but SHAC has denied knowledge of the group's actions and claims that it does not support violence.

ALF member Keith Mann, convicted of terrorist activities in Britain, said in 1998, "No one has died yet [as a result of animal rightists' attacks], but that time will come."[35] In fact, it appears to have come already. On May 6, 2002, a popular Dutch politician named Pim Fortuyn was shot to death in a radio station parking lot in Amsterdam, and Volkert van der Graaf, founder of a group called Environmental Offensive, was arrested and charged with the crime. Van der Graaf's group opposed animal agriculture, and he may have been incensed by Fortuyn's statement that the politician intended to work toward lifting a ban on breeding mink and other animals for fur. Van der Graaf later admitted to the killing, and in April 2003 he was sentenced to 18 years in prison for it. Both the defense and the prosecution (which had hoped for a life term) are planning to appeal the sentence.

Some animal rights activists feel that extreme tactics are necessary because nothing else will bring about the results they desire. Speaking of the ALF, British activist Tim Dailey said, "In a war you have to take up arms and people will get killed. . . . It's a war, and there's no other way you can stop vivisectors [people who operate or experiment on living animals]."[36] Some groups that say they do not use or advocate violence themselves have supported ALF's actions morally and sometimes financially. PETA, for example, contributed more than $45,000 in 1995 toward the cost of defending ALF member Rodney Coronado, who was convicted of a firebombing at Michigan State University. PETA's web site has compared the ALF to the Underground Railroad and the French Resistance.

Most animal rights groups, however, strongly disavow the use of violence. In a joint resolution published in the *New York Times* in 1991, for instance, the ASPCA, the HSUS, and more than 100 other animal protection groups stated that they opposed "threats and acts of violence against people and willful destruction and theft of property."[37] This disapproval may be as much strategic as moral. A 1994 editorial in the magazine *Animal People* complained that "the ALF and imitators are practically singlehandedly responsible for rationalizing the organized backlash against the animal rights movement,"[38] and the HSUS's Andrew Rowan points out, "As a matter of historical fact, threats of bodily harm and acts of destruction . . . are nearly always counterproductive in the long term."[39] Most of Lyle Munro's interviewees said that legal tactics were more effective, as well as more justifiable, than illegal ones.

In contrast to the ALF or even PETA, many animal rights groups choose tactical approaches that encourage dialogue and compromise with those whose behavior they seek to change. For example, the late Henry Spira, founder of Animal Rights International and leader of a successful campaign against product testing on animals in the 1980s, was famous for his willingness to meet opponents halfway and his refusal to verbally attack them as individuals, no matter how strongly he might criticize their actions. According to Lyle Munro, Spira claimed that

> *his strategy of accommodation, a version of reintegrative shaming that favours reinforcement and forgiveness, leads to less animal suffering and is more effective than the vilification and stigmatisation of opponents is. . . . According to how the theory of reintegrative shaming [by Australian criminologist J. Braithwaite] works, the crime, not the offender, is the focus of the moralising effort.*[40]

OPPONENTS OF THE ANIMAL RIGHTS MOVEMENT

Lyle Munro writes that "one measure of a social movement's success is the intensity of opposition to it," and by that standard, the animal rights movement has been successful indeed.[41] At first, farmers, scientists, hunters, and others targeted by animal rights protests often simply ignored what they regarded as fringe activity. As the protests stirred up increasing public pressure, however, groups opposing them faced the fact that, as critic Marlene Halverson said in 1991, "social concerns regarding the treatment of animals are [not] going to go away or . . . continue to be answer[able] by denial and resistance," and they began actively fighting back.[42] Existing trade associations such as the Animal Industry Foundation set up committees and campaigns to respond to animal rightists' attacks, and some new organizations, such as the National Association for Biomedical Research, were established solely for the purpose of defending particular industries.

Particularly since the 1990s, anti–animal rights groups have used many of the same tactics as the animal rightists in campaigns to defend their treatment of animals. They publish pamphlets and videotapes, present position statements on their web sites, and offer fact packets to teachers and journalists to counteract what they say is misrepresentation or outright lying by animal rights organizations. "For years scientists have not been good at informing the public about the benefits of what they do. A lot of propaganda has been allowed to fill the gap," says Andrew Gay, marketing director of Huntingdon Life Sciences.[43] Similarly, the Animal Industry Foundation, which represents agricultural interests, says that "agriculture must realize that . . . consumers . . . must be the focal point [of education campaigns] . . . Agriculture [needs] to become more open about why animals are raised the way they are."[44]

Following the example set by animal rights organizations, opposition groups have learned to appeal powerfully to emotion. For instance, to counter antivivisectionists' pictures of what Andrew Gay calls "cuddly animals with things sticking out of their heads," animal research advocacy groups such as the British Research Defence Society have published testimonials from seriously ill people who say they would not be alive if research on animals had not taken place.[45] "We have now realized the issue is about people," not scientific information, says Mark Matfield, the society's executive director.[46]

Just as with some animal rights groups, a few opposition groups have apparently resorted to underhanded or even illegal tactics, although none has been accused of physical violence. Janice Pottker, a freelance writer who published material critical of the Ringling Bros. and Barnum & Bailey Circus and its head, Ken Feld, sued Feld and the circus in 1999, claiming that Feld had hired (among others) a former head of covert operations at the Central Intelligence Agency (CIA) to spy on her and attempt to derail her career. According to court records, the ex-CIA official, Clair George, admitted overseeing operations against Pottker and also against animal rights groups that opposed the circus, including the Performing Animal Welfare Society (PAWS) and PETA. Pottker's suit is still pending as of late 2003. Meanwhile, a jury in Washington, D.C., awarded $500,000 to Shan Sparshott, a former Ringling Bros. employee, in May 2001 after finding that a former executive vice president of the circus had Sparshott's phones illegally wiretapped.

ANIMALS AS COMPANIONS

The chief way in which most people consciously interact with animals is by having pets—or, as animal rights activists urge others to call them, "companion animals." Almost two-thirds of American households are estimated to have at least one resident cat, dog, bird, or reptile. James Serpell wrote in *In the Company of Animals* that people are drawn to share their lives with animals because "they do not judge us, criticize us, lie to us or betray our trust."[47] Trained companion animals help some physically disabled people lead independent lives, and elderly or mentally disabled people often respond to animals when they have all but lost the ability to respond to other humans. The companionship of animals has even been credited with healing powers. In turn, many human "guardians" pamper and cherish their companion animals and view them as members of their family.

Of all relationships between humans and animals, the companion animal one surely comes the closest to being symbiotic, or equally beneficial to both partners. Nonetheless, some radical animal rightists consider even the keeping of companion animals to be a kind of slavery because the animal usually has no choice about whether to be part of the relationship. Ingrid Newkirk, for instance, calls it an "absolutely abysmal situation brought about by human manipulation"[48] and says it should be "phased out" and be replaced by "enjoyment at a distance."[49] Similarly, John Bryant, author of a 1990 British book called *Fettered Kingdoms*, writes, "Pet animals are slaves and prisoners, and I am opposed to both slavery and imprisonment."[50]

Most animal protectionists do not share this view, however. On the contrary, as Lyle Munro writes, "the keeping of companion animals is one of the distinguishing characteristics of animal protectionists."[51] Surveys have shown that some 90 percent of self-identified animal rights supporters or activists in the United States share their household with one or more animals, and each household has an average of 4.7 animals, about five times the national average. Many animal rightists cite an experience or relationship with a companion animal as the reason they were drawn to the cause.

THE FIRST ANIMAL PROTECTION SOCIETIES

The public's close relationship with companion animals, Lyle Munro believes, "is . . . the basis for the reservoir of good will that the animal movement depends on in its campaigns."[52] It was also the basis for the animal protection movement itself. Concern for companion animals, or at least for domesticated working animals, was the reason for the formation of the first animal protection laws and organizations.

England passed the first national animal protection law, the Ill Treatment of Horses and Cattle Bill, or Martin Act (named after Richard Martin, the Irish Minister of Parliament, who introduced it), in 1822. It forbade "any Person [from] wantonly and cruelly beat[ing], abus[ing] or ill treat[ing] any Horse, Mare, Gelding, Mule, Ass, Ox, Cow, Heifer, Steer, Sheep or other Cattle."[53] The law was expanded to cover all domestic animals, including the bulls used in bullbaiting (which judges had not considered to be cattle) and the cocks used in cockfighting, in 1835. These common lower-class amusements thus became illegal.

Two years after the original Martin Act was passed, Britisher Arthur Broome founded the Society for the Prevention of Cruelty to Animals

(SPCA), the West's first national animal protection organization. (It had been preceded by the Liverpool Society for Preventing Wanton Cruelty to Brute Animals, founded in 1809, which is said to be the world's oldest known animal welfare group.) The group worked to make sure the Martin Act was enforced, particularly in regard to the treatment of the horses that filled the streets of British cities. Queen Victoria lent the society her patronage, allowing it to add *Royal* to its name, in 1840.

The group was influential, probably because, according to historian B. Harrison, it kept its views and tactics firmly in line with middle- and upperclass Victorian mores. By the end of the century it had persuaded British legislators to pass laws that protected wild and domestic animals in a variety of situations, from use in scientific laboratories to drawing of carts, and had made kindness to animals a widely accepted concept, at least among relatively affluent people in the cities. The idea was much less well received in rural England, where activities such as fox hunting remained popular and the slaughter of animals on farms was a daily occurrence.

The United States followed England's example thanks to Henry Bergh, a wealthy New Yorker whose thoughts had been turned toward animals by experiences during his career as a diplomat. In Russia he had been greatly disturbed by the sight of peasants beating their horses, and in England he observed the RSPCA and decided to establish a similar group in America. He founded the American Society for the Prevention of Cruelty to Animals (ASPCA) in 1866 and, a mere year later, succeeded in persuading the New York legislature to pass an anticruelty law that became a model for most later laws. Numerous similar groups (despite its name, Bergh's organization at that time was active only in New York) and laws sprang up in the following decades in the United States, Britain, and other nations that followed the traditions of these countries. By 1921, every state in the United States had some sort of law forbidding cruelty to animals, and most countries in Europe did, too.

BREEDING AND SALE OF COMPANION ANIMALS

State anticruelty laws are still the chief laws that protect companion animals, but some other laws also affect them. For instance, the federal Animal Welfare Act, passed in 1970, covers (among many other things) breeding facilities that sell dogs to pet stores. So far, however, this law has proved unable to control what animal rightists call "puppy mills": large kennels in which purebred puppies are crowded together in unsanitary housing, sometimes given inadequate food and veterinary care, and taken away from their mothers at an early age to be sold through brokers or dealers. Because of the conditions in which they have been raised, these animals frequently have health problems that are revealed only after they have been adopted.

21

Animal protectionists say that the U.S. Department of Agriculture's lax enforcement of the AWA has allowed puppy mills to continue. They also have criticized the American Kennel Club (AKC) for accepting money from breeders to certify the ancestry of purebred dogs regardless of the animals' health, a practice that they say encourages puppy mills. Some animal welfare groups have worked for the passage of federal or state laws that would force more strict control of dog breeding, such as specifying how many litters a mother dog would be allowed to have each year. (In puppy mills, female dogs are kept pregnant almost constantly.) The AKC has also expressed disapproval of puppy mills, but it opposes laws that restrict breeding and states that establishing the health of a dog is the buyer's responsibility. Several states have passed "lemon laws" that require businesses that sell dogs to replace, pay for treatment of, or refund the purchase price of any dog found to have a serious disease or congenital defect soon after purchase.

Animal protectionists' criticism extends to pet stores, which are not covered by the Animal Welfare Act. PETA and some other animal rights groups have called for a national boycott of Petco, a large pet store chain, claiming that sick or dead small animals, such as birds and turtles, have been seen in Petco stores. Some animal protectionists disapprove of even humanely run pet stores because, they say, people should adopt homeless animals from shelters rather than adding to pet overpopulation by buying specially bred animals in stores.

CRUELTY TO COMPANION ANIMALS

State animal cruelty laws differ in their level of detail, but all specify to some degree the kinds of animals protected, the actions prohibited, the mental state required to establish liability, and the uses of animals that are exempted. Most do not cover socially approved uses of animals, such as killing certain animals for meat or using them for experiments in licensed laboratories.

However they are defined, laws against animal cruelty have resulted in few prosecutions and even fewer convictions. One estimate in the late 1990s stated that about 50,000 complaints of cruelty are probably filed in the United States each year, but they produce only about 500 prosecutions and 50 convictions. When a conviction does occur, punishments are usually what many animal protectionists consider woefully inadequate. Even the most egregious examples of animal torture and murder have been classified as misdemeanors in many states, punishable by seizure of the animals plus a fine or, at most, perhaps a year in jail.

In the last 10 or 20 years, however, thanks in part to the activities of animal protection groups, the public has become much less tolerant of companion animal abuse. This change in opinion was shown clearly during a nationally publicized California case in 2000, in which animal rights groups and concerned citizens established a $120,000 reward for the identification and capture of a man who threw a woman's dog into traffic, causing its death—a far greater sum, critics pointed out, than was offered for information on most kidnapped children. The man was eventually found, arrested, convicted, and given the state's maximum sentence for cruelty to animals, three years in prison. In 1998, a Wisconsin judge meted out an even harsher sentence, a prison term of 12 years, to a man who had tortured and killed numerous kittens and puppies. By 2001, 33 states and the District of Columbia classified severe animal abuse as a felony.

Sociologists and law enforcement officers, meanwhile, are paying increasing attention to abuse of companion animals because research has shown that many people who became serial killers or other violent criminals as adults abused animals as children. The relationship between cruelty to animals and violence to humans remains complex and poorly understood, but evidence for some link between the two has become strong enough to warrant the founding of programs in which animal control officers, law enforcement officers, and social workers cooperate to uncover cases of childhood animal abuse and obtain psychiatric help for young offenders. In addition, experts say that animal abuse often occurs in the same households as child abuse and domestic violence, and the discovery of any one of these crimes should prompt a search for the others.

SHELTERS FOR HOMELESS COMPANION ANIMALS

Unfortunately, many potential companion animals do not have human guardians. They may be born on the streets, run away or become lost, or be surrendered or abandoned by people who can no longer keep them or have simply grown tired of them. According to one estimate, some 8 million to 12 million dogs and cats arrive at pounds or shelters in the United States every year. (Facilities for homeless animals are often called pounds when they are managed by cities and shelters when they are managed by private groups, but in reality the two often overlap, as when cities hire local SPCAs or humane societies to run their animal control facilities.) These facilities, originally set up in the early 1800s to prevent public nuisances and the spread of diseases such as rabies by rounding up stray dogs, began to be overwhelmed with animals in the years following World War II, when postwar prosperity allowed the pet population to burgeon.

In an attempt to stem the growing tide of homeless dogs and cats, shelters started aggressive adoption outreach programs. In addition, in the late 1970s, the animal welfare groups that ran many shelters began to promote the idea that companion animals should be spayed or neutered as early in their lives as possible. Since the operations (spaying especially) were expensive, some shelters opened low-cost spay and neuter clinics to help low-income people afford them. This action produced an outcry from veterinarians, who felt that the shelter groups were unfairly using the tax advantages of their nonprofit status to offer services at a lower price than the veterinarians could. Some veterinarians, as well as some pet owners, also questioned whether sterilization was good for the animals.

Today, virtually all animal protection groups, and many people who adopt companion animals as well, agree that the animals should be sterilized. Veterinarians now say that the operations can be safely performed when the animals are as little as eight weeks old, so many shelters sterilize even the youngest animals before making them available for adoption. Alternatively, shelters may require adopters to sign a contract promising to have the animals neutered within a certain time period or even to pay a deposit, which is returned when the adopters present a signed certificate from a veterinarian saying that the operation has been done. No state law forces owners to spay or neuter their animals, but 24 states require all animals adopted from shelters or pounds to be sterilized. (Some groups have urged the passage of legislation that would prohibit the breeding of dogs and cats until shelter populations are considerably reduced, but this move has not been popular.) In addition to sterilizing animals turned in to them, some shelters work with feral cat colony caregivers to have adult cats sterilized and rereleased and kittens collected for socialization and adoption.

Spay/neuter campaigns have had a substantial effect on the companion animal overpopulation problem, especially in reducing the population of very young animals, but they have by no means eliminated it. In addition to promoting spaying and neutering, therefore, many shelters now seek ways to keep more adopted animals in their existing homes. They may guide people to landlords who accept pets, help to pay animal care costs for low-income families or senior citizens, provide dog training programs, or hire animal behaviorists to work with owners to find solutions to problems such as barking, house soiling, and clawing furniture.

Once animals are turned in to a shelter or picked up by animal control officers and taken to a pound, their lives are likely to be short. If an animal is not reclaimed by its original owner or adopted by a new one within a week or two, it probably will be euthanized, even if it is healthy. Estimates say that about half of the animals turned in to or collected by pounds and shelters—a minimum of 4 million a year—are killed there.

In an attempt to change this depressing state of affairs, some animal welfare organizations around the mid-1980s began to establish no-kill shelters, in which animals, once accepted, remain until they are adopted—no matter how long that takes. These shelters keep their populations at a manageable size by limiting the number of animals they accept, taking only the most adoptable ones and usually rejecting those that are old, ill, or have behavior problems. Critics say that the no-kill shelters thereby simply force someone else, such as a pound, to do their killing for them or indirectly encourage owners to abandon the animals that the shelters reject. Even the "lucky" animals that the shelters accept may spend months or years in small, barren cages if they are not adopted quickly. Nonetheless, no-kill shelters have become popular and are increasing in number.

More controversially, rather than euthanizing animals considered unadoptable, some shelters sell such animals to laboratories for research or education, or to dealers who, in turn, sell them to laboratories. Supporters of this practice say that since the animals are slated to die anyway, they might as well benefit science first, but because of fears, justified or otherwise, about what might be done to animals in a lab, many shelter organizations and members of the public oppose this practice. By early 2003, 14 states had passed laws barring shelters from selling animals directly for research or education. Even in those states, however, shelters can still sell to "middleman" animal dealers.

THEFT OF COMPANION ANIMALS

The dealers who buy animals from shelters are classified by the Animal Welfare Act as class B dealers, meaning that they buy animals from "random sources" rather than breeding them specifically for sale as so-called class A dealers do. The AWA stipulates that class B dealers must be licensed by the USDA and must keep careful records showing the sources of their animals, but animal rights groups such as the American Anti-Vivisection Society claim that these records are sometimes incomplete or falsified.

Animal rightists say that some class B dealers or the "bunchers" they buy from (who are not licensed or inspected by the USDA) do not limit themselves to purchasing animals from shelters. According to these critics, bunchers may send people masquerading as families, sometimes complete with children, to claim animals described in "free to good home" advertisements, or they may steal pets outright. Shelters and pounds as well as animal protection organizations estimate that hundreds of thousands of pets are stolen each year, and Patricia Jensen, a former USDA assistant secretary, stated in 1996 that laboratories' (usually unknowing) use of "stolen and fraudulently acquired pets . . . [is] one of the most egregious problems in research."[54] The National Association for Biomedical Research, however, says the accusation that laboratories frequently buy stolen animals is a "myth."

The latest attempt to counteract misappropriation of pets for use in laboratories was the Pet Protection Act, passed in 1990. This amendment to the

AWA requires pounds and shelters to hold animals for at least five days before selling them to dealers. (Dealers were already required to hold animals for five days, but owners are not likely to know where to find animal dealers, whereas shelters and pounds are easy to locate.) Some state and local laws also specify holding periods. These laws are seldom enforced, however, and, even on the rare occasions when conviction is obtained, penalties are small.

Because of class B dealers' often dubious sources, as well as the fact that the genetics and health of the animals they supply are unknown, many laboratories avoid such dealers, and animal protection groups and even some USDA officials have recommended that this category be eliminated entirely. Researchers defending class B dealers, however, say that small scientific facilities often cannot afford to buy purpose-bred animals from class A dealers. Furthermore, they point out, requiring laboratories to buy research animals only from breeders unnecessarily adds to the overpopulation of cats and dogs.

ANIMALS IN AGRICULTURE

Although 19th-century anticruelty laws such as Britain's Martin Act forbade farmers to beat cattle or other farm animals, they did not regulate the way the animals were raised or the methods by which those intended for meat or other destructive uses were killed. Concern about these issues arose only in the 1950s and 1960s, following the growth of large, intensive farms after World War II. Today, many animal rights activists see the issue of animals in agriculture as equally or perhaps even more important than the ever-popular subject of animals in research.

RAISING OF FARM ANIMALS

The United Nations Food and Agricultural Organization estimated that 1.9 billion cattle, sheep, and pigs and 39.7 billion chickens and turkeys were killed for food worldwide in 1998. In 2001, according to the National Agricultural Statistics Service, the United States alone possessed a total of 8,824,439,000 animals being raised for meat, of which 8,389,000,000 were broiler chickens. The number of fish and other aquatic creatures being raised for food is also rising rapidly.

Animal rightists claim that most of these animals, along with others being raised for eggs, milk, and fur, live under abysmal conditions. One of the first descriptions of these conditions appeared in a 1964 British book called *Animal Machines*, in which Ruth Harrison described life on what she called factory farms:

*The old lichen covered barns are being replaced by . . . industrial type build-
ings into which the animals are put. . . . The sense of unity with his stock
which characterizes the traditional farmer is condemned as being uneconomic
and sentimental. . . . The factory farmer . . . uses new systems . . . which subject the animals to conditions to which they are not adapted . . . characterized
by extreme restriction of freedom, enforced uniformity of experience, the sub-
mission of life processes to automatic controlling devices and inflexible time
scheduling.*[55]

Farms of the type Harrison described began to replace the classic family
farm of Old MacDonald and childhood readers in the United States and
other developed countries in the late 1940s, when agricultural and shipping
technology advanced and a rising population increased the demand for
meat. Today they are becoming common in certain developing countries,
such as China, as well. One study estimated that 79 percent of the poultry,
68 percent of the eggs, and 39 percent of the pork produced worldwide during 1996 came from intensive farms. These large farms permit economies
of scale and efficiency that make their survival possible on the low profit
margin that exists in agriculture.

Although interpretations of the conditions' effects differ, the nature of
the conditions under which animals are raised on intensive farms usually is
not disputed. For instance, egg-laying hens are housed in wire cages with
three to six birds to a cage, allowing each hen about 55 square inches of
space. By comparison, the cover of a big-city telephone book is about 102
square inches. The cages, few of which contain nesting material, slant
downward slightly so that the hens' eggs can roll onto a conveyor belt for
easy removal. The cages are stacked in rows and tiers to make a huge battery that may hold thousands or even tens of thousands of birds. A layer
house, or warehouse full of such batteries, may contain 80,000 hens.

Once a year the hens are forced to begin molting, or dropping their
feathers, usually by being deprived of food, water, and sometimes light for
several days. Molting, during which the hens do not lay eggs, is a natural
part of the birds' yearly cycle. The purpose of forcing it is to make all the
hens molt at once and make the process last as short a time as possible so
that its effect on egg production is minimized. Kept on this schedule and
bred for high production volume, battery hens may lay 280 or more eggs a
year, as opposed to the 12 to 20 eggs that hens would lay during the same
period in their natural state.

Most of the eggs are sold, but some are kept to produce new chickens.
Since they cannot be egg layers, males are killed almost immediately after
birth. Females, which will become new laying hens, usually have the ends of
their beaks and sometimes their toes cut off with a hot blade so that they will

not be able to peck or scratch one another, a natural aggressive tendency that can develop into cannibalism in the close confines of the battery cages.

Broiler chickens—those intended to be sold as meat—are bred from different lines and raised on different farms. Most are males. They, too, are kept in huge warehouses, with 10,000 to 20,000 birds in a building. Unlike laying hens, they are not caged, but instead stay on the floor of the warehouses. Broiler chickens are genetically selected to grow rapidly and reach a relatively large weight, four to five pounds, in about six weeks. Broiler breeders, which produce new broilers, are kept much like broilers except that, as with laying hens, their beaks and toes are trimmed to prevent aggressive behavior. To prevent fertility problems associated with the obesity to which they are genetically prone, they are often fed very restricted diets.

Cattle, too, lead lifestyles that depend on the purpose for which they have been bred. Those intended for consumption as beef are usually males. A few weeks after birth they are branded and castrated, and the buds on their heads that would normally grow into horns usually are burned so the animals will not develop weapons that can be used against other cattle or people. Anesthesia is seldom used during these procedures. The cattle are allowed to graze in pastures for about nine months, after which they are shipped, usually by truck, to feedlots for finishing. Some 10,000 animals may be crowded together on the packed dirt surface of a feedlot. For several months the cattle in feedlots are fed high-calorie corn and soy meal, sometimes treated with growth promoters, to make them gain weight rapidly. When they reach their market weight of 1,000 pounds or so, they are sent to slaughter.

Dairy cattle are treated differently from beef cattle. Cows on some large farms are allowed to graze in pastures, but many dairy cattle spend part or all of their time in packed dirt lots or concrete-floored stalls, where they are mechanically milked two or three times a day. They must be made pregnant once a year to keep their milk flowing, but their calves are removed right after birth.

Male calves born into a dairy herd are either killed at birth or raised as veal. Animal rights groups' publicization of the treatment of veal calves, featuring pictures of calves imprisoned without bedding in stalls so small that the animals could not lie down or turn around, caused considerable public outrage in the 1980s. The animal rightists also reported that the calves were deliberately fed iron-poor diets to make them anemic so that their flesh would remain desirably pale. This kind of treatment is still legal in the United States, but veal producers say that calves today are less tightly confined, fed adequate diets, and kept under more sanitary conditions.

Pigs have their own version of intensive farming. Like broiler chickens, they are kept in large, warehouselike buildings. Sows, or female pigs, used for breeding (and therefore kept pregnant or nursing almost constantly) spend most of their adult lives in gestation stalls (when they are pregnant) and farrowing crates (in the weeks around the time they give birth), some of which are so narrow that they cannot turn around. Their piglets, if they are male, are castrated about two weeks after birth. The teeth of both males and females are clipped and their tails are cut short, or docked, to keep them from injuring or being injured by other pigs. Nonbreeding pigs spend about 20 weeks in a growing building or sometimes in a pasture before being sent to slaughter. The growing buildings usually lack bedding and have slatted floors so that the animals' manure can fall into a pit below.

As intensively farmed animals go, sheep and lambs lead a relatively easy life. They are the only major food animal still normally allowed to live outside for most of their lives.

Not all farmed animals are raised for food, of course. Sheep provide wool as well as meat, and other animals, primarily mink, a relative of the weasel, are farmed for their fur. Mink and other fur animals, such as foxes, are usually raised in pens or cages, then killed and skinned.

Efforts to control problems resulting from intensive farming conditions can sometimes create other problems. Crowding, for instance, can make animals unusually susceptible to disease because of easy transmission of microorganisms and immune suppression due to stress. Many intensive farmers therefore dose their animals with antibiotics, both to prevent disease and to stimulate growth by allowing the animals to digest their feed more completely. In the late 1990s, the World Health Organization and the U.S. National Academy of Sciences' National Research Council reported studies showing a link between the use of antibiotics in food animals and the development of antibiotic-resistant bacteria in those animals. The Animal Health Institute, a trade organization for the makers of animal health care products, says that the National Research Council study found the incidence of human disease caused by such bacteria to be very low. Animal rights groups and other critics of the practice reply, however, that these bacteria can easily pass their resistance genes to other bacteria that cause human illness.

Intensive farmers also sometimes give animals hormones or other substances to promote growth and productivity. A 1995 USDA study estimated that more than 90 percent of beef cattle in the United States were given hormones for this purpose. Bovine growth hormone (BGH) is given to 10 percent to 25 percent of dairy cows in the United States to increase milk production. These measures, combined with genetic selection for economically desirable traits, have proven very effective, but animal rights organizations say that they also increase the likelihood of disability and illness, such as udder inflammation (mastitis).

Pigs and broiler chickens bred for fast growth and laying hens and dairy cattle bred for high output, the Animal Protection Institute says, often become so heavy or develop such fragile bones that walking becomes painful or even impossible. The likelihood of lameness is increased by the bare concrete or slatted floors common in animal warehouses and by the packed dirt of paddocks and feedlots. Dairy cows treated with BGH are more likely than others to develop mastitis, a painful udder inflammation. Pigs genetically selected for fast growth and leanness are highly excitable and, therefore, are likely to damage themselves or suffer stress reactions during transport. Turkeys must be artificially inseminated because the males are too fat to mate normally. "One of my biggest concerns is the possibility that producers are pushing animals beyond their biological limits," writes livestock expert Temple Grandin.[56]

Animal rights groups claim that intensive farming causes unimaginable suffering. Close confinement and crowding prevent animals from indulging in natural behaviors, resulting in boredom, frustration, and abnormal aggression. This aggression, in turn, must be prevented by physical mutilations such as debeaking and dehorning, which can produce lifelong pain.

Some intensive farming practices also endanger human health, animal rightists say. In addition to the possible increase in drug-resistant bacteria caused by feeding healthy animals antibiotics, they point out, a deadly human brain disease may have sprung up because some ranchers in Europe and North America fed cattle feed that contained the ground-up remains of other cattle and sheep. In the late 1980s, a form of fatal brain infection called bovine spongiform encephalopathy (BSE), dubbed "mad cow disease" by the media, became widespread in Britain, where the use of such feed was common. The disease, caused by poorly understood malformed proteins called prions, proved to be spread when cattle ate brain or nerve tissue in animal feed made from animals with the illness. Worse still, the British government admitted in March 1996 that about 10 people had died of a similar disease, called variant Creutzfeldt-Jakob disease in humans, and they might have caught it from eating beef from cattle afflicted with BSE. It was rancher Howard Lyman's warnings that the disease might also appear in the United States that caused Texas cattlemen to sue him and Oprah Winfrey, host of a 1996 television talk show on which he appeared, for product defamation. By late 2003, about 150 people, almost all Britons, had died of the disease.

Britain quickly outlawed the use of ruminant remains in cattle feed, and in August 1997 the United States and Canada did so as well. U.S. agriculture officials admit, however, that only about 75 percent of ranchers complied with the ruling at first. (They claim that more than 99 percent had complied by 2003.) Furthermore, the disease takes years to develop, and cattle that could have eaten tainted feed before the ban were still alive in the early 2000s. Critics of this feeding practice, and of intensive farming in general, thus were not surprised when a cow with BSE was discovered in Alberta, Canada, in May 2003 and another, also apparently born in Canada, was found in the state of Washington in December 2003.

Reports about these animals led to widespread concern both in the United States and abroad. Some 30 countries, together making up about 90 percent of the U.S. beef export market, halted their importation of American beef within a week of the December report. (The United States, similarly, had banned importation of Canadian beef after the May report.) Although they admitted that the U.S. cow had been processed as meat before its illness was diagnosed and recalled some meat, government officials played down the risk to the human food supply, as well as announcing numerous changes in testing and slaughtering rules aimed at eliminating future threats. Nonetheless, numerous animal rights and vegetarian groups seized on this highly publicized occurrence as another reason why people should give up eating meat.

Trade organizations such as the American Meat Institute say that animal rightists exaggerate the problems caused by intensive farming. Many of the worst conditions the animal groups cite, they claim, occur on only a small number of farms or no longer occur on any farms. Furthermore, the trade groups say, there is no verifiable way to tell what emotions—if any—intensively farmed animals experience.

Animal rights organizations never mention the positive features of intensive farming, supporters of the practice point out. Keeping animals indoors protects them from weather, attacks by predators, and some diseases. Intensive farming technology has produced more nutritionally balanced feeding and more effective veterinary care than was possible on traditional farms. Confinement systems can be kept cleaner than open lots. Confining hens or pigs in separate enclosures protects them from attacks by other animals and ensures that each receives an appropriate amount of food. Farrowing stalls keep sows from accidentally crushing their piglets. Industry trade groups point out that the American Veterinary Medical Association approves of most of the practices that animal rightists criticize, including beak trimming and stalls or tethers for sows, as long as they are monitored carefully. Farmers have a powerful economic incentive to keep their animals healthy and productive, these supporters say, and therefore will care for the animals as well as possible.

Canadian animal welfare professor David Fraser and his coauthors, writing in *The State of the Animals: 2001*, may provide the best summary of the situation. "Proponents of each of these highly simplified [pro and con] views can cite facts and examples to support their claims," they say, "yet neither one provides an adequate or accurate description of animal agriculture."[57]

31

Even within a small region, they point out, farms and agricultural practices can be quite diverse.

ATTEMPTS TO CHANGE CONDITIONS ON INTENSIVE FARMS

Animal rights groups have had little success in persuading state or federal governments to regulate, let alone ban, intensive farming practices in the United States. Both federal laws such as the Animal Welfare Act and most state animal cruelty laws specifically exempt animals in agriculture treated in accordance with "normal practice." Animal rightists have had better luck, however, in using public opinion to persuade businesses to require certain changes.

Some of the original groups' most effective campaigns have targeted large restaurant and supermarket chains, particularly fast food chains such as McDonald's. These campaigns publicized the alleged misery of factory farmed animals and urged the public to boycott the chains unless the chains insisted that their meat suppliers make certain improvements in the conditions of the animals they raise. Following such campaigns, McDonald's issued revised guidelines for its suppliers in August 2000, and Burger King and Wendy's did likewise in June 2001. In early 2003, PETA was moving on to the Colonel Sanders Kentucky Fried Chicken chain.

In its August 2000 settlement, McDonald's agreed to buy eggs only from producers who do not use starvation to force molting and who provide 72 square inches of space for each hen in a battery cage. Wendy's also agreed to these conditions, as well as requiring that chickens be stunned with electricity before they are slaughtered. Meanwhile, in October 2000, United Egg Producers (UEP), a trade organization that represents 85 percent of egg producers in the United States, issued new guidelines that promised to gradually increase the size of battery cages by up to 40 percent, make debeaking less painful, and develop ways to force molting without starvation. Al Pope, president of the organization, said the guidelines were issued partly in response to animal rights protests but chiefly because "it is the right thing to do" and "will benefit the industry in the long run."[58] The McDonald's and UEP guidelines were similar, although McDonald's demanded that the changes be implemented sooner than UEP wished.

Animal rights groups' crusade against fur farming and the fur trade has also been cited as one of the movement's success stories. Beginning in the 1970s, organizations such as PETA waged attention-getting campaigns against the wearing of fur, using tactics ranging from pictures of supermodels such as Naomi Campbell saying (and showing, to a limited extent) that they would rather go naked than wear fur to spraying red paint on the fur coats of women in the streets. The protests appeared to work. There were more than 1,200 mink farms in the United States in 1968, for instance, but by 1999 the number had dropped to less than 450. However, it is not really clear whether the decline in fur use is due to a change in public feeling brought about by the rights organizations or simply to changes in fashion. There were signs, too, that the industry was recovering somewhat in the late 1990s.

Europe has been a more fertile ground than the United States for legislative control of intensive farming. As far back as 1964, in response to Ruth Harrison's book about "factory" farming, the British Parliament set up a committee to investigate conditions on intensive farms. The so-called Brambell Committee's report, issued in 1965, set standards for treatment of various kinds of farm animals and inspired Parliament to pass the Agriculture (Miscellaneous Provisions) Act in 1968, which put some of these standards into law.

The European Union (EU) has banned hormonal growth promoters since 1988 and BGH since 2000. Switzerland outlawed battery cages for laying hens in 1991, and Sweden did the same in 1998; the EU decided in 1999 to phase out such cages in all member nations by 2012. Britain banned crates for veal calves in 1990 and confinement for sows in 1999 and, in 2003, even passed a law requiring farmers to put balls in pigsties to give the animals "environmental enrichment." Sweden, Finland, and the Netherlands have made sow gestation crates illegal, and the EU is phasing them out on a schedule similar to that for battery cages. The EU has agreed to ban forced molting outright and phase out veal crates by 2007. Britain outlawed fur farming in November 2000. However, a 2002 EU study of farm animal welfare laws in 73 countries concluded that such laws, as well as their enforcement, differ considerably from country to country and that many countries' laws are not as stringent as those of the EU. This fact places EU farmers at an economic disadvantage compared to farmers in countries where standards are more lax.

Future success of efforts to modify intensive farming in either Europe or the United States is likely to depend on animal rights groups and the animal agriculture industry being willing to meet each other halfway. Such compromise may be hard to achieve. Some industry spokespeople claim that the rightists' ultimate agenda is not merely improving conditions for farm animals but completely destroying animal agriculture, and some rightist groups in fact admit to this. PETA spokesman Bruce Friedrich, for instance, says that PETA will not be satisfied until "no corporations are serving up animal products."[59]

Because they feel that animal rights organizations will not compromise with them, some animal industry members have decided to take a hard line against the rightists' attacks. A few have tried using lawsuits to stop criticism, but so far these attempts have not been very successful. In 1998, after seven years of litigation in the so-called McLibel case, a judge in England ruled against McDonald's, which had sued two London activists for libel for distributing pamphlets that accused it of the "torture and murder" of millions of animals.[60] The judge said that the activists had not proved all their claims, but a number of the factory farming practices they described could be considered cruel. Similarly, when cattlemen sued American talk show host Oprah Winfrey and others under a Texas food disparagement law after a guest on a 1996 Winfrey program warned of possible health dangers from American beef, allegedly causing a sharp drop in beef prices, a jury acquitted the defendants in 1998 because they concluded that the guest's claims, while possibly exaggerated, were not false.

Other representatives of both sides of the animal agriculture controversy, however, are willing to work toward compromise goals, if only because each side has faced the fact that the other is not going to go away. Animal rights groups realize that, whatever they might desire, most people are not likely to stop eating or wearing all animal products. Similarly, the agriculture industry understands that, whether justified or not, public concern about how farm animals are treated can have a significant effect on its sales figures, and it hopes that voluntarily making changes will help it avoid what it sees as overly restrictive government regulation. Some industry members also agree with animal agriculture expert Temple Grandin, who stresses that humane treatment is profitable as well as moral: "Good stockmanship can improve productivity of pigs and dairy cattle by more than 10 percent," she writes, and "costs very little."[61]

Whatever their motives, animal agriculture and related industries are continuing to develop both improved practice standards and better methods of making sure the standards are followed. For instance, in 2002 the Food Marketing Institute and the National Council of Chain Restaurants released a set of guidelines for food suppliers that covers laying hens, dairy cattle, pigs, poultry, and beef and includes new requirements for castration and dehorning and increased space for pregnant sows. The USDA's Agricultural Research Service is working on new ways to measure and control stress in farm animals. Animal agriculturists are trying to design more humane housing for confined animals, such as cages for laying hens that are not only roomier but include perches, nest boxes, and nesting material. Improvements in electronic systems may allow dairy cows to be kept in open pens and come into milking stations at will to be milked by robotic milkers.

Some animal rights groups, in turn, are telling people that if they must eat meat, they should buy it from sources that treat their animals relatively well. Consumers can purchase "organic" or "free-range" meat at health food stores, for instance, or buy meat from farms with verified high standards of animal care. The American Humane Association has created a "free farmed" label to designate food that comes from animals raised under conditions deemed likely to leave them free of fear, stress, and disease and able to enjoy normal behaviors and the companionship of other animals. However, some critics both within and outside the animal rights movement say that terms such as *free range* can be unclear or misleading and that it is often hard to determine which methods of keeping animals actually contribute to improved animal welfare.

Regardless of who instigates them, improvements in farm animal care are likely to raise the cost of meat and other animal products. Commentators disagree on both the probable amount of increase and the willingness of consumers to accept it. "In 1999 we succeeded in having sow stalls banned [in Britain], and the extra cost now for a meal that includes pork or ham is less than a penny," maintains Peter Stevenson, political and legal director of the British anti–factory farming group Compassion in World Farming.[62] Industry organizations, however, have predicted that the EU's forthcoming ban on battery cages for hens will boost European egg producers' costs by 24 percent. Sixty-four percent of people questioned in a 1993 poll said they would be willing to pay more for meat from humanely treated animals, and more recent surveys have found similar results, but what people say is not always what they do.

TRANSPORTATION AND SLAUGHTERING

The only two federal laws that apply directly to farm animals affect them near the end of their lives. The first law, the Twenty-eight-Hour Act, governs shipping of live animals to feedlots and slaughterhouses. It grew out of the fact that in the late 19th century, when shipping livestock by railroad for long distances first became common, cattle, sheep, and pigs were jammed together into boxcars and sent on journeys of three to six days, usually without food, water, or bedding. Not surprisingly, by the time they arrived at slaughterhouses, 30 to 40 percent of these animals were already dead, and most of the others were in poor condition.

When newspapers in Boston and Chicago publicized this situation, animal welfare organizations such as the Massachusetts Society for Prevention of Cruelty to Animals, as well as some members of the public, demanded changes. In 1873, therefore, after two years of debate and resistance from representatives of the railroad and livestock industries, Congress passed a law requiring that cattle, sheep, and pigs be rested and given access to food and water on any rail or ship journey that lasts more than 28 hours. Jordan Curnutt explains that this was the first federal law intended, at least in part, to mitigate cruel conditions for animals.

The Twenty-eight-Hour Act was revised and expanded in 1994 to cover truck transportation, regulate conditions during loading and unloading, and specify five hours for the rest period. As with most other federal laws affecting animals, the Animal and Plant Health Inspection Service (APHIS) of the U.S. Department of Agriculture has the job of enforcing this law. It appears to be used rarely, and fines for violation are minor. It does not apply to poultry.

The second federal law governs slaughterhouses. In a normal slaughter-house, cattle or pigs are run along a chute into a restraint device where each animal is supposed to be stunned (rendered unconscious), usually by a blow to the head. It is then hoisted by its legs onto a conveyor line and killed by having its throat slit, causing it to bleed to death within seconds. In the first half of the century, however, stunning methods were sometimes ineffective, resulting in animals being bled out or even occasionally dismembered or skinned while still conscious.

Animal welfare groups such as the Humane Society of the United States, as well as prominent senator Hubert Humphrey, protested against this state of affairs, and in 1958 their complaints finally produced passage of the Humane Slaughter Act, which required that pigs, cattle, and sheep be made unconscious by some rapid method before being cut, chained, hoisted, or knocked down. The law was revised and somewhat expanded in 1978, at which time it became the Humane Methods of Slaughter Act. It is enforced by a branch of the USDA called the Food Safety and Inspection Service (FSIS). It does not apply to birds or to animals killed by the methods of Jewish (kosher) and Muslim (halal) ritual slaughter, which require animals to be conscious at the time of killing.

Articles published in the *Washington Post* in 1997 claimed that the Humane Methods of Slaughter Act was being violated routinely. Since then, however, Congress has increased the USDA's budget for slaughterhouse inspections, and large meat purchasers such as the McDonald's fast food chain have demanded improvements. A 2001 audit of 44 beef plants and 20 pork plants revealed that almost all animals were successfully stunned the first time.

Animal rightists have also complained that the Humane Methods of Slaughter Act does not cover another practice of which they disapprove, the killing of "downer" animals—those too sick or injured to walk into a slaughterhouse on their own. The animals are pushed, carried, or dragged to slaughter, causing great suffering, according to groups such as Farm Sanctuary. The National Cattlemen's Beef Association maintains that less than 1 percent of cattle slaughtered for meat are downers and that most downer cattle do not suffer from conditions that make them a threat to the food supply, and the cattle and meat industries had successfully fought off animal rights groups' attempts to persuade Congress to ban the use of downer cattle as meat. On December 30, 2003, however, a week after a slaughtered downer cow in Washington state was found to have BSE ("mad cow disease"), which may be transmissible to humans who eat meat from sick animals, Agriculture Secretary Ann Veneman announced that downer cattle would no longer be allowed to enter the human food supply.

Most other industrialized countries have laws similar to the Twenty-eight-Hour Act and the Humane Methods of Slaughter Act, some of which were passed or strengthened because of massive public protests. Such protests broke out in Australia in the 1980s and in Britain in 1995, for example, following publicity about the stressful conditions during long-distance (especially overseas) transport of live animals.

ANIMALS IN SCIENCE

Australian sociology professor Lyle Munro writes that "for many people inside or outside of the [animal protection] movement, . . . experimentation [on animals] remains the most important moral dilemma, as well as the most controversial question."[63] It is also, after cruelty to working and companion animals, the issue that has concerned the movement longest.

RESEARCH

Ancient Greek thinkers such as Hippocrates made the first systematic explorations of anatomy and helped to lay the foundations of Western medicine more than 2,000 years ago by performing surgical experiments on living animals, a practice called vivisection. Vivisection was common in Rome and, after languishing during the Middle Ages, revived during the Renaissance. Major medical advances such as English physician William Harvey's discovery of the circulation of the blood, which he first described in 1628, grew out of vivisection (Harvey cut open dogs, snakes, and deer captured in hunts by his friend and patron, King Charles I). By the early 18th century, research on animals was widespread in Europe.

Concern about vivisection began in Britain in 1875, when a scientist named George Hoggan published an account of his time in the laboratory of famed French physiologist Claude Bernard that included descriptions of Bernard's many painful experiments on unanesthetized animals. When the Royal Society for the Prevention of Cruelty to Animals refused to take a strong stand against vivisection, several animal protectionists formed a new group, the Victoria Street Society for the Protection of Animals from Vivisection, specifically to combat the practice.

In 1876, following the recommendations of a commission set up by Queen Victoria, Parliament passed the Cruelty to Animals Act, the first law to regulate the use of animals in research. It required anyone planning to experiment on living vertebrates to obtain a license from the home secretary, which would be granted only after the experimenter described the laboratory and proposed procedures and showed that the research would be likely to produce significant new medical knowledge.

Antivivisectionist societies were also established in the United States, but they failed to obtain any legislation against the practice, and interest in the subject faded away after World War I. Then, just as happened with animal agriculture, a surge of activity brought on by the prosperity following World War II revived American concern about vivisection. In this case the activity was government-supported medical research, and its rise produced a corresponding increase in the demand for laboratory animals. By 1957, U.S. laboratories were using some 17 million animals a year, and their activities were almost completely unregulated. No federal law covered laboratory animals, and, like farm animals, they were explicitly exempted from most state anticruelty laws.

Then, as now, the vast majority of laboratory animals were rats and mice, but some were cats and dogs, and researchers began to ask pounds and shelters to supply these. When some private shelters refused to surrender their animals, groups such as the National Society for Medical Research persuaded several states and cities to pass laws requiring them to do so. The American Humane Association (AHA), then the largest animal welfare organization in the United States, made little attempt to fight these pound seizure laws, so some disaffected AHA members left to form more active groups such as the Animal Welfare Institute (1951) and the Humane Society of the United States (1954).

These organizations had little luck in reversing the pound seizure laws or obtaining any other research regulations, however, until a case in which a Pennsylvania family's dog was stolen and sold to a laboratory received considerable publicity in 1965. A few months later, in February 1966, an exposé in *Life* magazine revealed the filthy conditions under which one animal dealer kept dogs before selling them. The combination of these two events caused the American public to flood Congress with more letters than it was receiving about civil rights or the Vietnam War. Faced with this outcry, legislators quickly passed the Laboratory Animal Welfare Act (LAWA), which became law in August 1966.

Perhaps not surprisingly given its background, the LAWA was designed chiefly to protect family pets. It focused on animal dealers, requiring them to obtain licenses from the USDA, which was given responsibility for enforcing the law (after 1972 this duty fell to the department's Animal and Plant Health Inspection Service [APHIS]), and keep records of all dogs and cats they sold. The law also ordered the secretary of agriculture to "promulgate standards to govern the humane handling, care, treatment, and transportation of animals by dealers and research facilities" but stated that no rules were to be made affecting the handling or care of animals "during actual research or experimentation."[64]

Congress expanded the LAWA in 1970 and renamed it the Animal Welfare Act (AWA). Among other things, the new law required the USDA to monitor records and perform inspections to verify that facilities were meeting the act's standards of animal care. The USDA set forth those standards in regulations issued in 1972.

Public concern about the conditions under which animals are kept in laboratories and about the nature of the experiments carried out on them skyrocketed in the early 1980s because of two widely publicized scandals, both centering on videotapes made clandestinely inside laboratories by members of animal rights groups. The first of these horror stories began in May 1981, when Alex Pacheco, who had recently joined Ingrid Newkirk in founding PETA, obtained a volunteer position in the Edward Taub laboratory's, part of the Institute for Behavioral Research in Silver Spring, Maryland. In an effort to discover whether regrowth of nerves and perhaps restoration of function was possible following injuries or strokes, Taub had cut nerves leading from the spinal cords to the arms of macaque monkeys so that the animals could no longer feel pain or other sensations in the limbs. He then tried to force the monkeys to use the numbed limbs (over which they still had muscle control) to see whether such use would stimulate regrowth in the cut nerves.

APHIS had inspected Taub's laboratory, as the AWA required, and had found it to be in compliance with the law. Pacheco, however, saw the monkeys living under what he described as truly horrible conditions.

The smell was incredible. . . . I saw filth caked on the wires of the cages, feces piled in the bottom of the cages, urine and rust encrusting every surface. There, amid this rotting stench sat seventeen monkeys, their lives limited to metal boxes just 17¾ inches wide.[65]

Perhaps worst of all, the monkeys apparently no longer recognized their treated limbs as part of their bodies and had viciously bitten and chewed them, producing wounds that often became infected and were left untreated.

Working alone in the laboratory at night, Pacheco videotaped the monkeys and their miserable surroundings. He also brought in local primate experts to witness what he had seen. He then took his film, notes, and the experts' sworn statements to local police. On September 11 the police searched the laboratory, confiscated 17 monkeys, and charged Taub with 17 counts of animal cruelty, one for each monkey—the first time a federally funded researcher had been charged under a state animal cruelty law. Taub was convicted of six counts of animal cruelty in December 1981, but the convictions were overturned on appeal in 1982 and 1983, partly because the higher courts ruled that the animals' sufferings were not "unnecessary or unjustifiable," as the law required, but rather were part of the "purely incidental and unavoidable pain" that can occur during research.[66]

The second scandal, revealed in a similar way, took place at the University of Pennsylvania's Head Injury Clinical Research Laboratory in Philadelphia in 1984. In this case the incriminating videotape was made by the researchers themselves. Members of the Animal Liberation Front stole 60 hours of it when they broke into the laboratory in May, and PETA edited the footage into a half-hour documentary, which it distributed widely. The PETA video (which researcher Adrian Morrison calls "cleverly edited" and "grossly distorted") showed live baboons being used essentially as crash test dummies, with helmets glued to their heads and then struck with pistons.[67] It also pictured the baboons being operated on without anesthesia, under clearly nonsterile conditions, while the surgeons smoked pipes and cigarettes. For many viewers, the most unsettling aspect of the footage was the apparently callous attitude of the experimenters and technicians, some of whom were shown making fun of the writhing animals.

Public outrage about these two high-profile cases played a part in persuading Congress to expand and toughen the AWA in 1985. The new amendments, collectively called the Improved Standards for Laboratory Animals Act, emphasized the importance of "minimiz[ing] pain and distress" to animals during experiments.[68] It also mandated exercise programs for dogs and "a physical environment adequate to promote the psychological well-being of primates."[69]

Finally, the 1985 AWA amendments required institutions using animals to set up Institutional Animal Care and Use Committees (IACUCs) to review proposals for all new experiments that used animals and to monitor ongoing experiments and the overall care of animals in the institution. Each committee was to have a minimum of three members, one of whom was a veterinarian and one of whom was a person who represented "general community interests in the proper care and treatment of animals" and was not affiliated with the institution or related to anyone who was.[70] Animal rightists, however, have complained that people with ties to their organizations are very rarely chosen to serve on IACUCs and that IACUC meetings or their records are seldom open to the public. "Their effectiveness in screening inappropriate, redundant, and/or inhumane experiments is questionable," animal rights advocate Martin Stephens maintains.[71]

In general, animal rights groups have not been happy with either the AWA's standards or the USDA's enforcement of them. In the 1990s, for instance, some groups filed a series of petitions and lawsuits aimed at forcing the USDA to remove a controversial feature of its 1972 AWA regulations that explicitly excluded rats, mice, and birds from coverage by the law, even though these species make up about 95 percent of all laboratory animals. The USDA claimed that it lacked the funds and staff to handle the paperwork and inspections that covering this huge number of animals would require. Furthermore, it said, including rats, mice, and birds in the AWA was unnecessary because their care was already regulated by guidelines published by the Public Health Service and the National Institutes of Health, which all federally funded researchers must follow.

The groups' early lawsuits were thrown out, either directly or on appeal, because the organizations could not demonstrate standing to sue, but in September 2000 a district court judge granted standing to one plaintiff, a student who worked in a college psychology laboratory and claimed aesthetic injury from seeing mistreatment of the rats there. After the USDA's legal counsel advised the agency that a judge might well rule against it if the suit came to trial, it settled the suit out of court by promising to remove the controversial exemption. Agriculture Secretary Dan Glickman, writing in the *Journal of the American Medical Association* in February 2001, claimed that the USDA's decision "was in the best interest of all involved . . . and will not jeopardize important research,"[72] but an opposing article in the same issue called the move "a complete capitulation . . . to the demands" of the rights groups.[73]

Before the animal rightists had finished celebrating, however, scientists and others who supported the use of animals in experimentation, represented by such groups as the National Association for Biomedical Research (NABR), persuaded Congress that this change would drown researchers in paperwork, cost $280 million or more per year, and impede research necessary to improve human health. The legislature therefore blocked the proposed alteration, first for a year and then, in May 2002, permanently. Animal rights groups have vowed to continue fighting for the change.

As with intensive farming, public feeling against the use of animals in experiments has been stronger in Europe than in the United States, and legislation has been more strict and appeared sooner. Britain began to regulate laboratory animal use 90 years before the United States did, for example. In 1986 that country replaced its 1876 act with the Animals (Scientific Procedures) Act, which covers all experiments using vertebrates, including rats and mice, and this act was further expanded in 1999. Numerous commentators have said, approvingly or otherwise, that British regulations governing use of laboratory animals are the most comprehensive in the world. (Some British scientists have complained that the rules are so complex and bureaucratic that they force animal research out of the country, to Britain's scientific and economic loss.) Britain has also been the site of the most violent protests against alleged laboratory animal abuse, those directed against Huntingdon Life Sciences.

In 1986, the same year that Britain passed its new act and a similarly rigorous law took effect in West Germany, the European Union approved the Animal Experiments Directive (86/609/EEC), which established uniform animal welfare provisions for all member countries and required member countries to develop legislation promoting alternatives to laboratory animal use. In June 2002, after 10 years of debate, Germany went even further by becoming the first European Union country to guarantee protection to animals in its constitution. (Switzerland, which is not a member of the EU, passed a constitutional amendment in 1992 that recognized animals as beings rather than things.)

The issue of animal use in science continues to produce confrontational rhetoric on both sides. The more extreme animal rightists maintain that the use of animals in science, like every other human use of animals, is simply wrong, no matter how great its potential benefit for humans. "Even if animal research produced a cure for AIDS, we'd be against it," says PETA's Ingrid Newkirk.[74] Not surprisingly, statements such as Newkirk's produce equally intransigent reactions from some scientists. For instance, Frederick Goodwin, a former director of the National Institute of Mental Health, has said that attempting to compromise with animal rightists is a mistake because they see doing so as an admission of guilt.

Both sides of the debate often present arguments that rely on science (as they interpret it) as well as emotion. Animal rights groups claim that experiments and drug tests on animals are invalid and even dangerously misleading because of biological differences between animals and people. They point out that some widely used drugs such as aspirin are poisonous to animals but not to humans, for instance, and other drugs have passed animal tests but have later had to be withdrawn because they proved to have dangerous side effects in people. They say that lack of supporting evidence from animal studies held up campaigns linking smoking and lung cancer in the late 1950s and early 1960s, long after clinical studies of human patients strongly suggested such a link. "Not a single animal test has gone through a validation process [to demonstrate relevance] to human health," claims Jessica Sandler, a spokesperson for PETA.[75]

Scientists who support animal research, on the other hand, say that two-thirds of the Nobel Prizes in physiology or medicine were awarded for discoveries that grew at least partly out of experiments on animals. Major scientific organizations, including the Institute of Medicine of the National Academy of Sciences and the American Medical Association, also unequivocally support the use of animals in research. Scientists admit that comparisons between animals and humans are not perfect, but most maintain

42

that the anatomy and physiology of humans and other mammals are similar enough to make animal experiments a highly accurate means of testing drugs and learning about diseases. To be sure, this line of reasoning brings up what animal rights philosopher Peter Singer calls the researcher's central dilemma:

> *Either the animal is not like us, in which case there is no reason for performing the experiment; or else the animal is like us, in which case we ought not to perform an experiment on the animal which would be considered wrong if performed on one of us.*[76]

Animal rightists also claim that most of the health gains of the last hundred years have come about because of improvements in sanitation and diet, not because of the drugs and vaccines developed through animal experiments. Similarly, they believe that scientists who wish to improve human health today should concentrate more on methods of disease prevention, such as lifestyle changes, rather than on the creation of new drugs or other treatments. Animal research supporters such as Adrian Morrison and Frederick Goodwin reply that many preventive methods, like methods of treatment, were and are developed on the basis of animal experiments.

Responding to accusations that they are indifferent to the suffering of the animals they use, some researchers admit to being emotionally torn when they must hurt or kill animals. Others point out that, whatever their feelings, they have practical incentives to use as few animals as possible and to treat them gently. Animals are expensive, they say, and animals that are excessively stressed or sick with any disease other than one being studied are worthless as experimental subjects. "We have to have them in exquisite health," says Michael Hayre, vice president of comparative medicine at St. Jude Children's Research Hospital in Memphis. "Any stress in the animal will throw off the study results."[77]

One issue within the subject of animal research that has proved particularly difficult to settle is the use of primates (monkeys and apes), particularly great apes such as chimpanzees, in medical experiments. On the one hand, these animals' close biological similarity to human beings makes them seemingly essential for certain types of experiments. Chimpanzees, for instance, are the only nonhuman animals that HIV, the virus that causes AIDS, will infect, so a number of them have been used in attempts to develop a vaccine against the disease. (They do not actually develop AIDS, however. Animal rightists say this fact makes them useless for studying the disease, but some scientists feel that discovering how they are able to resist the virus could be very valuable.) On the other hand, these animals' intelligence and seemingly humanlike emotions and behaviors make many people see experimenting on them as perilously close to experimenting on, say, brain-damaged children. Chimpanzees are also endangered in the wild, which makes capturing them for use in experiments problematic at best.

Because of these concerns, Britain and New Zealand have essentially banned research on chimpanzees, and many other countries are trying to phase out ape experiments. Countries that regulate animal research, including the United States, usually have particularly strict rules about housing primates, including requirements for their psychological well-being such as allowing contact with other members of their species and providing objects for play. In December 2000, Congress passed the Chimpanzee Health Improvement, Maintenance, and Protection (CHIMP) Act, which authorizes the secretary of health and human services to set up and operate a system of sanctuaries to which chimpanzees no longer needed for research can be "retired." Animal rightists have criticized this act, however, because it allows the animals to be reclaimed for further experiments if there is a good scientific reason for doing so.

PRODUCT TESTING

A second way of using animals in science, product testing, has also been the subject of major animal rights campaigns. The U.S. Food and Drug Administration (FDA) and similar agencies in most other industrialized countries require drugs and other medical treatments to be tested on animals before being tried on humans. Even when animal tests are not legally required, as is the case with most cosmetics and household products, many companies use them as a way to guarantee the safety of their products and protect themselves against lawsuits. Products are often tested for acute toxicity (their ability to act as poisons with immediate effects) and the ability to irritate the eyes and skin. Product testing today accounts for between a fifth and a quarter of all animals used in science. Most of these animals are used to test drugs.

In the 1970s, almost all safety testing of products was done on living animals, using several standard procedures. The usual test for acute toxicity was the LD50 ("lethal dose for 50 percent") test, in which groups of about 100 animals (usually rats) were given (usually by force feeding) varying doses of the test substance until half of one group died. The other animals were killed after two weeks so they could be autopsied to determine sublethal toxic effects of the substance. This test, invented in Britain in 1927, produced numerical data from which the toxic dose of a substance could be computed. It was popular because it was easy to carry out and produced the kind of quantitative data that regulatory agencies liked. However, its critics have said that it not only causes great suffering in the animals but is too crude to provide much useful information.

The two standard irritancy tests were called Draize tests, after their inventor, John Draize of the FDA, who created them in the 1940s. In the skin irritation test, a patch of skin on the body of a rabbit was shaved and then scraped to create a slight abrasion. The substance being tested was placed on a piece of gauze and taped over the abrasion. The spot was examined for redness, blistering, or other signs of irritation after one day and again after three days. In the Draize eye irritation test, rabbits were restrained in devices that kept them from touching their heads, and the tested material was placed in their eyes. The eyes were examined at varying intervals, ranging from 1 to 7 days, to find out whether they were irritated. (Signs of irritation could range from mild reddening to complete destruction of the eye.) Rabbits were preferred for this test because, unlike humans and many other mammals, they have no tear ducts to produce fluid that can wash irritating substances out of their eyes. Like the LD50 test, the Draize tests have been criticized for their inaccuracy as well as their cruelty.

Animal rights activist Henry Spira established the Coalition to Abolish the Draize Test in the late 1970s. In 1980, the group targeted Revlon, the leading company in the cosmetics industry, by placing a full-page advertisement in the *New York Times* showing a rabbit with bandaged eyes and asking, "How Many Rabbits Does Revlon Blind for Beauty's Sake?" Most readers had never heard of these tests and were shocked to learn about them. After further campaigns and an outpouring of letters from the public, Revlon and several other cosmetics companies agreed not to test new products on animals. Spira's campaign, which grew to involve 400 animal protection organizations, also generated more than $1.75 million in funding for research into alternatives to animal tests within its first year. Probably largely because of Spira's and similar campaigns, use of the Draize test fell by 87 percent during the 1980s.

Campaigns against the testing of cosmetics and household products on animals continued to be successful during the 1990s. Gillette agreed to stop testing its products on animals in 1997, and Mary Kay Cosmetics and Procter and Gamble followed suit in 1999. The LD50 test has been refined to reduce the number of animals used and to use nonfatal doses, and increasing numbers of government regulatory agencies are accepting nonanimal alternatives to this and other animal tests for nondrug products. Britain, Austria, and the Netherlands have banned all testing of cosmetics on animals, and in January 2003 the European Union voted to ban all such tests and the sale of cosmetics tested on animals anywhere in the world by 2009.

Nonetheless, at least 50 major companies in the cosmetics and household products industries were still testing their products on animals in some way in 2000. Furthermore, some regulatory agencies still require or at least encourage animal tests. The FDA requires them for all eye care products as well as drugs, and the Consumer Product Safety Commission, another U.S. government agency, requires the LD50 test and the eye irritancy test for "highly toxic" products. The Environmental Protection Agency (EPA) prefers, although it does not necessarily require, animal tests for possibly toxic substances.

The EPA, in fact, has been the focus of a recent major campaign by animal rights groups. In 1998, the agency asked manufacturing companies to provide health and environmental safety information for 2,800 high-production-volume (HPV) chemicals—those manufactured at the rate of 1 million pounds or more per year. These substances are everywhere in the environment, the EPA said, yet many of them have never been tested in ways that meet current safety standards, or else data from the tests is not available to the public. Companies could fulfill the agency's request either by releasing existing test data or by performing new tests.

PETA and other animal rights organizations attacked the EPA proposal, claiming that tests it requested would kill 1.3 million animals. The groups also stated that standard animal tests were unreliable and that "modern, reliable, non-animal tests are available but are being ignored."[78] On this issue, as on some others such as wildlife management, animal rights and environmental protection organizations have found themselves on opposite sides, since many environmental groups feel that at least some animal tests of potentially toxic chemicals are necessary. "We would prefer that a small number of lab rats are used to save the rest of us," Gina Solomon, a senior scientist with the National Resources Defense Council, said in 2002.[79]

Responding to the animal groups' pressure, the EPA and the Clinton administration agreed in late 1999 to permit nonanimal tests in part of the EPA program, to provide funding for development and validation of nonanimal tests, and to delay acute toxicity testing for two years so that alternatives to the LD50 test could be developed. Animal rights organizations are still critical of the program, however, maintaining, for instance, that many proposed new tests are unnecessary because the information demanded by the EPA already exists in some form. PETA and others have tried to use lawsuits to stop the HPV testing program, but as of early 2003 they have not been successful.

EDUCATION

The use of animals in education, which accounts for about 10 percent of all laboratory animal use, is also controversial. College, high school, and sometimes even elementary school students are frequently required to dissect the bodies of animals such as frogs in their biology classes, and some medical and veterinary students practice surgical and medical techniques on living or dead dogs and other animals. An estimated 10 million animals a year, more than half of which are frogs, are used in this way. Although the frogs are usually taken from the wild, most of the remaining corpses or body parts come from animals that would have been killed anyway, such as euthanized dogs and cats (or those scheduled to be euthanized) from pounds and parts of cattle, sheep, and pigs from slaughterhouses.

Many animal rights groups maintain that killing animals for educational purposes is unnecessary, and some students have protested or even sued to be relieved of dissection requirements because they felt that killing an animal in order to dissect it was morally wrong. Several states now require that students be allowed to use alternative methods, such as "virtual dissection" computer programs, if they ask to.

Opinions differ, however, about whether these alternatives are as effective as actual dissections. "Repetition is the most important aspect of learning, and you can only dissect an animal once," Jonathan Balcombe of the Humane Society of the United States points out.[80] However, the National Association of Biology Teachers and the National Science Teachers Association say that real dissection still has its place in schools. "Dissection gives students a unique opportunity to observe how animals are structured to function the way they do," says Adrian Morrison, a strong supporter of the use of animals in science.[81] Similar differences of opinion exist about computer programs or other alternatives to the use of animals in surgery practice for medical and veterinary students.

THE SEARCH FOR ALTERNATIVES

Just as many animal rights groups would like all eating and wearing of animal products to cease, so many ultimately hope to see all research and testing on animals end. Most of these, however, recognize that neither aim is likely to be achieved in the foreseeable future and, therefore, are willing to work toward lesser but more practical goals. The most commonly accepted path toward reduction of animal use in science and improvement of conditions for animals in laboratories was first laid out in 1959 by two British scientists, W. M. S. Russell and Rex Burch. In *The Principles of Humane Experimental Technique*, Russell and Burch described what they called the "three Rs" of alternatives to animal research: Replace—substitute tests and experiments using such things as cultured cells or computer simulations for tests and experiments on whole animals; reduce—redesign tests and experiments so that they can be performed on smaller numbers of animals; and refine—redesign tests or experiments to cause less pain and distress to animals.

For the most part, both scientists and animal protectionists ignored Russell and Burch's book when it was first published. When the animal rights movement became active in the 1970s, however, some antivivisection groups began promoting the three Rs as a way of weaning scientists and regulators away from reliance on animals.

Some scientists and legislators embraced this approach as well. The governments of the Netherlands and some other European countries began promoting and funding the search for alternatives to animal research as early as the late 1970s. The European Union established the European Centre for the Validation of Alternative Methods (ECVAM) in 1991. In the United States, the National Institutes of Health (NIH) Revitalization Act, passed in 1993, ordered the director of the NIH, the federal government's chief research facility, to develop, validate, and support tests that fulfill the three Rs. To carry out this mandate, the NIH established the Interagency Coordinating Committee on the Validation of Alternative Methods (ICCVAM) in 1994. Temporary at first, the ICCVAM was made a permanent standing committee in December 2000.

Today, the three Rs are a mainstream concept. Most countries' legislation governing laboratory animals incorporates this approach, and most research institutions and IACUCs have written it into their policy. Many regulatory agencies also accept the word of ICCVAM and ECVAM regarding the validity of alternative tests and have substituted nonanimal methods for the LD50, Draize, and similar tests under at least some circumstances. Scientists and businesses such as drug companies are often willing, even eager, to adopt alternative tests because they are usually cheaper, faster, and easier to execute than animal tests. "The beauty of the three Rs is that they provide a way for all parties to work together to advance the cause of both animals and humans," Richard Smith wrote in an editorial in the *British Medical Journal* in 2001.[82]

"The prospects for making steady progress [in having alternatives substituted for animal tests] is very good," Michael Balls, the director of ECVAM, said in 1999, but he added that "many individuals, especially in government and in animal welfare, have unrealistic expectations of the rate at which progress can be made in replacing current animal procedures."[83] Alternatives work better for some purposes than others. Drug companies find computer programs and cell culture techniques very useful for initial screening of possible new drugs, for instance, but tests carried out later in the development of a drug still usually involve animals, to meet regulatory requirements if nothing else. Although some animal rights groups claim that most, if not all, animal research can now be replaced by methods that do not use whole animals, most scientists disagree. A spokesperson for the National Association for Biomedical

Research, for instance, says, "Many of the processes that occur within the human body remain too complex to be simulated by a computer or a cell culture."[84]

In addition to replacing animal tests with ones that do not use animals and reducing the number of animals needed in certain tests, scientists are trying to refine experiments on animals by developing better ways to define, measure, and relieve pain and stress, including stress caused by inadequate housing. For one thing, they increasingly recognize that stress can change animals' physiology enough to invalidate the results of some experiments. University of California, Davis, animal behaviorist Joseph Garner, for one, maintains that animals kept in barren conditions show signs of actual brain damage. Hanno Wurbel of the Institute of Laboratory Animal Sciences in Zurich adds

It took some time for scientists to realize that using 'dirty' animals [animals exposed to disease-causing microorganisms] can compromise the validity of experiments. Today, we are about to realize that the same could hold true if we use animals with impaired welfare. It is time to improve housing conditions for scientific, if not for ethical reasons.[85]

At least partly because of the new emphasis on alternatives, the number of animals used yearly in experiments has declined sharply over the past 30 years. In the United States, according to the Foundation for Biomedical Research's citation of USDA statistics, the number of dogs used in research declined by 61 percent, the number of cats by 62 percent, and rabbits by 35 percent between 1973, about the time laboratory animal use is thought to have peaked, and 1998. Similar decreases have occurred in Britain, Germany, the Netherlands, and Switzerland.

Nonetheless, about 24 million animals were still used for scientific work in the United States in 1998, and the worldwide total was estimated at 41 million. Some commentators, furthermore, feel that the decline in animal numbers has leveled off and may even begin to reverse. Much research in the rapidly growing field of biotechnology and genetic engineering, for instance, is done on mice. Some scientists also hope to use cloned, transgenic farm animals (those engineered to carry genes from another species, usually humans) as "factories" to make medically useful compounds or to provide organs for transplantation into humans.

On the other hand, new genetic technology may also offer more ways around animal experiments. DNA microarrays, or "chips," which contain hundreds or even thousands of short strands of DNA that act as probes for different genes, are held to be a likely tool for toxicity testing, for example. New methods of freezing and storing mouse embryos could allow special genetic strains to be preserved that way rather than by breeding stock, thus greatly reducing the number of adult animals that must be housed in laboratories. New methods of imaging and recording data from animals without operating on or killing them could also reduce suffering.

ANIMALS IN ENTERTAINMENT

What could be more wholesome and innocent than a day at the circus or a zoo? Plenty of things, animal rights supporters say. Many animal rights organizations claim that animals in circuses are abused to make them perform tricks for the public and, in between performances, spend their lives in confining, uncomfortable cages. Some zoos provide better habitats for their animals than others, the groups admit, but they believe that no benefits in even the best zoos justify keeping wild animals in captivity. There is even less excuse, they believe, for most other forms of animal "entertainment," such as animal fighting, rodeos, and even racing. "To treat animals as objects for our amusement is to treat them without the respect they deserve," states a fact sheet published by the animal rights magazine *Animals Voice*.[86] Nonetheless, many people continue to enjoy being entertained by animals and say that doing so can have educational as well as aesthetic value.

ANIMAL FIGHTING

Watching animals fight each other (or humans), and often betting on the outcome, has been a popular form of entertainment since ancient times. Most people have read about the Roman emperors' famous displays of lions and other beasts in arenas such as the Circus Maximus (from which the term *circus* comes). Ordinary people could not afford lions, but in many societies they enjoyed watching pairs of dogs or roosters (the latter often fitted out with knife-sharp "spurs") fight one another in open pits. Bullbaiting, in which dogs were allowed to attack a bull tethered to a stake, was the target of the world's first attempt at passage of an anti–animal cruelty law, proposed in Britain in 1800. Opponents defeated the measure, arguing that ending this "sport" would deprive the working class of one of its few forms of amusement. Bullbaiting, however, was finally outlawed in Britain in 1835.

Most people in North America and Europe today, whether animal rightists or not, disapprove of animal fighting. The Protection of Animals Act outlawed all animal fighting in Britain in 1911. Cockfighting is presently illegal in 46 states of the United States and dog fighting in all 50; the latter is a felony in 45 states. Animal fighting is also prohibited by the federal Animal Fighting Venture Prohibition Act, a 1976 amendment to the Animal Welfare Act, although an exception is made for cockfighting in states where it is legal. Nonetheless, these activities remain popular with certain groups and continue underground.

Animal rightists point out that in addition to causing obvious pain and injury to the animals—the losers, if not killed outright, are often abandoned to die of their wounds—fighting, at least in the case of dogs, presents potential danger to humans as well, since dogs bred to fight other dogs (a process that often involves systematic abuse) are also likely to attack people. Certain breeds used frequently for fighting or aggressive guarding, such as pit bulls (bull terriers), have become so notorious that some cities ban anyone from keeping them. Some dog owners and animal protectionists have protested such breed-specific legislation, emphasizing that dogs of any breed can be gentle and loving if given proper training and socialization.

RODEOS

Some people see rodeos as exciting contests of cowboy skill and a symbol of America's wild frontier past, but animal rights groups say that rodeos are almost as hard on animals as fighting. In roping contests, calves or even fullgrown steers are brought to a sudden halt and then thrown to the ground, sometimes breaking bones or dislocating joints. Leather straps tied tightly around their loins irritate horses and bulls into bucking so that riders will face a thrilling challenge in trying to stay on them.

The Professional Rodeo Cowboys Association (PRCA), which oversees major rodeos and sets standards for the treatment of animals during them, claims that injury to animals in modern rodeos is uncommon. The group has done its best to eliminate some cruel practices, such as the addition of spikes to bucking straps (indeed, it requires that the leather straps be padded to minimize tissue damage). However, animal rightists point out, less than half of all American rodeos are accredited by the PRCA or any other standard-setting organization. Furthermore, the PRCA's own survey cited 38 animal injuries at 57 PRCA-sanctioned rodeos in 2000, more than one for every two rodeos.

Most animal rights groups would like to see rodeos legally banned, but they have had little success in obtaining such legislation. Rodeos are exempt from the Animal Welfare Act, and no other federal law affects them, although the Twenty-eight-Hour Law applies to the transportation of animals to and from rodeos. No one connected with rodeos apparently has ever been convicted of violating this law or any state animal cruelty law. Only two states, Rhode Island and Ohio, regulate rodeos.

SHOWING AND RACING

Animals are not usually visibly injured during horse and dog showing or racing, but some animal rights organizations say that these activities have a hidden abusive side as well. Most notorious was the practice of "soring," in which the high-stepping gait of a breed called the Tennessee walking horse was accentuated by blistering the horses' front legs with chemicals and then wrapping chains or wires around the blisters to irritate them further, making the legs so painful so the animals took their weight off their feet as often as possible. One of the few federal laws specifically governing animals in entertainment, the Horse Protection Act, was passed in 1970 to outlaw this practice. USDA regulations let managers of horse events choose their own soring inspectors, however, and critics say that lax inspection and enforcement allow soring to continue.

In another form of abuse now illegal in many states, live animals, usually rabbits, were used as lures to train greyhounds to race, and the dogs were allowed to tear the animals apart when they caught them. Greyhound racing spokespeople say that live lures are now seldom used, but an investigator from the Humane Society of the United States claimed that 90 percent of greyhound trainers used them in 1991.

One would think that, for economic reasons if nothing else, racing animals themselves would be well cared for, but animal rightists say that this is not always the case. Although the practice is illegal, horses are sometimes given excessive doses of painkillers before a race so they will continue to run even when injured. Between races, dogs or horses may be kept in crowded, unsanitary facilities. Furthermore, except for champions kept for breeding purposes, the lives of racing horses and dogs often come to an abrupt end when the animals stop winning. Some horses go to slaughterhouses, while other, somewhat luckier ones begin "second careers," for instance working in riding stables or pulling carriages for tourists. Greyhounds are usually killed or sold to laboratories after about two years of racing.

Like rodeos, horse and dog races and shows are exempted from the Animal Welfare Act, although the Twenty-eight-Hour Act governs the transportation of racing animals. Most states leave control of racing to state racing commissions, which are more concerned with gambling at the races than with animal welfare. Racing personnel have rarely been charged under state anticruelty laws and even more rarely convicted.

CIRCUSES AND ANIMAL SHOWS

Most people probably think of a trip to the circus as a harmless family outing, but animal rights groups such as PETA say that circuses are anything but harmless to their animals. These organizations claim that many smaller circuses lack the funding, expertise, and sometimes the will to care for exotic animals properly. Furthermore, they point out, even well-cared-for circus animals cannot live in a natural environment or carry out most normal behaviors and social relationships. "When I look at animals held captive by circuses, I think of slavery," says African-American former comedian Dick Gregory.[87]

Animals in circuses, zoos, and other exhibitions (with the exception of rodeos, races, and dog, horse, and cat shows) are protected by the Animal Welfare Act, but animal rightists say that the law's regulations often are not followed, and the USDA's APHIS lacks sufficient inspectors to check up on exhibition conditions regularly. Animal groups claim that the same spotty enforcement hampers the Twenty-eight-Hour Act, which governs care of exhibited animals during transportation, and state anticruelty laws as applied to circus animals. Animal rights supporters have persuaded a few cities to ban circuses and other exhibitions that include animals, but no states have done so.

Some animal rights groups claim that trainers of performing animals regularly use whips, electric prods, or other pain-inducing devices. Most animal trainers vehemently deny this charge, saying that they train the animals by means of food and other rewards and maintain close, affectionate relationships with them. "Sara the Tiger Whisperer," a performer with Ringling Bros. and Barnum & Bailey Circus, says, "I have an awesome relationship with my tigers, and we spend lots of time together even when we're not performing. I do everything I can to make their lives as comfy as possible."[88] If nothing else, trainers maintain, reward is a more effective tool for shaping behavior than punishment, and it is also safer for the trainer.

The truth is almost surely that, as in every other area of human-animal relationships, a wide range of training situations exists. In one highly publicized case, PETA publicly claimed that a popular Las Vegas entertainer, Bobby Berosini, abused the orangutans in his animal act. The animal rights group distributed a videotape taken by a dancer at the hotel where Berosini worked that appeared to show the entertainer hitting one of the animals backstage. In 1989, Berosini sued PETA and other animal rights organizations that had attacked him for invasion of privacy and defamation of character. He claimed that the dancer had deliberately upset the orangutans, making it necessary for Berosini to control them and that the videotape had been heavily edited to produce a false effect. A jury supported Berosini in 1990, but in 1994 the Nevada Supreme Court ruled that the videotape did show abuse.

On the other hand, a jury in San Jose, California, took less than two hours in December 2001 to bring an acquittal in a PETA suit against Mark

Gebel, an elephant trainer for the Ringling Bros. and Barnum & Bailey Circus, who was accused of violating a state law against abusing elephants. A San Jose policewoman and an officer of the Humane Society of Santa Clara claimed that they had seen Gebel strike an elephant with an ankus, or bullhook (a device with a blunted tip that is frequently used for controlling elephants), during a parade in the preceding August. They said they saw a dime-sized red spot, which appeared to be blood, on the elephant's leg shortly afterward. Under cross-examination, however, they admitted that they had not actually witnessed the ankus touching the elephant but had only seen Gebel lunge at the animal. The "blood" spot disappeared after the elephant was bathed, and a circus veterinarian testified that he found no injuries. The attorney representing Gebel and the circus did not even present a defense because, he said, the prosecution's case was so weak that none was needed. The jury apparently agreed, and the jury foreman said afterward that the case never should have been brought to trial.

Several individuals and organizations have established sanctuaries for former performing animals that have been sold after becoming too old, injured, or ill to work. Some of these sanctuaries also take in exotic animals that ill-advised people adopted as pets, usually when the animals were babies, and then either abused or abandoned when the animals grew up and began to be destructive rather than "cute." (Several animal protection groups and even the USDA are working for passage of legislation that would prohibit individuals from keeping big cats and most other exotic pets.) For example, Jonathan Kraft, a former Las Vegas showman, has established a refuge for big cats and other wild predators in the Arizona desert. Carol Buckley, a former circus trainer and performer, has set up the Elephant Sanctuary in Tennessee for Asian elephants.

ZOOS

Zoos and aquariums have an even better public reputation than circuses—but Richard Farinato, director of the captive wildlife program of the Humane Society of the United States (HSUS), claims it is "a better reputation than they deserve."[89] Many zoos stress the naturalistic environments in which they house their animals, their captive breeding programs for endangered species, and their efforts to educate the public about animals and nature, but animal rightists say that all of these are inadequate at best and actually harmful at worst.

Even critics admit that the best zoos today offer their occupants state-of-the-art veterinary care and nutrition as well as attendance by well-educated, devoted keepers, resulting in a longer life than the animals usually would have in the wild. No matter how well cared for they are, however, a fact sheet published by *Animals Voice* claims that "keeping animals in zoos harms them, by denying them freedom of movement and association, which is important to social animals, and frustrates many of their natural behavior patterns, leaving them at least bored, and at worst seriously neurotic."[90] A study from Oxford University published in late 2003 states that animals with large home ranges in the wild, such as polar bears and lions, do particularly poorly in captivity, showing high infant mortality and incidence of pacing, a neurotic behavior.

Following ideas first presented by German zoo builder Carl Hagenbeck in 1907 and Heini Hediger, director of the Basel Zoo in Switzerland, in the 1950s, state-of-the-art zoos try to make their animal habitats as natural looking as possible and offer plenty of room for animals to roam or hide from the public. Landscape architect Grant Jones, who designed the first of these new habitats for Seattle's Woodland Park Zoo in the mid-1970s, called this approach "landscape immersion." As Hediger recommended, it includes features of the animals' native habitat that help them engage in normal behaviors, such as trees for them to rub against or sharpen their claws upon. It is also intended to make visitors appreciate the grandeur of the world's natural landscapes, in which they are supposed to feel immersed.

Critics such as David Hancocks, director of the Open Range Zoo in Victoria, Australia, say, however, that even these naturalistic environments may be more restrictive than they seem. Some are made chiefly of plastic and concrete rather than natural materials. In other cases, the animals are restricted to a small part of these beautiful landscapes by electric fences or other invisible barriers. Even when that is not true, animals may spend much of their time, such as the night hours, "off display" in small holding cages.

Furthermore, plenty of zoos still house their animals in the traditional and depressing barred, barren, concrete-floored cages, limiting their activities so severely that the animals resort to abnormal, stereotyped behaviors such as pacing or chewing the bars. The Animal Welfare Act prescribes minimum housing requirements for zoos as well as circuses and other animal exhibits, and it was the primate housing at a zoo that drove New Yorker Marc Jurnove and others to sue for violation of the AWA in the late 1990s, resulting in the first granting of standing to an individual in an AWA case. The European Commission also has a directive setting standards for zoos, 1999/22/EC, which includes a requirement for research and education programs as well as appropriate housing conditions for the animals.

Zoos say that their captive breeding programs offer one of the best hopes for preserving endangered species, most of which have lost their habitats through land clearing or are threatened by poaching in the wild. Animal rights groups claim, however, that although these programs have reduced the numbers of animals taken from the wild to replenish zoo stock, they are of little use in preserving rare species. Some breeding efforts (such as those for pandas) have failed, requiring importation from the wild to continue. Others are forced to work with a limited pool of animals, contributing to increases in birth defects and genetic problems related to inbreeding.

Still other breeding programs, such as the ones for tigers and other big cats, apparently have been entirely too successful, creating more animals than the zoos can afford to house or exhibit. Richard Farinato of the HSUS says there are now more tigers in private hands—about 10,000 in the United States alone—than in the wild. Guidelines established in 2000 by the American Zoo and Aquarium Association (AZA), which accredits the most respected zoos, require zoos to give or sell "surplus" animals only to other zoos with AZA accreditation or equivalent standards, but an investigation by *U.S. News & World Report* in 2002 revealed that this does not always happen. Even much admired zoos such as those in the Bronx (New York) and San Diego (California) sell some animals to substandard facilities or dealers, who in turn may auction them off to roadside zoos, owners of game ranches that provide so-called canned hunts, or people looking for exotic pets.

The AZA began addressing some of these problems in the 1980s with its Species Survival Plan. Even zoo critic David Hancocks admits that the plan has been an overall success and that "animals in accredited zoos are now bred sensibly and wisely."[91] He is not sure how useful even the best breeding programs are in the long run, however, because "the problem is not loss of species but loss of entire habitats and the eradication of complete, functioning, balanced ecosystems."[92] Furthermore, only a small percentage of zoos are accredited by the AZA and follow their regulations.

Richard Farinato also questions the conservation value of zoo-sponsored scientific research, which, he says, "has limited application to the conservation of free-living populations" and chiefly "addresses husbandry techniques or other issues specifically aimed at the management of animals in captivity."[93] However, the AZA says that in 1998 alone, its member organizations supported almost 700 field conservation projects in 80 countries.

Hancocks and other animal rightists doubt the educational benefits of zoos as well. Hancocks says that by emphasizing the colorful and "cute" rather than trying to present whole natural ecosystems, most zoos produce "a kindergarten view of the natural world" that is "upside down" because it stresses big mammals rather than the tiny invertebrates that constitute the bulk of nature.[94] Zoo critics claim that people can learn more about animals by watching them in their natural habitats on television nature documentaries or reading articles in magazines like *National Geographic* than they can from any zoo or animal show. "What we . . . teach children in a place like Connyland [a marine park in Switzerland that displays captive dolphins] is a lesson in domination, a lack of respect for other living things," says Noelle Delaquis, an animal rights activist who is trying to end the keeping of dolphins in captivity.[95]

Some animal rights groups believe that it would be better to maintain endangered animals in large wilderness reserves or sanctuaries than in zoos, although they do not say where such reserves might be found or created or who would pay for them. Alternatively, David Hancocks suggests, zoos could be redesigned to be part of "natural history institutions that can reveal the connectedness . . . of the natural world," including complex interdependencies between plants and animals.[96] Such institutions, he says, would represent partnerships between traditional zoos, botanical gardens, natural history and geology museums, aquariums, science centers, and even perhaps libraries and art galleries. Some of the most farsighted zoos today, in fact, are pursuing just such a goal.

ANIMALS IN THE WILD

The idea of protecting wild animals for their own sake, like most aspects of what is now called animal rights, is a product chiefly of the late 20th century. It is an outgrowth at least as much of the environmental movement as the animal rights movement, and it has produced both some of the most striking instances of cooperation and the deepest disagreements between the two.

ENDANGERED SPECIES

The killing of wild animals, especially in the United States, was seldom restricted before the 20th century, and as the country expanded, excesses frequently occurred. Hunters on the Great Plains shot bison ("buffalo") by the millions for meat, hides, and other products. The last passenger pigeons and Carolina parakeets died in zoos in 1914, victims of the fashion for putting feathers in women's hats. Sealers, feeding another fashion of the 1870s, reduced the northern fur seal population in Alaska's Pribiloff Islands, the animals' primary breeding ground, from about 3 million when the United States bought Alaska from Russia in 1868 to about 800,000 by 1890. Whalers made similar incursions into whale populations during the same period.

The threatened or actual extinction of wildlife species, along with loss of their wilderness habitats, began to attract government attention around the end of the 19th century as even some hunters realized that, unless they employed some degree of restraint, their "geese that laid golden eggs" would soon cease to exist. With the encouragement of sport hunters, states started to establish permanent agencies to regulate hunting and manage wildlife populations to produce a sustained yield of game animals for future hunters.

Regulation of hunting and wildlife was at first considered to be the province of the states. The Supreme Court spelled this out in its ruling on an 1896 case called *Geer v. Connecticut,* in which Justice Edward White wrote that each state had the right to regulate its "common property in game" in order to "preserve for its people a valuable food supply," even if doing so affected the movement of animals out of the state.[97] The federal government, however, banned hunting in Alaska's Afognak Island and in Wyoming's Yellowstone National Park in the 1890s, and in 1900 Congress passed the Lacey Act, which prohibited interstate movement of birds or other animals killed or captured in violation of state laws (or parts of their bodies, such as feathers), invoking the federal legislature's constitutional right to regulate interstate commerce. The Lacey Act, one of the first laws to protect nongame species, was an attempt to stop market hunters' wholesale slaughter of birds to provide feathers for women's hats.

This somewhat schizophrenic state of legal affairs continued until 1928, when the Supreme Court ruled in *Hunt v. United States* that the federal government could regulate activity on federal lands such as national forests, even if its regulations contradicted hunting laws in the states where the lands were located. The court based this authority on the Constitution's Property Clause (Article IV, Section 3), which states that "Congress shall have the Power to dispose of and make all needful Rules and Regulations respecting the Territory or other Property belonging to the United States." In a second decision, *Kleppe v. New Mexico* (1976), the court extended the power of the Property Clause to wildlife on public land as well as the land itself.

Meanwhile, international treaties entered the wildlife conservation picture in the early 20th century. The first one involving the United States was the Fur Seal Treaty of 1911, which was signed by the United States, Britain (for Canada), Russia, and Japan, the four nations responsible for most of the decimation of northern fur seals that had taken place in the late 19th century. In this treaty, the countries agreed not to hunt fur seals on the open ocean, a practice recognized as wasteful because the dead animals usually sank before they could be collected. When the United States signed such agreements, Congress eventually passed laws to implement them within the country. The Migratory Bird Treaty Act, passed in 1918, was the first such law, passed to execute an agreement made with Canada in 1913 to protect nongame migratory birds and limit the hunting of game birds. (No law was made regarding sealing until 1966, when the Fur Seal Act was passed.)

The Lacey Act, the Migratory Bird Treaty Act, and the Fur Seal Act all protected particular groups of species. The same was true of several other federal wildlife laws: the Bald Eagle Protection Act (1940), the Whaling Convention Act (1949), the Wild Free-Roaming Horses and Burros Act (1971), and the Marine Mammal Protection Act (1972). The idea of preserving all endangered or threatened species as such, on the other hand, did not arise until the 1960s, when the writings of Rachel Carson and others made Americans realize the extent to which human activities were destroying not only animals themselves but their habitats through such activities as logging and land clearing.

Extinction—the complete disappearance of particular species—has always been a part of nature, but humans, it appeared, were speeding up tremendously the rate at which extinction occurred. Preservationists argued that some vanishing species might contain materials valuable for medicine or other human uses. More important, they said, all species contribute to the complex interactions that scientists were beginning to recognize in ecosystems, and the loss of biological diversity brought about by the increased extinction rate might doom other species or even whole ecosystems.

Wildlife-oriented animal protection groups such as Friends of Animals joined general-purpose environmentalist organizations in helping to persuade Congress to pass the Endangered Species Preservation Act in 1966, an expanded version of the act in 1969, and, finally, the Endangered Species Act (ESA), which President Richard Nixon signed into law in December 1973. This law states that its purpose is to protect species of plants and animals classified as endangered ("in danger of extinction throughout all or a significant portion of its range") or threatened ("likely to become endangered . . . in the foreseeable future"), along with "the ecosystems upon which endangered and threatened species depend."[98] Although the act was amended in 1978, 1982, and 1988, the 1973 version is still in force today. Jordan Curnutt calls the ESA "the most comprehensive, controversial, and perhaps the most complicated wildlife protection law in the world."[99]

The Endangered Species Act provides elaborate procedures for classifying a species, subspecies, or population as endangered or threatened. Any species of plant or animal, anywhere in the world, is potentially eligible. In 1973, 109 species were listed; by 2002, 1,818 species worldwide, including 1,260 found in the United States, were on the list, and only 31 had been removed, including 11 that no longer seemed to be in danger and seven that had actually become extinct. The law forbids anyone to take ("harass, harm, pursue, hunt, shoot, wound, kill, trap, capture, or collect") or attempt to take members of listed species in the United States, its territorial waters, or the open ocean and to export, import, possess, sell, or transport endangered species or any part of their bodies.[100] It also forbids government agencies to authorize, fund, or carry out projects that will harm a listed species or damage its so-called critical habitat. The U.S. Fish and Wildlife Service, part of the Department of the Interior, is in charge of enforcing this law.

The Endangered Species Act also implements a major international agreement, the Convention on International Trade in Endangered Species of Wild Fauna and Flora (CITES), as it applies to the United States. This agreement was established in March 1973 and signed by 80 countries. Today 160 countries are signatories, making CITES one of the largest conservation agreements in existence. CITES maintains its own list of endangered and threatened species worldwide, numbering more than 30,000 species in 2003. The signatory countries have agreed to limit or ban trade in these plants and animals or any materials made from them to the degree CITES determines. CITES boasts that no species protected by the agreement has gone extinct as a result of trade since it has been in force. Part of the Endangered Species Act implements CITES as U.S. federal law.

One of the most important parts of the Endangered Species Act from the standpoint of environmental and animal welfare groups is its so-called citizen suit provision, which states that any person can file a civil suit against another person, organization, or government entity claiming violations of the act. Citizens may also charge the secretary of the interior with failure to list a species as threatened or endangered or to remove a recovered species from the list. The Supreme Court ruled in 1997 that landowners who feel that actions taken to protect species have damaged their interests can also sue under this provision.

Environmental and animal rights groups have frequently attempted to use the ESA's citizen suit provision. The courts have often ruled that they did not have standing to sue, but in a few cases, judges have granted standing to the wildlife species themselves. One such species was a Hawaiian native bird, the palila, which, the Ninth Circuit Court of Appeals wrote in 1988, "as an endangered species under the Endangered Species Act . . . [has] a legal status and wings its way into federal court as a plaintiff in its own right."[101]

One aspect of the ESA that has caused considerable conflict between conservation groups and businesses such as logging companies is the question of how a species' critical habitat is to be determined and protected. A 1975 Fish and Wildlife Service regulation stated that "environmental modification or degradation [that] . . . disrupts essential behavior patterns" was to be included in the definition of *harm* in the act.[102] In 1992, however, after logging projects in Oregon's old-growth forests had been halted because they degraded the habitat of the endangered northern spotted owl, a pro-logging group called the Sweet Home Chapter of Communities for a Great Oregon sued the secretary of the interior, claiming that Congress had never intended the ESA to cover habitat degradation, or at least that it had intended that such damage should be prevented by purchase of land rather than halting of activities. The district court for the District of Columbia rejected the suit, but the D.C. Circuit Court reversed the decision on appeal. In 1995 the Supreme Court upheld the inclusion of environmental degradation in the definition of *harm*.

Determination of the critical habitat that must be protected for particular species (defined as geographic areas "on which are found those physical or biological features essential to the conservation of the species and which may require special management considerations or protection") is also a contentious issue, particularly when the economic impact of setting lands aside or halting projects on those lands is large.[103] The ESA does require that economic impacts be considered before designating an area as critical habitat, and the Fish and Wildlife Service says that it tries very hard to work with project designers and landowners to resolve conflicts and find ways for projects to proceed or land to be used without harming species, but some landowners have complained that they are not compensated for loss of use of their land or reduction in property values resulting from actions taken to conserve species. Conflicts between human economic needs and the needs of endangered species have frequently made headlines, as when a three-inch-long endangered fish called the snail darter nearly stopped the building of the gigantic Tellico Dam in Tennessee in the mid-1970s.

HUNTING

Among wildlife issues addressed by animal rights groups, by far the strongest emotions seem to be stirred up by hunting. Most such groups see modern hunting as completely indefensible. The Fund for Animals, for example, terms recreational hunting "a piteously unfair and cruel slaughter of innocent animals," and one animal rights ethicist called it the equivalent of child abuse.[104] Hunters, for their part, have an almost religious devotion to their sport, describing it as their way of expressing a bond with nature. Hunting supporter Ward Clark calls it "a matchless experience, a communion,"[105] and British baroness Anne Mallalieu, head of the pro-hunting group Countryside Alliance, writes that hunting is "our [rural people's] music, it is our poetry, it is our art, it is our pleasure. . . . It is our whole way of life."[106]

As hunters and their supporters never tire of pointing out, humans have hunted throughout their evolution; humanity's closest animal relatives, chimpanzees, also hunt and eat meat. Traditionally, the chief purpose of hunting was to provide meat, clothing, and other materials necessary for survival. Today, although almost half of hunters in the United States are said to eat what they kill, few rely on hunting as a major food source. They hunt primarily for enjoyment, and it is chiefly this sport aspect of hunting that rouses animal rightists' ire.

In England, the most common form of sport hunting is the pursuit of foxes, deer, or hares with dogs. According to the Burns Report, a report on hunting with dogs that was commissioned by the British Parliament and released in June 2000, hunts are an important and sometimes "dominant" feature of social life in rural Britain. In the United States, hunting is usually done with guns, and the most common prey animals—amounting to about half of the 134 million animals killed in the country by hunters each year—are birds, mainly doves, ducks, grouse, quail, and partridges. Another third of the animals killed are squirrels, rabbits, and raccoons. Larger prey include deer (more than 6 million a year) and bears.

Hunting in both countries is largely a rural pursuit, whereas most of the people who oppose hunting come from cities. The animosity between hunters and their opponents is therefore increased by mutual misunderstanding and clashes between urban and rural cultures. Ted Kerasote, an American supporter of hunting, complains that the sport "stands in jeopardy at the hand of a mostly urban society that has come to know wildlife largely through TV and computer screens."[107] In Britain, class is involved in the hunting dispute as well because many Britons see fox hunting as primarily an upper-class activity, although British hunters and their supporters maintain that hunting is popular with all classes in the countryside.

Especially in the United States, hunters claim that hunting is a form of wildlife management. Because settlers killed most wolves and other natural predators of game animals such as deer in the 18th and 19th centuries, hunting supporters say, these prey animals overpopulate if not culled by their only remaining predator, humankind. When such overpopulation occurs, the animals consume all the edible plant matter in their habitat, depriving other animals of food and damaging the ecosystem as a whole. They then succumb to starvation and disease, a far more painful and lingering death than one brought about by a skilled hunter's bullet. Hunting, its defenders say, controls animal populations the same way nature does.

Animal rights groups grant that deer and some other animals tend to overpopulate and that this can be destructive to the animals and their environment. Jordan Curnutt points out in his book on animal law, however, that doves, ducks, and squirrels, the most commonly hunted animals in the United States, do not usually overpopulate. Furthermore, animal rightists question whether hunting is the best, let alone the only, way to control overpopulation when it does occur. Other possibilities exist, including reintroduction of natural predators, relocation, and contraception. (One contraception method is PZP or porcine zona pellucida vaccine, a vaccine against part of the mammalian egg developed in the 1970s, which can be injected by means of a dart.) Hunters say that at least at present, all these methods are expensive, labor intensive, and unreliable.

Discussions about the value of hunting as a wildlife management tool highlight a philosophical disagreement that sometimes divides animal rights organizations from environmental ones. Environmental groups usually try to preserve species and habitats rather than individuals. Some environmental and wildlife preservation organizations, such as the National Wildlife Federation, therefore accept sport hunting under some conditions or want government agents to hunt, trap, or otherwise kill certain types of animals in order to prevent overpopulation or excessive predation on endangered species. Animal rights groups, on the other hand, focus on individual animals and thus usually oppose all hunting and trapping.

This disagreement about management techniques often underlies a deeper clash about whether wildlife should be "managed" at all. Whether as a responsibility entailed by humankind's traditional dominion over other animals or as an attempt to correct the damage already done to ecosystems by human activities such as land clearing, many environmental groups, as well as many scientists and most government wildlife agencies, feel that scientists and wildlife experts should closely monitor wild animal populations and take whatever steps seem necessary to keep them healthy and in balance with their food supply. In line with their hands-off policy on other human-animal interactions, however, many animal rightists say that people should interfere with nature as little as possible, especially when the interference involves killing.

Hunters also argue that, at least in the United States, they are among the foremost preservers of wildlife habitat. They must purchase licenses from their states in order to hunt legally, and the money from license fees is used to buy wilderness land and support wildlife management programs. State fish and wildlife agencies, in fact, receive most of their funding from hunters. (For this very reason, such agencies tend to support hunters' interests.) Hunters of waterbirds must also buy so-called duck stamps as a sort of secondary license or tax, and the revenue from these is used to maintain duck habitat. Money to preserve and restore wildlife habitat comes from federal taxes on sporting guns, handguns, ammunition, and archery tackle as well. Finally, private hunting groups such as Ducks Unlimited spend considerable money to buy, preserve, or even create habitats for their chosen game animals. No one has more motivation than hunters themselves, hunting supporters say, to maintain healthy, sustainable populations of game animals—and when game animals benefit, other animals that live in the same ecosystem usually do as well.

Hunters and animal rights activists disagree about how cruel hunting is. Hunters maintain that they usually accomplish a clean kill, in which the animal dies instantly, whereas animal rights organizations say that at least one animal is wounded and escapes, to die a lingering death from blood loss and infection, for every one that dies on the spot. Similarly, British anti-hunting web sites frequently feature pictures of foxes being torn to bits by dogs, but hunt supporters say that this occurs only after the fox has been killed by the hunters and its dead body is thrown to the dogs as a reward. Britain's Burns Report concluded that the killing in a fox hunt is no more cruel than most other methods used to dispose of foxes, which many farmers see as pests. Hunting advocates say that hunters who eat their kill are at least as moral as people who buy meat at the supermarket—perhaps, in fact, more so because, until they are taken, hunted animals live free and natural lives, whereas animals on factory farms are tightly confined and may be abused in other ways. Food animals that come from the wild also do not contribute to pollution and habitat destruction, as farmed food animals are said to do.

Certain practices have caused controversy within the hunting community as well as between it and animal rights groups. Most hunters feel that high-technology devices such as laser sights, spotlights, explosives, automatic weapons, and aircraft are not sporting, and most states have outlawed the use of such devices in hunting. Hunters are more divided over the use of bait to attract game animals, particularly bears and waterbirds. In the United States, federal Fish and Wildlife Service regulations have forbidden the use of bait in hunting migratory birds since the 1920s, but baiting bears is permitted. About a third of the states completely outlaw the use of bait, and many others limit it. The use of dogs, too, is sometimes outlawed. Many hunters feel that any practice that virtually guarantees a kill is not fair to the prey. Naturally, animal rights groups feel even more strongly that such activities should be banned.

Another practice that has garnered much disapproval from hunters as well as animal rights activists is the canned hunt, in which hunters pay for the chance to shoot game animals, often exotic ones such as African antelopes, zebras, or tigers, and take home their heads, horns, or skin as trophies. The animals frequently are half-tame creatures raised on the game ranch or preserve where the hunt takes place or purchased from circuses or zoos. Although some game preserves have large acreages through which the hunters may pursue their prey, others pen the animals in small enclosures where they cannot escape. They guarantee a kill to any hunter who pays their fee. "That ain't hunting. That's a slaughter," says Florida hunter Perry Arnold.[108] Some states have restricted or banned canned hunting, and animal rights groups and some pro-hunting groups such as the Izaak Walton League have tried to obtain a federal law against it as well, though so far without success.

Animal rights groups have used a variety of tactics in efforts to stop hunting. The League Against Cruel Sports (LACS), founded in Britain in 1924 to stop fox hunting, concentrated on trying to have the sport banned by law. It also bought large tracts of land in hunting territory and used them as wildlife sanctuaries. When these approaches failed to have much effect on hunting, a new group called the Hunt Saboteurs Association (HSA) split off from the LACS in 1964, becoming the first British animal rights group to focus on direct action. It broke up hunts nonviolently, usually by distracting dogs with bait, scents, or noise. In the early 1970s, disgruntled members of the HSA formed a still more radical group called the Band of Mercy, which damaged cars and other property of hunters and their supporters with vandalism and even bombs. This group later became the highly controversial Animal Liberation Front, which targets anyone it classifies as animal abusers.

Sabotaging hunts and harassing hunters also became popular in the United States in the late 1960s and 1970s. There the preferred technique was to frighten prey animals away by such methods as talking loudly or playing music. Although these methods were nonviolent, they irritated hunters into demanding help from their legislators. States began to pass laws against harassment of hunters, beginning with Arizona in 1981, and by 1995, every state had such a law. In addition, a pro-hunting group, the Wildlife Legislative Fund of America (now the U.S. Sportsmen's Alliance), began working for a federal antiharassment law. In 1994 the group obtained passage of the Recreational Hunting Safety and Preservation Act, which makes it illegal to "engage in any physical conduct that hinders a lawful hunt."[109]

At the start of the 21st century, the British government has repeatedly been on the verge of outlawing all or almost all hunting with dogs (hunting with guns and fishing are not expected to be affected). Scotland passed a bill prohibiting the hunting of mammals with hounds in March 2002. On June 30, 2003, despite massive demonstrations by the Countryside Alliance and others (who opposed all regulation of hunting) and the disapproval of Prime Minister Tony Blair (who favored compromise legislation), the British Parliament's House of Commons voted 362 to 154 to ban foxhunting. The House of Lords, Parliament's upper house, contains many members who favor hunting, however, and on October 21 it voted by 261 to 49 to allow fox, hare (rabbit), and stag (deer) hunts with dogs to continue with regulation.

The battle over hunting in Britain seemed sure to continue in 2004, as representatives of the House of Commons threatened to invoke a rule called the Parliament Act to enforce their will on the Lords. Most other European countries permit hunting.

The United States is unlikely to outlaw hunting as a whole, although federal and state laws ban or limit the hunting of certain species, and thousands of other laws, administered by state wildlife agencies or commissions, regulate the sport in various ways. Common types of laws limit the times of year during which hunting is allowed (open and closed seasons), the number of animals of particular types that each hunter can kill (bag limits), and the kinds of weapons that may be used. Hunters must normally purchase both hunting licenses and permits to kill particular kinds of animals; the number of permits issued depends on the number of animals that a state wildlife agency thinks can be safely harvested. Many states also require hunters to take education courses that cover gun safety, hunting ethics, and principles of wildlife management and conservation.

Although hunting remains legal in the United States, its popularity seems to be declining. The number of hunting licenses sold dropped by 11 percent between 1982 and 1997, according to the Fish and Wildlife Service. Some 14 million Americans, about 6 percent of the U.S. population, bought hunting licenses in 2000. Paul G. Irwin, president and chief executive officer (CEO) of the Humane Society of the United States, claims that "the decline in hunting has [chiefly] to do with . . . a growing rejection of the idea of killing for fun," but other commentators say that many factors probably are involved, including a growing lack of leisure time and a decrease in hunting areas that can be reached without spending considerable time and money.[110]

TRAPPING

About 4 million animals were estimated to have been trapped, primarily for their fur, in the United States in 2000. (Some trapping is done for food or to remove animals that humans in the area regard as nuisances, such as coyotes.) Animals trapped commercially include rabbits, foxes, raccoons, and beavers. Like fur farming, trapping has declined since animal rights groups began attempting to persuade people not to wear fur. In the late 1980s, for instance, about 20 million animals were trapped yearly.

Animal rights groups have protested trapping as well as hunting. The National Trappers Association claims that "the professional wildlife conservation community universally endorses traps and trapping as critical and essential wildlife management tools" to keep populations at optimum size and prevent the spread of disease, but animal rightists say that almost all traps cause terribly painful injuries and deaths.[111] They also estimate that for every targeted animal, from two to five "nontargeted" ones, including endangered species and family pets, are caught in traps. The National Trappers Association denies this.

The type of trap that has caused the most controversy is the steel-jawed leghold trap, which is used in about 80 percent of trappings in the United States. Of 15 practices that could be considered harmful to animals, both Australian and American animal activists indicated in surveys that they considered use of these traps the worst. The National Trappers Association claims that fish and wildlife agencies regularly use steel-jawed leghold traps to capture animals for study or transportation to other sites and that they would not do so if the traps usually harmed the animals caught in them. However, the American Veterinary Medical Association and the American Animal Hospital Association both say that the traps can cause severe tissue damage.

A second type of trap, the Conibear or body-gripping trap, is supposed to kill animals quickly by snapping shut on their necks and breaking them. Opponents of the traps say that the traps sometimes close on an animal's chest or hips instead, producing a slow death from shock and suffocation as the trap crushes its body. Snares, a third type of trap, are wire loops that tighten around an animal's leg or neck. The National Trappers Association compares them to "a dog collar and leash," but if the wire is uncoated, as is often the case, it can cut through flesh to the bone.[112] The only kind of trap that dependably does not injure an animal is the live trap, in which food bait essentially lures an animal into a cage with a door that then shuts, but commercial trappers seldom use such traps because they are expensive.

No federal law governs trapping as a whole, but many states have laws or regulations that limit the activity. Like hunting, trapping requires a license in all states, and some states limit trapping by season, bag limit, size and placement of trap, or all of these. Steel-jawed leghold traps have been outlawed in eight states (as well as in 89 other countries, including all members of the European Union) and are restricted in most others. Four states have outlawed body-gripping traps, nine have banned snares, and some others restrict size or placement of these devices. Forty-five states also have laws that require trappers to check their traps at stated intervals so that animals caught in them can be either killed or released. Other state laws specify minimum distances by which traps must be separated from roads or human habitations, to minimize the capture of pets or other disturbance to humans. California stands alone in banning all trapping of furbearing animals for either commercial purposes or sport.

THE FUTURE OF ANIMAL RIGHTS

Although the ideas and tactics of its more extreme members have caused considerable controversy and its basic aims are still far from being achieved, the animal rights movement has certainly succeeded in establishing itself as a social and political force during the past 30 years. It has made people think about subjects that most had never considered before, such as the conditions under which cattle and chickens live before reaching their dinner tables. As a result, the public has begun to examine the ethical implications of lifestyle choices ranging from eating meat to buying eye makeup and taking their children to the zoo.

Polls show that public opinion in the United States and Europe on many issues involving human treatment of animals has become more animal-friendly since the crusade for animal rights began. To some extent, behavior has changed as well. Robert Garner wrote in the British magazine *Parliamentary Affairs* in 1998, for instance, that because of the animal rights movement, "a social stigma is now attached to the wearing of fur; the number of vegetarians has increased markedly, creating a new marketing niche; [and] the demand for 'cruelty free' cosmetic products has played an important role in the decision of many manufacturers to seek alternative testing methods."[113]

Nonetheless, most people still eat meat, wear at least some animal products (such as leather shoes), and approve of research on animals if it seems likely to contribute substantially to human health and safety. Intensive farming and widespread habitat destruction continue worldwide. Although there has been some tightening of laws and regulations governing treatment of animals, especially in Europe, the animal rights movement has had much less effect on government and law than on the public, and many uses of animals remain virtually unregulated (or existing regulations are seldom enforced).

Most commentators doubt that animal rightists will achieve their more extreme aims, such as full legal rights for animals, in the next 50 years. However, the influence of the animal rights crusade is likely to continue to bring changes as people increasingly examine their consciences about what uses of animals they can accept and what sacrifices of effort and money they will make to improve animals' lot. Futurist Lee Shupp, strategic director of Cheskin Research in Redwood Shores, California, said in an interview published in *American Demographics* in 2001 that he believes that

> *within the next 10 to 20 years, the idea that animals . . . have some individual rights will become a generally accepted notion. . . . I don't think we're going to become a nation of vegetarians [but] I think it's likely that we're going to pay a lot more attention to how animals are treated, not only as pets, but as sources of food.*[114]

Issues in Animal Welfare and Animal Rights

Animal rights activists and their opponents will continue to compete for the hearts and minds of the public as each side increasingly recognizes that the other is here to stay. Corporations and individuals who work with or use animals will try harder to explain their activities as they realize that responding to consumers' concern about treatment of animals makes good business sense. All but the most extreme animal rightists, for their part, most likely will face the fact that some human relationship with, and probably some human use of, animals will continue for the foreseeable future, and they will concentrate on shaping that relationship rather than trying to end it. Both sides of the animal rights debate may come to understand that willingness to listen to and respect each other's point of view, discuss issues rationally, and make compromises will work better than moral intransigence in advancing their aims.

Many observers both within and outside the animal rights movement say that the movement's future success will depend to a very large extent on whether it forms alliances with other social movements and groups that share some of its goals. Possible allies include groups devoted to consumer issues, human health, and the environment, as well as academics and even representatives of business and industry. Such alliances could greatly increase the movement's ability to influence governments as well as the public. Andrew Rowan and Bernard Unti of the Humane Society of the United States write that the relationship between animal protection and environmentalism will be particularly important because "among all new social movements, environmentalism elicits the most support and the greatest degree of consensus" and "has emerged as the pivotal foundation of new social movements worldwide."[115]

Indeed, whatever their position on the many debates within the area of animal rights, it seems likely that increasing numbers of people will come to recognize that humans' treatment of animals is simply one aspect of their treatment of nature as a whole. In a much-quoted statement, Mohandas Gandhi said, "The greatness of a nation and its moral progress can be judged by the way its animals are treated."[116] More than greatness or even morality may be at stake, however. The way human beings treat the other creatures with whom they share the planet, as a reflection of the way they treat the planet itself, may be what determines their species' survival.

---

[1] Gary Francione, quoted in Harold D. Guither, *Animal Rights: History and Scope of a Radical Social Movement.* Carbondale: Southern Illinois University Press, 1998, p. 23.

[2] Genesis, 1: 28.

[3] Thomas Aquinas, quoted in Frank R. Ascione and Randall Lockwood, "Cruelty to Animals: Changing Psychological, Social, and Legislative Perspectives," in Deborah J. Salem and Andrew N. Rowan, eds., *The State of the Animals: 2001.* Washington, D.C.: Humane Society Press, 2001, p. 39.

[4] Jeremy Bentham, quoted in Lyle Munro, *Compassionate Beasts: The Quest for Animal Rights*. Westport, Conn.: Praeger, 2001, p. 17.

[5] Jeremy Bentham, quoted in Jordan Curnutt, *Animals and the Law: A Sourcebook*. Santa Barbara, Calif.: ABC-CLIO, 2001, p. 435.

[6] Richard Ryder, quoted in Edward Skidelsky, "Nonsense upon Stilts," *New Statesman*, vol. 129, June 5, 2000, p. 53.

[7] Peter Singer, quoted in Adam Kolber, "Standing Upright: The Moral and Legal Standing of Humans and Other Apes," *Stanford Law Review*, vol. 54, October 2001, p. 193.

[8] Peter Singer, quoted in Lewis Petrinovich, *Darwinian Dominion: Animal Welfare and Human Interests*. Cambridge, Mass.: MIT Press, 1999, p. 211.

[9] Tom Regan, quoted in Guither, *Animal Rights*, p. 20.

[10] Michael Fox, quoted in Ward M. Clark, *Misplaced Compassion: The Animal Rights Movement Exposed*. San Jose, Calif.: Writers Club Press, 2001, p. 13.

[11] Roger Scruton and Andrew Tyler, "Do Animals Have Rights?" *The Ecologist*, vol. 31, March 2001, p. 24.

[12] David S. Oderberg, "The Illusion of Animal Rights," *Human Life Review*, Spring–Summer 2000, p. 42.

[13] Matthew Scully, quoted in Michael Mountain, "Speaking for the Animal Right," *Best Friends Magazine*, January–February 2003, p. 22.

[14] Curnutt, *Animals and the Law*, p. 29.

[15] *Black's Law Dictionary*, quoted in Guither, *Animal Rights*, p. 163.

[16] Antonin Scalia, quoted in Curnutt, *Animals and the Law*, p. 48.

[17] Patricia Wald, quoted in Curnutt, *Animals and the Law*, p. 62.

[18] Rob Roy Smith, "Standing on Their Own Four Legs: The Future of Animal Welfare Litigation after *Animal Legal Defense Fund, Inc. v. Glickman*," *Environmental Law*, vol. 29, Winter 1999, p. 990.

[19] Steven Wise, quoted in Josie Glausiusz, "He Speaks for the Speechless," *Discover*, vol. 22, September 2001, p. 18.

[20] Richard A. Epstein, "The Next Rights Revolution? It's Bowser's Time at Last," *National Review*, vol. 51, November 8, 1999, p. 44.

[21] Eric Glitzenstein, quoted in Shawn Zeller, "Counsel for a Menagerie of Clients," *National Journal*, vol. 32, March 4, 2000, p. 715.

[22] Gary L. Francione and Lee Hall, "Confused Animal Rights Movement," *San Francisco Chronicle*, August 21, 2002, p. A21.

[23] Stephen Fox, quoted in Munro, *Compassionate Beasts*, p. 73.

[24] Roger, quoted in Munro, *Compassionate Beasts*, p. 95.

[25] Clark, *Misplaced Compassion*, p. 41.

[26] Tom Regan, quoted in Munro, *Compassionate Beasts*, p. 39.

[27] Munro, *Compassionate Beasts*, p. 5.

[28] Bernard Unti and Andrew N. Rowan, "A Social History of Postwar Animal Protection," in Salem and Rowan, eds., *The State of the Animals: 2001*, p. 29.

[29] Ingrid Newkirk, quoted in Clark, *Misplaced Compassion*, p. 36.

[30] Betsy Cummings, "Shock Treatment," *Sales and Marketing Management*, vol. 153, January 2001, p. 64.

[31] Andrew Tyler, quoted in Munro, *Compassionate Beasts*, p. 131.

[32] Munro, *Compassionate Beasts*, p. 190.

[33] Animal Liberation Front, quoted in Mike Weiss, "Eco-Terrorists Frustrate FBI," *San Francisco Chronicle*, February 3, 2002, p. A1.

[34] James Jarboe, quoted in Sean Higgins, "The Terrorist Tactics of Radical Environmentalists," *Insight on the News*, vol. 18, p. 45.

[35] Keith Mann, quoted in Terry O'Neill, "Bambi's Vigilantes," *The Report Newsmagazine*, vol. 28, February 5, 2001, p. 25.

[36] Tim Dailey, quoted in Guither, *Animal Rights*, pp. 159–160.

[37] Joint resolution, quoted in Guither, *Animal Rights*, p. 57.

[38] *Animal People*, quoted in Guither, *Animal Rights*, p. 161.

[39] Unti and Rowan, "A Social History of Postwar Animal Protection," p. 31.

[40] Munro, *Compassionate Beasts*, p. 165.

[41] Munro, *Compassionate Beasts*, p. 31.

[42] Marlene Halverson, quoted in Guither, *Animal Rights*, p. 22.

[43] Andrew Gay, quoted in Ed Shelton, "New Comms Tactics Test Animal Research Groups," *PR Week*, January 25, 2002, p. 9.

[44] Animal Industry Foundation, quoted in "Agriculture's Efforts Must Be Focused on Building Image," *Feedstuffs*, vol. 71, October 11, 1999, p. 8.

[45] Andrew Gay, quoted in Shelton, "New Comms Tactics Test Animal Research Groups," p. 9.

[46] Mark Matfield, quoted in Shelton, "New Comms Tactics Test Animal Research Groups," p. 9.

[47] James Serpell, quoted in Munro, *Compassionate Beasts*, p. 178.

[48] Ingrid Newkirk, quoted in Guither, *Animal Rights*, p. 68.

[49] Ingrid Newkirk, quoted in Clark, *Misplaced Compassion*, p. 38.

[50] John Bryant, quoted in Munro, *Compassionate Beasts*, p. 177.

[51] Munro, *Compassionate Beasts*, p. 176.

[52] Munro, *Compassionate Beasts*, p. 178.

[53] Martin Act, quoted in Curnutt, *Animals and the Law*, p. 71.

[54] Patricia Jensen, quoted in Judith Reitman, "From the Leash to the Laboratory," *Atlantic Monthly*, p. 17.

[55] Ruth Harrison, quoted in Guither, *Animal Rights*, pp. 2, 87.

[56] Temple Grandin, "Progress in Livestock Handling and Slaughter Techniques in the United States, 1970–2000," in Salem and Rowan, eds., *The State of the Animals: 2001*, p. 108.

[57] David Fraser, Joy Mench, and Suzanne Millman, "Farm Animals and Their Welfare in 2000," in Salem and Rowan, eds., *The State of the Animals: 2001*, p. 98.

[58] Al Pope, quoted in Sally Schuff, "Inside Washington," *Feedstuffs*, vol. 74, May 20, 2002, p. 5.

[59] Bruce Friedrich, quoted in Megan Steintrager, "Duty and the Beast," *Restaurant Business*, vol. 101, June 15, 2002, p. 24.

[60] Animal rights pamphlet, quoted in Curnutt, *Animals and the Law*, p. 164.

[61] Grandin, "Progress in Livestock Handling and Slaughter Techniques in the United States, 1970–2000," p. 108.

[62] Peter Stevenson, quoted in Tessa Fox, "Animal Passions," *Caterer & Hotelkeeper*, June 13, 2002, p. 20.

[63] Munro, *Compassionate Beasts*, p. 157.

[64] Laboratory Animal Welfare Act, quoted in Curnutt, *Animals and the Law*, pp. 442–443.

[65] Alex Pacheco, quoted in Charles Patterson, *Animal Rights*. Lincoln, Neb.: iuniverse.com, 2000, pp. 52–53.

[66] Quoted in Curnutt, *Animals and the Law*, p. 52.

[67] Adrian R. Morrison, "Personal Reflections on the 'Animal-Rights' Phenomenon," *Perspectives in Biology and Medicine*, vol. 44, Winter 2001, p. 62.

[68] 1985 revision of Animal Welfare Act, quoted in Curnutt, *Animals and the Law*, p. 446.

[69] 1985 revision of Animal Welfare Act, quoted in Curnutt, *Animals and the Law*, p. 447.

[70] 1985 revision of Animal Welfare Act, quoted in Curnutt, *Animals and the Law*, p. 446.

[71] Martin Stephens, quoted in Lisa Yount, *Issues in Biomedical Ethics*. San Diego, Calif.: Lucent Books, 1998, p. 70.

[72] Dan Glickman, "Regulations for the Use of Laboratory Animals," *Journal of the American Medical Association*, vol. 285, February 21, 2001, p. 941.

[73] Estelle A. Fishbein, "What Price Mice?" *Journal of the American Medical Association*, vol. 285, February 21, 2001, p. 939.

[74] Ingrid Newkirk, quoted in Clark, *Misplaced Compassion*, p. 37.

[75] Jessica Sandler, quoted in Glen Martin, "It's PETA vs. Greens in Tiff over Lab Rats," *San Francisco Chronicle*, July 22, 2002, p. A6.

[76] Peter Singer, quoted in Yount, *Issues in Biomedical Ethics*, p. 62.

[77] Michael Hayre, quoted in Scott Shepard, "Animal Protection Law Targets 70,000 Mice in St. Jude Labs," *Memphis Business Journal*, vol. 22, November 17, 2000, p. 1.

[78] PETA advertisement, quoted in Deborah Rudacille, *The Scalpel and the Butterfly*. Berkeley: University of California Press, 2000, p. 299.

[79] Gina Solomon, quoted in Martin, "It's PETA vs. Greens in Tiff over Lab Rats," p. A6.

[80] Jonathan Balcombe, quoted in Virginia McCord, "More Frogs Live to Croak," *Insight on the News*, vol. 14, March 30, 1998, p. 42.

[81] Adrian Morrison, quoted in Patterson, *Animal Rights*, p. 33.

[82] Richard Smith, "Animal Research: The Need for a Middle Ground," *British Medical Journal*, vol. 322, February 3, 2001, p. 248.

[83] Michael Balls, quoted in Robert Koenig, "European Researchers Grapple with Animal Rights," *Science*, vol. 284, June 4, 1999, p. 1604.

[84] National Association for Biomedical Research, quoted in Guither, *Animal Rights*, p. 80.

[85] Hanno Wurbel, "Better Housing for Better Science," *Chemistry and Industry*, April 16, 2001, p. 237.

[86] "Animal Rights FAQ: Section 9, Animals for Entertainment," www.animal-rights.com/arsec9q.htm, p. 3, downloaded on January 9, 2003.

[87] Dick Gregory, quoted in Catherine Gourley, "Animal Welfare or Animal Rights?" *Writing!*, vol. 24, January 2002, p. 9.

[88] "Sara the Tiger Whisperer," quoted in Denise Martin, "Ringling Bros. Waging a Campaign to Combat Allegations of Animal Abuse," *Orange County Register*, July 26, 2002, p. K3830.

[89] Richard Farinato, "Another View of Zoos," in Salem and Rowan, eds., *The State of the Animals: 2001*, p. 145.

[90] "Animal Rights FAQ: Section 9, Animals for Entertainment," p. 2.

[91] David Hancocks, "Is There a Place in the World for Zoos?" in Salem and Rowan, eds., *The State of the Animals: 2001*, p. 143.

[92] Hancocks, "Is There a Place in the World for Zoos?" p. 143.

[93] Farinato, "Another View of Zoos," p. 147.

[94] Hancocks, "Is There a Place in the World for Zoos?" p. 138.

[95] Noelle Delaquis, quoted in "When Dolphins Cry," *Swiss News*, March 2001, p. 10.

[96] Hancocks, "Is There a Place in the World for Zoos?" p. 139.

[97] Edward White, decision in *Geer v. Connecticut*, quoted in Curnutt, *Animals and the Law*, p. 318.

[98] U.S. Fish & Wildlife Service, "ESA Basics," http://endangered.fws.gov, downloaded in December 2002, p. 1.

[99] Curnutt, *Animals and the Law*, p. 369.

[100] Endangered Species Act, quoted in Curnutt, *Animals and the Law*, p. 373.

[101] Ninth Circuit Court of Appeals decision in *Palila v. Hawaii Department of Land and Natural Resources (Palila II)*, quoted in Curnutt, *Animals and the Law*, p. 35.

[102] Fish and Wildlife Service ESA regulation, quoted in Curnutt, *Animals and the Law*, p. 374.

[103] Endangered Species Act, quoted in Fish and Wildlife Service, "ESA Basics," p. 2.

[104] Fund for Animals, quoted in Clark, *Misplaced Compassion*, p. 94.

[105] Clark, *Misplaced Compassion*, p. 68.

[106] Anne Mallalieu, quoted in Munro, *Compassionate Beasts*, p. 205.

[107] Ted Kerasote, "Straight Talk on Hunting," *Sports Afield*, vol. 223, August 2000, p. 34.

[108] Perry Arnold, quoted in Jeffrey Kluger, "Hunting Made Easy," *Time*, vol. 159, March 11, 2002, p. 62.

[109] Recreational Hunting Safety and Preservation Act, quoted in Curnutt, *Animals and the Law*, p. 305.

[110] Paul G. Irwin, "Overview: The State of Animals in 2001," in Salem and Rowan, eds., *The State of the Animals: 2001*, p. 4.

[111] National Trappers Association, "Factual Rebuttals to HSUS Non-factual 'Facts about Trapping,'" www.nationaltrappers.com/Facts.html, downloaded on February 8, 2003, pp. 3–4.

[112] National Trappers Association, "Factual Rebuttals to HSUS Non-factual 'Facts about Trapping,'" pp. 1–2.

[113] Robert Garner, "Defending Animal Rights," *Parliamentary Affairs*, vol. 51, July 1998, p. 459.

[114] Lee Shupp, quoted in "Futurespeak," *American Demographics*, May 1, 2001, p. 56.

[115] Unti and Rowan, "A Social History of Postwar Animal Protection," p. 31.

[116] Mohandas Gandhi, quoted in Margaret C. Jasper, *Animal Rights Law*. Dobbs Ferry, N.Y.: Oceana Publications, Inc., 2002, p. vii.

CHAPTER 2

THE LAW AND ANIMAL RIGHTS

LAWS AND REGULATIONS

Hundreds of pieces of state and local legislation, and a handful of federal laws, affect humans' treatment of animals in the United States. Compared to rulings in other areas of legislative interest, however, laws concerning animals are scant.

The roles of federal and state legislation differ depending on the situations in which animals are kept. Virtually all laws against cruelty to cats and dogs as companion animals are state laws, for example, but treatment of those same species in laboratories is governed almost entirely by federal law. The states normally regulate hunting and trapping unless endangered species are involved, in which case the federal Endangered Species Act takes over.

The amount of legal regulation also varies in different industries and in different aspects of the same industry. For instance, the federal Humane Slaughter Act regulates the way food animals are killed, but their treatment before that time is hardly regulated. The Animal Welfare Act and its regulations describe in some detail the minimum housing and care required for different kinds of animals in laboratories and animal exhibitions, but the act specifically forbids any direct regulation of experimental procedures performed on the animals. The same act covers zoos, circuses, and animal shows but not animal races or rodeos.

This section describes the federal and state laws that have had the most significant effects on the animal welfare issues discussed in Chapter 1. The laws are arranged by date, with the oldest first.

ANIMAL WELFARE ACT (1970)

Government-funded medical research in the United States increased substantially in the late 1940s, and so did the demand for laboratory animals, including cats and dogs. Stories in the mid-1960s about the theft of pets and the miserable conditions in which some dealers held animals destined for sale to laboratories produced a public outcry that made Congress pass the Laboratory Animal Welfare Act (LAWA) in 1966.

The LAWA's chief purpose was clearly the protection of family pets. It required dealers who sold dogs and cats (but not other animals) to obtain licenses from the U.S. Department of Agriculture (USDA), which was given responsibility for enforcing the law, and to identify and keep records of all animals they sold. Similarly, laboratories that used dogs and cats, but no others, had to buy them from licensed dealers and keep records of them. The law also ordered the secretary of agriculture to "promulgate standards to govern the humane handling, care, treatment, and transportation of animals by dealers and research facilities," including primates, cats, dogs, rabbits, guinea pigs, and hamsters, but no rules were to be made affecting the handling or care of animals "during actual research or experimentation."

In 1970, Congress gave the LAWA a shorter name, the Animal Welfare Act (AWA), and expanded it considerably. The AWA (7 U.S.C. 2131-2157) is the only significant federal law that regulates the use of animals in research, product testing, and education. It applies to all laboratories carrying out research supported in whole or in part by federal funds or using animals that have been transported across state lines, which, according to Jordan Curnutt's *Animals and the Law*, means "virtually all research using laboratory animals" of the covered types in the United States.[1]

Unlike its predecessor, the AWA regulated animal exhibitors as well as wholesale dealers and laboratories. It also covered "any warm-blooded animal," not just the six species mentioned in the LAWA. The new law specified the meanings of certain terms and the penalties for violation more clearly than the old one had, and it required monitoring and inspections to verify that research and exhibition facilities were meeting its standards of animal care, which the LAWA had not. These inspections, along with other aspects of implementing and enforcing the AWA, were assigned to the USDA's Animal and Plant Health Inspection Service (APHIS) in 1972.

APHIS issued regulations implementing the AWA later in 1972. They provide minimum requirements (which are sometimes, though not always, quite detailed) for the housing of different species of laboratory animals, specify the kinds of records that dealers and laboratories must keep, and so on. They also require training programs for all personnel who handle animals. Probably the most controversial aspect of these regulations is their redefinition of "animal" to exclude rats, mice, and birds, which make up about 95 percent of all laboratory animals. Farm animals are also exempted from the AWA.

The AWA was revised in 1976, 1983, 1985, 1990, and 1991, with the 1985 amendments (collectively termed the Improved Standards for Laboratory Animals Act) being the most significant. Partly in response to two high-profile cases of apparent animal abuse in laboratories in the early 1980s, the AWA's 1985 amendments specifically require scientists to "minimize pain and distress" to animals during experiments, to consult with a veterinarian about pain control as well as general care, and to provide anesthesia or analgesia unless withholding such medication is deemed "scientifically necessary." They also mention for the first time the desirability of seeking nonanimal alternatives to animal testing and of avoiding unnecessary duplication of animal experiments. They mandate exercise programs for dogs and "a physical environment adequate to promote the psychological well-being of primates," but they let the regulated institutions and the veterinarians decide how to fulfill these requirements.

The 1985 revision of the AWA also requires institutions using animals to set up Institutional Animal Care and Use Committees (IACUCs). Each committee must have at least three members, including a veterinarian and a person who represents "general community interests in the proper care and treatment of animals" and is not affiliated with the institution or related to anyone who is. The IACUC reviews proposals for all new experiments using animals at its institution as well as monitoring ongoing experiments and the overall care of the institution's animals. It is supposed to judge whether each use of animals is scientifically necessary and to evaluate steps taken to minimize the animals' pain and distress. However, although it can reject a research plan completely (which apparently rarely happens), it cannot prescribe or alter such a plan.

The Pet Protection Act is a further amendment to the AWA made in 1990. It requires all animal control facilities (pounds and shelters) to hold cats and dogs brought to them for at least five days before selling them to dealers who may sell them to laboratories. This is similar to the requirement for dealers in the original 1966 LAWA, but it is more useful because pet owners are more likely to be able to find animal control facilities than animal dealers and thus should have a better chance of retrieving lost or stolen pets. The requirement also gives animals a somewhat better chance to be adopted. The Pet Protection Act increases record-keeping requirements for dealers and animal control facilities as well.

ENDANGERED SPECIES ACT
(1973—AMENDED 1978, 1982, 1988)

Several federal laws, such as the Bald Eagle Protection Act (1940) and the Marine Mammal Protection Act (1972), protect particular wildlife species or groups of species. In addition, calls for a law to protect all endangered or threatened species began in the 1960s, when Americans started to realize the extent to which human activities were destroying not only animals themselves but their habitat through such activities as logging and clearing land for agriculture or housing. The result of this destruction was a rapid rise in the rate at which species were vanishing completely, or becoming extinct.

Congress passed the first federal law aimed at protecting endangered species, the Endangered Species Preservation Act, in 1966. It directed the secretary of the interior to identify every endangered native fish and wildlife species and preserve the species and their habitats where possible, but, amazingly, it did not prohibit hunting of identified species, except on federal lands, or their commercial transportation across state borders. In 1969, this weak act was replaced by the Endangered Species Conservation Act, which expanded the types of animals covered and extended the range of the endangered species list to the entire world. However, the new act still did not cover plants, and it left most species protection up to the states.

Environmental groups demanded that these acts be strengthened, and the final result was the Endangered Species Act (ESA), signed into law in December 1973. It appears in the U.S. Code as 16 U.S.C. 1531-1544. The ESA's purpose is to protect species of plants and animals classified as endangered ("in danger of extinction throughout all or a significant portion of its range") or threatened ("likely to become endangered . . . in the foreseeable future"), along with "the ecosystems upon which endangered and threatened species depend." Such species should be preserved, the act said, because they are of "aesthetic, ecological, educational, historical, recreational, and scientific value to the Nation and its people." The act covers all plant and animal species worldwide, including subspecies and, in the case of vertebrates, populations (thus a vertebrate species may be declared to be endangered in a particular area, even though it is thriving elsewhere). Although the ESA was amended in 1978, 1982, and 1988, the 1973 version is basically still in force today. In 1978, the Supreme Court called this law "the most comprehensive legislation for the preservation of endangered species ever enacted by any nation."[2]

The Endangered Species Act provides elaborate procedures for classifying a species, subspecies, or population as endangered or threatened. Individuals or groups may petition to have a species considered for listing, or the department of the interior's Fish and Wildlife Service (FWS), which is in charge of implementing the law except in the oceans, may determine on its own that a species needs to be added to the list. The law forbids anyone to take ("harass, harm, pursue, hunt, shoot, wound, kill, trap, capture, or collect") or attempt to take members of listed species in the United States, its territorial waters, or the open ocean and to export, import, possess, sell, or transport endangered species or any part of their bodies. It also forbids government agencies to authorize, fund, or carry out projects that will harm a listed species or damage its "critical habitat" unless they receive an exemption from a cabinet-level committee. Violation of the law can result in fines of up to $100,000 and jail terms of up to six months.

The FWS, the Commerce Department's National Marine Fisheries Service (which administers the ESA in the oceans), and the USDA's Forest Service are required to devise plans for helping endangered species "recover" to the point where they are no longer endangered or threatened. These agencies work with the states and private landowners to develop conservation programs. As authorized by the ESA, they also administer the provisions of the Convention on International Trade in Endangered Species of Wild Fauna and Flora (CITES) as these apply to the United States. This international agreement was signed in 1973.

One of the most important parts of the ESA from the standpoint of environmental and animal welfare groups is its so-called citizen suit provision, which states that any person can file a civil suit against another person, organization, or government entity, claiming violations of the act. Citizens may also charge the secretary of the interior with failure to list a species as threatened or endangered or to remove a recovered species from the list. Environmental and animal rights groups have attempted to use the citizen suit provision frequently, although courts have usually ruled that they did not have standing to sue. Landowners who feel that actions taken to protect species have damaged their interests can also sue under this provision.

FWS regulations and, sometimes, court challenges have refined the definition of particular terms in the ESA. For instance, a 1975 FWS regulation specified that "environmental modification or degradation [that] . . . disrupts essential behavior patterns" was to be included in the act's definition of "harm." The Supreme Court upheld this inclusion in a 1995 case, *Babbitt v. Sweet Home Chapter of Communities for a Great Oregon*. Determination of the "critical habitat" that must be protected for particular species (defined as geographic areas "on which are found those physical or biological features essential to the conservation of the species and which may require special management considerations or protection" has also been a contentious issue. The ESA specifies that economic impacts are not to be considered when deciding whether to list a species as threatened or endangered, but they must be considered when determining critical habitat.

As the Endangered Species Act became 30 years old in December 2003, the George W. Bush administration and Republicans in Congress were making plans to change it in ways that, if approved, will be sure to rouse the ire of animal protection and environmental groups. Proposed alterations include allowing American hunters to kill, capture, or import certain endangered animals overseas, permitting some resumption in international trade of ivory from African elephants, limiting the ESA's ability to set aside "critical habitat" for endangered species, and exempting military installations from critical habitat requirements. Supporters of the changes say that relaxation of the overseas rules will help poor countries raise money for wildlife and habitat conservation and that tightening the rules about critical habitat will allow the government to spend money on conservation programs rather than on defending itself against environmentalists' suits regarding habitat. Environmentalists and animal rights groups see the changes as attempts to weaken the act's ability to protect endangered species.

HUMANE METHODS OF SLAUGHTER ACT (1978)

In the first half of the 20th century, large meat animals (cattle, sheep, and pigs) slaughtered at meatpacking plants were normally stunned, usually by being hit over the head with a hammer, before their throats were slit. The stunning sometimes failed, however, resulting in animals being bled out or even occasionally dismembered or skinned while still conscious. In response to pressure from prominent senator Hubert Humphrey and several national animal welfare groups, Congress passed the Humane Slaughter Act in 1958 to end this cruel state of affairs. The law, which covered pigs, cattle, and sheep killed in U.S. packing plants that supplied meat to the federal government, required that these animals be "rendered insensible to pain by a single blow or gunshot or an electrical, chemical or other means that is rapid and effective" before being cut, chained, hoisted, or knocked down. It also specified procedures for handling the animals just before slaughter. The USDA was given the job of implementing and enforcing the law.

The slaughter law was revised in 1978, at which time it became the Humane Methods of Slaughter Act, 7 U.S.C. 1901-1906. This version of the law covers all U.S. plants subject to federal inspection (required for plants engaging in interstate commerce)—about 95 percent of all U.S. meatpackers—and plants in all foreign countries that export meat to the United States. Unlike its predecessor, it provides a way for the government to verify that meatpackers are following its regulations. Inspectors working for a branch of the USDA called the Food Safety and Inspection Service (FSIS) are stationed in slaughterhouses and have the authority to stop the production line if they see either violations of handling and slaughter regulations or signs of diseased animals or meat. FSIS inspectors also periodically examine plants in countries that export meat to the United States, although they do not remain there all the time.

The Humane Methods of Slaughter Act, like the earlier slaughter law, has two important and controversial exceptions. First, it does not apply to birds, which make up more than 95 percent of the animals killed in slaughterhouses. Chickens and turkeys therefore may legally be killed while they are still conscious. Many poultry slaughterhouses dip their birds in a tank of electrically charged water to stun them, but only California has a law that requires them to do so.

The Humane Methods of Slaughter Act also does not apply to Jewish kosher slaughter, which requires that animals be conscious and standing when they are killed. (The original purpose of this religious rule was probably to ensure that people ate fresh meat from healthy animals. Kosher killing is done by slitting the throat with an extremely sharp knife and, properly carried out, is said to be almost painless and to induce unconsciousness within seconds.) The exemption also covers halal, rules of slaughter in the Muslim religion that are similar to kosher. Although this exception has been challenged in court as showing favoritism to particular religions, the Supreme Court in a 1974 case, *Jones v. Butz*, affirmed a district court ruling that the law is constitutional.

ANIMAL ENTERPRISE PROTECTION ACT (1992)

Congress passed the Animal Enterprise Protection Act (P.L. 102-346) in 1992 in response to the violent activities of a handful of extremist animal rights groups such as the Animal Liberation Front. The act makes physical disruption of animal production and research facilities a violation of federal law. Facilities covered under the law include "commercial or academic enterprise[s] that use animals for food or fiber production, agriculture, research, or testing" as well as zoos, aquariums, circuses, rodeos, fairs, and competitive animal events such as races. Disruption is defined as "intentionally stealing, damaging, or causing the loss of, any property (including animals or records) used by the animal enterprise, . . . thereby caus[ing] economic damage exceeding $10,000 to that enterprise." The law specifies monetary restitution and other penalties, but critics say that these penalties are less severe than those many state laws mandate for similar crimes.

State Laws Against Cruelty to Animals

The first clear legal statement of a responsibility toward animals in themselves, rather than as someone's property, was part of the "Body of Liberties," a set of 100 rules of conduct which the Reverend Nathaniel Ward drew up for the Pilgrims' Massachusetts Bay Colony in 1641. Liberty 92 stated that "No man shall exercise any tirranny or crueltie towards any bruite creature which are usuallie kept for man's use."[3]

This statement was far ahead of its time. No other American colonies wrote laws or rulings forbidding animal abuse, nor did the new states of the fledgling United States, until Maine passed one in 1821. This law, like the better-known one that wealthy ex-diplomat Henry Bergh wrote and persuaded the New York legislature to pass in 1867, focused chiefly on horses and cattle. The more expansive New York law, however, forbade beating, overworking, torturing, or killing "any living creature," depriving animals of sustenance (neglect), or abandoning old, maimed, or sick horses or mules.

All states of the United States had laws against cruelty to animals by 1921, and all still do today. These laws differ in their level of detail and specific requirements, but, according to Jordan Curnutt's *Animals and the Law*, all specify to some degree the kinds of animals protected, the actions prohibited, the mental state required to establish liability, and the uses of animals that are exempted.

Many state anticruelty laws apply to "any animal," but others cover only mammals or mammals and birds. "Cruel" actions forbidden usually include killing, maiming, torturing, mutilating, and tormenting—terms which may or may not be defined and are often qualified by the adjectives *unnecessary, needless,* or *unjustifiable,* leaving it up to judges to decide when killing, injuring, or causing pain is necessary or justifiable. Neglect, including deprivation of food and water and, sometimes, shelter or veterinary care, is also usually included, and abandonment is illegal in three-fourths of the states. Most anticruelty laws require that cruel acts be done "knowingly" or with some similar type of guilty mental state, which is often hard to prove. People are almost always exempted from animal cruelty laws if they harm an animal in defense of themselves or others or for purposes of euthanasia to end suffering. Some states also exempt particular types of activities, including research, agricultural, or veterinary practices that are "generally accepted," hunting done in compliance with state law, and sometimes forms of entertainment such as rodeos and circuses.

Until recently, convictions under state animal cruelty laws were few and sentences usually light because the laws considered animal cruelty to be merely a misdemeanor crime against "public order" or "public morals." In the last 10 or 20 years, however, thanks in part to the activities of animal protection groups, this situation has been changing. By 2001, 33 states and the District of Columbia classified severe animal abuse as a felony.

COURT CASES

A number of court cases, including some that reached the Supreme Court, have affected judicial views of animal welfare and animal rights. Some were criminal cases involving alleged cruelty to animals, while others addressed more basic legal issues such as the requirements an animal protection or environmental organization must meet in order to have the right ("standing") to bring a civil suit against a government agency. The remainder of this chapter discusses some key cases in this field.

SIERRA CLUB V. MORTON
405 U.S. 727 (1972)

Background

Mineral King Valley is a wilderness area in Tulare County, California, on the western side of the Sierra Nevada near Sequoia National Park. It has long been beloved as a beautiful, unspoiled spot for hiking and similar recreational activities. In 1965, the U.S. Forest Service, which controls the land (the valley is part of the Sequoia National Forest), invited private developers to submit proposals for constructing and operating a ski resort there. Four years later, it accepted the proposal of Walt Disney Enterprises, Inc., to build a $35 million complex of motels, restaurants, ski lifts, and other facilities that ultimately could accommodate 14,000 visitors a day.

Environmental groups, including the renowned Sierra Club, feared that such a huge resort would destroy Mineral King's natural beauty. The club filed suit against Rogers Morton, secretary of the interior and head of the Forest Service, in the U.S. District Court for the Northern District of California in June 1969 on the grounds that the development would violate several laws governing the preservation of national forests, parks, and game refuges (which Mineral King also was). It claimed that, if the agency gave permission for the resort to be built, the club would be injured by the resulting damage to the aesthetics and ecology of the area. It asked for a permanent injunction to stop federal officials from allowing the development to proceed.

Legal Issues

The Sierra Club's suit invoked section 10 of the Administrative Procedures Act (5 U.S.C. 702), which allows "a person suffering legal wrong because of [federal government] agency action, or adversely affected or aggrieved by agency action within the meaning of a relevant statute," to demand judicial review of an agency's actions. It claimed that as a membership corporation with "a special interest in the conservation and sound maintenance of the national parks, game refuges, and forests of the country," it met the act's, and the Constitution's, requirements for grievance and therefore had the right, or standing, to sue in this case. Whether the Sierra Club in fact met those requirements was the chief issue before the courts; they never actually ruled on whether the proposed Disney development was legal.

The ability to establish standing to sue was extremely important to environmental and animal protection groups because they could not use lawsuits to pressure government agencies to enforce protective federal laws unless they could obtain standing. To be granted standing, plaintiffs had to prove that they had "a personal stake in the outcome of the controversy." Specifically, according to rulings in previous court cases, they had to establish that the action they challenged had caused them "injury in fact" and that the injury was to an interest "arguably within the zone of interests to be protected or regulated" by the statutes that the agencies supposedly had violated. In most of these previous cases the injuries had been economic, but some decisions had suggested that noneconomic injuries could also be considered.

Decision

After two days of hearings, the district court granted the Sierra Club the preliminary injunction it had requested. The Forest Service's attorneys appealed the decision, however, and the Ninth Circuit Court of Appeals reversed it, saying that the club did not have standing to sue because there was "no allegation in the complaint that members of the Sierra Club would be affected by the actions of [the defendants] other than the fact that the actions are personally displeasing or distasteful to them." The Sierra Club appealed the decision to the Supreme Court, which agreed to review it.

The Supreme Court issued its decision, written by Justice Potter Stewart, on April 19, 1972. Stewart agreed that the type of injury alleged fell within the zone of protected interests because "esthetic and environmental well-being, like economic well-being, are important ingredients of the quality of life in our society, . . . deserving of legal protection through the judicial process." However, he found, as the appeals court had, that the Sierra Club's lawyers had not proved that the club's members were among those injured. "Nowhere in the pleadings or affidavits did the Club state that its members use Mineral King for any purpose, much less that they use it in any way that would be significantly affected by the proposed actions of the respondents," Stewart wrote. The club apparently had thought that its expertise in environmental matters was sufficient to give it standing as a "representative of the public" in the suit, but Stewart said that this was not the case: a personal injury or grievance also had to be shown before standing was granted. Stewart's majority opinion therefore upheld the appeals court's ruling that the Sierra Club did not have standing to sue in this case.

Several members of the court, most notably William O. Douglas, dissented from Stewart's decision, however. Douglas stated:

> *The critical question of "standing" would be simplified and also put neatly in focus if we fashioned a federal rule that allowed environmental issues to be litigated . . . in the name of the inanimate object about to be despoiled, defaced, or invaded. . . . This suit would therefore be more properly labeled as* Mineral King v. Morton.

Douglas pointed out that other types of inanimate objects, such as ships and corporations, were sometimes considered to be legal persons and granted standing to sue. "So it should be as respects valleys, alpine meadows, rivers, lakes. . . . The voice of the inanimate object . . . should not be stilled." Furthermore, he wrote, "Those who hike [the Mineral King Valley], fish it, hunt it, camp in it, or frequent it . . . are legitimate spokesmen for it."

Justice Harry A. Blackmun also dissented from the majority's decision, writing, "Must our law be so rigid and our procedural concepts so inflexible that we render ourselves helpless when the existing methods and the traditional concepts do not quite fit . . . new issues?" Like Douglas, he decried the likely effects of the proposed development on the Mineral King Valley. He recommended either that a preliminary injunction be granted on condition that the Sierra Club amend its complaint to include proof that some of its members regularly visited the valley and therefore would be personally injured by damage to it or else that concepts of standing be expanded to include organizations that have "a provable, sincere, dedicated, and established" interest in a particular issue.

Impact

Even though the Sierra Club lost this case, the Supreme Court's ruling outlined the approach that environmental and animal protection groups needed to take in order to gain standing. An animal rights group followed this approach successfully in a later case, *Animal Legal Defense Fund v. Glickman.*

Furthermore, even though the dissenting opinions of Justices Douglas and Blackmun carried no legal weight, animal rights groups were encouraged by their proposals that inanimate objects or their defenders be granted standing under certain conditions. If a valley or a river had a possible right to standing, then surely, they reasoned, an ape or a dolphin ought to have an even greater one. As of early 2003, no court has allowed an individual animal to be a plaintiff in a lawsuit, but in a few cases a species of animal has been granted that status, appearing along with human coplaintiffs.

Finally, the Sierra Club may have lost in the courts, but it won on the slopes of Mineral King. Neither the Disney development nor any other has been built there.

TENNESSEE VALLEY AUTHORITY V. HILL
437 U.S. 153 (1978)

Background

The Tennessee Valley Authority (TVA), a corporation wholly owned by the U.S. federal government, began constructing the Tellico Dam and Reservoir Project in the area of the Little Tennessee River in 1967. The project, which included a proposed dam on the river that would create a 30-mile-long reservoir, was intended to stimulate shoreline development, generate electricity for 20,000 homes, provide flatwater recreation and flood control, and improve economic conditions in a depressed area.

Several environmental groups, chiefly the Environmental Defense Fund (now Environmental Defense), and some local citizens opposed the Tellico Dam because it would obliterate what the Supreme Court later described as "clear, free-flowing waters [moving] through an area of great natural beauty . . . much of which represents valuable and productive farmland." They filed lawsuits claiming that the project violated the National Environmental Policy Act of 1969 and obtained a temporary injunction from a district court that stopped work on the dam for almost two years (1972–1973). After TVA provided an improved environmental impact statement in late 1973, however, the court allowed the project to proceed.

In August 1973, a few months before the dam building started again, a University of Tennessee biologist discovered a previously unknown type of perch, a three-inch-long tan fish that became known as the snail darter *(Percina imostoma tonasi)*. This new species appeared to live only in the Little Tennessee River, although about 130 other species of darters were found elsewhere.

Four months after the snail darter was identified, the Endangered Species Act (ESA) became law. In January 1975, the biologist who had found the new fish and the groups who had been trying to stop the Tellico Dam petitioned the secretary of the interior to classify the snail darter as an endangered species, and it was so classified in November. The secretary also designated the stretch of river that would be flooded by the dam as critical habitat for the fish and stated, "The proposed impoundment of water behind the proposed Tellico Dam would result in total destruction of the snail darter's habitat."

Working with the Fish and Wildlife Service, the TVA attempted to relocate a number of snail darters to the nearby Hiwassee River, but the agency said that more than a decade might be needed to determine whether the transplantation "took" to the extent of producing a breeding population. In April 1975, even before the darter was listed as endangered, TVA representatives also told a Congressional subcommittee that they did not believe that the ESA prohibited (or at least should prohibit) completion of a project that was more than half finished by the time the law was passed. The committee agreed and approved additional funding for the project. By the time the snail darter was classified as endangered, the dam was 80 percent completed.

In February 1976, the groups who opposed the Tellico Dam, including a local citizen named Hiram Hill, filed a new lawsuit, claiming that completion of the dam would violate section 7 of the ESA (16 U.S.C. 1536), which requires all federal agencies to "tak[e] . . . action necessary to insure that actions authorized, funded, or carried out by them do not jeopardize the continued existence of . . . endangered . . . and threatened species or result in the destruction or modification of habitat of such species which is determined by the Secretary . . . to be critical." At the end of April, the district court agreed that the dam would probably cause the extinction of the snail darter but nonetheless refused to grant the injunction the groups had requested because, if the dam were scrapped permanently, "some $53 million [of the $78 million spent on the project to date] would be lost in nonrecoverable obligations," which the court considered an "absurd result" of applying the law—one that Congress surely had never intended. (The environmental groups later claimed, based on a General Accounting Office study, that the loss in fact might be considerably less.) The court pointed out that Congress had continued to grant funds for the project even after its likely effect on the endangered fish had been brought up, which suggested that it had not meant the ESA to apply in this case.

The environmentalists appealed the case, and on January 31, 1977, the Sixth Circuit Court of Appeals reversed the lower court's decision. The appeals court granted a permanent injunction to keep the dam from closing until Congress passed legislation to specifically exempt it from the ESA, the snail darter was no longer classified as endangered, or the fish's critical habitat had been substantially redefined. Neither the dam's stage of completion nor Congress's granting of funds for it was relevant, the judges ruled.

Even after this decision, Congress continued to approve funds for the dam. In June 1977, the House Appropriations Committee stated, "It is the Committee's view that the Endangered Species Act was not intended to halt projects such as these in their advanced stage of completion." The equivalent Senate committee agreed. Meanwhile, the TVA appealed the legal case to the Supreme Court, which agreed to review it.

The Law and Animal Rights

Legal Issues

One issue before the court was whether the ESA required cancellation of a project that was mostly finished before the law was passed and, by the time of the court's decision, was "virtually completed and . . . essentially ready for operation." A second question was whether Congress had intended the needs of endangered species to outweigh all other considerations, including the irrecoverable loss of millions of dollars in public funds. TVA attorneys contended that, on the contrary, Congress had by implication repealed the relevant portion of the ESA as applied to the Tellico Dam by continuing to grant funds for the dam project after the snail darter had been classified as endangered.

Decision

On June 15, 1978, the Supreme Court voted to uphold the appeals court's decision and its injunction. Chief Justice Warren Burger wrote the court's majority opinion.

Burger stated that "one would be hard pressed to find a statutory provision whose terms were any plainer than those in Section 7 of the Endangered Species Act." The requirement for government agencies to ensure that their actions did not jeopardize or destroy the habitat of endangered species "admits of no exception," he wrote. Furthermore, he claimed, "examination of the language, history and structure of the legislation under review here indicates beyond doubt that Congress intended endangered species to be afforded the highest of priorities." He cited examples to prove that Congress foresaw and accepted the possibility that section 7 might require agencies to alter or halt ongoing projects. It was not the court's job, he wrote, to weigh the monetary loss of stopping a project, no matter how great, against the value of an endangered species, which Congress had called "incalculable."

Burger denied that Congress's continued granting of funds for the Tellico Dam amounted to an "implied repeal" of Section 7 as it applied to that project. For one thing, he wrote, it was court policy to find "implied repeal" only when an old law was completely incompatible with a newly passed one, which he did not believe was true in this case. Furthermore, the statements maintaining that the ESA did not require halting the dam came only from subcommittees, not from the whole Congress, and therefore did not override the plain language of the ESA itself.

Having found that there was "an irreconcilable conflict between operation of the Tellico Dam and the explicit provisions of Section 7 of the Endangered Species Act," Burger went on to consider whether an injunction against the dam's completion was an appropriate remedy. The

TVA had asked the court to view the ESA "reasonably" and choose a remedy for the legal conflict "that accords with some modicum of commonsense and the public weal." However, Burger felt that defining such a settlement was both beyond the court's expertise and an overstepping of its authority relative to Congress. "Once the meaning of an enactment is discerned and its constitutionality determined, the judicial process comes to an end," he wrote. Since the court had found that completion of the dam would violate the ESA, he concluded that the dam should be stopped.

Justices Lewis F. Powell, Jr. and Harry A. Blackmun filed a dissent, written by Justice Powell. Powell claimed that "this decision casts a long shadow over the operation of even the most important [government] projects, serving vital needs of society and national defense." He held that Congress had not intended Section 7 of the ESA to apply to projects that were completed or nearly so and that using the law in this way essentially made it retroactive. He disagreed with Burger about the "plainness" of Section 7's language, holding that "actions" in the law referred only to actions an agency is deciding whether to perform—that is, actions not yet accomplished. He also interpreted the ESA's and the dam project's legislative history differently, finding Congress's continued voting of funds for the dam more significant than Burger had. He labeled Burger's decision "an extreme example of a literalist construction, not required by the language of the Act and adopted without regard to its manifest purpose." Justice Rehnquist also dissented, saying that the district court was right not to issue an injunction against the dam because of the very unclearness of Congress's intention, as evidenced by the other justices' differing interpretations.

Impact

Congress's first response to the Supreme Court's decision was to develop a process through which federal agencies could seek an exemption from Section 7 of the ESA. It put this procedure into law as an ESA amendment in late 1978. The amendment stated that an "Endangered Species Committee," chaired by the secretary of the interior, would decide whether an exemption would be granted.

Not surprisingly, the first agency to ask for an exemption was TVA. What perhaps *was* surprising was that the committee unanimously rejected the request. Not daunted, Congress then passed a bill specifically ordering completion of the Tellico Dam and waiving any federal laws that might oppose it. The dam went into operation in November 1979.

Although the environmentalists (and animal protectionists who shared their interest in saving the snail darter) lost the battle to stop the Tellico

Dam, *TVA v. Hill* took them a step forward in the overall war to protect endangered species. Congress might have opened a loophole to allow federal agencies—with some difficulty—to avoid the ESA in selected cases, but the Supreme Court's statement of the primacy of preserving endangered species over economic or other considerations nonetheless still stood overall.

The snail darter also survived. A year after the Tellico Dam closed its gates, the biologist who had discovered the species found another population of the fish in South Chickamauga Creek, which was unaffected by the dam. Additional groups were found in other waterways during the next several years. In 1984, the Fish and Wildlife Service reclassified the snail darter as merely threatened rather than endangered, a classification it still holds.

INTERNATIONAL PRIMATE PROTECTION LEAGUE V. INSTITUTE FOR BEHAVIORAL RESEARCH 799 F.2D 934 (1986)

Background

In May 1981, Alex Pacheco, who had recently joined Ingrid Newkirk in founding People for the Ethical Treatment of Animals (PETA), decided to personally investigate the conditions under which laboratory animals were kept. Pacheco, then an undergraduate student at George Washington University, chose the laboratory of Edward Taub, chief of the Behavioral Biology Center of the Institute for Behavioral Research in Silver Spring, Maryland, because it was near his home.

In an effort to discover whether regrowth of nerves and perhaps restoration of function was possible following injuries or strokes, Taub had cut nerves leading from the spinal cords to the arms of macaque monkeys so that the animals could no longer feel pain or other sensations in the operated limbs. He then tried to force the monkeys to use the numbed arms (over which they still had muscle control) to see whether such use would stimulate regrowth in the cut nerves. After a certain length of time he planned to euthanize the monkeys and examine their spinal cords to check for regrowth. His work was funded by the National Institutes of Health (NIH)—in other words, by the federal government.

Taub signed Pacheco on as a volunteer and immediately allowed him to work with the monkeys in spite of Pacheco's admitted lack of experience in caring for laboratory animals. Pacheco discovered to his horror that the creatures were kept in small cages under filthy conditions—despite the fact that, as required by the Animal Welfare Act (AWA), the laboratory had been inspected by representatives of the U.S. Department of Agriculture (USDA) and found to be in compliance with the law. Furthermore, the monkeys apparently no longer recognized the treated limbs as part of their bodies and had viciously bitten and chewed them, producing wounds that often became infected and were left untreated.

Working alone in the laboratory at night, Pacheco filmed the animals and their miserable surroundings. He also brought in several primate experts to witness the conditions. He then took his film, notes, and witnesses' sworn statements to local police. On September 11, the police searched the laboratory, confiscated 17 monkeys, and charged Taub with 17 counts of animal cruelty, one for each monkey. The seized monkeys were sent to a facility run by the NIH.

Legal Issues

What came to be known as "the Silver Spring monkey case" marked the first time a federally funded researcher had been charged under a state animal cruelty law or raided by police. Most anticruelty laws specifically exempted scientific researchers or at least were never enforced in regard to them. Maryland's law, however, contained no such exemption.

The case took on even greater legal importance because of several civil suits filed in connection with it. In early 1982, PETA and the Humane Society of the United States sued the USDA to demand that it enforce the AWA, provisions of which they claimed that Taub had violated. This lawsuit was the first time that animal protection groups had tried this approach, which environmentalist organizations had already attempted in regard to the Endangered Species Act. As the environmental groups had done in cases such as *Sierra Club v. Morton*, the animal rightists faced the stiff legal challenge of convincing the courts that they had standing to sue.

Two other suits, one filed by the Fund for Animals in 1982 and another by the International Primate Protection League (IPPL) and PETA in 1984, brought up the same problem. The first suit attempted to stop the NIH from returning the monkeys to Taub and the Institute for Behavioral Research on the grounds that the scientists had violated the AWA, and the second suit asked for legal guardianship of the monkeys and claimed that the groups' members would suffer financial and other injuries if the research organization was allowed to reacquire the monkeys.

Decision

In December 1981, the District Court for Montgomery County convicted Edward Taub of six counts of cruelty for failing to provide adequate veterinary care for his monkeys, but it acquitted him on the other 11 counts. Taub appealed the conviction, swearing that no one else in the laboratory had observed the mistreatment Pacheco had alleged. A jury in a local circuit court overturned five of the six convictions after a new trial, and a state appeals court reversed the remaining one in 1983. The courts ruled that the monkeys' suffering was not "unnecessary or unjustifiable," as the Maryland anticruelty law required, but rather was part of the "purely incidental and unavoidable pain" that can occur during research, which, they concluded, state legislators had not meant the law to cover. The appeals court also ruled that the state law did not apply to research done with federal funding.

All the civil suits were dismissed. In the 1982 suits, the courts ruled that the USDA was entitled to decide when and how to enforce the AWA and that nothing in the AWA obliged the NIH to do what the Fund for Animals asked. In March 1985, a federal district court denied PETA and the IPPL standing to sue in the guardianship case. The animal rights groups appealed the decision, but the Fourth Circuit Court of Appeals upheld the lower court's ruling in September 1986. As the Supreme Court had done in *Sierra Club v. Morton*, the appeals court held that an organization's general interest in a problem was not enough to constitute an "injury in fact." Furthermore, Judge Wilkinson wrote in his majority opinion,

> to imply a cause of action in [i.e., to grant standing to] these plaintiffs . . . might open the use of animals in biomedical research to the hazards and vicissitudes of courtroom litigation. . . . It might unleash a spate of private lawsuits that would impede advances made by medical science in the alleviation of human suffering. To risk consequences of this magnitude in the absence of clear direction from the Congress would be ill-advised.

In addition to denying standing, Wilkinson pointed out that, unlike the Endangered Species Act, the AWA contains no provision for private individuals to sue for enforcement of the law, and he claimed that Congress had not wanted it to have any such provision. Citizen monitoring of the AWA as it applied to laboratories was expected to occur only through the Institutional Animal Care and Use Committees authorized by the 1985 amendments to the AWA. Most important, Wilkinson said the AWA was not intended to allow citizens or courts to pass judgment on the conduct of medical research. He quoted a congressional statement that under the AWA "the research scientist still holds the key to the laboratory door."

Impact

Supporters of animal research such as Adrian Morrison have claimed that Edward Taub's eventual acquittal on all charges of animal cruelty showed that Alex Pacheco's accusations were false. Animal rightists, for their part, say that Taub was freed merely on a technicality. In any case, the publicity surrounding Taub's trials made his monkeys what Jordan Curnutt calls "perhaps the most famous lab animals in the history of science."[4] Public horror at the conditions in Taub's laboratory, as Pacheco described them, helped to pressure Congress to strengthen the AWA considerably in 1985. Maryland lawmakers also revised the state anticruelty law in 1992 to explicitly cover "all animals . . . [used in] federally funded scientific medical activities."

The failure of the animal rights groups' civil suits showed that the difficulties in obtaining standing to sue that had hamstrung environmental groups in cases such as *Sierra Club v. Morton* applied to animal protection groups as well. Supporters of animal research were heartened by the dismissal of the rightists' suits. Nonetheless, PETA, the Animal Legal Defense Fund, and others continued to attempt to use lawsuits against what they saw as the USDA's inadequate enforcement of the AWA, and in a later case *(Animal Legal Defense Fund v. Glickman)* they were successful at least in obtaining standing as regards the AWA's application to animal exhibitors.

The legal battles over Taub's monkeys, which continued throughout the 1980s, allowed most of the animals to live far longer than Taub had originally planned. When several of the surviving monkeys were finally returned to Taub and killed in 1990 and 1991—more than 10 years after their original operations—autopsies showed that many of their cut nerve fibers had in fact regrown. This discovery suggested that Taub's research, whatever its moral or other drawbacks, did have potential medical value.

THE BOBBY BEROSINI ORANGUTAN CASE

Background

Entertainer Bobby Berosini used five orangutans in a comedy act at the Stardust Hotel and Casino in Las Vegas, Nevada, in the 1980s. Ottavio Gesmundo, a dancer working at the Stardust, made a videotape that appeared to show Berosini striking the animals with a rod or baton backstage before several performances in July 1989. As part of an ongoing campaign to end the use of animals in entertainment, the animal rights groups People for the Ethical Treatment of Animals (PETA) and the Performing Animal Welfare Society (PAWS) distributed the tape and publicly accused Berosini of animal abuse. PETA also said that Berosini violated the Animal Welfare Act by keeping the orangutans "in refrigerator-sized metal containers" on a bus between shows.[5]

In August 1989, soon after the tape was made public, Berosini sued PETA and other animal rights activists in a Clark County district court for defamation of character and invasion of privacy. He claimed that Gesmundo and others had deliberately made noises that upset the orangutans, forcing Berosini to use the rod to quiet them, and that the backstage tape had been edited to produce a false effect. The USDA had just inspected the animals' housing, he said, and found no signs of abuse. PETA filed a countersuit, requesting custody of the orangutans.

Legal Issues

The Berosini case brought into question the degree of proof an animal rights group needs to have in order to publicly call someone an animal abuser. It also spotlighted possible remedies that either an accused person or institution or an animal rightist accuser might find in the courts. Finally, the case and comments about it illustrate how opposing biases can cause different people to perceive the same actions differently.

Decision

In August 1990, after a five-week trial that included a court appearance by Berosini's orangutans, a jury in the district court ruled against the animal rightists and ordered them to pay a total of $3.1 million in damages to Berosini. PETA appealed the case, however, and in January 1994 and again in May 1995 the Nevada State Supreme Court unanimously reversed the decision. According to PETA, the judges wrote:

> All of the members of the court have viewed the tape; and what is shown on the tape is clear and unequivocal; Berosini is shown, immediately before going on stage, grabbing, slapping, punching and shaking the animals while several handlers hold the animals in position.[6]

The court ordered Berosini to pay PETA's court costs. According to a PETA news release, Berosini gave the organization $340,230 in May 2000.

Impact

The state supreme court ruling has so far marked the end of the Berosini case from a legal standpoint, although he and PETA have continued to argue both in and out of court. The court records may not tell the whole story, however. In an article published in *Harper's Magazine* in 1993, animal trainer Vicki Hearne described spending a week with Berosini (whom she had not previously known) and seeing his act a dozen times in an attempt to ascertain the truth of PETA's accusations. She saw no signs of abuse; she pointed out, for instance, that the orangutans were unconfined during their stage performances and could have attempted to escape if they had felt threatened. On the contrary, she perceived the relationship between Berosini and the apes as close and loving, supporting his claim that the animals were "comedians" like himself and developed the act collaboratively with him. Ward Clark, a strong critic of animal rights groups, reported similar experiences in his 2001 book, *Misplaced Compassion*. On a visit to the Berosini home, he wrote, he found all the orangutans "obviously happy, content, loved and well cared for."[7]

Who has the true picture of the way Bobby Berosini treats his coperformers? Only the orangutans really know.

BABBITT V. SWEET HOME CHAPTER OF COMMUNITIES FOR A GREAT OREGON 515 U.S. 687 (1995)

Background

As the Supreme Court's decision in *TVA v. Hill* showed, the Endangered Species Act (ESA) could be read very broadly, and the court interpreted its requirements as overriding economic or other considerations under almost all circumstances. Groups who suffered economic losses as a result of the act, however, continued trying to persuade the courts to set limits on it.

In the late 1980s, several logging projects on private land were halted because their continuation was expected to damage the habitats of the endangered red cockaded woodpecker and the threatened northern spotted owl to an extent that would result in injury or death of members of these species. In response, a group of logging companies and individuals who supported or earned their living from forest products industries in the Pacific Northwest and Southeast, calling themselves the Sweet Home Chapter of Communities for a Great Oregon, sued the secretary of the interior, Bruce Babbitt, and the director of the Fish and Wildlife Service (FWS), John F. Turner, in the federal district court for the District of Columbia in 1992. Halting logging to preserve endangered species habitat, they said, had injured them economically.

Legal Issues

Section 9(a)(1) of the Endangered Species Act forbids anyone in the United States to take endangered species, and section 3(19) further defines *take* as "to harass, harm, pursue, hunt, shoot, wound, kill, trap, capture, or collect, or to attempt to engage in any such conduct." The act itself does not further define *harm*. However, a 1975 Fish and Wildlife Service (FWS) regulation defines *harm* as

> *an act which actually kills or injures wildlife. Such act may include significant habitat modification or degradation where it actually kills or injures wildlife by significantly impairing essential behavioral patterns, including breeding, feeding, or sheltering.*

The logging group challenged the validity of the 1975 regulation "on its face," rather than as applied to any particular situation, claiming that the regulation's definition of *harm* as including significant habitat modification went further than Congress had intended. It offered three arguments to support its position:

1. that the Senate had deleted from its version of the ESA language that would have defined *take* to include "destruction, modification, or curtailment of [the] habitat or range" of endangered wildlife;
2. that Congress intended habitat to be preserved only by government purchase of relevant private land, as provided for in section 5 of the act; and
3. that because the Senate had added *harm* to the definition of *take* without debate, it should not be given much weight.

The district court rejected all three arguments and ruled that a definition of *take* that included habitat modification was a reasonable interpretation of the ESA. When the Sweet Home group appealed the case, a divided panel of the District of Columbia Court of Appeals initially agreed with the district court, but on rehearing, a majority of the court reversed the decision. Based on the meanings of the words around *harm* in the ESA's definition of *take*, the court read *harm* as requiring "the perpetrator's direct application of force against the animal taken." They also claimed that the inclusion of habitat modification in the definition of *harm* was not supported by the legislative history of the ESA and its amendments.

The appeals court's decision was in conflict with a decision by the Ninth Circuit Court of Appeals in a 1988 case, *Palila v. Hawaii Department of Land and Natural Resources (Palila II)*. In that case (one of the rare examples in which a species of animal was named as a plaintiff, in this case an endangered species of Hawaiian bird), the appeals court had concluded that inclusion of habitat modification that might endanger a species in the future in the ESA's definition of *harm* was appropriate. The Supreme Court agreed to hear the Sweet Home case in order to resolve this conflict.

Decision

The high court rendered its decision on June 29, 1995, reversing the appeals court by a 6-3 vote. Justice John Paul Stevens wrote the court's majority opinion. In supporting the idea that the meaning of *harm* could include habitat modification, as the 1975 regulation stated, Stevens first maintained that the dictionary definition of *harm* supported the interpretation that the word could include indirect and unintended as well as direct and willful damage. Furthermore, he said, if the word did not include indirect damage, there would have been no reason to add it to the definition of *take*.

Next, Stevens reiterated the court's conclusion in *TVA v. Hill* that "the plain intent of Congress in enacting . . . [the ESA] was to halt and reverse the trend toward species extinction, whatever the cost." This understanding of the ESA's broad scope made inclusion of habitat modification in the definition of *harm* reasonable, whether the modification came from a federal agency, as in *TVA v. Hill*, or private industry. Third, Stevens wrote, the fact that Congress had added an amendment to the ESA in 1982 that allowed groups to obtain permits for taking that the ESA would otherwise forbid "if such taking is incidental to . . . the carrying out of an otherwise lawful activity" suggested that "taking" had been meant to include indirect actions—otherwise there would have been no need for the amendment, since permits for direct, deliberate destruction of members of a threatened or endangered species were hardly likely to be requested or granted.

Stevens went on to cite several more general reasons for disagreeing with the appeals court. First, he wrote, buying land might be the best method for preserving habitat under some circumstances, but Stevens believed that Congress did not intend it to be the only method available. Second, drawing by analogy on the court's ruling in a previous key case, *Chevron U.S.A., Inc., v. Natural Resources Defense Council*, Stevens stated that the authority that Congress had granted to the secretary of the interior for enforcing and interpreting the ESA, as well as the secretary's regulatory expertise, was great enough that the court should accept the secretary's interpretations unless they were shown to be obviously unreasonable, which he did not believe they were in this case. Finally, he maintained that the legislative history of the ESA and its amendments supported the belief that Congress intended *take* to encompass indirect as well as direct actions.

Justice Antonin Scalia wrote a dissenting opinion (in which Chief Justice William H. Rehnquist and Justice Clarence Thomas concurred) in which he offered several reasons for believing that the 1975 regulation should be declared invalid because it was far broader than Congress had intended the ESA to be. Justice Sandra Day O'Connor wrote a concurring opinion in which, among other things, she claimed that *Palila II* had been wrongly decided because the harm to the palila resulting from destruction of plant seedlings by sheep and goats was speculative rather than actual.

Impact

The Supreme Court's decision carried even further the tendency it had shown in *TVA v. Hill* to interpret Congress's intention in passing the ESA as being to preserve endangered species literally "at any cost." Shelli Lyn Iovino, writing in the *Villanova Environmental Law Journal* in 1996, maintained that the decision "is consistent with jurisdictional trends." She claimed that most jurisdictions have recognized that some degree of destructive habitat modification can reasonably be included under the "harm" provision in Section 9 of the ESA.

The court's decision removed the inconsistency between the appeals court ruling in this case and that in *Palila II*, providing "a clear and concise interpretation of the section 9 taking provision" for future courts. It emphasized the discretion of government agencies to establish reasonable regulations and, above all, strengthened and expanded the power of the ESA. Environmentalists and animal rights groups would be expected to regard the decision as a victory, while those whose businesses brought them into potential conflict with the ESA no doubt viewed it with dismay. Such businesses include not only logging companies and other large corporations but builders of low-income housing and other projects of potential social benefit.

ANIMAL LEGAL DEFENSE FUND V. GLICKMAN
154 F.3D 426 (1998) 204 F.3D 229 (2000)

Background

Marc Jurnove, a member of several animal protection organizations who was "very familiar with the needs of and proper treatment of wildlife," paid frequent visits to (among others) the Long Island Game Park Farm and Zoo during 1995 and early 1996. There he saw apes and monkeys living under conditions that distressed him because he believed that the conditions were inhumane. For instance, a chimpanzee and a Japanese snow macaque (a type of monkey) were kept in cages out of sight of other primates, which Jurnove knew was likely to make the animals unhappy because primates are social animals and like to be with others of their kind. The only object in the cage with the macaque was a swing, which the animal did not use. In another cage, squirrel monkeys were kept near a cage that contained bears. The bears could not actually harm the monkeys, but the smell of them upset the smaller creatures.

In Jurnove's opinion, these arrangements were violations of the Animal Welfare Act (AWA), which specifies the minimum conditions under which animals in exhibitions such as the Long Island zoo must be kept. Amendments to the AWA passed in 1985 state that exhibitors must establish programs to promote "the psychological well-being of primates," and AWA regulations recommended (but did not require) housing primates together, providing enrichment objects in their enclosures, and keeping them separate from predator animals. Beginning on the day after his first visit to the

Long Island zoo in 1995, Jurnove complained repeatedly to the U.S. Department of Agriculture (USDA), which administers and enforces the AWA. In response, the USDA sent inspectors to the zoo four times, but they found no significant AWA violations. As far as the USDA was concerned, the zoo animals' housing was perfectly legal.

In June 1996, Jurnove, the Animal Legal Defense Fund (ALDF), and several other plaintiffs sued Daniel Glickman, the secretary of agriculture, in a federal district court. They claimed that Glickman had not fulfilled the AWA's requirement to "promulgate standards to govern the humane handling, care, treatment, and transportation of animals by dealers, research facilities, and exhibitors" because the USDA's regulations allowed the regulated institutions to design their own programs for primate well-being rather than specifying such programs in detail.

Jurnove, in particular, alleged that seeing the primates kept as they were in the zoo caused him "extreme aesthetic harm and emotional and physical distress" and would continue to do so unless the conditions changed. He explicitly stated that he planned to "return to the [Long Island Game] Farm in the next several weeks" and to "continue visiting the Farm to see the animals there" in the future. He claimed that the conditions that distressed him would not be legal if the USDA issued and implemented regulations detailed enough to meet the AWA requirements, so improvements in the regulations would end his injury.

Legal Issues

As in *Sierra Club v. Morton* and numerous other lawsuits filed by environmental and animal rights groups, the first hurdle the plaintiffs had to leap was establishment of standing to sue. In cases such as *Lujan v. Defenders of Wildlife* (1992), the Supreme Court had elaborated on the requirements for gaining standing in a particular case. Plaintiffs, they stated, had to prove that they suffered from an "injury in fact," that the injury is "fairly traceable" to the defendants' conduct, and that a court ruling in the plaintiffs' favor would be likely to "redress" the injury—repair it or stop it from continuing. Plaintiffs also had to fulfill "prudential" requirements for standing, which meant that their "grievance must arguably fall within the zone of interests protected or regulated by the statutory provision or constitutional guarantee invoked in the suit." At the time Jurnove and the other plaintiffs filed their suit, no individual or group had succeeded in establishing standing to sue for a violation of the AWA.

If standing to sue could be established, the case would then be tried on its merits. Such a trial would produce a ruling on whether the USDA had violated Congress's intention in passing the AWA in the way the agency wrote and, perhaps, enforced the regulations that implemented the act.

The Law and Animal Rights

Decision

In October 1996, District Court Judge Charles R. Richey granted the plaintiffs standing to sue and ruled in their favor, holding that the USDA's lack of detailed regulations regarding promotion of primate well-being violated the Administrative Procedure Act (APA), a 1946 law establishing procedural requirements for rule making by federal agencies, as well as the AWA. The agriculture department's lawyers appealed, however, and in March 1997, two judges out of a three-judge panel from the District of Columbia Circuit Court of Appeals reversed the decision, saying that the plaintiffs did not have standing to sue because they failed to meet the requirements of cause and redressability.

The ALDF demanded a rehearing by all 11 judges of the circuit court, claiming that the appeals panel's majority opinion not only went against previous court rulings but set such high standards for proving causation and redressability that this decision essentially made it impossible for third parties to sue a government agency for failing to comply with legislation's requirement to issue appropriate regulations. If allowed to stand, the ruling, therefore, "would virtually end judicial review of agency action."[8] The rehearing was granted and occurred on May 13, 1998. On September 1, the full appeals court granted Marc Jurnove standing to sue by a 7-4 vote. Once one plaintiff was granted standing, the court did not need to rule on the others.

Judge Patricia Wald, who had cast a dissenting vote in the previous appeals court ruling, wrote the court's majority opinion. She said Jurnove had established that he had been injured "in a personal and individual way . . . by seeing with his own eyes the particular animals whose condition caused him aesthetic injury." He had thus suffered the required "injury in fact." She also held that Jurnove had satisfactorily demonstrated that the lack of specificity in USDA regulations concerning primate housing had caused his injury because the conditions that distressed him were legal under the present regulations but (the plaintiffs alleged) would not have been so if the regulations had been as specific as the AWA required. Finally, Wald wrote, Jurnove had satisfied the redressibility requirement of standing because he had described specific plans to visit the zoo in the future and had claimed that more stringent USDA regulations would be likely to prevent future aesthetic injury by improving the conditions he witnessed.

Jurnove also met the prudential requirements for standing, Wald wrote, because Supreme Court decisions in *Sierra Club v. Morton* and other cases had established that aesthetic interest, including an interest in "view[ing] animals free from . . . 'inhumane treatment,'" was a protected interest. Wald held that it was specifically an interest protected by the AWA, since "the very purpose of animal exhibitions is . . . to entertain and educate people." She pointed out that the legislative history of the AWA also indicated that Congress had expected and desired that "humane societies and their members" would monitor animal exhibitions "to ensure that the purposes of the Act were honored."

Judge Sentelle wrote a dissenting opinion for the en banc hearing, in which Judges Silberman, Ginsburg, and Henderson joined. Sentelle wrote that by allowing Jurnove standing to sue, the majority "significantly weakens existing requirements of constitutional standing." He claimed that aesthetic injury regarding animals so far had been accepted only for circumstances in which the numbers of a species were reduced, not for conditions under which individual animals were viewed. Expanding the doctrine, he said, "opens an expanse of standing bounded only by what a given plaintiff finds to be aesthetically pleasing." There is no precise, objective definition for "humane treatment," he noted, and exactly what Jurnove would require in this line was unknown.

Sentelle was not convinced that Jurnove had satisfied the causation requirement, either, because the actions that produced his alleged injury were those of a third party (the zoo), not the USDA. "I find frightening at a constitutional level the majority's assumption that the government causes everything that it does not prevent," he wrote. Finally, because the conditions that would satisfy Jurnove's definition of humaneness were unknown, Sentelle stated that there was no real reason for thinking that a judicial order requiring the USDA to write new regulations would be likely to redress his injury.

The USDA appealed the case to the U.S. Supreme Court, but the high court declined to hear it in 1999, thereby allowing the appeals court ruling to stand. Obtaining standing to sue proved to be insufficient for Jurnove and the ALDF to achieve their aims, however. District Court Judge Richey again ruled in their favor when he reheard the case on its merits, but the case was appealed, and in February 2000 another three-judge panel from the D.C. appeals court (including Sentelle but not Wald) ruled by a split vote (2-1) that the USDA regulations about primates did not violate either the AWA or the APA. Neither the USDA nor the zoo, therefore, had done anything illegal, so the suit was dismissed.

In the majority opinion for the 2000 appeals court hearing, Judge Williams wrote that regulations, including the USDA's regulations for implementing the AWA, normally contain one or both of two types of rules: engineering standards, which "dictate the required means to achieve a result," and performance standards, which "state the desired outcomes, leaving to the facility the choice of means." According to Williams, Jurnove and the other plaintiffs claimed that the USDA had issued no engineering standards for furthering the psychological well-being of primates. The USDA's response, which Williams supported, was that it had in fact issued such standards, for instance by requiring specific cage sizes and placing limits on the use of restraint devices.

Williams believed that the USDA had made most other requirements less specific because designing detailed regulations that would work well for all of the several hundred diverse species of primates was almost impossible. Even experts in the field disagreed about what the best social arrangements for captive primates should be, for instance. Because of such disagreement, Williams said, the vagueness of the USDA's regulations was not "arbitrary and capricious," as the district court had held.

Impact

The en banc appeals court decision in *ALDF v. Glickman I* in 1998 marked the first time that standing to sue had been granted for an alleged USDA violation of the AWA. Naturally, animal protection groups were delighted with the ruling. ALDF senior staff attorney Valerie Stanley called it "a landmark decision for anyone concerned about promoting humane treatment for animals."[9] Rob Roy Smith, a student at the Northwestern School of Law of Lewis and Clark College, wrote in 1999 that it "la[id] a foundation for animal welfare litigation to follow" and potentially would "spark a legal and political revolution in animal law."[10] On the other hand, Judge Santelle in his dissent expressed a fear that "allowing unrestricted taxpayer or citizen standing would significantly alter the allocation of power at the national level, with a shift away from a democratic form of government" because it would "increase federal judicial power at the expense of that of the political [legislative and executive] branches."

The ability to establish standing to sue in an AWA case probably does, as Smith wrote, "open a door to judicial review previously closed to animal welfare plaintiffs" and "provide a roadmap for future plaintiffs to follow."[11] However, the fact that the case was rejected on its merits shows that the door has hardly swung wide, and the road has more than a few bumpy places. Clearly, obtaining standing to sue is not enough to make the courts demand improvement in AWA regulations. Also, unlike the Endangered Species Act, the AWA lacks a "citizen suit" provision, so trying to sue for enforcement of parts of the AWA itself, as opposed to using the grounds of the USDA's failure to promulgate adequate rules (the legal theory the courts accepted in *ALDF v. Glickman*), may still be difficult. It is also unclear whether it will be as easy to establish standing in regard to laboratories, which are not normally open to the public, as for animal exhibitions, although one student laboratory worker was granted standing in a later (2000) AWA case.

Animal Rights

TEXAS BEEF GROUP V. WINFREY
201 F.3D 680 (2000)

Background

In the mid-1990s, a mysterious brain ailment called variant Creutzfeldt-Jakob disease killed 10 young people in Britain. A British Ministry of Health announcement in March 1996 linked this illness to a similar brain disease in cattle called bovine spongiform encephalopathy (BSE), or "mad cow disease," which had been common in British cattle since the late 1980s. Ministry scientists raised the terrifying possibility that the disease's human victims might have contracted it by eating beef from cattle with BSE, just as BSE itself appeared to have spread through cattle feed that contained the remains of cattle with BSE and sheep that had a similar disease called scrapie. Mad cow disease had never been reported in the United States, but some ranchers did feed cattle material that contained animal remains, and some people speculated that an outbreak of BSE and perhaps variant Creutzfeldt-Jakob disease could occur in this country as well.

One person who thought this might happen was Howard Lyman, a Montana rancher who had become an ardent vegetarian and believed that a diet high in animal foods caused numerous health problems. Famous talk show host Oprah Winfrey interviewed Lyman, among others, on an episode of her self-titled show called "Dangerous Food," which was broadcast on April 16, 1996. On the air, Lyman said that an epidemic of human brain disease spread by tainted beef could "make AIDS look like the common cold" by comparison. Winfrey exclaimed that his words had "stopped [her] cold from eating another burger."

Other guests on Winfrey's show gave reasons for thinking that eating American beef was safe, but in the weeks following the broadcast the nationwide price of cattle plummeted to its lowest level in four decades. Several Texas cattle ranchers sued Winfrey, Lyman, and the producers and distributors of her show in May 1996, claiming that they had violated the Texas False Disparagement of Perishable Food Products Act. This 1995 law, which stated that "a person may be held liable for damages sustained by the producer of a perishable food product if that person knowingly disseminates false information to the public stating or implying that the producer's product is not safe for public consumption," was one of the food disparagement, or "veggie libel," laws that 13 states had passed after a 1989 media scare about a chemical sprayed on apples had caused a catastrophic drop in apple prices. The ranchers also sued for business disparagement, defamation, and negligence.

The Law and Animal Rights

Legal Issues

This case was one of the first to be brought under the Texas food disparagement law, and both supporters and opponents of such laws hoped that the Winfrey suit could be used as a test case to determine the laws' constitutionality. However, Mary Lou Robinson, the judge of the federal district court to which the trial was moved, dismissed the food disparagement claim. The law applied only to perishable food products, which it defined as "food product[s] of agriculture or aquaculture that [are] sold or distributed in a form that will perish or decay beyond marketability within a limited period of time," and Robinson ruled that live cattle did not meet this definition. When she gave the case to a jury, she told the jurors that their only job was to rule on whether a business disparagement had occurred. She instructed them to find the defendants guilty only if they believed that the defendants had knowingly or recklessly published false, disparaging statements "of and concerning" the plaintiffs' cattle and that such statements had "played a substantial and direct part in inducing specific damage to the business interest of the Plaintiff[s]."

Decision

The jury found the defendants not guilty in February 1998. They and the judge agreed that Lyman's statements were based on "reasonable and reliable scientific inquiry, facts, [and] data." Furthermore, although those who edited the program for airing had removed some material from other interviewees that might have presented American beef in a better light (describing, for instance, some of the steps that government authorities were taking to prevent BSE's appearance in the United States and the fact that ranchers had agreed to a voluntary ban on feeding ruminant parts to cattle), their work also did not produce a result that was actually false.

The Texas Beef Group appealed the case, and a three-judge panel of the Fifth Circuit Court of Appeals gave its opinion in February 2000. The appeals court did not rule on the issue of whether cattle should be considered "perishable" for purposes of the food disparagement law, although one, Edith L. Jones, wrote in a concurring opinion that she believed that cattle should so qualify. The circuit court judges agreed with the district court that the defendants had not knowingly made false statements about the safety of eating American beef, and they therefore upheld the lower court's acquittal on the business disparagement charge. Some of Lyman's statements might have been overdramatic and exaggerated, the judges wrote, but they cited a ruling in another case that "exaggeration does not equal defamation." Similarly, they stated, "so long as the factual underpinnings remained accurate, as they did here, the editing did not give rise to an inference that knowingly false information was being disseminated."

Impact

The *Winfrey* case did not provide a ruling on the constitutionality of food disparagement laws, not only because the district court ruled that cattle were not perishable products but also because, as the appeals court wrote, "the insufficiency of the cattlemen's evidence . . . render[ed] unnecessary a complete inquiry into the [Texas] Act's scope." However, Winfrey and Lyman's victory, like that of the animal rightist defendants in a similar case in England involving hamburger giant McDonald's, the so-called McLibel case, showed that animal rights groups or others were entitled to criticize animal agriculture publicly as long as their statements were based on sound information.

The publicity surrounding Lyman's and Winfrey's statements may also have played a role in the fact that in August 1997, the U.S. Food and Drug Administration made the ban on the use of most animal products in food for cattle and other ruminants mandatory. Some people were sure to have recalled the case, too, in 2003, when mad cow disease was diagnosed for the first time in cattle from Canada (May) and the United States (December)—and hoped that Lyman's words were not prophetic.

THE CASE OF ANDREW BURNETT

Background

After a minor traffic accident in February 2000, a man in San Jose, California, Andrew Burnett, seized Leo, a small bichon frise dog riding with the woman whose car had bumped his black SUV, and threw him into the heavily traveled street. As his horrified owner, Lake Tahoe realtor Sara McBurnett, watched, the dog was hit by a passing car. He died of his injuries before he could reach a veterinarian. Meanwhile, Burnett, whose identity was not known at the time, left the scene.

The story of this incident produced headlines around the world, and people sent $120,000 in donations to a fund that the Humane Society of the United States established to provide a reward for the man's identification and capture. Thanks largely to the work of San Jose detective sergeant Phil Zaragoza and California Highway Patrol sergeant Jeff Rhea, the man was eventually identified as a former telephone repairman named Andrew Burnett. Burnett was arrested and charged with felony cruelty to animals in April 2001.

Legal Issues

Most state laws against cruelty to animals once termed that crime a misdemeanor. In recent years, however, more and more states, including California, have amended their laws to classify severe animal abuse as a felony. The

Burnett case brings up the question of how seriously the public and the legal system regard cruelty to animals today.

Decision

Andrew Burnett was convicted of felony animal cruelty in June 2001. Noting a likelihood that Burnett, who had shown a violent temper on other occasions, would go on to commit greater acts of violence, Judge Kevin Murphy sentenced him to three years in prison, the maximum term under the California law. Burnett challenged the decision, but a state appeals court upheld it in July 2003.

Impact

By 2001, 33 states and the District of Columbia had classified severe animal abuse as a felony. Although Sara McBurnett complained that the San Jose police—with the notable exception of Zaragoza—"treated me like a nuisance, and the case like a nuisance" because it involved a "mere dog," the national outrage generated by the death of Leo showed that the American public does not regard animal abuse as a minor matter.[12]

---

[1] Jordan Curnutt, *Animals and the Law: A Sourcebook*. Santa Barbara, Calif.: ABC-CLIO, 2001, p. 448.

[2] *Tennessee Valley Authority v. Hill*, 437 U.S. 153 (1978).

[3] Nathaniel Ward, quoted in Curnutt, *Animals and the Law*, p. 70.

[4] Curnutt, *Animals and the Law*, p. 50.

[5] "Orangutan Beater Pays PETA $340,320." People for the Ethical Treatment of Animals. Available online. URL: http://www.peta-online.org/news/500/500berov.html. Posted May 4, 2000.

[6] Nevada Supreme Court opinion, quoted in "Orangutan Beater Pays PETA $340,320."

[7] Ward Clark, *Misplaced Compassion: The Animal Rights Movement Exposed*. San Jose, Calif.: Writers Club Press, 2001, pp. 219–220.

[8] Animal Legal Defense Fund, quoted in Rob Roy Smith, "Standing on Their Own Four Legs," *Environmental Law*, vol. 29, Winter 1999, pp. 989 ff.

[9] Valerie Stanley, quoted in Rob Roy Smith, "Standing on Their Own Four Legs," pp. 989 ff.

[10] Rob Roy Smith, "Standing on Their Own Four Legs," pp. 989 ff.

[11] Rob Roy Smith, "Standing on Their Own Four Legs," pp. 989 ff.

[12] Sara McBurnett, quoted in Bill Hewitt, "Collared," *People Weekly*, April 30, 2001, p. 48.

CHAPTER 3

CHRONOLOGY

This chapter presents a chronology of important events that have affected development of attitudes and laws concerning animal welfare and animal rights. The focus is on events in the United States and Britain, although important events in some other countries are also mentioned.

circa 450 B.C.

■ Alcmeon of Croton performs the first recorded act of vivisection by cutting the optic nerve of a dog and showing that the dog becomes blind as a result.

1200s

■ Christian philosopher Thomas Aquinas states that animals deserve no consideration in themselves because they lack reason. They should be treated kindly, however, because being cruel to animals may lead one to be cruel to human beings.

early 1600s

■ French philosopher René Descartes maintains that animals are mere machines that cannot really suffer because they lack reason, soul, and feeling.

1628

■ British physician William Harvey publishes a groundbreaking book, *On the Movement of the Heart and Blood in Animals*, describing the circulation of the blood accurately for the first time. It is based on his dissections of dead and living animals.

Chronology

1641

- Reverend Nathaniel Ward draws up the "Body of Liberties" to govern the Massachusetts Bay Colony, including Liberty 92, the first known Western law against cruelty to animals.

1789

- British utilitarian philosopher Jeremy Bentham states that even if animals cannot reason, they can suffer, and their right to avoid suffering should be respected.

1809

- The Liverpool Society for Preventing Wanton Cruelty to Brute Animals, the world's oldest known animal protection society, is founded.

1821

- Maine passes the first U.S. state law against animal cruelty, forbidding the beating of horses or cattle.

1822

- Britain passes the Martin Act, the first national law against animal cruelty; it outlaws cruelty to horses and cattle.

1824

- Arthur Broome founds the Society for the Prevention of Cruelty to Animals (later the Royal Society for the Prevention of Cruelty to Animals, or RSPCA), the world's first national animal protection society, in England.

1835

- The Martin Act is expanded to cover all domestic animals, thereby making bullbaiting and cockfighting illegal in Britain.

1866

- Henry Bergh, a wealthy New York diplomat, founds the American Society for the Prevention of Cruelty to Animals.

1867

- Bergh persuades the New York legislature to pass a law against cruelty to animals that becomes the model for most later anticruelty laws.

1873

- U.S. Congress passes the Twenty-eight-Hour Act, which requires rest and access to food and water every 28 hours for mammalian livestock being transported by rail or ship.

1875

- Publication of a description of vivisection in the laboratory of French physiologist Claude Bernard arouses British sentiment against the practice.

1876

- Britain passes Cruelty to Animals Act, the world's first law to regulate the use of animals in scientific research.

1896

- U.S. Supreme Court rules in *Geer v. Connecticut* that states have the right to regulate actions that affect wild animals, even if the actions involve interstate commerce.

1900

- U.S. Congress passes the Lacey Act, which forbids interstate transportation of birds or other animals killed in violation of state laws.

1911

- The United States, Britain (for Canada), Japan, and Russia sign the Fur Seal Treaty, which forbids hunting of fur seals on the open ocean; this is the first international agreement aimed at conservation of wildlife that involves the United States.

1914

- The last passenger pigeons and Carolina parakeets die in zoos, rendered extinct by excessive hunting.

1918

- U.S. Congress passes the Migratory Bird Treaty Act, which implements a treaty that the United States and Canada had agreed to in 1913. This is the first U.S. law that implements that country's share of an international treaty concerning animal protection.

Chronology

1924

- The League Against Cruel Sports is founded to work toward outlawing fox hunting in Britain.

1927

- The LD50 ("lethal dose for 50 percent") test, a commonly used but controversial animal test for acute toxicity, is invented in Britain.

1928

- Basing its decision on the Constitution's property clause, the U.S. Supreme Court rules in *Hunt v. United States* that the federal government can regulate activity on federal lands such as national forests, even if such regulations contradict state hunting and wildlife laws.

late 1940s

- In response to a growing need for animals to be used in biomedical research, some states and cities pass laws that force pounds and shelters to release homeless dogs and cats to researchers on demand.
- The practice of intensive farming, which involves keeping large numbers of animals indoors, develops in response to growing demand for meat.
- U.S. Food and Drug Administration researcher John Draize invents tests for eye and skin irritation using rabbits that later become commonly used on cosmetics and household products.

early 1950s

- Groups such as the Animal Welfare Institute (1951) and the Humane Society of the United States (1954) spin off from the American Humane Society because of what they see as the Humane Society's weak stand on vivisection.
- Heini Hediger, director of the Basel Zoo in Switzerland, recommends that zoos create habitats for their animals that allow the animals to engage in as many of their natural behaviors as possible.

1958

- U.S. Congress passes the Humane Slaughter Act, which requires all livestock except birds to be rendered unconscious before being slaughtered.

1959

- British scientists W. M. S. Russell and Rex Burch publish *The Principles of Humane Experimental Technique*, which describes the "three Rs" (reducing, replacing, and refining) of developing alternatives for research and testing on animals.

1964

- Ruth Harrison's book *Animal Machines* makes the British public aware of animal abuses involved in what she calls factory farming.
- The Hunt Saboteurs Association splits off from the League Against Cruel Sports because it believes that direct action in the field is necessary to stop fox hunting in Britain.

1965

- The Brambell Committee, established by the British Parliament after publication of Ruth Harrison's book, recommends standards for treatment of farm animals and urges that such standards be made legally binding.
- *July:* Publicity following a Pennsylvania family's discovery that their lost dog has been sold to a research laboratory produces a demand for federal legislation to regulate animal dealers and laboratories that use animals.

1966

- U.S. Congress passes the Fur Seal Act, implementing the Fur Seal Treaty of 1911 and later sealing treaties.
- The Tennessee Valley Authority, a federal agency, begins building the Tellico Dam on the Little Tennessee River.
- U.S. Congress passes the Endangered Species Preservation Act, the first federal law aimed at protecting endangered species as such.
- *February 4:* *Life* magazine publishes an article that describes miserable conditions in the kennels of a dealer who sells animals to laboratories, producing many letters to Congress.
- *August:* President Lyndon Johnson signs into law the Laboratory Animal Welfare Act, which chiefly regulates the way cats and dogs used in medical research are bought and sold.

1968

- British Parliament passes the Agriculture (Miscellaneous Provisions) Act, which establishes standards for housing and treatment of livestock on intensive farms.

Chronology

1970

- Animal rights philosopher Richard Ryder coins the term *speciesism*, which Peter Singer later adopts and makes famous.
- U.S. Congress passes the Animal Welfare Act (AWA), which revises and expands the Laboratory Animal Welfare Act to cover more kinds of animals and regulate animals used in exhibitions as well as laboratories.
- U.S. Congress passes the Horse Protection Act, which outlaws soring, a practice in which horses' feet are deliberately made sore in order to produce a gait valued in shows.

1970s

- Landscape architect Grant Jones creates the first "landscape immersion" habitat for the Woodland Park Zoo in Seattle, Washington.
- Animal protection groups that run shelters for homeless dogs and cats begin promoting the idea that pet owners should spay and neuter their pets to prevent overpopulation.
- Animal rights groups begin campaigns against the wearing of fur.
- Animal rights activist Henry Spira establishes the Coalition to Abolish the Draize Test.
- American scientists develop the Porcine Zona Pellucida (PZP) vaccine, an animal contraceptive that can be injected by dart and thus can be used on wildlife.
- The Band of Mercy breaks off from the Hunt Saboteurs Association and begins using violence, primarily property damage, in attempts to stop fox hunting in Britain; this group later becomes the Animal Liberation Front.

1972

- U.S. Department of Agriculture issues regulations implementing the Animal Welfare Act, including the stipulation that the act will not cover mice, rats, and birds.
- U.S. Supreme Court rules in *Sierra Club v. Morton* that the club has no standing to sue to stop development of a wilderness area because it has not proved that the development would cause an "injury in fact" to its members.

1973

- *March:* Representatives of 80 countries establish the Convention on International Trade in Endangered Species of Wild Fauna and Flora

(CITES), the chief international agreement that regulates or bans trade in endangered species or materials made from them.

- *August:* A biologist discovers a new species of fish, the snail darter, in the Little Tennessee River, site of the Tellico Dam and Reservoir Project.
- *December:* President Richard Nixon signs into law the Endangered Species Act, the chief U.S. law protecting endangered and threatened species.

1974

- U.S. Supreme Court affirms in *Jones v. Butz* that the Humane Slaughter Act's exemptions for kosher and halal slaughter do not violate the Constitution's prohibition against making laws concerning religion.

1975

- Australian philosopher Peter Singer's *Animal Liberation*, called "the Bible of the animal rights movement," is published; this event is often considered to be the start of the modern crusade for animal rights.
- U.S. Fish and Wildlife Service issues regulations implementing the Endangered Species Act, one of which states that the term *harm* in the act can include "significant habitat modification or degradation."
- *November:* The snail darter is listed as endangered.

1976

- U.S. Congress passes the Animal Fighting Venture Prohibition Act, an amendment to the Animal Welfare Act, which prohibits all animal fighting (except cockfighting in states where it is legal).
- U.S. Supreme Court rules in *Kleppe v. New Mexico* that the federal government can regulate disposition of wildlife on public lands, even when doing so contradicts state laws.

1978

- U.S. Congress revises and expands the Humane Slaughter Act (1958) and the Meat Inspection Act (1906) to produce the Humane Methods of Slaughter Act, which specifies stunning and slaughter methods for mammalian livestock (but not birds).
- U.S. Supreme Court rules in *Tennessee Valley Authority v. Hill* that the almost-completed Tellico Dam violates the Endangered Species Act because closing the dam would destroy the critical habitat of the endangered snail darter. The court issues a permanent injunction to stop building on the dam.

Chronology

1979

- *November:* After Congress passes a bill specifically exempting the Tellico Dam from the Endangered Species Act, the dam goes into operation.

1980

- Henry Spira launches a campaign against cosmetics giant Revlon, criticizing its use of the painful Draize rabbit eye irritancy test.
- Ingrid Newkirk, Alex Pacheco, and others found People for the Ethical Treatment of Animals (PETA).

1981

- *May:* Alex Pacheco begins work at Edward Taub's laboratory in Silver Spring, Maryland, where federally funded research on monkeys is taking place.
- *September 11:* After seeing videotapes made by Pacheco and statements from witnesses about conditions in Taub's laboratory, local police charge Taub with 17 counts of animal cruelty—the first time a research scientist has been so charged.
- *December:* A district court convicts Taub of six counts of animal cruelty.

1983

- On appeal, Taub is acquitted of all charges.

1984

- American philosopher Tom Regan publishes *The Case for Animal Rights*, which says that all human uses of animals that cause animal suffering are morally wrong and should be abolished.
- PETA circulates a documentary made from videotapes stolen from the University of Pennsylvania's Head Injury Clinical Research Laboratory, showing researchers making fun of injured baboons.

1985

- Congress makes substantial revisions to the Animal Welfare Act, including establishment of Institutional Animal Care and Use Committees (IACUCs) to oversee experiments using animals and addition of a requirement for programs to promote the psychological well-being of primates.

late 1980s

- Cosmetics giants Revlon and Avon, responding to campaigns by animal rights groups, agree to stop testing their products on animals.
- "No-kill" animal shelters begin to be established.

1986

- Britain passes the Animals (Scientific Procedures) Act, an extremely comprehensive set of regulations governing experiments on animals, and West Germany passes a similarly rigorous law.
- The European Union passes a directive that provides a legal framework for the regulation of experiments on animals in member countries.
- The Fourth Circuit Court of Appeals denies standing to PETA in a suit in which that group asks for guardianship of the Silver Spring monkeys. The court claims that granting standing could unleash a spate of lawsuits that would impede medical research.
- "Mad cow disease" (bovine spongiform encephalopathy) appears in Britain, probably spread by the intensive-farming practice of using cattle feed that contains ground-up remains of other cattle and sheep.

1988

- In *Palila v. Hawaii Department of Land and Natural Resources*, the Ninth Circuit Court of Appeals grants the palila, an endangered species of Hawaiian bird, standing to sue under the Endangered Species Act.
- California passes a law requiring that students who have moral objections to performing dissections in biology classes be given alternative assignments.

1989

- Bobby Berosini, a Las Vegas entertainer, sues PETA and other animal rights groups for defamation of character after they distribute a videotape appearing to show him abusing the orangutans in his nightclub act before a performance.

1990

- U.S. Congress passes the Pet Protection Act, an amendment to the Animal Welfare Act that requires pounds and shelters to hold animals for at least five days before selling them to dealers.

Chronology

- *August:* A jury awards Bobby Berosini damages against PETA and other groups for defamation of character.

1991

- The American Society for the Prevention of Cruelty to Animals, the Humane Society of the United States, and more than 100 other animal protection groups publish a joint resolution in the *New York Times* stating that they oppose use of threats or violence against people or property.
- The European Union establishes the European Centre for Validation of Alternative Methods (ECVAM) to develop and validate nonanimal alternatives to tests and experimental methods using animals.

1992

- In its ruling on *Lujan v. Defenders of Wildlife*, the U.S. Supreme Court lists three criteria that plaintiffs, including environmental and animal rights organizations, must fulfill in order to have standing to sue.
- U.S. Congress passes the Animal Enterprise Protection Act, which makes physical disruption of animal production and research facilities a federal crime.

1993

- U.S. Congress passes the NIH Revitalization Act, which, among other things, orders the director of the National Institutes of Health to develop, validate, and promote nonanimal alternatives to animal tests and experiments.

1994

- U.S. Congress passes the Recreational Hunting Safety and Preservation Act, which makes it illegal to "engage in any physical conduct that hinders a lawful hunt."
- U.S. Congress modernizes the Twenty-eight-Hour Act and expands it to include animals transported by truck.
- The National Institutes of Health (NIH) establishes the Interagency Coordinating Committee on the Validation of Alternative Methods (ICCVAM) as an ad hoc (temporary) committee to carry out the requirements of the NIH Revitalization Act concerning establishment, validation, and promotion of nonanimal tests.
- The Nevada Supreme Court reverses a lower court's decision in the Bobby Berosini case, ruling that PETA's videotape did show that Berosini

abused his orangutans. It orders Berosini to pay a substantial sum to cover PETA's court costs.

1995

- Massive protests at British ports attempt to halt the export of live animals, which animal rights groups claim often occurs under cruel conditions.
- *June 29:* U.S. Supreme Court rules in *Babbitt v. Sweet Home Chapter of Communities for a Great Oregon* that environmental degradation can be included in the definition of *harm* in the Endangered Species Act.

1996

- Britain bans biomedical research on great apes.
- *March:* The British government announces that 10 people have died of a brain disease similar to "mad cow disease," by then widespread among British cattle, and may have contracted the disease from infected beef.
- *May:* Texas cattlemen sue prominent television host Oprah Winfrey under a state food disparagement law after a guest on her program warns that the practice of giving American cattle feed that contains the ground-up bodies of other animals, linked to the spread of mad cow disease and possible infection of humans in Britain, could lead to a devastating outbreak of human brain disease in the United States.

1997

- Gillette Corporation agrees to stop testing its products on animals.
- U.S. Supreme Court rules that landowners as well as animal and environmental protection groups can use the citizen suit provision of the Endangered Species Act.
- *August:* The United States and Canada ban use of cattle feed containing ground-up animal parts, which can spread mad cow disease (bovine spongiform encephalopathy).

1998

- A Wisconsin judge sentences a man to 12 years in prison for severe animal abuse, probably the longest sentence ever given for such a crime.
- After seven years of litigation, a British judge rules against McDonald's in the "McLibel" case, holding that London animal rights activists did not libel the fast food giant because some of the conditions they described in their pamphlets could in fact be considered cruel.

- The Environmental Protection Agency asks companies to provide health and safety test information for 2,800 high-production-volume chemicals.
- *February:* A Texas judge acquits Oprah Winfrey, Howard Lyman, and other defendants of violating the state food disparagement law.
- *September 1:* In *Animal Legal Defense Fund v. Glickman I,* the District of Columbia Circuit Court rules that Marc Jurnove has standing to sue the USDA for not making specific regulations under the Animal Welfare Act for promoting the psychological well-being of primates—the first time an individual has been granted standing to sue for a violation of the AWA.

1999

- New Zealand passes a law that essentially bans research on great apes.
- The law schools of Harvard and Georgetown Universities begin offering courses in animal law.
- Writer Jan Pottker files suit against Ringling Bros. and Barnum & Bailey Circus and its owner, Ken Feld, claiming that Feld hired people to harass and spy on her after she published an article critical of the circus and the Feld family.
- Mary Kay Cosmetics and Procter & Gamble agree to stop testing their products on animals.
- The Animal Liberation Front in Britain kidnaps documentary filmmaker Graham Hall and burns the group's initials into his back.
- The European Union agrees to phase out battery cages for laying hens in all member nations by 2012.
- Responding to criticism from animal rights groups, the Environmental Protection Agency and the Clinton administration agree to modify the EPA's planned testing program for high-production-volume chemicals so that it will use fewer animals.
- *October:* The Justice Department, an extremist animal rights group, mails razor blades and threats to 87 American scientists who do research on primates.
- *December:* A group called Stop Huntingdon Animal Cruelty (SHAC) begins a campaign to close British-based Huntingdon Life Sciences, the world's second-largest commercial animal testing facility, because of alleged animal abuse.

2000

- A PETA campaign featuring a picture of then-New York mayor Rudolph Giuliani, who had recently been found to have prostate cancer, in an

117

attempt to link a diet high in dairy products with the disease draws widespread criticism for exploiting Giuliani's illness and is withdrawn. Mothers Against Drunk Driving criticizes a second PETA antimilk campaign, which claims that beer is more healthful than milk, and forces its withdrawal as well.

- *February:* Following a minor traffic accident, a man in San Jose, California, throws a small dog belonging to the woman who hit him into traffic, where the dog is killed. Animal rights groups and an outraged public establish a $120,000 reward for the man's identification and arrest.
- *February:* The Fifth Circuit Court of Appeals upholds a district court's acquittal of Oprah Winfrey and others in a food disparagement case.
- *February:* Hearing Marc Jurnove's case against the USDA for violation of the Animal Welfare Act *(ALDF v. Glickman II)* on its merits, a three-judge panel from the District of Columbia Court of Appeals reverses a lower court's decision and finds that the department's regulations for promoting the psychological well-being of primates meet the AWA's requirements.
- *June:* A committee set up by the British Parliament releases the Burns Report, which says that hunting with dogs is an important feature of social life in rural Britain and is no more cruel to foxes than other common methods of exterminating them.
- *August:* Following a PETA campaign accusing it of animal cruelty, fast-food giant McDonald's agrees to make changes in its requirements for meat suppliers' treatment of animals.
- *September:* A district court grants standing to sue to a plaintiff in a suit against the U.S. Department of Agriculture (USDA) that is aimed at making the USDA remove its controversial exclusion of mice, rats, and birds from the Animal Welfare Act. Within days, the USDA settles the suit out of court by promising to remove the exemption.
- *October:* United Egg Producers, a large industry trade group, issues new guidelines that promise to gradually increase the size of cages in which laying hens are kept and make other improvements to their care.
- *November:* Britain passes the Fur Farming (Prohibition) Act, which essentially outlaws breeding animals for their fur.
- *December:* U.S. Congress makes the Interagency Coordinating Committee for the Validation of Alternative Methods (ICCVAM) a permanent standing body.
- *December:* U.S. Congress passes the Chimpanzee Health Improvement, Maintenance, and Protection (CHIMP) Act, which authorizes establishment of a system of sanctuaries to which chimpanzees no longer needed for medical research can be "retired."

Chronology

- **February:** British animal rights protesters attack Brian Cass, managing director of Huntingdon Life Sciences, breaking one of his ribs and inflicting a head wound that requires 10 stitches.
- **May:** A jury in Washington, D.C., awards $500,000 to Shan Sparshott, a former employee of the Ringling Bros. and Barnum & Bailey Circus, because a former executive vice president of the circus had Sparshott's telephone illegally wiretapped.
- **June:** Following PETA campaigns, Wendy's and Burger King issue revised guidelines for their suppliers' treatment of animals, similar to those that McDonald's issued the previous year.
- **June:** Andrew Burnett, identified as the man who threw a small dog into traffic in a road rage incident in February 2000, causing its death, is convicted of felony animal abuse and sentenced to three years in prison.
- **December:** After less than two hours of deliberation, a jury in San Jose, California, acquits Ringling Bros. and Barnum & Bailey Circus animal trainer Mark Gebel of abusing an elephant.

2002

- The Food Marketing Institute and the National Council of Chain Restaurants release new guidelines for food suppliers' treatment of animals, including such requirements as increased confinement space for pregnant sows (female pigs).
- **March:** Scotland passes a bill prohibiting hunting of mammals with hounds.
- **May:** Congress permanently blocks the USDA from expanding Animal Welfare Act regulations to cover rats, mice, and birds.
- **May 6:** Pim Fortuyn, a popular Dutch politician who had expressed support for fur farming, is shot to death in Amsterdam. Animal rights activist Volkert van der Graaf is accused of his murder.
- **June:** Germany becomes the first country in the European Union to guarantee protection of animals in its constitution.
- **December:** A compromise bill that would regulate hunting rather than banning it is introduced into the British Parliament.

2003

- **January:** The European Union votes to ban all cosmetics testing on animals and most sales of cosmetics tested on animals elsewhere in the world by 2009.
- **April 16:** Animal rights activist Volkert van der Graaf, who had confessed to the murder of Dutch politician Pim Fortuyn, is sentenced to 18 years in prison.

- *May:* A cow with mad cow disease (bovine spongiform encephalopathy) is discovered in Alberta, Canada, the first report of the disease in North America.
- *June 30:* British Parliament's House of Commons votes by 362 to 154 to ban foxhunting.
- *July 7:* People for the Ethical Treatment of Animals files a lawsuit in California Superior Court in Los Angeles to stop what it alleges are deceptive statements on fast food chain Kentucky Fried Chicken's website and customer hotline. PETA claims that the company misleads people about the treatment of the chickens whose meat they sell.
- *August 28:* A group calling itself Revolutionary Cells sets off two pipe bombs at California-based Chiron Corporation, a biotechnology company that pays Huntingdon Life Sciences to test Chiron's new drugs on animals. No one is injured, but the group's use of explosives marks an escalation in violence in support of animal rights in the United States.
- *September 2:* People for the Ethical Treatment of Animals drops its lawsuit against Kentucky Fried Chicken after the company agrees to change allegedly false statements on its website and customer hotline.
- *October 21:* British Parliament's House of Lords votes by 261 to 49 to allow regulated hunting to continue.
- *late 2003:* As the Endangered Species Act's 30th anniversary nears, Congress considers revising it in ways that would limit its powers.
- *December 22:* A Holstein cow in Washington state, slaughtered for meat on December 9, is discovered to have had mad cow disease, the first case of this illness reported in the United States. The USDA recalls 10,000 pounds of meat that the meat factory that processed the sick cow handled on the same day. Several Asian countries immediately ban beef imports from the United States; within a week, the ban includes 30 countries that make up 90 percent of the U.S. beef export market.
- *December 30:* Agriculture Secretary Ann Veneman proposes new regulations aimed at controlling the possible spread of mad cow disease and easing the fears of consumers, including a ban on slaughtering of "downer" cattle—those too sick or lame to stand and walk on their own—for use as meat.

CHAPTER 4

BIOGRAPHICAL LISTING

This chapter offers brief biographical information on people who have played major roles in development of crusades for animal welfare and animal rights. Most of these people were or are active in the United States or Britain, but some important figures from other countries are also included.

Alcmeon of Croton, ancient Greek physiologist. Around 450 B.C., he performed the first recorded act of vivisection by cutting the optic nerve of a dog and showing that the dog became blind as a result.

Thomas Aquinas, 13th-century Christian theologian and philosopher. Aquinas stated that animals deserve no consideration in themselves because they lack reason. He professed that they should be treated kindly only because cruelty to animals may lead to cruelty to human beings.

Jeremy Bentham, British philosopher. In 1789, he opposed cruelty to animals on the grounds that animals could suffer, even though they might not possess reason or language, and inflicting such suffering was in itself an immoral act. He also speculated that eventually animals, as sentient beings, might be granted certain legal rights.

Henry Bergh, 19th-century American diplomat. Upset by abuse to animals, especially horses, that he had seen during his diplomatic career and inspired by the work of the Royal Society for the Prevention of Cruelty to Animals in Britain, Bergh, a wealthy New Yorker, founded the American Society for the Prevention of Cruelty to Animals in 1866 and, a year later, persuaded New York legislators to pass one of the first state laws against animal cruelty.

Claude Bernard, French physiologist. Bernard stated that he saw nothing wrong with performing painful or fatal experiments on animals if the experiments seemed likely to benefit humans. A scientist's account of the suffering caused by Bernard's innumerable operations stirred strong opposition to vivisection in Britain in the late 1870s.

Bobby Berosini, Las Vegas entertainer. Berosini, who used orangutans in his act, sued People for the Ethical Treatment of Animals (PETA) and other groups for defamation of character in 1989 after they accused him of abusing the animals. A lower court supported Berosini in 1990, but in 1994 the Nevada Supreme Court reversed that decision and ordered Berosini to pay a large sum to the animal rights groups.

Arthur Broome, British minister. He founded the Society for the Prevention of Cruelty to Animals, the first national animal welfare society, in 1824.

Rex Burch, British scientist. With W. M. S. Russell, he codeveloped the concept of the "three Rs" of alternatives to animal research: *replace* animal tests with nonanimal ones whenever possible, *reduce* the number of animals needed per test, and *refine* tests so that they cause less pain and stress to animals. Russell and Burch first described the three Rs in *The Principles of Humane Experimental Technique*, published in 1959.

Andrew Burnett, California man convicted of animal cruelty in a highly publicized case. Following a minor traffic accident in the city of San Jose in February 2000, Burnett seized Leo, a small dog riding with the woman whose car had bumped his, and threw him into passing traffic, where he was killed. Burnett, whose identity was unknown at the time, then left the scene. Donations from the public and animal rights groups established a $120,000 reward for his identification and capture. In June 2001, he was convicted of felony cruelty to animals and sentenced to three years in prison.

Brian Cass, managing director of Huntingdon Life Sciences, a large animal testing firm in Britain. Animal rightists attacked Cass with baseball bats in front of his home in February 2001, breaking one of his ribs and inflicting a head injury that required 10 stitches.

Frances Power Cobbe, British animal welfare activist and antivivisectionist. She cofounded the Victoria Street Society for the Protection of Animals from Vivisection in 1875. She drew an explicit parallel between abuse of animals and mistreatment of women.

Rodney Coronado, Animal Liberation Front activist convicted of a firebombing at Michigan State University in the early 1990s. People for the Ethical Treatment of Animals (PETA) helped to pay for his defense.

René Descartes, 17th-century French philosopher. He maintained that animals cannot really suffer because they lack reason, a soul, and feeling.

John Draize, researcher with the U.S. Food and Drug Administration. In the 1940s, he developed two tests using rabbits that became standard for discovering whether cosmetics, household products, or other substances could irritate eyes and skin.

Ken Feld, owner of the Ringling Bros. and Barnum & Bailey Circus. Feld takes an aggressive stand against animal rights groups who say that the circus is cruel to its animals. Several people have accused him of spying on and harassing those who disagree with him.

Biographical Listing

Pim Fortuyn, Dutch politician. Fortuyn, a popular leader who had expressed support for the fur industry, was shot to death in Amsterdam on May 6, 2002. Animal rights activist Volkert van der Graaf was convicted of the murder and sentenced to 18 years in prison in April 2003.

Michael Fox, bioethicist, currently a senior scholar in bioethics with the Humane Society of the United States. He is famous for radical animal rights statements such as: "The life of an ant and the life of my child should be granted equal consideration."

Gary Francione, law and philosophy professor at Rutgers University. He is a leading advocate of the idea that chimpanzees and bonobos, and perhaps some other animals, should have legal rights.

Mark Gebel, animal trainer with Ringling Bros. and Barnum & Bailey Circus. Two animal rightists claimed that they saw Gebel strike an elephant with an ankus, or bullhook, during a parade in San Jose, California, in August 2001, and he was brought to trial on charges of abusing an elephant. The witnesses admitted under cross-examination that they had actually only seen Gebel lunge at the animal, and a veterinarian testified that he had found no injuries on the elephant. The jury deliberated less than two hours before acquitting Gebel.

Jane Goodall, British primatologist. Goodall's long-running studies of chimpanzees in the wild in Tanzania showed that the animals exhibit many humanlike behaviors, including the making of tools. Goodall now works for numerous environmental and animal welfare causes, including efforts to end medical research on great apes.

Frederick Goodwin, former director of the National Institute of Mental Health, part of the National Institutes of Health. Goodwin is a major supporter of the use of animals in biomedical research.

Volkert van der Graaf, Dutch animal rights activist. Van der Graaf, founder of a group called Environmental Offensive, which opposed animal agriculture, was charged with the murder of popular Dutch politician Pim Fortuyn on May 6, 2002. He confessed and was sentenced to 18 years in prison on April 16, 2003.

Temple Grandin, American expert on treatment and slaughter of livestock. She has invented simple, inexpensive improvements in the design of slaughterhouses and other animal handling facilities that greatly reduce stress on the animals.

Graham Hall, British documentary filmmaker. After Hall made a film about the British arm of the Animal Liberation Front, the group kidnapped him and branded the organization's initials on his back.

David Hancocks, director of the Open Range Zoo in Victoria, Australia. Hancocks criticizes conventional zoos' animal environments and educational benefits and says that zoos do not present an accurate picture of the complexity of nature.

Ruth Harrison, British author. Her book *Animal Machines,* published in 1964, drew the British public's attention to abuses of animals involved in what she called "factory farming," a term she probably coined.

William Harvey, British physician. In 1628, he published a groundbreaking book describing the heart and circulation of the blood, based on discoveries he had made by dissecting dead and living animals. Harvey's work is one of many major medical breakthroughs that supporters of research on animals cite.

Heini Hediger, director of the Basel Zoo in Switzerland. In the 1950s, Hediger suggested that zoo environments should be designed to allow animals to carry out as many of their normal behaviors as possible. His ideas influenced zoo designers to create more naturalistic habitats.

George Hoggan, British scientist. His account of experiences in the laboratory of French physiologist Claude Bernard, who experimented extensively on living animals, stirred British opposition to vivisection in 1875.

Hubert Humphrey, Democratic senator from Minnesota, vice president from 1965 to 1969. Humphrey's support was important in achieving passage of the Humane Slaughter Act, which was intended to reduce the suffering of livestock in slaughterhouses, in 1958.

Grant Jones, landscape designer. In the mid-1970s, he designed a new type of habitat for the Woodland Zoo in Seattle, Washington, that he called "landscape immersion." It was intended to make visitors feel surrounded by a natural landscape and experience its grandeur, while at the same time providing features that allow the habitat's animal occupants to carry out normal behaviors. Other zoos soon adapted his ideas.

Marc Jurnove, plaintiff in a landmark 1998 legal case *(ALDF v. Glickman).* He gained standing to sue the Department of Agriculture for not establishing adequate regulations for promoting the psychological well-being of primates as mandated by the Animal Welfare Act, leading to conditions in a Long Island zoo that caused Jurnove aesthetic distress during his frequent visits there.

Howard Lyman, Montana rancher turned ardent vegetarian. Lyman's prediction on a 1996 Oprah Winfrey talk show that contaminated American beef might cause an outbreak of "mad cow disease," a deadly human brain disease, resulted in his being sued under a Texas food disparagement law. He was acquitted in 1998.

Richard Martin, Irish Minister of Parliament. In 1822, he introduced a bill prohibiting mistreatment of horses and cattle into the British Parliament that, when passed, became the first national law against mistreatment of animals.

Sara McBurnett, a Lake Tahoe realtor. Her small dog, Leo, was thrown into traffic by an enraged motorist whose car she had bumped in San Jose, California, in February 2000. The man, later identified as Andrew Burnett, was convicted of felony cruelty to animals and sentenced to three years in prison in June 2001.

Adrian Morrison, American researcher and defender of biomedical research on animals. Morrison, a veterinarian, is the former director of the Office of Animal Research Issues at the Substance Abuse and Mental Health Services Administration, part of the U.S. Department of Health and Human Services. He now does research on the brain's function during sleep at the University of Pennsylvania's School of Veterinary Medicine. Animal rightists have criticized both his own experiments, which use animals, and his defense of other researchers such as Edward Taub. Morrison, in turn, is highly critical of the animal rights movement.

Ingrid Newkirk, American animal rights activist. In 1980, she and four friends, including Alex Pacheco, founded People for the Ethical Treatment of Animals (PETA), described in 2001 as "the world's largest and most controversial animal rights organization." Newkirk has become famous for such attention-getting statements as "A rat is a pig is a dog is a boy."

Alex Pacheco, cofounder of PETA with Ingrid Newkirk and three of Newkirk's friends. After obtaining volunteer employment in 1981 in the laboratory of Edward Taub, a researcher in Silver Spring, Maryland, Pacheco secretly filmed monkeys being kept there under filthy conditions. His exposé of these conditions led to Taub's arrest, several court cases, and considerable publicity supporting animal rights groups' claim that animals in laboratories were mistreated.

Lewis Petrinovich, emeritus professor of psychology at the University of California, Riverside. Petrinovich maintains that a desire to put the interests of one's own species over those of others, which Peter Singer calls speciesism, is built into humans (and all other animals) by evolution.

Janice Pottker, American writer. In a 1999 suit against Ringling Bros. and Barnum & Bailey Circus, Pottker claimed that the circus's owner, Ken Feld, had hired people to spy on her, harass her, and derail her career after she published an article critical of the circus and the Feld family.

Tom Regan, North Carolina State University philosopher. Regan's 1984 book, *The Case for Animal Rights,* provides the philosophical rationale for the more radical wing of the animal rights movement. He claims that animals have basic rights, such as the right to life and bodily integrity, that must be respected, and he demands an end to essentially all human uses of animals.

Andrew N. Rowan, senior vice president for research, education, and international issues at the Humane Society of the United States. He is also a professor at Tufts University and a faculty member of the Johns Hopkins University Center for Alternatives to Animal Testing. He writes frequently about animal welfare issues.

W. M. S. Russell, British scientist. With Rex Burch, he codeveloped the concept of the "three Rs" of alternatives to animal research: *replace* animal tests with nonanimal ones whenever possible, *reduce* the number of animals needed per test, and *refine* tests so that they cause less pain and stress to animals. Russell and Burch first described the three Rs in *The Principles of Humane Experimental Technique,* published in 1959.

Richard Ryder, British philosopher and bioethicist. He is credited with coining the term *speciesism,* later adopted by Peter Singer, in 1970. He is a former chairman of the Royal Society for Prevention of Cruelty to Animals and currently directs animal welfare studies for the International Fund for Animal Welfare. He has been called "the Moses of the animal rights movement" and "the stormy petrel of the RSPCA."

Peter Singer, Australian philosopher, now at Princeton University. Singer's book *Animal Liberation,* first published in 1975, has frequently been called the Bible of the animal rights movement, and its publication is often held to mark the start of that movement. Singer, a utilitarian, believes that human uses of animals may be permissible if they do more good than harm overall. However, he says that animals deserve as much consideration as other sentient beings that can feel pain but cannot reason, such as human babies.

Henry Spira, American animal rights leader. Spira, a veteran of many social movements, founded Animal Rights International in 1976. He introduced tactics that had been effective in other movements into the fledgling animal rights movement and helped to establish dialogues among the new groups, traditional animal welfare societies, and the industries that animal rights groups opposed. In the early 1980s, he led a campaign that persuaded cosmetics giant Revlon to stop using the painful Draize irritancy tests on rabbits.

Edward Taub, American researcher. While conducting federally funded studies of nerve regrowth after injury at the Institute for Behavioral Research in Silver Spring, Maryland, in 1981, Taub allowed his experimental subjects, 17 rhesus monkeys, to be kept under substandard conditions that were secretly documented by animal rights activist Alex Pacheco. When Pacheco took his films to the police, Taub was arrested and charged with cruelty to animals. Taub was convicted of six counts of animal abuse, but the convictions were overturned on appeal in 1982 and 1983.

Frankie Trull, president of the National Association for Biomedical Research. The association, based in Washington, D.C., is a lobbying group that works to protect the interests of scientists who experiment on animals.

Queen Victoria (Victoria I), 19th-century British monarch. In 1840, she lent her patronage to the Society for the Prevention of Cruelty to Animals, allowing it to add "Royal" to its name. She also appointed a royal commission to investigate vivisection in the early 1870s.

Nathaniel Ward, English Puritan minister and lawyer. In 1641, Ward drew up a set of laws for the Massachusetts Bay Colony called the "Body of Liberties," which included (as Liberty 92) the first known specific statute against cruelty to animals.

Caroline White, 19th-century animal activist. White cofounded the Pennsylvania Society for the Prevention of Cruelty to Animals (SPCA) in 1868. In 1870, she helped establish the first animal shelter, which was intended to provide more humane living conditions and more painless deaths for stray animals than were available at pounds. White also cofounded the American Anti-Vivisection Society in 1883.

Oprah Winfrey, American talk show host. After a 1996 program in which Winfrey supported an interviewee (Howard Lyman) who predicted that the practice of giving beef cattle food that contained animal remains might lead to an outbreak in the United States of "mad cow disease" and an equivalent illness in humans, a group of Texas cattlemen sued her and others involved with the show for violating a state food disparagement law. Winfrey and the others were acquitted in 1998.

Steven Wise, professor of law at Harvard University. Wise maintains that chimpanzees and bonobos, and perhaps some other animals, should be entitled to legal personhood because of their intellectual and emotional similarities to humans, and he works toward this end with groups such as the Great Ape Project. He has written several books to explain his ideas, including *Rattling the Cage* and *Drawing the Line*.

Clive D. L. Wynne, senior lecture in the Department of Psychology at the University of Western Australia. Wynne is among those who say that behavioral studies of great apes do not necessarily prove that the animals possess such humanlike abilities as self-awareness and the power to understand and use language.

CHAPTER 5

GLOSSARY

Discussions about animal welfare and animal rights draw on their own specialized vocabulary as well as those of science, agriculture, philosophy, law, medicine, and other fields. This chapter presents some of the terms that the general reader is likely to encounter while researching these subjects.

Animal and Plant Health Inspection Service (APHIS)   The agency of the U.S. Department of Agriculture that implements and enforces the Animal Welfare Act.

Animal Enterprise Protection Act   A U.S. law, passed in 1992, that makes physical disruption of animal production and research facilities a federal crime.

animal law   The body of law covering human actions that affect animals.

animal protection organizations   A term often used to encompass both animal welfare and animal rights organizations.

animal rights movement   A social movement dedicated to the idea that nonhuman animals possess, or should possess, at least some of the moral and legal rights granted to humans, including the right not to be killed, injured, or held captive. Some organizations in the animal rights movement see all human use of animals as inherently cruel and work to abolish it.

Animal Welfare Act (AWA)   A U.S. law, passed in 1970, that regulates the housing and care of animals in laboratories and most types of animal exhibitions.

animal welfare organizations   Organizations holding that humans should harm animals as little as possible but accepting the morality of human uses of animals. The American and Royal (British) Societies for the Prevention of Cruelty to Animals are examples.

anthropomorphism   Attribution of human emotions and thoughts to animals.

bag limit   A limit on the number of animals of a certain type that a hunter may kill.

Glossary

battery cage A wire cage in which three to six laying hens are kept in intensive farming. The cages are stacked in rows and tiers to form "batteries" that may contain thousands of birds.

body-gripping trap A type of trap, also called the Conibear trap, which is intended to kill an animal by snapping shut on its neck and breaking it. Animal rightists say the traps are cruel because they may close on an animal's chest or hips instead, producing a slow death from shock and suffocation.

bonobo A great ape formerly called a pygmy chimpanzee but now considered a separate species *(Pan paniscus)*.

bovine growth hormone (BGH) A hormone sometimes given to dairy cattle to increase milk production. Animal rights groups often object to use of this hormone, and some countries and the European Union have outlawed it.

bovine spongiform encephalopathy (BSE) A brain-destroying disease of cattle, popularly called "mad cow disease," that is transmitted by feeding cattle the remains of other ruminants that have died of the disease. It may be transmissible to humans who eat meat from cattle with the disease. The human form of the illness is called variant Creutzfeldt-Jakob disease.

buncher A person who collects animals from random sources for an animal dealer to sell. Animal rightists say that some bunchers obtain pet cats and dogs under false pretenses or even steal them.

canned hunt Derogatory term for a hunt in which a hunter pays a private game preserve for the chance to hunt an animal, often an exotic species, on the preserve. A kill and a trophy (head or skin) are often guaranteed.

Chimpanzee Health Improvement, Maintenance, and Protection Act (CHIMP Act) A U.S. law, passed in 2000, that authorizes the establishment of sanctuaries to which chimpanzees formerly used in medical research may be "retired" when they are no longer needed.

class A dealer As defined in the Animal Welfare Act, a dealer who breeds animals specifically for the purpose of selling them.

class B dealer As defined in the Animal Welfare Act, a dealer who obtains animals from random sources and then sells them. These sources are often shelters, pounds, and animal auctions, but they may also include "bunchers" who, animal rightists allege, steal or fraudulently obtain family pets.

closed season The time of year during which a particular type of game animal may not be hunted.

companion animal Animal rights and some animal welfare organizations prefer this term for what is commonly known as a pet.

Convention on International Trade in Endangered Species of Wild Flora and Fauna (CITES) An international agreement, established by representatives of 80 countries in 1973, that limits or bans trade in endangered plant and animal species or any material made from them.

critical habitat   As defined in the Endangered Species Act, the geographic areas "on which are found those physical or biological features essential to the conservation of [an endangered] species and which may require special management considerations or protection."

DNA chip   Also called DNA microarray. Each "chip" contains hundreds or even thousands of short strands of DNA that act as probes for different genes. DNA chips may replace animals in some toxicity tests.

"downer cattle"   Animals too sick or lame to walk to slaughter. Until December 2003 in the United States they could be carried to the slaughterhouse, killed, and used as meat, a practice animal rightists called cruel as well as a threat to the human-food supply. The U.S. Secretary of Agriculture banned their use after a case of mad cow disease was discovered in that country.

Draize tests   Tests commonly used to determine whether a cosmetic or other product is likely to irritate skin or eyes. The tests, which usually use rabbits, were invented by John Draize, a scientist working for the U.S. Food and Drug Administration, in the 1940s. Animal rightists oppose the tests because they are painful to the animals involved.

duck stamp   Informal name for the Migratory Bird Hunting Stamp, which a federal law passed in 1934 requires adult waterfowl hunters to purchase each year in addition to hunting licenses. The U.S. Fish and Wildlife Service uses the resulting money to buy or lease land for waterfowl habitat.

endangered species   As defined in the Endangered Species Act, a species that is "in danger of extinction throughout all or a significant portion of its range."

Endangered Species Act   A U.S. law, passed in 1973, that protects species classified as endangered or threatened, along with their "critical habitat."

factory farming   A derogatory term (probably coined by British author Ruth Harrison in a 1964 book) often used by animal rights activists to describe what is more neutrally called intensive farming.

farrowing crate   A tight enclosure in which a sow (female pig) is kept while she is nursing her piglets. The crate's purpose is to keep the sow from lying on and crushing the piglets, but animal rightists say it is excessively confining.

Fish and Wildlife Service   The agency of the U.S. Department of the Interior that implements and enforces the Endangered Species Act.

food disparagement law   A type of law that forbids intentional dissemination of false information claiming that a food product is unsafe for consumption. Sometimes called "veggie libel law."

Glossary

Food Safety and Inspection Service (FSIS)   The agency of the U.S. Department of Agriculture that inspects slaughterhouses and meatpacking plants in the United States and other countries that import meat to the United States to ensure that (among other things) the Humane Methods of Slaughter Act is followed.

forced molting   The practice, often used with laying hens in intensive farming, of forcing all the hens to molt (lose their feathers) at once, usually by temporarily depriving them of food and sometimes water and light.

Fur Seal Act   A U.S. law, passed in 1966, that implements international agreements limiting hunting of fur seals that the United States signed in 1911 and 1957.

gestation stall   A small enclosure in which a sow (female pig) is kept while she is pregnant. Many animal rights groups object to gestation stalls.

great apes   Primates belonging to the family *Pongidae*, including chimpanzees, bonobos, gorillas, and orangutans.

halal slaughter   Slaughter of meat animals carried out in accordance with the dietary practices of the Muslim religion, which, like Jewish kosher slaughter, requires animals to be conscious at the time of death. The Humane Methods of Slaughter Act exempts halal slaughter from its requirement that livestock be stunned before it is killed.

high-production-volume chemicals (HPV chemicals)   Chemicals manufactured at the rate of 1 million pounds or more per year. In 1998, the U.S. Environmental Protection Agency began a program requiring additional safety testing data for these chemicals, which animal rightists objected to because they said it would cost the lives of more than 1 million animals.

Horse Protection Act   A U.S. law, passed in 1970, which bans soring of horses.

Humane Methods of Slaughter Act   A U.S. law, passed in 1978, that establishes rules for treatment of livestock (except for birds) in and around slaughterhouses, including a requirement that the animals be rendered unconscious before being killed unless they are being killed according to kosher or halal slaughter.

inherent value   Value that is inseparable or inborn, not determined by how a living thing is used or what experiences it has had.

Institutional Animal Care and Use Committee (IACUC)   A committee charged with ensuring the proper care and minimal harm of experimental animals, which every scientific institution that uses animals must establish, according to the 1985 revision of the Animal Welfare Act.

intensive farming   Farming in which hundreds or thousands of animals are kept together indoors in close quarters for part or all of their lives and usually fed and watered automatically. Animal rightists disapprove of this type of farming, which they call factory farming.

kosher slaughter Slaughter of meat animals carried out according to the dietary rules of the Jewish religion, which, among other things, requires animals to be conscious and standing when they are killed. The Humane Methods of Slaughter Act exempts kosher slaughter from its requirement that livestock be stunned before it is killed.

Lacey Act A U.S. law, passed in 1900, that forbids movement of protected birds or their body parts across state lines.

landscape immersion A style of zoo habitat first developed by landscape architect Grant Jones for Seattle's Woodland Park Zoo in the mid-1970s. It is intended to make both resident animals and human visitors feel immersed in a natural landscape and to allow the animals to carry out natural behaviors.

LD50 ("lethal dose for 50 percent") test A widely used test for acute toxicity, developed in Britain in 1927, in which groups of about 100 animals (usually rats) are given (usually by force feeding) varying doses of the test substance until half of one group dies. Animal rightists call this test crude as well as cruel.

legal personhood The status of possessing certain legal rights, including the right to be a plaintiff in a lawsuit. All humans are considered legal persons, whether or not they can understand or take an active part in legal proceedings; so, by convention, are certain other entities, such as corporations and ships. Some animal rightists believe that legal personhood should be extended to great apes and, perhaps, certain other animals.

legal standing The quality of being recognized by law as having value and dignity in one's own right, rather than simply because of one's usefulness to others. Animals do not have legal standing at present, but some animal rightists believe that they should.

mad cow disease Popular name for bovine spongiform encephalopathy. See **bovine spongiform encephalopathy** and **Variant Creutzfeldt-Jakob disease**.

Martin Act The name sometimes given to the Ill Treatment of Horses and Cattle Bill, which the British Parliament passed in 1822. Aimed at preventing cruelty to horses, cattle, and other livestock, it was the first national animal protection law.

mastitis A painful inflammation of the udder that dairy cows often suffer, particularly in intensive farms.

Migratory Bird Treaty Act A U.S. law, passed in 1918, that implemented an agreement the government had made with Canada in 1913 to protect nongame migratory birds and limit the hunting of game birds. It was the first U.S. law that implemented that country's share of an international treaty concerning animal protection.

no-kill shelter A shelter in which animals are kept until they are adopted, no matter how long this takes.

open season The time of year during which hunters may legally kill a particular type of animal.

orangutan A type of great ape, now endangered, indigenous to Indonesia.

Pet Protection Act An amendment to the Animal Welfare Act, passed in 1990, that requires pounds and shelters to hold animals for a minimum of five days before selling them to dealers.

pound A facility for holding stray dogs or (sometimes) other animals, usually run by a city or other municipality, as opposed to a shelter, which is generally operated by a private organization.

pound seizure laws Laws that some U.S. states passed in the late 1940s and 1950s that required pounds and shelters to surrender animals to research laboratories on demand. Also called pound procurement laws.

primate Any member of the order of animals that includes lemurs, monkeys, apes, and humans.

puppy mill A large dog-breeding facility that keeps its animals in substandard conditions, thereby making them likely to have health problems.

PZP vaccine (porcine zona pellucida vaccine) A form of animal contraceptive, invented in the 1970s, that can be injected with a dart and, therefore, can be used on wildlife such as deer.

Recreational Hunting Safety and Preservation Act A U.S. law, passed in 1994, that makes it a federal crime to physically interfere with a lawful hunt.

sentient being A living thing capable of feeling pleasure and pain.

shelter A facility that takes in unwanted or homeless animals, chiefly cats and dogs, and usually tries to find homes for them. Unlike pounds, shelters are generally operated by private organizations.

Silver Spring monkey case A case of alleged abuse of monkeys in the laboratory of Edward Taub in Silver Spring, Maryland, in the early 1980s, revealed by film shot by PETA cofounder Alex Pacheco. Taub was initially convicted of six counts of animal abuse, but the convictions were reversed on appeal.

snail darter A three-inch-long fish whose designation as endangered in 1975 almost stopped the building of the Tellico Dam in Tennessee because the dam would destroy the fish's critical habitat, thus violating the Endangered Species Act.

snare A trap in which a wire loop, which may or may not be coated, tightens around an animal's leg or neck.

soring   A practice of deliberately injuring and irritating a horse's front legs to make it perform a type of high-stepping gait valued in shows. The Horse Protection Act (1970) makes soring illegal.

speciesism   Term, coined by Richard Ryder and made popular by Peter Singer's use of it in *Animal Liberation*, defined as automatically placing the interests of one's own species ahead of those of other species.

standing to sue   The right to be a plaintiff in a particular lawsuit. Justice Antonin Scalia spelled out the requirements for having standing to sue in a 1992 Supreme Court case, *Lujan v. Defenders of Wildlife*.

steel-jawed leghold trap   A commonly used type of trap that animal rightists say is particularly cruel and causes extensive tissue damage.

threatened species   As defined in the Endangered Species Act, a species that is "likely to become endangered ... in the foreseeable future."

three Rs   The approach to reducing the use of animals in science first described by British scientists W. M. S. Russell and Rex Burch in 1959. Russell and Burch said that scientists should *replace* tests that use animals with nonanimal tests wherever possible, *reduce* the number of animals used in each test, and *refine* tests and experiments to make them cause less pain and distress to animals.

Twenty-eight-Hour Act   A U.S. law, passed in 1873, that requires animals being transported over long distances to be given rest, food, and water every 28 hours.

utilitarianism   A school of philosophy, founded by British philosopher Jeremy Bentham, that states that the most moral choice of action is the one that produces the best outcome (greatest amount of pleasure) for all those involved in a situation.

variant Creutzfeldt-Jakob disease   A mysterious and deadly human brain-destroying ailment that may be transmitted by eating beef from cattle infected with bovine spongiform encephalopathy, popularly called "mad cow disease."

vegan   A person whose diet contains no meat or animal products.

vegetarian   A person who eats no meat but may eat animal products such as milk and cheese.

veggie libel law   Slang term for a food disparagement law.

vivisection   Performing surgery on a living animal for experimental purposes; sometimes, performing any painful or stressful experiment on an animal.

PART II

GUIDE TO FURTHER RESEARCH

CHAPTER 6

━━━━━━━━

HOW TO RESEARCH
ANIMAL RIGHTS ISSUES

The subject of animal welfare and animal rights has generated a considerable amount of information in recent years. This chapter presents a selection of resources, techniques, and research suggestions for investigating issues related to human treatment and uses of animals.

Although students, teachers, journalists, and other investigators may ultimately have different objectives, all are likely to begin with the same basic steps. The following general approach should be suitable for most purposes:

- Gain a general orientation by reading the first part of this book. Chapter 1 can be read as a narrative, while Chapters 2–5 are best skimmed to get an idea of what is covered. They can then be used as a reference source for helping make sense of the events and issues encountered in subsequent reading.

- Skim some of the general books listed in the first section of the bibliography (Chapter 7). Neutral overviews and books that provide pro and con essays on various issues in the field are particularly recommended.

- Browse the many web sites provided by organizations involved in animal welfare and animal rights (see Chapter 8), including those of groups that support industries that animal rightists criticize. Their pages are rich in news, articles, and links to other organizations, as well as describing particular cases and discussing the pros and cons of various practices involving animals.

- Use the relevant sections of Chapter 7 to find more books, articles, and online publications on particular topics of interest.

- Find more (and more recent) materials by using the bibliographic tools such as the library catalogs and periodical indexes discussed later.

- To keep up with current events and breaking news, check back periodically with media and organization web sites and periodically search the catalogs and indexes for recent material.

The rest of this chapter is organized according to the various types of resources and tools. The three major categories are online resources, print resources, and the special area of law, legislation, and legal research.

ONLINE RESOURCES

With the increasing amount of information being made available online, turning to the World Wide Web is a logical way to begin any research project. It is easy to drown in the sea of information the Web reveals, but starting with a few well-organized, resource-rich sites and then applying selective Web searching can provide a logical thread through the labyrinth.

GENERAL SITES ON ANIMAL WELFARE ISSUES

As Chapter 8 shows, dozens of groups present information or take stands on various animal-related issues. The following major sites (listed in alphabetical order) are recommended as good starting places for research. They offer well-organized overviews of issues, provide numerous resources and links, and answer frequently asked questions. As described in the annotations for the sites, some favor animal rights, some explicitly oppose animal rights, and others are neutral or advocate animal welfare but not necessarily animal rights.

Animals Voice
URL: http://animalsvoice.com/PAGES/home.html
Sponsored by *The Animals Voice Magazine*, a leading animal rights journal published between 1986 and 1997. Includes numerous links and access to fact sheets from a variety of animal rights groups, news stories, audio and video, and more.

Animal Welfare Institute
URL: http://www.awionline.org
Includes extensive collection of articles and other material on animal-related topics. Supports animal welfare but not necessarily animal rights.

Cambridge University Animal Welfare Center Animal Information Network
URL: http://www.animal-info.net
Neutral site includes lists of books, reports, links, and other resources on a wide variety of animal-related topics.

Envirolink
URL: http://www.envirolink.org
Large web site devoted to environmental issues; includes some material that covers animal welfare/animal rights issues, such as wildlife preservation and animals in agriculture.

The Humane Society of the United States
URL: http://www.hsus.org
Provides numerous reports and news stories from an animal rights point of view on animals in research, pets/companion animals, farm animals, marine mammals, and wildlife.

Man in Nature
URL: http://www.maninnature. com
Provides access to an assortment of articles that oppose animal rights and support hunting and other uses of animals.

National Animal Interest Alliance (NAIA)
URL: http://www.naiaonline.org
Animal industry trade association site provides news articles, including archived ones, on topics including animals and the law and what the NAIA views as animal rights extremism.

U.S. Department of Agriculture Animal Welfare Information Center
URL: http://www.nal.usda.gov/ awic
Extensive government web site with many links is devoted primarily to care and use of animals in science but also includes material on animals in agriculture, animals in entertainment, and companion animals.

World Animal Net Directory
URL: http://worldanimalnet.org
Claims to be the world's largest database of animal protection societies (grouped by categories as well as searchable individually), with listings for more than 13,000 international animal rights and welfare organizations and links to more than 6,000 web sites. Resources include material on animal protection laws in various countries.

SITES ON SPECIFIC ANIMAL TOPICS

The following sites feature material on the specific areas of animal use discussed in Chapter 1. As with the general sites, some of the specific sites are neutral, while others support or oppose particular human uses of animals.

Companion Animals

International Society for Animal Rights
URL: http://www.isaronline.org
Provides reports on such subjects as pet overpopulation, spay/neuter, and puppy mills.

National Council on Pet Population Study and Policy
URL: http://www.petpopulation. org
Provides abstracts of academic studies on companion animals and shelters, chiefly studies examining why people give up their pets.

Animals in Agriculture

Compassion in World Farming
URL: http://www.ciwf.co.uk
British animal rights organization has detailed reports on allegedly harmful conditions on intensive farms, as well as on such subjects as genetic engineering of farm animals and the effect of World Trade Organization rules on animal welfare.

U.S. Department of Agriculture, Agricultural Research Service (ARS)
URL: http://www.nps.ars.usda. gov
Describes ARS's national programs, including several related to farm animal health and welfare. Includes yearly reports from each program.

U.S. Department of Agriculture, National Agricultural Statistics Service (NASS)
URL: http://www.usda.gov/nass
Includes information on the numbers and different types of animals in U.S. agriculture.

Animals in Research, Testing, and Education

Alternatives to Animal Testing on the Web
URL: http://altweb.jhsph.edu
Sponsored by Johns Hopkins University, this site provides miscellaneous news, conference proceedings, and more on development of alternatives to tests on animals.

Americans for Medical Progress
URL: http://www.ampef.org
Offers news stories and other information supporting the use of animals in research and criticizing animal rights groups.

Animals in Laboratories Information Service (ALIS)
URL: http://www.alisdatabase.org
Sponsored by the Humane Education Network, this site contains summaries of books, articles, and other documents related to the use and care of and alternatives to animals in laboratories. Urges reform or abolition of animal use in science.

National Institutes of Health (NIH), Office of Laboratory Animal Welfare
URL: http://www.grants.nih. gov/grants/olaw/olaw.htm
Government site includes news stories, policies and laws, guidance in meeting regulations, general information, foreign and domestic institutions holding animal welfare assurances, and links, as well as the Public Health Service and NIH policies and laws for care of laboratory animals.

Norwegian Inventory of Alternatives (NORINA)
URL: http://oslovet.veths.no/ NORINA
Provided by the Norwegian Reference Centre for Laboratory Animal Science & Alternatives, this database lists alternatives or supplements to use of animals in education.

Animals in Entertainment

**Performing Animal Welfare
 Society**
URL: http://www.pawsweb.org
Gives background information and news stories on alleged abuses of elephants and other performing animals, places that have banned animal entertainment, and contact information for the entertainment industry.

**Ringling Bros. and Barnum &
 Bailey Circus**
URL: http://www.ringling.com/
 animals
Includes material on training and care of animals in this famous circus as well as descriptions of particular types of animals such as elephants and big cats.

Wildlife

**Convention on International
 Trade in Endangered Species
 of Wild Fauna and Flora
 (CITES)**
URL: http://www.cites.org
Contains material describing and related to CITES, the chief international agreement for preservation and limitation of trade in endangered species.

Defenders of Wildlife
URL: http://www.defenders.org
Includes publications regarding the Endangered Species Act and preservation of wildlife.

National Wildlife Federation
URL: http://www.nwf.org
Includes a directory of more than 4,000 environmental groups.

**New Mexico School of Law
 Institute of Public Law
 Center for Wildlife Law**
URL: http://ipl.unm.edu/cwl
Includes handbooks of federal and state wildlife laws and reports on biodiversity and on the Endangered Species Act arranged by state.

**U.S. Fish and Wildlife Service
 Endangered Species Program**
URL: http://endangered.fws.gov
Provides information about the Endangered Species Act and the program designed to implement it, as well as news, information on the state of particular species, and other features.

MEDIA SITES

News (wire) services, most newspapers, and many magazines have web sites that include breaking news stories and links to additional information. The following media sites have substantial listings for stories on animal rights and animal welfare:

- Cable News Network (CNN)
  URL: http://www.cnn.com
- Reuters
  URL: http://www.reuters.com

- *New York Times*
  URL: http://www.nytimes.com (offers only abstracts for free; full-text stories available for a fee)
- *Time* magazine
  URL: http://www.time.com/time

Yahoo! maintains a large set of links to many newspapers that have web sites or online editions: http://dir.yahoo.com/News_and_Media/Newspapers/ Web_ Directories

FINDING MORE ON THE WEB

Although the resource sites mentioned earlier provide a convenient way to view a wide variety of information, the researcher will eventually want to seek additional data or views elsewhere. The two main approaches to Web research are the portal (guide or index) and the search engine.

Web Portals

A web guide or index is a site that offers a structured, hierarchical outline of subject areas. This format enables the researcher to zero in on a particular aspect of a subject and find links to web sites for further exploration. The links are constantly being compiled and updated by a staff of researchers.

The best known (and largest) web index is Yahoo! (http://www.yahoo. com). Its home page gives a top-level list of topics, which researchers simply click to find more specific areas. Alternatively, there is a search box into which researchers can type one or more keywords and receive a list of matching categories and sites. (The box is rather confusingly labeled "Search the Web," but it also searches Yahoo!'s directories, and the results of this search appear at the top of the page.)

Web indexes such as Yahoo! have two major advantages over undirected "web surfing." First, the structured hierarchy of topics makes it easy to find a particular topic or subtopic and then explore its links. Second, Yahoo! does not make an attempt to compile every link on the Internet (a task that is virtually impossible, given the size of the Web). Instead, Yahoo!'s indexers evaluate sites for usefulness and quality, giving the researcher a better chance of finding more substantial and accurate information. The disadvantage of web indexes is the flip side of their selectivity: researchers are dependent on the indexer's judgment for determining what sites are worth exploring.

To research animal rights via Yahoo!, the researcher should follow these links: "Science," then "Biology," then "Zoology," then "Animals, Insects, and Pets," and finally, "Animal Rights." At the time of writing, the following topics appeared under Animal Rights:

- Animal Abuse
- Animal Experimentation
- Bear Farming Issues
- Bullfighting Views
- Cat Declawing
- Circus Animals
- Dog Ear Cropping
- Dog Meat
- Dog Tail Docking
- Endangered Animals
- Factory Farming
- Fishing Views
- Fur
- Humane and Rescue Societies
- Hunting Views
- Magazines
- Opposing Views
- Organizations
- Petitions
- Puppy Mill Issues
- Vegetarianism
- Web Directories
- Zoos

A variety of sites selected by the editors are available for browsing. Several other subtopics under "Animals, Insects, and Pets" are also worth examining, including "Animal Abuse," "Organizations," "Pets," "Wildlife," and "Zoos." *Animal welfare* does not have its own subdirectory, but typing these words into the Yahoo! search engine will pull up some relevant web sites and news stories. The two topics, of course, also overlap to a moderate extent. In any case, there is clearly no shortage of links that can be explored using Yahoo! as a starting point.

About.com run by About, formerly The Mining Company (http://www.about.com), is rather similar to Yahoo! but emphasizes overviews or guides prepared by self-declared experts in various topics. The site does a good job of creating a guide page "on the fly" when a keyword or phrase is entered in the search box. At present, *animal rights and welfare* is a subcategory under *News and Issues / Liberal Politics: U.S.* The About listing provides many pages both within the About network itself (the one on animal rights recommends seeing *animal rights activists, anti-animal rights, cruelty to animals, defenders of animal rights, animal rights groups, information on animal rights, animal welfare, animal rights laws, animal rights issues,* and *PETA*) and on the Web in general. Note that About generates special URLs that keep pages "tied" to the About site, so for bookmarking purposes it is probably a good idea when visiting the linked site to reload it under its own URL.

New guide and index sites are constantly being developed, and capabilities are improving as the Web matures.

Search Engines

Search engines take a very different approach to finding materials on the Web. Instead of organizing topically in a "top down" fashion, search engines work their way "from the bottom up," scanning through web documents and indexing them. There are hundreds of search engines, but some of the most widely used include:

- AltaVista: http://www.altavista.com
- Excite: http://www.excite.com
- Google: http://www.google.com
- Hotbot: http://www.hotbot.com
- Lycos: http://www.lycos.com
- WebCrawler: http://www.webcrawler.com

To search with a search engine, one can employ the same sorts of keywords that work in library catalogs. There are a variety of Web search tutorials available online (try entering "web search tutorial" in a search engine to find some). One good one is published by Bright Planet at http://www.brightplanet.com/deepcontent/tutorials/search/index.asp.

Here are a few basic rules for using search engines:

- When looking for something specific, use the most specific term or phrase. For example, when looking for information about slaughterhouses, use that specific term.

- Phrases should be surrounded by quotation marks if you want them to be matched as phrases rather than as individual words. Examples include "animal rights movement," "Draize test," and "battery cages."
- When looking for a general topic that might be expressed using several different words or phrases, use several descriptive words (nouns are more reliable than verbs), such as *circus animal training*. Most engines will automatically put pages that match all terms first on the results list.
- Use "wildcards" when a desired word may have more than one ending. For example, *animal** will include results containing both "animal" and "animals."
- Most search engines support Boolean *(and, or, not)* operators, which can be used to broaden or narrow a search.
- Use AND to narrow a search. For example, *circuses* **and** *zoos* will match only pages that have both terms.
- Use OR to broaden a search: *"companion animals"* **or** *pets* will match any page that has *either* term, and since these terms are often used interchangeably, this type of search is necessary to retrieve the widest range of results.
- Use NOT to exclude unwanted results: *horses* **not** *racing* finds articles about horses but not horse racing.

Since each search engine indexes somewhat differently and offers somewhat different ways of searching, it is a good idea to use several search engines, especially for a general query. Some "metasearch" programs, such as Metacrawler (http://www.metacrawler.com) and SurfWax (http://www.surfwax.com), automate the process of submitting a query to multiple search engines. Metasearch engines may overwhelm you with results (and insufficiently prune duplicates), however, and they often do not use some of the more popular search engines, such as Google.

There are also search utilities that can be run from the researcher's own computer rather than through a web site. A good example is Copernic (http://www.copernic.com).

Finding Organizations and People

Chapter 8 of this book provides a list of organizations involved with research, advocacy, or opposition to animal rights. New organizations continue to emerge, however. The resource sites and Web portals mentioned earlier are good places to look for information and links to organizations. If the name of an unfamiliar organization turns up during reading or browsing, the name can be entered in a search engine. For best results, the complete name should be put in quotation marks (for instance, "San Francisco

Society for the Prevention of Cruelty to Animals"), although some search engines, such as Google, do not require this. If omitting the quotation marks, also omit common words such as *the* and *of;* for instance, type *San francisco society prevention cruelty animals* rather than the organization's complete name. Including these words will confuse the search engine.

Another approach is to take a guess at the organization's likely Web address. For example, People for the Ethical Treatment of Animals is commonly known by the acronym PETA, so it is not a surprise that the organization's web site is at http://www.peta.org. (Note that noncommercial organization sites normally use the *.org* suffix, government agencies use *.gov,* educational institutions have *.edu,* and businesses use *.com.*) This technique can save time, but it does not always work. In particular, watch out for "spoof" sites that mimic or parody organizational sites. For instance, an animal rights opponent named Michael Doughney originally reserved the domain name www.peta.org for a site on which the acronym was used to stand for "People Eating Tasty Animals." (PETA sued him for trademark infringement, and he was forced to give up the domain name.) Of course, parody sites may be of interest in themselves as forms of criticism or dissent.

When reading materials by an unfamiliar author, it is often useful to learn about that person's affiliation, credentials, and other achievements. There are several ways to find a person on the Internet:

- Put the person's name (in quotes) in a search engine, which may lead you to that person's home page or a biographical sketch listed by the institution for which the person works.

- Contact the person's employer (such as a university for an academic or a corporation for a technical professional). Most such organizations have web pages that include a searchable faculty or employee directory.

- Try a people-finder service, such as Yahoo! People Search (http://people.yahoo.com) or BigFoot (http://www.bigfoot.com). These services may yield contact information, including an e-mail address, regular address, and/or phone number.

PRINT SOURCES

As useful as the Web is for quickly finding information and the latest news, in-depth research can still require trips to the library or bookstore. Getting the most out of the library, in turn, requires the use of bibliographic tools and resources. *Bibliographic resources* is a general term for catalogs, indexes, bibliographies, and other guides that identify the books, periodical articles, and other printed materials that deal with a particular subject. They are essential tools for researchers.

LIBRARY CATALOGS

Most readers are probably familiar with the basics of using a library catalog, but they may not know that many catalogs besides that of their local library can be searched online. The largest library catalog, that of the Library of Congress, can be accessed at http://catalog.loc.gov, a page that includes a guide to using the catalog as well as both basic and advanced catalog searches. Yahoo! offers a categorized listing of libraries at http://dir. yahoo.com/Reference/Libraries.

Most catalogs can be searched in at least the following ways:

- An author search is most useful if researchers know or suspect that a person has written a number of works of interest. However, it may fail if they do not know the person's exact name. (Cross-references are intended to deal with this problem, but they cannot cover all possible variations.)

- A title search is best if a researcher knows the exact title of a book and just wants to know if a particular library has it. Generally, researchers need only use the first few words of the title, excluding initial articles (*a, an,* or *the*). This search will fail if a researcher does not have the exact title.

- A keyword search will match words found anywhere in the title. It is thus broader and more flexible than a title search, although it may still fail if all keywords are not present.

- A subject search will find all works to which a library has assigned that subject heading. The advantage of a subject search is that it does not depend on certain words being in a book's title. However, using this kind of search can require knowing the appropriate Library of Congress subject headings for a topic. These can be obtained from the Library of Congress catalog site (http://catalog.loc.gov) by clicking on Basic Search, then selecting Subject Browse and typing in a term such as *animal rights*. On the next list that appears, researchers should click "Subject Headings."

Once the record for a book or other item is found, it is a good idea to see what additional subject headings and name headings have been assigned to that item. These, in turn, can be used for further searching. For instance, in addition to *animal rights*, researchers will probably also want to check out *animal welfare* and *animal rights activists*.

BOOKSTORE CATALOGS

Many people have discovered that online bookstores such as Amazon.com (http://www.amazon.com) and Barnes & Noble (http://www.barnesandnoble. com) provide convenient ways to shop for books. A less-known benefit of online bookstore catalogs is that they often include publisher information, book reviews, and reader comments about a given title. They can thus serve as a form of annotated bibliography. Out-of-print or highly specialized materials may not appear in such catalogs, however.

BIBLIOGRAPHIES, INDEXES, AND DATABASES

Printed or online bibliographies provide a convenient way to find books, periodical articles, and other materials. Some bibliographies include abstracts (brief summaries of content), while others provide only citations. Some bibliographies and indexes are available online (at least for recent years), but researchers may be able to access them only through a library where they hold a card. (When searching on a college campus, researchers can ask a university reference librarian for help.) There are two good indexes with unrestricted search access, however. UnCover Web (http://www.ingenta.com) contains brief descriptions of about 13 million documents from about 27,000 journals in almost every subject area. Copies of complete documents can be ordered with a credit card, or they may be obtained free at a local library.

PERIODICAL INDEXES

Most public libraries subscribe to database services such as InfoTrac or EBSCOhost, which index articles from hundreds of general-interest periodicals (and some moderately specialized ones). This kind of database can be searched by author or by words in the title, subject headings, and sometimes words found anywhere in the article text. Depending on the database used, "hits" can produce just a bibliographical citation (author, title, pages, periodical name, issue date, and other information), a citation and abstract, or the full text of the article. Before using such an index, it is a good idea to view the list of newspapers and magazines covered and determine the years of coverage.

Many libraries provide dial-in, Internet, or telnet access to their periodical databases as an option in their catalog menu. However, licensing restrictions usually mean that only researchers who have a library card for that particular library can access the database (by typing in their name and card number). Check with local public or school libraries to see what databases are available.

For periodicals not indexed by InfoTrac or another index (or for which only abstracts rather than complete text is available), check to see whether the publication has its own web site (most now do). Some scholarly publications are putting most or all of their articles online. Popular publications tend to offer only a limited selection. Some publications of both types offer archives of several years' back issues that can be searched by author or keyword.

Nearly all newspapers now have web sites with current news and features. Generally a newspaper offers recent articles (perhaps from the last 30 days) for free online access. Earlier material can often be found in an archive section. A citation and, perhaps, an abstract is frequently available for free, but a fee of a few dollars may be charged for the complete article. One can sometimes buy a "pack" of articles at a discount as long as the articles are retrieved within a specified time. Of course, back issues of newspapers and magazines may also be available in hard copy, bound, or on microfilm at local libraries.

LEGAL RESEARCH

As with all complex and controversial topics, animal welfare and animal rights have been the subject of intense litigation in the courts. Animal rights groups have often used lawsuits in attempts to pressure government agencies to enforce animal protection laws such as the Animal Welfare Act and the Endangered Species Act, and these groups in turn have been sued by some of the individuals and businesses they have attacked. Although one can find news coverage of some important cases in the general media, many researchers will need to find specific court opinions or the text of existing or pending legislation.

Because of the specialized terminology of the law, legal research can be more difficult to master than bibliographical or general research tools. Fortunately, the Internet has also come to the rescue in this area, offering a variety of ways to look up laws and court cases without having to pore through huge bound volumes in law libraries (which may not be easily accessible to the general public, anyway.) To begin with, simply entering the name of a law, bill, or court case into a search engine will often lead the researcher directly to both text and commentary.

Finding Laws

Federal legislation is compiled into the massive U.S. Code. The U.S. Code can be searched online in several locations, but the easiest site to use is probably that of Cornell Law School: http://www4.law.cornell.edu/uscode. The fastest way to retrieve a law is by its title and section citation (listed for all laws discussed in Chapter 2), but popular names (Animal Welfare Act, Endangered Species Act, and so on) and keywords can also be used.

Many state agencies have home pages that can be accessed through the FindLaw state resources website (http://findlaw.com/11stategov). This site also has links to state law codes. These links may or may not provide access to the text of specific regulations, however.

Animal Rights

Keeping Up with Legislative Developments

Pending legislation is often tracked by advocacy groups, both national and those based in particular states. See Chapter 8, "Organizations and Agencies," for contact information for particular groups.

The Library of Congress Thomas web site (http://thomas.loc.gov) includes files summarizing legislation by the number of the Congress (each two-year session of Congress has a consecutive number; for example, the 108th Congress was in session in 2002 and 2003. Legislation can be searched for by the name of its sponsor(s), the bill number, or by topical keywords. (Laws that have been passed can be looked up under their Public Law number.) For instance, selecting the 108th Congress and typing the phrase "animal protection" into the search box at the time of writing retrieved four bills containing that phrase. Further details retrievable by clicking on the bill number and then the link to the bill summary and status file include sponsors, committee action, and amendments.

A second extremely useful site is maintained by the Government Printing Office (http://www.gpoaccess.gov/index.html). This site has links to the Code of Federal Regulations (which contains federal regulations that have been finalized), the Federal Register (which contains announcements of new federal agency regulations), the Congressional Record, the U.S. Code, congressional bills, a catalog of U.S. government publications, and other databases. It also provides links to individual agencies, grouped under government branch (legislative, executive, judicial), and to regulatory agencies, administrative decisions, core documents of U.S. democracy such as the Constitution, and web sites hosted by the federal government.

Finding Court Decisions

Legislation is only part of the story, of course. The Supreme Court and state courts make important decisions every year that determine how laws are interpreted. Like laws, legal decisions are organized using a system of citations. The general form is: *Party1* v. *Party2 volume reporter* [optional start page] *(court, year)*. Here are some examples:

Sierra Club v. Morton, 405 U.S. 727 (1972)

Here the parties are Sierra Club and Morton (the first listed is the plaintiff or appellant, the second the defendant). The case is in volume 405 of the *U.S. Supreme Court Reports,* beginning on page 727, and the case was decided in 1972. (For the U.S. Supreme Court, the name of the court is omitted).

The following case was decided by the 3rd U.S. Circuit Court of Appeals in 1998:

Animal Legal Defense Fund v. Glickman, 154 F.3d 426 (1998)

A state court decision can generally be identified because it includes the state's name. For example, in *Texas Beef Group v. Winfrey*, 11 F. Supp. 2d 858 (N.D. Tex. 1998), *F. Supp. 2d* refers to the federal district court to which the case was transferred, but *N.D. Tex.* refers to the Texas state court where it was first heard.

Once the jurisdiction for a case has been determined, a researcher can then go to a number of places on the Internet to find cases by citation and sometimes by the names of the parties or by subject keywords. Some of the most useful sites are:

The Legal Information Institute (http://supct.law.cornell.edu/supct/index.html) supplies all Supreme Court decisions since 1990, plus 610 of "the most important historic" decisions.

Washlaw Web (http://www.washlaw.edu) lists a variety of courts (including state courts) and legal topics, making it a good jumping-off place for many sorts of legal research. However, the actual accessibility of state court opinions (and the formats they are provided in) varies widely.

Lexis and Westlaw

Lexis and Westlaw are commercial legal databases that have extensive information, including an elaborate system of notes, legal subject headings, and ways to show relationships among cases. Unfortunately, these services are too expensive for most individual researchers to use unless they can access the services through a university or corporate library.

Sites Specific to Animal Law

Several animal welfare/animal rights sites feature access to the text of major laws and court cases specific to animal law. Some of the best are the following:

- **International Institute for Animal Law**
  URL: http://www.animallaw.com
  This site's extensive database allows searching for legislation/laws (by state). It also has a bibliography, divided by topic and type of material (book, magazine article, government documents, law journal articles, and more). The items are not annotated, however, and many appear to be quite old.
- **Rutgers University School of Law Animal Rights Law Project**
  URL: http://www.animal-law.org

This site contains papers by Gary Francione and Anna E. Charlton, leading advocates of legal rights for animals. It also includes the text of some major federal and state laws pertaining to animals, handbooks on protest and on renters' rights regarding companion animals, and the text of key court cases.

More Help on Legal Research

For more information on conducting legal research, see the "Legal Research FAQ" at http://www.faqs.org/faqs/law/research. After a certain point, however, the researcher who lacks formal legal training may need to consult with or rely on the efforts of professional researchers or academics in the field.

A WORD OF CAUTION

Thanks to the Web, there is more information from more sources available than ever before. There is also a greater diversity of voices since any person or group with a computer and Internet service can put up a web site—in some cases a site that looks as polished and professional as that of an "established" group. One benefit of this situation is that dissenting views can be found in abundance, including even sites maintained by more-radical groups such as the Animal Liberation Front or their supporters.

However, the other side of the coin is that the researcher—whether journalist, analyst, teacher, or student—must take extra care to try to verify facts and to understand the possible biases of each source. Some good questions to ask include:

- Who is responsible for this web site?
- What is the background or reputation of the person or group?
- Does the person or group have a stated objective or agenda?
- What biases might this person or group have?
- Do a number of high-quality sites link to this one?
- What is the source given for a particular fact? Does that source actually say what or whom is quoted? Where did *they* get the information?

In a sense, in the age of the Internet each person must be his or her own journalist, verifying sources and evaluating the extent to which they can be relied upon.

CHAPTER 7

ANNOTATED BIBLIOGRAPHY

Hundreds of books, articles, and Internet documents related to animal protection and animal rights have appeared in recent years, as this issue has attracted increasing attention in the United States, Britain, and other industrialized countries. This bibliography lists a representative sample of serious nonfiction sources dealing with various aspects of this subject. Sources have been selected for clarity and usefulness to the general reader, recent publication (mostly from 1998 or later), and variety of points of view.

Listings are grouped in the following subject categories:

- general and historical works on animal protection and human relationships with animals
- the philosophy of animal rights
- animals and the law
- the animal rights movement, its opponents, and their tactics
- companion animals and animal shelters
- animals in agriculture
- animals in research, testing, and education
- animals in entertainment
- wildlife

Items are listed only once, under what appears to be their most important category, even though they might also fit under other categories.

Within each category, items are listed by type (books, articles, and web documents). Newspaper articles have not been included because magazines usually cover the same material and back issues of magazines are easier to obtain than those of most newspapers. Magazine articles available on the Internet are listed as articles, not as Internet documents.

GENERAL AND HISTORICAL WORKS ON ANIMAL PROTECTION AND HUMAN RELATIONSHIPS WITH ANIMALS

BOOKS

Appleby, Michael C. *What Should We Do About Animal Welfare?* Oxford, U.K.: Blackwell, 1999. Discusses the science and ethics of animal welfare. Claims that some uses of animals should be phased out, while others can continue but under improved conditions.

Arluke, Arnold, and Clinton R. Sanders. *Regarding Animals: Animals, Culture, and Society.* Philadelphia, Pa.: Temple University Press, 1996. The authors, ethnographers and professors of sociology, provide a detailed analysis of what the contradictory ways in which Western society has treated animals say about human individuals within that society.

Baker, Steve, and Carol J. Adams. *Picturing the Beast: Animals, Identity and Representation.* Champaign: University of Illinois Press, 2001. Describes images of animals in politics, entertainment, and social interactions and considers how such images distort the way people perceive and treat animals.

Beck, Benjamin B., et al., eds. *Great Apes and Humans: The Ethics of Coexistence.* Washington, D.C.: Smithsonian Institution Press, 2001. Outgrowth of a 1998 workshop on the welfare of captive gorillas, bonobos, chimpanzees, and orangutans. Includes a discussion of apes' cognitive skills, similarities and differences between apes and humans, and the current moral and legal status of great apes.

Bekoff, Marc, and Carron A. Meaney, eds. *Encyclopedia of Animal Rights and Animal Welfare.* Westport, Conn.: Greenwood Press, 1998. Focuses more on animal rights than animal welfare, especially on the animal rights movement's impact on medical research. Includes short biographies (only of deceased persons), philosophical essays, and discussions of scientific topics such as genetic engineering. Covers a variety of viewpoints.

Clark, Ward M. *Misplaced Compassion: The Animal Rights Movement Exposed.* San Jose, Calif.: Writers Club Press, 2001. Highly critical description of the philosophy and tactics of the animal rights movement, written by a supporter of hunting and other activities that use animals for human benefit.

Damron, W. Stephen. *Introduction to Animal Science: Global, Biological, Social, and Industry Perspectives.* Upper Saddle River, N.J.: Prentice-Hall, 2002. College textbook focuses on animals in agriculture but also discusses companion animals. Includes material on animal welfare and animal rights.

Annotated Bibliography

Eurogroup for Animal Welfare. *Analysis of Major Areas of Concern for Animal Welfare in Europe.* Brussels, Belgium: Eurogroup for Animal Welfare, 2001. Animal legislation group provides a guide to the main aspects of animal welfare that are or could be affected by European Community legislation and suggests ways in which these areas of concern might be addressed. Includes sections on farmed animals, wild animals, companion animals, animals in research, and animals in entertainment.

Fouts, Roger, and Steve Tukel Mills. *Next of Kin: What Chimpanzees Have Taught Me About Who We Are.* Collingdale, Pa.: Diane Publishing Co., 2000. Joined by wildlife writer Mills, primatologist Fouts, who has worked on language studies with captive chimpanzees for 30 years, describes what he has learned about the animals' mental powers. Includes an introduction by Jane Goodall.

Franklin, Adrian. *Animals and Modern Culture: A Sociology of Human-Animal Relations in Modernity.* Thousand Oaks, Calif.: Corwin Press, 1999. Describes the dramatic changes in views of relationships between humans and animals that occurred during the 20th century as society moved away from a strict focus on human needs to one that encompasses animals' needs as well.

Gold, Mark. *Animal Century: A Celebration of Changing Attitudes to Animals.* Charlbury, Oxfordshire, U.K.: Jon Carpenter Publishing, 1999. Uses illustrations and the words of prominent animal protectionists such as Jane Goodall and Peter Singer to portray the growing concern for animal welfare and liberation against a backdrop of overall acceleration in political and social change.

Griffin, Donald R. *Animal Minds: Beyond Cognition to Consciousness.* Rev. ed. Chicago: University of Chicago Press, 2001. Claims that animals have complex communication skills analogous to human language and that these abilities suggest a sense of time and the future, complex memory, and perhaps even consciousness.

Henninger-Voss, Mary, ed. *Animals in Human Histories: The Mirror of Nature and Culture.* Rochester, N.Y.: University of Rochester Press, 2002. Anthology of essays explores human interaction with animals and uses animals as a lens to view human social interactions. Compares cultural images of animals during different periods of history and contrasts them with reality.

Kean, Hilda. *Animal Rights: Political and Social Change in Britain since 1800.* London: Reaktion Books, 1998. Describes 200 years of controversy over vivisection, zoos, and hunting in Britain.

Kistler, John M. *Animal Rights: A Subject Guide, Bibliography, and Internet Companion.* Westport, Conn.: Greenwood Press, 2000. Divides material into general works, animal natures, fatal uses of animals, nonfatal uses of animals, animal populations, and animal speculations (religious and philosophical views of animals and how animals should be treated).

Masson, Jeffrey Moussiaeff, and Susan McCarthy. *When Elephants Weep: The Emotional Lives of Animals.* New York: Delta, 1996. Argues that many animals possess an emotional sensibility and, possibly, a consciousness similar to that of humans.

Preece, Rod, ed. *Awe for the Tiger, Love for the Lamb: A Chronicle of Sensibility to Animals.* New York: Routledge, 2002. Statements of sensibility to animals from ancient times to the present show humanity's ongoing concern for nonhumans as part of the moral community.

Primatt, Humphry. *The Duty of Mercy and the Sin of Cruelty to Brute Animals.* Fontwell, Sussex, U.K.: Centaur Press, 1992. Reprint of a book first published in 1776, which contained most of the arguments against cruelty to animals that would shape the 19th-century animal welfare movement.

Ritvo, Harriet. *The Animal Estate: The English and Other Creatures in the Victorian Age.* Cambridge, Mass.: Harvard University Press, 1989. Describes attitudes to animals in Victorian Britain.

Roleff, Tamara L., and Jennifer A. Hurley, eds. *The Rights of Animals: Current Controversies.* San Diego, Calif.: Greenhaven Press, 1999. Anthology of articles and book excerpts presents different viewpoints on several issues within the animal rights debate.

Rothfels, Nigel, ed. *Representing Animals.* Bloomington: Indiana University Press, 2002. Collection of scholarly articles shows deep connections between the ways people in different cultures and times think about animals and the ways they think about themselves and their societies.

Salem, Deborah J., and Andrew N. Rowan, eds. *The State of the Animals 2001.* Washington, D.C.: Humane Society Press, 2001. Anthology of articles published by the Humane Society of the United States surveys the condition of animals in various industries and discusses issues related to animal protection, such as social attitudes to animals and progress in livestock handling and slaughter techniques.

Savage-Rumbaugh, Sue, and Roger Lewin. *Kanzi: The Ape at the Brink of the Human Mind.* Hoboken, N.J.: John Wiley & Sons, 1996. Savage-Rumbaugh, a specialist in language studies with apes, and Lewin, a science writer, describe the history of this research and evaluate what has been learned from it, focusing on the bonobo Kanzi.

Serpell, James. *In the Company of Animals: A Study of Human-Animal Relationships.* Rev. ed. New York: Cambridge University Press, 2002. Studies human attitudes to different kinds of animals and the natural world, including inherent contradictions.

Shepard, Paul. *The Others: How Animals Made Us Human.* Washington, D.C.: Island Press, 1997. The author, an ecologist, maintains that humans have always depended on animals and that their dependence has shaped humans' views of themselves.

Simons, John. *Animal Rights and the Politics of Literary Representation.* New York: Palgrave Macmillan, 2002. Asks what literary studies would look like if animal rights were taken seriously. Examines a wide range of literary texts and discusses positions and themes in the history and philosophy of animal rights.

Singer, Peter, ed. *In Defense of Animals.* New York: HarperCollins, 1986. Classic anthology of animal rights writings includes Alex Pacheco's description of allegedly abusive conditions in Edward Taub's laboratory as presented in the "Silver Spring monkeys case."

Spedding, Colin. *Animal Welfare.* London: Earthscan Publications, 2000. Describes nature and scale of today's animal welfare problems, what regulations and standards might ease them, and what part the concept of citizenship plays in ensuring that animals are treated humanely.

Stallwood, Kim W., ed. *A Primer on Animal Rights: Leading Animal Experts Write about Animal Cruelty and Exploitation.* New York: Lantern Books, 2002. Collection of articles from animal rights magazine *The Animals' Agenda,* chosen by the magazine's editor-in-chief, describes alleged exploitation and mistreatment of animals in six areas.

———. *Speaking Out for Animals: True Stories about Real People Who Rescue Animals.* New York: Lantern Books, 2001. Collection of interviews and profiles of animal rights activists and celebrity supporters from *The Animals' Agenda.* Includes a foreword by Jane Goodall.

Stevens, Karen Lee. *All for Animals: Tips and Inspiration for Living a More Compassionate Life.* Santa Barbara, Calif.: Fithian Press, 2001. Helps people learn how they can get along better with companion animals, curb pet overpopulation, avoid products made from or tested on animals, and coexist with wildlife.

Thomas, Keith. *Man and the Natural World: Changing Attitudes in England 1500–1800.* New York: Oxford University Press, 1996. Combines studies of history and literature to show how the profound social changes that occurred in England between the 16th and late 18th centuries led people to conclude that the unaltered "natural" world had healing powers and should be preserved.

Tobias, Michael. *Voices from the Underground: For the Love of Animals.* Pasadena, Calif.: Hope Publishing House, 1999. Profiles people who have founded well-known animal rights or animal welfare organizations such as PETA or in other ways devoted their lives to stopping cruelty to animals.

Turner, James. *Reckoning with the Beast: Animals, Pain, and Humanity in the Victorian Mind.* Baltimore, Md.: Johns Hopkins University Press, 2001. Discusses the 19th-century rise of concern for humane treatment of animals in relation to Victorian culture as a whole. Concludes that the shocks of urbanization and industrialization pushed people into closer emotional identification with the natural world.

Waals, Frans de. *The Ape and the Sushi Master: Cultural Reflections by a Primatologist.* Cambridge, Mass.: Perseus Publishing, 2001. Suggests that apes and some other animals transmit culture (convey knowledge and habits to others) much as humans do.

Wolfe, Cary, ed. *Zoontologies: The Question of the Animal.* Minneapolis: University of Minnesota Press, 2003. Anthology of contemporary writings includes philosophical and ethical essays, personal investigations of slaughterhouses, artistic renderings, and discussions of animal themes in literature and popular culture.

ARTICLES

Carson, Gerald. "The Great Meddler." *American Heritage,* vol. 19, December 1967, pp. 28–33, 94–97. Biographical article about Henry Bergh describes his founding of the American Society for the Prevention of Cruelty to Animals in 1866, the society's early work, and reactions to the fledgling animal protection movement.

Dawkins, Marian Stamp. "Evolution and Animal Welfare." *Quarterly Review of Biology,* vol. 73, September 1998, pp. 305–328. Discusses methods of assessment, covering a range of biological phenomena but focusing on the animals' own choices and reinforcement mechanisms. Also raises the possibility that nonhuman animals have conscious experiences of suffering and considers how these might be evaluated.

Einwohner, Rachel L. "Practices, Opportunity, and Protest Effectiveness: Illustrations from Four Animal Rights Campaigns." *Social Problems,* vol. 46, May 1999, pp. 169 ff. Interviews with members of groups targeted by animal rights campaigns in the Seattle area suggest that people are more likely to change challenged behavior if they do not see the behavior as necessary or as part of their personal identity.

Franklin, Adrian, and Robert White. "Animals and Modernity: Changing Human-Animal Relations, 1949–1998." *Journal of Sociology,* vol. 37, September 2001, pp. 219–241. Content analysis of more than 1,000 articles published in an Australian newspaper over a 50-year period served as an empirical test of author Franklin's use of theories of reflexive modernization to explain the modern shift to more animal-centered and sentimentalized relationships with animals. Results generally supported Franklin's conclusions but identified some local and historical exceptions.

Mullin, Molly H. "Mirrors and Windows: Sociocultural Studies of Human-Animal Relationships." *Annual Review of Anthropology,* vol. 28, 1999, pp.

201–224. Discusses human-animal relationships from a sociocultural perspective, including animal rights, animals as products, pets, and hunting.

Picker, Lauren. "Wild about Animals." *Town & Country*, June 1999, pp. 152 ff. Profiles nine women who help animals in various ways.

Praded, Joni. "One Who Made a Difference." *Animals*, November 1998, p. 30. Obituary for animal rights activist Henry Spira, who led successful campaigns against alleged abuses in product testing and factory farming.

Richard, Julie. "Animal 007's—Shaken and Stirred." *Best Friends Magazine*, January–February 2002, pp. 18–20. Profiles two men who have risked their lives in undercover work to bring animal abusers and illegal traders in animals to justice.

———. "Continental Divide." *Best Friends Magazine*, July–August 2002, pp. 20–23. Presents brief descriptions of laws and attitudes about animals in different European countries.

Shupp, Lee. "Futurespeak." *American Demographics*, May 1, 2001, p. 56. Futurist Lee Shupp predicts that most people will accept the idea of some legal rights for animals 10 to 20 years from now.

Singer, Barnett. "Brigitte Bardot: Animal Activist." *Contemporary Review*, vol. 275, November 1999, pp. 249–250. Profiles onetime "sex kitten" movie star who has devoted much of her life to animal rights activism, including protests against bullfighting and the killing of baby seals.

Singer, Peter. "Henry Spira." *The Animals' Agenda*, vol. 18, November–December 1998, pp. 10–11. Obituary of Spira, a highly respected animal rights activist, including excerpts from an interview.

Thomas, Sydney Carroll, and Piers Beirne. "Humane Education and Humanistic Philosophy: Toward a New Curriculum." *Journal of Humanistic Counseling, Education and Development*, vol. 41, Fall 2002, pp. 90–99. Claims that humane education should be an integral part of humanistic philosophy. Describes what authors see as humane education's two chief components: an understanding of the sociological and psychological dimensions of animal abuse and the cultivation of empathy for nonhuman animals.

Unti, Bernard. "Cleveland Amory." *The Animals' Agenda*, vol. 18, November–December 1998, pp. 12–13. Obituary of the famous writer and founder of the Fund for Animals.

Wolf, David B. "Social Work and Speciesism." *Social Work*, vol. 45, January 2000, pp. 88 ff. Urges social workers to become informed about the economic, environmental, and political issues connected with treatment of animals and adds speciesism to the list of noxious -isms that the profession combats.

Wynne, Clive D. L. "The Soul of the Ape." *American Scientist*, vol. 89, March 2001, pp. 120 ff. A psychologist evaluates several types of experiments purporting to show that great apes are self-aware and concludes that the evidence for this assertion is exaggerated.

WEB DOCUMENTS

"Animal Care: A New Era in Animal Welfare." U.S. Department of Agriculture Animal and Plant Health Inspection Service. Available online. URL: http://www.aphis.usda.gov/lpa/pubs/fsheet_faq_notice/fs_awnewera.html. Posted in February 2002. Describes new strategies for inspections and enforcement of the Animal Welfare Act, as well as new requirements for animal welfare.

"Animal Welfare Issues Compendium." U.S. Department of Agriculture Animal Welfare Information Center. Available online. URL: http://www.nal.usda.gov/awic/pubs/97issues.htm. Posted in September 1997. Fourteen discussion papers on topics related to animal welfare with an emphasis on agriculture.

Stevenson, Peter. "The World Trade Organisation Rules: A Legal Analysis of Their Adverse Impact on Animal Welfare." Compassion in World Farming. Available online. URL: http://www.ciwf.co.uk/Pubs/Reports/art9454.pdf. Accessed on April 18, 2003. Examines World Trade Organisation rules and how they have been interpreted by case law. Suggests ways for reforming the rules so that they will not have a harmful effect on animal welfare.

THE PHILOSOPHY OF ANIMAL RIGHTS

BOOKS

Adams, Carol J., and Josephine Donovan, eds. *Animals and Women: Feminist Theoretical Explorations.* Durham, N.C.: Duke University Press, 1995. Explores links between the treatment of animals and the treatment of women, including connections between sexist and speciesist language and between animal abuse and battering of women.

Cavalieri, Paola. *The Animal Question: Why Non-Human Animals Deserve Human Rights.* Translated by Catherine Woollard. New York: Oxford University Press, 2001. Argues that nonhuman animals should have the same rights as humans and should not be treated merely as things or means to an end.

Coetzee, J. M. *The Lives of Animals.* Princeton, N.J.: Princeton University Press, 2001. Uses a fictional framework to present essays on the ethics of human treatment of animals. Four experts in different fields, including animal rights philosopher Peter Singer, comment on the essays.

Annotated Bibliography

Cohen, Carl, and Tom Regan. *The Animal Rights Debate*. Lanham, Md.: Rowman and Littlefield, 2001. Two philosophy professors argue opposite sides of the debate on animal rights.

DeGrazia, David. *Animal Rights: A Very Short Introduction*. New York: Oxford University Press, 2002. Provides an overview of the philosophical and ethical issues involved in animal rights. Presents models for understanding animals' moral status and rights and explores their implications for the way humans should treat animals.

Dolins, Francine L., ed. *Attitudes to Animals: Views in Animal Welfare*. New York: Cambridge University Press, 1999. Offers philosophical, ethical, and scientific views of the nature of humans and animals and the relationships between the two groups. Considers how attitudes to animals are shaped by families, education, media, jobs, and society as a whole.

Dombrowski, Daniel A. *Babies and Beasts: The Argument from Marginal Cases*. Champaign: University of Illinois Press, 1997. Analyzes philosophical arguments for and against animal rights, focusing on the comparison of animals with noncompetent humans.

Donovan, Josephine, and Carol J. Adams, eds. *Beyond Animal Rights: A Feminist Caring Ethic for the Treatment of Animals*. New York: Continuum Publishing Group, 2000. Proposes a feminist-oriented "caring ethic" as an alternative to the rights approach to better treatment for animals.

Dunayer, Joan. *Animal Equality: Language and Liberation*. Derwood, Md.: Ryce Publishing, 2001. The author argues that biased language supports speciesism and mistreatment of animals and contends that humans and nonhuman animals deserve equal consideration and protection.

Francione, Gary. *Introduction to Animal Rights: Your Child or the Dog?* Philadelphia, Pa.: Temple University Press, 2000. Leading animal rights lawyer discusses dilemmas in animal ethics and the "moral schizophrenia" with which Western society views animals.

Fudge, Erica. *Perceiving Animals: Humans and Beasts in Early Modern English Culture*. Champaign: University of Illinois Press, 2002. Considers anthropocentrism and views of human superiority to animals in political, religious, legal, scientific, and literary works written from 1558 to 1649.

Hursthouse, Rosalind. *Ethics, Humans, and Other Animals: An Introduction with Readings*. New York: Routledge, 2000. Considers treatment of animals from the view of three common approaches to ethical theory: utilitarianism, rights theory, and virtue ethics. Provides exercises that help students use the subject as a way to understand philosophy.

Jamieson, Dale, ed. *Singer and His Critics*. Oxford, U.K.: Blackwell, 1999. Essays by a variety of philosophers discuss Peter Singer's controversial views, including his ideas about animal liberation.

Kalechofsky, Roberta, ed. *Judaism and Animal Rights*. Marblehead, Mass.: Micah Publications, 1992. More than 40 essays from writers throughout history discuss Jewish laws and customs that affect the treatment of animals.

Leahy, Michael P. T. *Against Liberation: Putting Animals in Perspective*. New York: Routledge, 1994. Claims that the animal rights movement is based on a mistakenly anthropomorphic view of animals and that most human uses of animals are justified as long as they are carried out humanely.

Linzey, Andrew. *Animal Gospel*. Louisville, Ky.: Westminster John Knox Press, 1999. Shows how Christian doctrine supports compassion for animals and describes Christian theologians' views of the animal rights movement.

Midgley, Mary. *Animals and Why They Matter*. Athens: University of Georgia Press, 1998. Considered a moderate animal rightist, Midgley presents a range of philosophical views of animals but does not strongly attach herself to any.

Nibert, David Alan. *Animal Rights/Human Rights*. Translated by Raf Casert. Lanham, Md.: Rowman and Littlefield, 2002. Uses social theory to explain oppression of animals and tie it to the human oppression produced by capitalism.

Orlans, F. Barbara, et al., eds. *The Human Use of Animals: Case Studies in Ethical Choice*. New York: Oxford University Press, 1998. Presents case studies that show the complexity of moral issues related to animal welfare. Includes 16 essays by experts in various fields, covering a variety of viewpoints and types of human use of animals, with an emphasis on use of animals in research.

Patterson, Charles. *Eternal Treblinka: Our Treatment of Animals and the Holocaust*. New York: Lantern Books, 2002. Suggests a causal link between social attitudes that encourage violence to animals and those that foster violence to other humans, as evidenced in the Holocaust.

Petrinovich, Lewis. *Darwinian Dominion: Animal Welfare and Human Interests*. Cambridge, Mass.: MIT Press, 2001. Argues that humans' tendency to place the interests of their own species ahead of those of others, which animal rightists call *speciesism*, is not morally wrong but, on the contrary, is built into all species by evolution.

Rachels, James. *Created from Animals: The Moral Implications of Darwinism*. New York: Oxford University Press, 1998. Claims that the theory of Darwinian evolution and scientific studies showing close similarities between humans and other primates undercut classic philosophical theories. Analyzes numerous theorists, including Darwin, his contemporary detractors, and modern animal rights philosopher Peter Singer.

Regan, Tom. *Defending Animal Rights*. Champaign: University of Illinois Press, 2001. Regan is considered the chief philosopher of the more radical wing of the animal rights movement. This volume of short essays written during the 1990s elaborates his thinking on animal rights issues.

Reichmann, James B. *Evolution, Animal "Rights," and the Environment.* Washington, D.C.: Catholic University of America Press, 2001. The author, a Jesuit, presents forceful arguments against claims that animals should have rights, whether they come from a philosophical/ethical/ moral or a biological (evolutionary or "Darwinian") point of view.

Rowlands, Mark. *Animal Rights: A Philosophical Defense.* New York: Palgrave Macmillan, 2000. Discusses philosophical concepts and viewpoints such as liberalism, utilitarianism, and inherent value in connection with animal rights.

Ryder, Richard D. *Animal Revolution: Changing Attitudes to Speciesism.* Oxford, U.K.: Berg Publishers, 2000. Describes historical changes in valuation of humans relative to animals, beginning with the ancient world.

———. *The Political Animal: The Conquest of Speciesism.* Jefferson, N.C.: McFarland and Co., 1998. Ryder, former head of the Royal Society for the Prevention of Cruelty to Animals and currently director of animal welfare studies for the International Fund for Animal Welfare, is a well-known British animal rights philosopher who coined the term *speciesism.* Here he discusses humans' relationships to other species from historical, ethical, scientific, and political points of view.

Salt, Henry S. *Animals' Rights Considered in Relation to Social Progress.* Clarke Summit, Pa.: International Society for Animal Rights, 1980. First published in 1892, this book is said to prefigure the main modern arguments in favor of animal rights.

Scruton, Roger. *Animal Rights and Wrongs.* 3d ed. Brinkworth, Wiltshire, U.K.: Claridge Press, 2003. Presents practical arguments on animal rights and human duties to animals, contradicting both the extreme animal rights position and the "weak welfarism" of those who think that being kind to their pets is sufficient to make them humane to animals.

Scully, Matthew. *Dominion: The Power of Man, the Suffering of Animals, and the Call to Mercy.* New York: St. Martin's Press, 2002. Conservative Christian Scully, a journalist and former speechwriter for President George W. Bush, criticizes the idea that animals are morally equal to humans but says that treating animals with respect and kindness is a moral imperative nonetheless.

Shapiro, Leland S. *Applied Animal Ethics.* Independence, Ky.: Delmar Learning, 1999. Textbook employs the ethics of different uses of animals as an example of applying ethics theory to practical situations. Includes case studies, a balanced selection of ethical viewpoints, and review and discussion questions.

Singer, Peter. *Animal Liberation: A New Ethics for Our Treatment of Animals.* Rev. ed. New York: HarperCollins/Ecco Press, 2001. Revised and expanded edition of seminal 1975 book by controversial Australian philosopher Singer (now teaching at Princeton University) that has frequently been called "the Bible of the animal rights movement." In this book, which is both a philosophy treatise and a practical call to action, Singer, a utilitarian, says that animals deserve respect because they are sentient, or able to feel pleasure and pain.

Sterba, James P., ed. *Earth Ethics: Introductory Readings on Animal Rights and Environmental Ethics.* Upper Saddle River, N.J.: Prentice-Hall, 1999. Anthology illustrates a range of positions on animal rights and environmental ethics. Sections include Judeo-Christian perspectives, deep ecology and ecofeminism, and non-Western religious and cultural perspectives.

Taylor, Angus. *Magpies, Monkeys, and Morals: What Philosophers Say about Animal Liberation.* Orchard Park, N.Y.: Broadview Press, 1999. Offers a thorough and balanced description of views on the subject, including historical background.

Varner, Gary E. *In Nature's Interests? Interests, Animal Rights, and Environmental Ethics.* New York: Oxford University Press, 2002. Argues against the assumptions that both animal rights philosophies and anthropocentric (human-centered) philosophies are enemies of sound environmental policy. Claims that giving priority to organisms with conscious desires and to certain interests of humans can provide vital support for environmental goals.

Waal, Frans de. *Good Natured: The Origins of Right and Wrong in Humans and Other Animals.* Reprint, Cambridge, Mass.: Harvard University Press, 1997. Critics of animal rights say that animals cannot have rights because they do not understand rights or other moral concepts, but animal behaviorist de Waal offers evidence from his studies that suggests that animals, particularly primates, do manifest moral behavior and, indeed, that such behavior is natural.

Wolfe, Alan. *The Human Difference: Animals, Computers, and the Necessity of Social Science.* Berkeley: University of California Press, 1993. Claims that completely eliminating all uses of animals that animal rightists deem cruel would produce a puritanical society and "a world without fantasy, excitement, and creativity."

ARTICLES

Bailey, Ronald. "The Pursuit of Happiness." *Reason*, vol. 32, December 2000, pp. 29 ff. Interview with philosopher Peter Singer includes discussion of his views on animal rights.

Bekoff, Marc. "Resisting Speciesism and Expanding the Community of Equals." *BioScience*, August 1998, pp. 638–641. Holds that all animals, not just great apes, should be included with humans in the "community of equals" and that to place animals in any hierarchical relationship is speciesist.

Carlin, David R. "Rights, Animal and Human." *First Things*, August 2000, p. 16. The animal rights movement claims to be trying to elevate the status of animals, but this author claims that its real purpose is to degrade humans.

Fjellstrom, Roger. "Equality Does Not Entail Equality across Species." *Environmental Ethics*, vol. 24, Winter 2002, pp. 339–352. Criticizes one minor and two major arguments that Peter Singer offers in support of his proposal that equality across species necessarily follows from general theories of equality.

Giannet, Stanley M. "The Human-Animal Divide: Interdisciplinary Ethical Reflections." *Journal of Evolutionary Psychology*, March 2003, pp. 9–13. Maintains that animals have many psychological features in common with humans and that religious teachings, properly viewed, mandate better treatment of animals because they ask people to act as "advocates for the powerless."

Lancaster, Clay. "Worship versus Investigation: Practices of Religion and Science." *The Animals' Agenda*, vol. 18, July–August 1998, pp. 44–45. Points out that several Eastern religions support what the West defines as animal rights, including prohibitions against killing sentient living things.

Li, Hon-Lam. "Animal Research, Non-Vegetarianism, and the Moral Status of Animals." *Journal of Medicine and Philosophy*, vol. 27, October 2002, pp. 589–615. Offers reasons for claiming that nonhuman animals have less intrinsic value than human beings.

Linker, Damon. "Rights for Rodents." *Commentary*, vol. 111, April 2001, pp. 41 ff. Critiques the arguments of animal rights philosopher Peter Singer and attorney Steven Wise and explains why humans are significantly different from nonhuman animals.

Moore, Eric. "The Case for Unequal Animal Rights." *Environmental Ethics*, vol. 24, Fall 2002, pp. 295–313. Maintains that the view of Tom Regan and Evelyn B. Pluhar that animals should have rights equal to those of humans should be rejected because it has what the author sees as unacceptable consequences. Describes an alternative theory that grants rights to both humans and animals but gives more rights to the former.

Neuhaus, Richard John. "A Curious Encounter with a Philosopher from Nowhere." *First Things*, February 2002, pp. 77–82. Article about philosopher Peter Singer, a strong supporter of animal rights, by an author who respects Singer but opposes many of his views.

Nussbaum, Martha C. "Animal Rights: The Need for a Theoretical Basis." *Harvard Law Review*, vol. 114, 2001, pp. 1509–1512. Provides a philosophically oriented and somewhat sympathetic review of Steven Wise's book *Rattling the Cage*, which calls for increased legal rights for great apes.

Oderberg, David S. "The Illusion of Animal Rights." *The Human Life Review*, Spring–Summer 2000, p. 37. Critiques philosophical arguments of animal rights supporters from the standpoint of "traditional morality." Maintains that knowledge and freedom, which only humans can possess, are the criteria for having rights.

O'Neil, Rick. "Animal Liberation versus Environmentalism: The Care Solution." *Environmental Ethics*, vol. 22, Summer 2000, pp. 183–190. Sees animal liberationism and environmentalism as complementary, rather than opposing, components of an environmental ethic, stressing moral standing and intrinsic value respectively.

Schalow, Frank. "Who Speaks for the Animals? Heidegger and the Question of Animal Welfare." *Environmental Ethics*, vol. 22, Fall 2000, pp. 259–272. Addresses the ethical treatment of animals from a Heideggerian perspective and concludes that it is necessary to develop a concept of freedom that is not human centered and to balance animal interests with human ones. Urges expansion of the concept of moral agency to allow the differences between humans and animals, rather than the similarities, to suggest reasons why humans should show benevolence toward animals.

Scholtmeijer, Marian. "Animals and Spirituality: A Skeptical Animal Rights Advocate Examines Literary Approaches to the Subject." *L I T: Literature Interpretation Theory*, vol. 10, March 2000, pp. 371–394. Maintains that literary imputation of a spiritual nature to animals probably contributes to animal rights and that views of spirituality that encompass animals treat humans more compassionately than many conventional belief systems do.

Schuh, Dwight. "Animal Rights?" *Bowhunter*, vol. 29, October–November 1999, pp. 36 ff. Offers evidence from the Bible to support claims that God did not intend humans and animals to be equal and that eating meat is morally acceptable.

Scruton, Roger, and Andrew Tyler. "Do Animals Have Rights?" *The Ecologist*, vol. 31, March 2001, pp. 20 ff. A philosopher and the leader of a large animal rights group debate the meaning, pros and cons, and implications of the idea of animal rights.

Singer, Peter. "Living and Dying." *Psychology Today*, vol. 32, January 1999, pp. 56 ff. Discusses how to perform the difficult task of drawing the line between moral and nonmoral treatment of animals.

Skidelsky, Edward. "Nonsense upon Stilts." *New Statesman*, vol. 129, June 5, 2000, pp. 53 ff. Review of several books on animal rights claims that the arguments for animal rights are sentimental and intellectually unsound.

Specter, Michael. "The Dangerous Philosopher." *The New Yorker*, vol. 75, September 6, 1999, pp. 46–54. Profile of controversial utilitarian philosopher and ethicist Peter Singer, including discussion of his views on animal liberation.

Wilde, Lawrence. "'The Creatures, Too, Must Become Free': Marx and the Animal/Human Distinction." *Capital and Class*, March 2000, pp. 37 ff. Holds that Marx's distinction between humans and other animals on the basis of how they produce is defensible, despite claims that it represents a disrespectful view of animals. Claims that movements exposing capitalistic cruelty to animals and those showing capitalistic degradation of humanity have common features.

WEB DOCUMENTS

Buyukmihci, Nedim C. "Serious Moral Concern Is Not Species-Limited." Association of Veterinarians for Animal Rights. Available online. URL: http://www.avar.org. Accessed on April 19, 2003. Gives philosophical and moral reasons for believing that humans do not have the right to use animals in ways that they would not use other human beings.

Schulman, J. Neil. "The Illogic of Animal Rights." Man in Nature. Available online. URL: http://www.maninnature.com/Management/ARights/Rights1f.html. Posted in 1995. States that if humans are no different from other animals, they will naturally advance their own species at the expense of others, as other animals do. Conversely, if they are superior, they are entitled to use nonhuman animals as they wish. In either case, author maintains, "animal rights do not exist."

ANIMALS AND THE LAW

BOOKS

Brooman, Simon, and Debbie Legge. *Law Relating to Animals.* London: Cavendish Publishing, 1997. Examines laws that relate to human treatment of animals in Britain, Europe, and Australia.

Curnutt, Jordan. *Animals and the Law: A Sourcebook.* Santa Barbara, Calif.: ABC-CLIO, 2001. Offers a comprehensive survey of laws and court cases affecting treatment of domestic and wild animals in a variety of situations and industries.

Francione, Gary. *Animals, Property, and the Law.* Philadelphia, Pa.: Temple University Press, 1995. Francione, a law professor at Rutgers University, is a leading proponent of the idea that animals should have legal rights. He claims that the law has failed to protect animals because they are viewed as property.

Frasch, Pamela D., et al., eds. *Animal Law*. Durham, N.C.: Carolina Academic Press, 1999. Thoroughly researched casebook on the new subject of animal law, covering laws related to many human uses of animals.

Waisman, Sonia S., et al. *Animal Law: Cases and Materials*. 2d ed. Durham, N.C.: Carolina Academic Press, 2002. Extensive reference book on laws and court cases affecting animals and human uses of them, divided into common subsets of law such as tort, criminal, and constitutional law.

Wise, Steven M. *Drawing the Line: Science and the Case for Animal Rights*. Cambridge, Mass.: Perseus Publishing, 2002. Wise, a Harvard law professor, is one of the chief advocates of the belief that animals should have legal rights. Here he offers evidence from scientific studies to bolster his claim that certain animal species, especially chimpanzees and bonobos, meet the criteria for legal personhood.

ARTICLES

Capone, Lisa. "Wise Counsel for Animals." *Animals*, vol. 133, March 2000, p. 30. Profiles attorney Steven Wise, who believes that chimpanzees, bonobos, and a few other types of animals should have legal rights equivalent to those granted to young children.

Epstein, Richard A. "Animal Rights Claims: Some Dangerous Implications." *Current*, October 2000, pp. 10–14. Claims that allowing animals to have legal rights, as some radical animal rightists desire, would have dangerous effects on the law.

Fields-Meyer, Thomas, and Vicki Bane. "Animal Magnetism." *People Weekly*, vol. 59, April 21, 2003, pp. 123–124. Profiles Gretchen Biggs, founder of the Animal Law Center in Boulder, Colorado, whose controversial legal practice uses environmental law to defend animals, even those considered "pests."

Frasch, Pamela D., et al. "State Animal Anti-Cruelty Statutes: An Overview." *Animal Law*, vol. 5, 1999, pp. 69–80. Reviews current state laws, including many that have upgraded severe animal abuse from a misdemeanor to a felony.

Kolber, Adam. "Standing Upright: The Moral and Legal Standing of Humans and Other Apes." *Stanford Law Review*, vol. 54, October 2001, pp. 163–204. Author presents philosophical and legal arguments for granting great apes the right to sue (through human intermediaries) for violations of the treatment standards mandated by the Animal Welfare Act.

Leo, John. "Another Monkey Trial." *U.S. News & World Report*, vol. 127, September 20, 1999, pp. 19 ff. Claims that the new focus on animal law and proposals to grant legal rights to animals attempt to force the courts to make social changes without the public's consent.

Annotated Bibliography

Marandino, Cristin. "A Modern Day Dr. Doolittle." *Vegetarian Times,* January 1998, pp. 90–92. Profiles attorney Gary Francione, a major proponent of the idea that animals should have legal rights, and Rutgers University's Animal Rights Law Center, which Francione cofounded in 1990 with his wife, Anna Charlton.

O'Neill, Terry. "I Bark, Therefore I Am." *The Report Newsmagazine,* April 1, 2002, p. 44. Asks whether a new British Columbia (Canada) law against cruelty to animals that includes psychological abuse goes too far.

Paige, Sean. "When America Went Animal Crackers." *Insight on the News,* vol. 18, April 1, 2002, p. 8. Describes recent court cases and other events which, Paige feels, show excessive concern for the rights of animals.

Smith, Rob Roy. "Standing on Their Own Four Legs: The Future of Animal Welfare Litigation After *Animal Legal Defense Fund, Inc., v. Glickman.*" *Environmental Law,* vol. 29, Winter 1999, pp. 989 ff. Analyzes a court case that the author believes will lay a foundation for future animal welfare litigation.

Walsh, Edward J. "The Animal Enterprise Protection Act: A Scientist's Perspective." *Lab Animal,* vol. 29, February 2000. Maintains that the Animal Enterprise Protection Act should be strengthened to protect scientists and others against terrorist acts of animal rights extremists and that proposals to grant legal standing or legal rights to nonhuman animals should be resisted.

Zeller, Shawn. "Counsel for a Menagerie of Clients." *National Journal,* vol. 32, March 4, 2000, pp. 714 ff. Profiles Washington lawyers Eric Glitzenstein and Kathy Mayer, a husband and wife who have successfully represented many animal rights groups in court.

WEB DOCUMENTS

Favre, David. "Overview of the U.S. Animal Welfare Act." Animal Legal and Historical Center, Michigan State University, Detroit College of Law. Available online. URL: http://www.animallaw.info/articles/ovusawa.htm#BM6_Regulatory_Process. Posted in May 2002. Article originally prepared by the Animal Law Web Center includes quotations from the act and its implementing regulations, as well as supporting data and links to relevant court cases.

Kreger, Michael, D'Anna Jensen, and Tim Allen, eds. "Animal Welfare Act: Historical Perspectives and Future Directions." Animal Welfare Information Center. Available online: URL: http://www.nal.usda.gov/awic/pubs/96symp/awasymp.htm. Posted on September 12, 1996. Proceedings of a symposium sponsored by the U.S. Department of Agriculture (USDA) reflect on the act's history, discuss its amendments, and offer comments from industry and humane groups as well as the USDA itself. Report considers future directions in several areas.

"Legal Protections for Companion Animals and Animals in Agriculture, Entertainment, and Research." Animal Protection Institute. Available online. URL: http://www.api4animals.org/73.htm. Accessed on January 9, 2003. Summarizes types of laws that affect animal welfare and tells researchers how they can contact agencies responsible for enforcing these laws.

THE ANIMAL RIGHTS MOVEMENT, ITS OPPONENTS, AND THEIR TACTICS

BOOKS

Finsen, Lawrence, and Susan Finsen. *The Animal Rights Movement in America: From Compassion to Respect.* New York: Twayne Publishers, 1994. Describes the history, tactics, issues, and philosophies of the movement, which the authors call the quintessential movement for social justice; also discusses the movement's opponents and related movements, such as environmentalism.

Garner, Robert. *Political Animals: Animal Protection Politics in Britain and the United States.* New York: Palgrave Macmillan, 1998. Analyzes and compares the politics of the animal protection and animal rights movements in the two countries.

Guither, Harold D. *Animal Rights: History and Scope of a Radical Social Movement.* Carbondale: Southern Illinois University Press, 1998. Presents a neutral overview of the animal rights movement, its history and philosophy, and different uses of animals with which it is concerned, including research and entertainment.

Jamison, Wesley, and William Lunch. *Results from Demographic, Attitudinal, and Behavioral Analysis of the Animal Rights Movement: A Preliminary Report.* Corvallis: Oregon State University College of Agricultural Sciences and Department of Political Science, 1991. Reports on a survey of 426 animal rights activists that two Oregon State University researchers conducted at the 1990 March for Animals in Washington, D.C.

Kistler, John M. *People Promoting and People Opposing Animal Rights: In Their Own Words.* Westport, Conn.: Greenwood Press, 2002. Collection of profiles written by and about people actively involved in supporting or opposing the animal rights and animal welfare movements.

Munro, Lyle. *Compassionate Beasts: The Quest for Animal Rights.* New York: Praeger, 2000. Describes and contrasts the animal rights movement and specific campaigns against animal abuse in the United States, Britain, and Australia from a sociological point of view, based on interviews with 53 members in the three countries.

Newkirk, Ingrid. *Free the Animals: The Story of the Animal Liberation Front.* New York: Lantern Books, 2000. PETA founder Newkirk describes the even more radical Animal Liberation Front (ALF), known for its violent tactics, and portrays its leader, "Valerie" (a pseudonym), in a sympathetic light.

Oliver, Daniel T. *Animal Rights: The Inhumane Crusade.* Bellevue, Wash.: Merril Press, 1999. Strongly criticizes the animal rights movement and its effects on society.

Singer, Peter. *Ethics into Action: Henry Spira and the Animal Rights Movement.* Lanham, Md.: Rowman and Littlefield, 2000. Premier animal rights philosopher Singer describes one of the former activist leaders of the movement, known both for his successful publicity campaigns and his willingness to treat opponents with respect even while working relentlessly to end their abusive actions. Singer shows how other activists can adapt Spira's approach.

Wand, Kelly, ed. *The Animal Rights Movement.* San Diego, Calif.: Greenhaven Press, 2002. Anthology of articles and book excerpts provides different viewpoints on several major organizations within the animal rights movement and their tactics.

Workman, Dave P. *PETA Files: The Dark Side of the Animal Rights Movement.* Bellevue, Wash.: Merril Press, 2003. Outdoor writer criticizes alleged extremism and tendencies to violence in the animal rights organization People for the Ethical Treatment of Animals (PETA).

ARTICLES

Baxter, Jim. "Intimidation and Harassment." *Chemistry and Industry,* February 5, 2001, p. 70. An officer at British animal testing firm Huntingdon Life Sciences describes animal rightists' violent harassment of scientists who work there and his reaction to this treatment.

Cheshes, Jay. "Investigations: The Scary Circus." *Columbia Journalism Review,* vol. 41, May–June 2002, p. 11. Alleges that Ken Feld, head of the Ringling Bros. and Barnum & Bailey Circus, waged covert operations against two writers who criticized his organization and that he may have used similar tactics against animal rights groups.

Cockrell, Susan. "Crusader Activists and the 1996 Colorado Anti-Trapping Campaign." *Wildlife Society Bulletin,* vol. 27, Spring 1999, p. 65. Uses information from a survey of top activists involved in passage of a Colorado ballot initiative to ban trapping to gain insights about animal rightists and their employment of the initiative process to affect wildlife management.

Cummings, Betsy. "Shock Treatment." *Sales & Marketing Management,* vol. 153, January 2001, pp. 64 ff. Shows why the tactics used by People for the Ethical Treatment of Animals (PETA) are effective marketing ploys.

Dancer, Helen. "Medium for a Message." *The Bulletin with Newsweek*, vol. 119, September 25, 2001, pp. 82–83. Discusses the effectiveness of electronic (Internet) animal rights protests, using examples of saving bears kept for extraction of their bile (a traditional medical ingredient) in China and dolphins mistreated in Mexico.

Dawson, Mildred Leinweber. "Scientists Brace for Animal Activism: Legal and Illegal Animal Rights Actions Continue." *The Scientist*, vol. 16, November 25, 2002, p. 53. Discusses ways that scientists whose research uses animals can prepare for and handle protests from animal rights groups.

Einwohner, Rachel L. "Gender, Class, and Social Movement Outcomes." *Gender and Society*, vol. 13, February 1999, p. 56. Considers the role of class and gender in the outcome of a Seattle animal rights group's campaigns against hunting and animal circuses. Hunters, but not circus patrons, made assumptions about the animal rightists based on the latter's class and gender and were less likely than circus patrons to take the protesters' views seriously because of these assumptions.

Evans, Lloyd. "The Animal Protection Racket." *The Spectator*, vol. 284, June 3, 2000, pp. 10–11. Undercover reporter describes a day spent with animal rightists picketing a research laboratory in Huntingdonshire, U.K., that uses animals and concludes that the protesters' tactics are counterproductive.

Fox, Tessa. "Animal Passions." *Caterer & Hotelkeeper*, June 13, 2002, pp. 20–21. Describes animal rights protests aimed at restaurants and discusses how restaurants and chefs can respond.

Garner, Robert. "Defending Animal Rights." *Parliamentary Affairs*, vol. 51, July 1998, pp. 458–469. In the last 20 years, animal rights activists have succeeded in heightening public awareness and concern about abuse of animals in laboratories and factory farms, but they have had little impact on legislation. Author believes that this might change if the groups become more willing to form coalitions with other groups who have overlapping aims.

Higgins, Sean. "The Terrorist Tactics of Radical Environmentalists." *Insight on the News*, vol. 18, April 22, 2002, pp. 44–47. Describes terrorist-style tactics used by the Earth Liberation Front and Animal Liberation Front.

Hileman, Bette. "The Animal Rights Movement's Impact." *Chemical and Engineering News*, vol. 79, January 22, 2001, pp. 45–49. Describes animal rights groups' campaigns against Procter & Gamble's use of animals in product toxicity testing, including a rise in illegal activities.

Kaiser, Jocelyn. "Booby-Trapped Letters Sent to 87 Researchers." *Science*, vol. 286, November 5, 1999, p. 1059. Describes how animal rights activists have targeted individual researchers in the United States for the first time, mailing letters containing razor blades to 87 scientists who conduct research on primates.

Kaufman, Stephen R. "Healing Anger, Nurturing Compassion." *The Animals' Agenda*, vol. 21, January–February 2001, pp. 42–43. Discusses how to avoid the discouragement and "burnout" that many animal rights activists feel when their initial enthusiasm fades and they see little direct result of their actions.

Kruse, Corwin R. "The Movement and the Media: Framing the Debate over Animal Experimentation." *Political Communication*, vol. 18, January–March 2001, pp. 67–99. Uses the example of animal rights groups' crusade against experimentation on animals to consider the role that mass media play in shaping social movements. Describes magazine and television coverage of the issue between 1984 and 1993, including differences between the two media.

Lefemine, Pat. "Wildlife Management Politics." *Bowhunter*, vol. 29, October–November 1999, pp. 78–79. Uses the ban on spring bear hunting in Ontario, Canada, as an example of techniques that animal rightists employ to obtain political action against hunters; suggests ways that hunters can fight back.

"Lessons from Huntingdon." *Nature*, vol. 409, January 25, 2001, p. 439. Editorial in eminent science magazine discusses issues raised by the vigorous campaign that animal rightists have waged against the British animal testing company Huntingdon Life Sciences.

Linzey, Andrew. "Investing in the Dream." *The Animals' Agenda*, vol. 20, November–December 2000, p. 21. Discusses the need for more funds for animal rights work, particularly education, and how the money might be raised through animal-related businesses.

Mason, Jim. "The Making of a Magazine." *The Animals' Agenda*, vol. 19, November–December 1999, pp. 42–43. The founder of this animal rights magazine, which ceased publication in March–April 2002, describes its beginnings and how it changed during 20 years.

McCartney, Jenny. "'We Wouldn't Hurt Anybody—Really!" *The Spectator*, February 6, 1999, pp. 13–14. Questions Animal Liberation Front activist John Curtin's claim that the group has never hurt anyone and points to material on the group's web site that appears to incite and provide methods for violence.

"Milk under Fire." *Dairy Industries International*, vol. 66, October 2001, p. 12. The milk industry criticizes a PETA campaign that attempts to persuade children to drink less milk by associating milk with health problems such as acne and obesity.

Mizejewski, Gerald. "Animal Crackers." *Insight on the News*, vol. 17, April 16, 2001, p. 24. Describes the range of media-savvy tactics used by

People for the Ethical Treatment of Animals (PETA), "the world's largest and most controversial animal rights organization."

Monaghan, Rachel. "Single-Issue Terrorism: A Neglected Phenomenon?" *Studies in Conflict and Terrorism*, vol. 23, October–December 2000, pp. 255–265. Uses the example of terrorism by animal rights groups in Britain to analyze single-issue political groups' use of threats and violence to target individuals, change behavior, and communicate goals.

Moretti, Laura A. "Rod Coronado." *The Animals' Agenda*, vol. 19, May–June 1999, pp. 22–27. Sympathetic profile of animal rights activist Coronado, who was convicted of firebombing Michigan State University's mink research facilities.

Morrison, Adrian R. "Perverting Medical History in the Service of 'Animal Rights.'" *Perspectives in Biology and Medicine*, vol. 45, Autumn 2002, pp. 606–619. Claims that animal rights supporters, including some who call themselves scientists, distort the truth about the importance of research on animals by such techniques as taking statements out of context and combining statements in ways that change their meaning.

Most, Doug. "On the Wild Side." *Boston Magazine*, vol. 93, November 2001, pp. 102–108. Describes International Fund for Animal Welfare president Fred O'Regan, who works to save whales, stop seal hunts, protect elephants, and relocate polar bears, using a variety of techniques and arguments.

Mugford, Sarah. "Young Animal Activists: Can They Work within Government?" *Vegetarian Journal*, vol. 21, January–February 2002, p. 20. Describes how animal activists can use different kinds of government jobs to further their cause.

Plous, S. "An Attitude Survey of Animal Rights Activists." *Psychological Science*, vol. 2, 1999, pp. 194–196. Key survey of attitudes and characteristics (gender, income, and so on) of animal rights activists, conducted at a large animal rights march.

———. "Signs of Change within the Animal Rights Movement." *Journal of Comparative Psychology*, vol. 112, March 1998, pp. 48–54. Comparison of surveys of animal rights activists made in 1990 and 1996 shows that the movement considered research on animals to be its chief target in 1990, but it stressed animal agriculture in 1996.

Roberts, Louisa. "Tried and Tested." *Financial Management*, December 2002, p. 16. Brian Cass, managing director of British animal testing firm Huntingdon Life Sciences, says he refuses to let violent animal rights protests or the company's past financial difficulties discourage him.

Satchell, Michael. "Terrorize People, Save Animals." *U.S. News & World Report*, April 8, 2002, p. 24. Recounts tactics, including violence, that animal rights groups have used in attempts to close down Huntingdon Life Sciences, a British facility that tests drugs and other substances on animals.

Schiermeier, Quirin. "Animal Rights Activists Turn the Screw." *Nature*, December 10, 1998, p. 505. Some animal rights activists in Britain and Germany are increasingly resorting to violence, causing biomedical researchers to ask research organizations and politicians for help, but others work within the system to bring about changes in laws.

Shapiro, K. "The Caring Sleuth: Portrait of an Animal Rights Activist." *Society and Animals*, vol. 2, 1994, pp. 145–165. Defines the characteristics and behavior of typical animal rights activists.

Shea, Michael P. "Beating Mitsubishi." *Campaigns & Elections*, vol. 21, July 2000, pp. 44 ff. Describes the complex campaign, employing a variety of techniques and professional publicity firms, by which the International Fund for Animal Welfare and the Natural Resources Defense Council pressured Mitsubishi, the world's largest corporation, and the Mexican government to abandon plans for building a large salt plant in an area in Baja California that harbors gray whales and other wildlife.

Shelton, Ed. "New Comms Tactics Test Animal Research Groups." *PR Week*, January 25, 2002, p. 9. Scientists defending the ethics of research on animals are turning to the same kinds of emotional appeals that have worked so well for their animal rightist opponents.

Smith, Gar. "Ringling Bros., Barnum & Spies." *Earth Island Journal*, vol. 17, Spring 2002, p. 22. Reportage and court testimony reveal the spying and "dirty tricks" that Ken Feld, chief executive officer (CEO) of the Ringling Bros. and Barnum & Bailey Circus, used against animal rights groups and a reporter who criticized his organization.

Southwick, Ron. "Animal Rights Groups Gain Ground with Subtler Approaches, Worrying Researchers." *Chronicle of Higher Education*, vol. 47, October 27, 2000, pp. A31–32. Discusses proposed changes in the Animal Welfare Act and how they might affect biomedical research. Also examines techniques animal rightists used in trying to bring about the changes, including political action committes.

———. "Fighting for Research on Animals: Frankie L. Trull Is a Lobbyist as Despised as She Is Respected." *Chronicle of Higher Education*, vol. 48, April 12, 2002, pp. A24–A25. Trull is the founder of the National Association for Biomedical Research, a major lobbying organization that defends animal research against attacks by animal rights groups.

Specter, Michael. "The Extremist: The Woman Behind the Most Successful Radical Group in America." *The New Yorker*, vol. 79, April 14, 2003, pp. 52 ff. Critical portrait of Ingrid Newkirk, head of People for the Ethical Treatment of Animals (PETA).

Stallwood, Kim W. "Joining the Party: Political Action for Animals." *The Animals' Agenda*, vol. 20, May–June 2000, pp. 22–27. Discusses the achievements of animal activists who use the democratic political process to mobilize public support for animals.

Watts, John. "Losing—and Winning." *Bowhunter*, vol. 29, October–November 1999, pp. 80–81. Describes how hunters and fishers can counter or prevent efforts of animal rights groups to ban these activities.

Welch, Aimee. "Fur Flies in PETA's Fight for Animals." *Insight on the News*, vol. 16, July 17, 2000, pp. 15 ff. Describes different tactics and campaigns used by PETA, especially in attempts to stop research on animals, as well as scientists' responses.

Wicklund, Freeman. "Direct Action—Progress, Peril, or Both?" *The Animals' Agenda*, vol. 18, July–August 1998, pp. 22–27. Animal rights groups are increasingly employing "direct action," which has worked well in swaying public opinion on past issues such as suffrage and civil rights.

Williams, Roger. "Under Pressure under Pressure under Pressure." *Business Review*, vol. 8, September 2001, pp. 18 ff. Using the animal rights campaign against British drug testing firm Huntingdon Life Sciences as a case study, author discusses how businesses can respond to pressure groups.

Zeller, Shawn. "Pet Causes." *National Journal*, vol. 32, January 1, 2000, pp. 32 ff. Author says that animal rights groups are becoming more sophisticated in their use of lobbying and other techniques to affect Congress, but he claims that they still have much to learn and points out that their opponents are skilled at fighting back.

Zumbo, Jim. "Battling the Antis." *Outdoor Life*, vol. 209, August 1, 2002, pp. 24–25. Describes how antihunting groups, including animal rights groups, try to influence legislators and the media.

WEB DOCUMENTS

Beirich, Heidi, and Bob Moser. "From Push to Shove." Man in Nature. Available online. URL: http://www.maninnature.com/Management/ARights/Rights1o.html. Posted in Fall 2002. This article from the Fall 2002 issue of the Southern Poverty Law Center's *Intelligence Report* describes an extremist animal rights group's harassment of a Chicago insurance company's employees.

Sizemore, Bill. "PETA's Zeal Pushes the Envelope Too Far for Some." Man in Nature. Available online. URL: http://www.maninnature.com/Management/ARights/Rights1b.html. Posted on December 3, 2000. This article, which originally appeared in the *Virginian-Pilot*, quotes disgruntled employees who describe PETA as having a cultlike atmosphere and being run ruthlessly by head "guru" Ingrid Newkirk, who tolerates no opposition in the organization.

Stein, Jeff. "The Greatest Vendetta on Earth." *Salon*. Available online. URL: http://archive.salon.com/news/feature/2001/08/30/circus. Posted on August 30, 2001. This article, the first of two, describes "dirty tricks" tactics that Ken Feld, head of the Ringling Brothers and Barnum & Bailey Circus, allegedly used against freelance writer Jan Pottker, who wrote an article critical of Feld's family and organization.

————. "Send in the Clowns." *Salon*. Available online. URL: http://archive. salon.com/news/feature/2001/08/31/circus. Posted on August 31, 2001. This article is the second of two describing circus mogul Ken Feld's alleged "dirty tricks."

Ward, Simon. "A Domino Too Far; UK Government Tells Animal Rightists 'Enough Is Enough.'" *Man in Nature*. Available online. URL: http://www.maninnature.com/Management/ARights/Rights1h.html. Posted in April 2001. This article, which originally appeared in the *Fur Farm Letter*, a trade newsletter, claims that the British government banned fur farming in November 2000 partly in return for large donations from animal rights groups.

COMPANION ANIMALS AND ANIMAL SHELTERS

BOOKS

Alger, Janet M., and Steven F. Alger. *Cat Culture: The Social World of a Cat Shelter*. Philadelphia, Pa.: Temple University Press, 2003. Academic study of interactions between cats and human caregivers at a no-kill shelter by two sociology professors who are also animal rights activists, owners of multiple cats, and participant-observers in the study.

American Veterinary Medical Association. *U.S. Pet Ownership and Demographics Sourcebook, 2002*. Schaumburg, Ill.: American Veterinary Medical Association, 2003. Extensive statistics about owners of dogs, cats, horses, and birds, including profiles of pet-owning households.

Ascioni, Frank, and P. Arkow, eds. *Child Abuse, Domestic Violence, and Animal Abuse: Linking the Circles of Compassion for Prevention and Intervention*. Lafayette, Ind.: Purdue University, 1999. Sourcebook of interdisciplinary essays explaining the likelihood that animal abuse, child abuse, and domestic violence will occur in the same households, stressing links between animal abuse and later violence to humans, and urging social workers and others to intervene early when animal abuse is detected.

Becker, Marty, and Danielle Morton. *The Healing Power of Pets: Harnessing the Ability of Pets to Make and Keep People Happy and Healthy*. New York: Hyperion, 2002. Describes how living with companion animals can improve human health and well-being.

Block, Rose, and Delilah Ahrendt. *Canine Caper: Real-Life Tales of a Female Pet Vigilante*. New York: Berkley Publishing Group, 2002. An encounter with an abused mother dog and her puppy turned Block (a pseudonym) into an almost obsessed "pet vigilante" who rescues, even sometimes steals, abused dogs, takes them to animal hospitals, and tries to find homes for them when they recover.

Brestrup, Craig. *Disposable Animals: Ending the Tragedy of Throwaway Pets.* Leander, Tex.: Camino Bay Books, 1998. Maintains that widespread "euthanasia" of healthy shelter animals works against shelters' ostensible message of respect for animal life and encourages people to think that pets are disposable commodities.

Bryant, John. *Fettered Kingdoms.* Washington, D.C.: People for the Ethical Treatment of Animals, 1982. Maintains that pet animals are "slaves and prisoners" and that pet ownership should be phased out.

Budiansky, Stephen. *The Covenant of the Wild: Why Animals Chose Domestication.* New Haven, Conn.: Yale University Press, 1999. Claims that domestication of animals is not exploitation but rather an evolutionary strategy that benefits both parts of the symbiotic human-animal partnership.

Christiansen, Bob. *Save Our Strays: How We Can End Pet Overpopulation and Stop Killing Healthy Cats and Dogs.* San Diego, Calif.: Canine Learning Centers, 1999. Discusses why animals in the United States enter shelters, how shelters influence cat and dog demographics, and what can be done to reduce shelter populations without euthanasia.

Drayer, Mary Ellen, ed. *The Animal Dealers.* Washington, D.C.: Animal Welfare Institute, 1997. Describes "Class B" dealers, who obtain animals, chiefly dogs and cats, from "random sources" (rather than raising them, as "Class A" dealers do) and sell them to research laboratories. Claims that some of these animals are obtained unethically, for instance by stealing pets. Discusses primates, birds, and reptiles, as well as dogs and cats.

Glen, Samantha. *Best Friends: The True Story of the World's Most Beloved Animal Sanctuary.* New York: Kensington Publishing Corporation, 2001. Describes formation of the sanctuary in Angel Canyon (formerly Kanab), Utah, which houses several thousand animals (cats, dogs, rabbits, birds, and farm animals), many of which have special needs.

Harbolt, Tami L. *Bridging the Bond: The Cultural Construction of the Shelter Pet.* Lafayette, Ind.: Purdue University Press, 2003. Scholarly study of humane societies, animal shelters, and rescue leagues from sociological and cultural perspectives is enriched by in-depth interviews with people who work at such institutions and the author's own experience with them.

Helton, J. R. *Man and Beast.* Austin, Tex.: Abiqua Press, 2001. Tells how the author and his wife formed the Southern Animal Rescue Association (SARA) Sanctuary, now one of the largest no-kill dog and cat sanctuaries in the South.

Annotated Bibliography

Hess, Elizabeth. *Lost and Found: Dogs, Cats, and Everyday Heroes at a Country Animal Shelter.* Orlando, Fla.: Harcourt, 1998. Describes author's experiences at the Columbia-Greene Humane Society, which she calls a "complex mix of people and animals, emotion and ideology."

Lockwood, Randall, and Frank R. Ascione, eds. *Cruelty to Animals and Interpersonal Violence: Readings in Research and Application.* Lafayette, Ind.: Purdue University Press, 1998. Includes essays from historical, philosophical, and research points of view that explore the connection between cruelty to animals and violence to humans.

Myers, Gene. *Children and Animals: Social Development and Our Connections to Other Species.* Boulder, Colo.: Westview Press, 1998. Discusses interactions between preschool children and animals and how these may affect the child's developing sense of self.

Podberscek, Anthony L., Elizabeth S. Paul, and James A. Serpell, eds. *Companion Animals and Us: Exploring the Relationships between People and Pets.* New York: Cambridge University Press, 2000. Seventeen papers, most originally presented at a 1996 conference, discuss people's relationships with companion animals. Subjects include human-pet relationships in earlier times and possible benefits of pet ownership for physical and mental health.

Slater, Margaret R. *Community Approaches to Feral Cats: Problems, Alternatives, and Recommendations.* Washington, D.C.: The Humane Society of the United States, 2002. Offers a comprehensive discussion of issues surrounding feral cats, which are often seen as pests, and solutions to the feral cat problem. Shows how feral cat caretakers, veterinarians, community agencies, and animal shelters can find common ground in dealing with cat colonies.

Wilson, Cindy C., and Dennis C. Turner, eds. *Companion Animals in Human Health.* Thousand Oaks, Calif.: Sage Publications, 1997. Seventeen papers from a conference explore the psychosocial and physiological effects of having companion animals and develops a framework for further research on the subject.

ARTICLES

"Animal Cruelty Often Tied to Family Abuse." *USA Today*, vol. 130, August 2001, p. 14. This article claims that many people who wound or kill other humans also abused animals at an earlier age and that intervention at the animal abuse stage may prevent escalation of violence.

Beirne, Piers. "For a Nonspeciesist Criminology: Animal Abuse as an Object of Study." *Criminology*, vol. 37, February 1999, pp. 117–119. Evaluates reasons for criminologists to study theories and research on animal abuse and concludes that such study is valuable, both for its own sake and because animal abuse is often connected with abuse of humans.

Ecenbarger, William. "Scandal of America's Puppy Mills." *Reader's Digest*, vol. 154, February 1999, pp. 114–119. Describes a visit to a puppy mill in Lancaster County, Pennsylvania, that revealed puppies living in crowded, unsanitary conditions similar to those of battery hens in intensive farms.

Foster, J. Todd. "Are These Animal Shelters Truly Humane?" *Reader's Digest*, vol. 157, July 2000, pp. 103–108. States that animal shelters range from luxurious, hotel-like accommodations to those that more nearly resemble concentration camps, in which animals are kept in overcrowded and unsanitary conditions with minimal veterinary care.

Gardner, Toni. "The Truth About Cats and Dogs." *Country Living*, vol. 22, September 1999, pp. 90–92. Corrects myths about these common companion animals, including the idea that neutering makes them fat and lazy; maintains that neutering benefits animal health and welfare.

Hewitt, Bill. "Collared." *People Weekly*, vol. 55, April 30, 2001, pp. 48 ff. Fourteen months after a road rage incident in which a man threw a woman's small dog into traffic, killing it, a Santa Clara, California, detective succeeded in identifying him as Andrew Burnett and having him arrested for felony animal cruelty.

Kenna, Amy. "Animal Abuse Laws That Bite." *Governing*, vol. 14, November 2000, pp. 52–54. Many states have recently passed, or are considering passing, legislation that raises cruelty to animals from a misdemeanor to a felony. Animal rights supporters say that cruelty penalties are still too light, whereas critics maintain that pets are being given more consideration than people.

New, John C., Jr. "Characteristics of Shelter-Relinquished Animals and Their Owners Compared with Animals and Their Owners in U.S. Pet-Owning Households." *Journal of Applied Animal Welfare Science*, vol. 3, no. 3, 2000, pp. 179–201. Reports on a study sponsored by the National Council on Pet Population Study and Policy, in which investigators interviewed people who relinquished dogs and cats at 12 shelters in four regions. The investigators then compared the results with similar data gathered from a sample of American households with companion animals.

Raina, Parminder, et al. "Influence of Companion Animals on the Physical and Psychological Health of Older People." *Journal of the American Geriatrics Society*, vol. 47, March 1999, pp. 323–329. Study shows a relationship between possession of a companion animal and enhanced well-being in older people.

Reitman, Judith. "From the Leash to the Laboratory." *Atlantic Monthly*, vol. 286, July 2000, pp. 17 ff. Claims that medical research institutions obtain many of their dog subjects from a black market in stolen and fraudulently obtained pets.

Righton, Barbara. "All the Sad Horses." *Maclean's*, February 10, 2003, p. 38. Claims that riding horses are often mistreated, for example at horse auctions in Canada.

Salman, Mo D. "Behavioral Reasons for Relinquishment of Dogs and Cats to 12 Shelters." *Journal of Applied Animal Welfare Science*, vol. 3, no. 2, 2000, pp. 93–106. Behavioral problems, including aggression toward other animals or people, were the most common reasons given for relinquishing dogs and the second most common for relinquishing cats.

WEB DOCUMENTS

"The American Kennel Club and Dog Overpopulation." International Society for Animal Rights web site. Available online. URL: http:// www. isaronline.org/special_reports.htm. Accessed on April 18, 2003. Claims that this organization devoted to purebred dogs encourages puppy mills and dog overpopulation by granting American Kennel Club (AKC) registration to puppy mill puppies. Also asserts that the AKC has questionable registration proceedings and contributes to genetic diseases in purebred dogs.

"Animal Behavior and Animal Rights." International Society for Animal Rights web site. Available online. URL: http://www.isaronline.org/special_reports.htm. Accessed on April 18, 2003. States that shelters can encourage people to keep their companion animals, and thereby save animal lives, by treating animal behavioral problems—the most common reason why animals are given to shelters—as both preventable and solvable.

"The Case against Random Source Dog and Cat Dealers." Animal Welfare Institute web site. Available online. URL: http://www.awionline.org/pubs/online_pub/casebdealers/bdealers.html. Accessed on April 18, 2003. Includes statements from scientists and information about stealing and fraudulent obtaining of pets, record keeping and enforcement problems, animal care violations, and information on the random source dealer network.

"The Exotic Pet Trade." Performing Animal Welfare Society web site. Available online. URL: http://www.pawsweb.org/site/resources/index_factsheets.htm. Accessed on April 20, 2003. Claims that tigers, bears, and other exotic pets are often improperly cared for and then dumped when they grow up and become dangerous or are no longer "cute." The exotic pet trade also threatens endangered species, the authors say.

Krebsbach, Susan B. "TNR—The Most Viable Option for Expedient Reduction of Stray and Feral Cat Populations." Alliance for Animals.

Available online. URL: http://www.allanimals.org/article2/html. Posted on February 1, 2002. Maintains that trapping, neutering, and releasing feral cats is a better way to control cat overpopulation than killing the cats.

"The Top Ten Reasons for Pet Relinquishment to Shelters in the United States." National Council on Pet Population Study and Policy web site. Available online. URL: http://www.petpopulation.org/topten.html. Accessed on April 20, 2003. Lists 10 reasons that cats and 10 reasons that dogs are given to shelters.

Winograd, Nathan J. "Feral Cats on the Firing Line." Alley Cat Allies web site. Available online. URL: http://www.alleycat.org/pdf/Feral%20Cats%20on%20the%20Firing.pdf. Accessed on April 19, 2003. Claims that feral cats are unfairly blamed for excess predation of birds and other small wildlife.

ANIMALS IN AGRICULTURE

BOOKS

Adams, Carol J. *The Sexual Politics of Meat.* New York: Continuum Publishing Group, 1999. Alleges hidden relationships between meat eating and patriarchy, on the one hand, and vegetarianism and feminism on the other.

Cheeke, Peter R. *Contemporary Issues in Animal Agriculture.* 2d ed. Upper Saddle River, N.J.: Prentice-Hall, 1998. Discusses controversial issues affecting animal production, including animal rights and use of drugs and other feed additives.

Curtis, Stanley E. *The Well-Being of Agricultural Animals.* Ames, Iowa: Council for Agricultural Science and Technology, 1997. Recommends that scientists become involved in the often politicized issue of farm animal welfare.

Davis, Karen. *Poisoned Chickens, Poisoned Eggs: A Look Inside the Modern Poultry Industry.* Summertown, Tenn.: Book Publishing Co., 1997. Author, president of United Poultry Concerns, an animal rights group, claims that intensive ("factory") farming is cruel to chickens, whether they are raised for eggs or meat, and that a high-poultry diet is no healthier than one high in red meat. Even so-called free range chickens, she says, are kept under cruel conditions.

Eisnitz, Gail A. *Slaughterhouse: The Shocking Story of Greed, Neglect, and Inhumane Treatment Inside the U.S. Meat Industry.* Loughton, Essex, U.K.: Prometheus Books, 1997. Claims that U.S. slaughterhouses are filthy and cruel to both animals and human workers.

Ewbank, R., F. Kim-Madslien, and C.B. Hart, eds. *Management and Welfare of Farm Animals: The UFAW Farm Handbook.* 4th ed. Wheathampstead, Hertfordshire, U.K.: Universities Federation for Animal Welfare, 1999. Comprehensive textbook for those concerned with improving standards of farm animal husbandry.

Hemsworth, Paul H., and Grahame J. Coleman. *Human-Livestock Interactions: The Stockperson and the Productivity and Welfare of Intensively Farmed Animals.* Cambridge, Mass.: CABI Publishing, 1998. Summarizes behavioral theories and research on human-animal interactions as they apply to agriculture.

Hodges, John, and In K. Han, eds. *Livestock, Ethics and the Quality of Life.* Cambridge, Mass.: CABI Publishing, 2000. Essays and papers from a 1998 symposium feature contributors from food sciences, agriculture, and philosophy who discuss the relationships between ethics and livestock agriculture, including an alternative ethic for animals, consumer ethical concerns, and the situation in developing countries.

Johnson, Andrew. *Factory Farming.* Oxford, U.K.: Blackwell, 2002. British book critical of intensive farming of animals.

Lovenheim, Peter. *Portrait of a Burger as a Young Calf: The True Story of One Man, Two Cows, and the Feeding of a Nation.* New York: Harmony Books, 2002. Relatively neutral firsthand account of a calf's life from birth to "burgerhood" by a man who bought two calves at a dairy farm (where they would be raised to become midprice beef) and was allowed to observe what happened to them throughout their lives.

National Research Council. *The Use of Drugs in Food Animals: Benefits and Risks.* Washington, D.C.: National Academy Press, 1999. The National Research Council, part of the National Academy of Sciences, reviews how and why drugs are used in animals raised for food and considers the likelihood of drug-resistant microorganisms being transferred from animal food and causing disease in humans.

Rampton, Sheldon, and John C. Stauber. *Mad Cow U.S.A.: Could the Nightmare Happen Here?* Monroe, Maine: Common Courage Press, 1997. Claims that both U.S. and British governments covered up important information about transmission of bovine spongiform encephalopathy (BSE, or "mad cow disease") to humans. Discusses food disparagement laws and the trial of Oprah Winfrey and others under a Texas law of this type after a 1996 broadcast of Winfrey's talk show in which one of Winfrey's guests said that a BSE outbreak could occur in the United States.

Tansey, Geoff, and Joyce D'Silva, eds. *The Meat Business: Devouring a Hungry Planet.* New York: Palgrave Macmillan, 1999. In sometimes inflammatory language, articles by 20 experts criticize intensive agriculture, particularly the meat industry, which they see as unsustainable, and offer alternatives.

Animal Rights

Vialles, Noélie. *Animal to Edible*. Translated by J. A. Underwood. New York: Cambridge University Press, 2002. Study of abbatoirs (slaughterhouses) in southwest France shows a complex system of ways to avoid thinking about what the abbatoirs actually do and how they do it.

Vidal, John. *McLibel: Burger Culture on Trial*. New York: New Press, 1998. Describes the trial—the longest in British history—that resulted when fast-food giant McDonald's sued two members of London Greenpeace for libel for distributing a flyer that accused the company of cruelty to animals and other "crimes," forcing the two to prove the truth of all the flyer's allegations.

ARTICLES

Bauston, Gene. "For a Mouthful of Flesh." *The Animals' Agenda*, vol. 18, January–February 1998, pp. 22–29. Examines the growth of the meat industry, which allegedly treats animals cruelly, and its implications for animal rights.

Comis, Don. "The Cyber Cow Whisperer and His Virtual Fence." *Agricultural Research*, vol. 48, November 2000, p. 4. Dean M. Anderson has developed techniques for using Global Positioning System signals to help in rounding up cattle and also a locator/controller cow collar that whispers commands to control a cow's movement and thus acts as both a director and a virtual fence. Author concludes that Anderson's roundup methods cause less stress for cattle than conventional techniques.

"The Cost of Fur." *The Economist*, March 3, 2001, p. 2. An "animal economy" study (which uses behavior to determine the relative values that animals place on different activities) of farmed mink suggests that swimming, an activity denied to the animals in fur farms, is as important to them as food.

Cox, David. "Silence of the Lambs' Champions." *New Statesman*, vol. 130, April 16, 2001, p. 12. Argues that animal rights groups should have protested the British government's mass killings of farm animals to stop the spread of foot-and-mouth disease and considers why they did not do so.

Dantzer, R. "Can We Understand Farm Animal Welfare without Taking into Account the Issues of Emotion and Cognition?" *Journal of Animal Science*, vol. 79, November 2001, p. S32. Farm animal welfare is usually assessed through physiological and behavioral measures of stress and coping, but this approach assumes that welfare is simply a matter of successful adaptation to the environment, which may not be the case. The author claims that new research in neuroscience may make it possible to measure farm animal cognition and emotion more directly.

Elliott, Ian. "EU Examines Animal Welfare Position." *Feedstuffs*, vol. 74, November 25, 2002, p. 5. Describes a European Commission report on animal welfare rules in 73 countries. The report suggests possible methods of rectifying the economic disadvantage that European Union farmers suffer because of the EU's high animal welfare standards.

"External Inquiries Require Understanding of True Intent: From Antibiotic, Welfare, Environmental Practices." *Feedstuffs*, vol. 74, June 3, 2002, p. 10. Suggests ways that agricultural firms can respond to queries about the use of antibiotics and other aspects of their treatment of animals.

Fraser, D. "The 'New Perception' of Animal Agriculture: Legless Cows, Featherless Chickens, and a Need for Genuine Analysis." *Journal of Animal Science*, vol. 79, March 2001, pp. 634 ff. Maintains that the public needs knowledgeable research and analysis to offset the simplistic views frequently offered by proponents (sometimes including scientists and ethicists) of both sides of the debate on the treatment of farm animals.

Langman, Brent. "Be Kind: Proper Handling and Stunning of Livestock Is Not Only Humane, It Can Improve the Quality of Your Product." *National Provisioner*, vol. 216, May 2002, pp. 82–83. Describes independent audit that showed high meat industry compliance with standards of humane slaughter. Recommends humane animal treatment as "good for business."

Maupin, Michael, and Judith Mandelbaum Schmid. "What Limit Religious Freedom?" *Swiss News*, April 2002, pp. 6–7. Conflicts about kosher slaughter in Switzerland involve issues of religious freedom and anti-Semitism as well as humane treatment of animals in slaughterhouses.

Metcalfe, Ed, and Iain Elliott. "The Pig Issue." *The Ecologist*, vol. 31, December 2001, pp. 52–56. Describes inhumanity of pork industry sow stalls, which the European Union is phasing out.

Motavalli, Jim. "Across the Great Divide: Environmentalists and Animal Rights Activists Battle over Vegetarianism." *E*, vol. 13, January–February 2002, pp. 34–39. States that many animal rights activists see vegetarianism as a necessary ethical choice, but few environmentalists agree. The resulting conflict causes strain in the two groups' relationship.

Muirhead, Sarah. "Animal Health, Welfare Concerns Linked to Recent Antibiotic Bans." *Feedstuffs*, vol. 74, November 18, 2002, pp. 4–5. Claims that a ban on giving antibiotics to meat animals for growth promotion in Denmark has led to an increase in animal disease, threatening the very welfare that supporters of the ban supposedly favor.

Priestly, Kate. "Is Humane Meat an Oxymoron?" *Natural Life*, May–June 2002, pp. 12–13. Discusses the meaning of labels such as *free range* and *humane meat.*

Rollin, Bernard E. "Farm Factories: The End of Animal Husbandry." *The Christian Century*, vol. 118, December 19, 2001, pp. 26–29. Explains the rise of intensive agriculture ("factory farming") after World War II and contrasts its practices and attitudes with those of traditional animal husbandry, which stressed humane treatment of farm animals.

Smith, Rod. "Consumer Views on Animal Production Pushing toward More Ethical Husbandry." *Feedstuffs*, vol. 73, January 1, 2001, p. 8. Surveys show that the percentage of American consumers demanding more humane treatment of farm animals is increasing. Author says the agriculture industry should take these demands seriously.

———. "McDonald's Guidelines Send Signal across All Animal Production Segments." *Feedstuffs*, vol. 72, August 28, 2000, pp. 3–4. Explains that McDonald's and United Egg Producers are working toward agreement on new guidelines for treating laying hens, but some issues remain, including timing for implementation of the guidelines.

Steintrager, Megan. "Duty and the Beast." *Restaurant Business*, vol. 101, June 15, 2002, pp. 20–24. Restaurants and fast-food chains are cooperating with animal rights activists to improve standards for their suppliers' treatment of farm animals, but the move could backfire if the industry does not maintain a united front against some groups' ultimate vegan agenda, this article claims.

Van Reenen, C. G., et al. "Transgenesis May Affect Farm Animal Welfare: A Case for Systematic Risk Assessment." *Journal of Animal Science*, vol. 79, July 2001, pp. 1763 ff. Claims that transgenesis (creation of animals containing genes of species other than their own) threatens farm animal health and welfare. Offers ways to study the welfare of transgenic farm animals.

Wagner, Susan. "Pissing Their Lives Away: How the Drug Industry Harms Horses." *The Animals' Agenda*, vol. 21, March–April 2001, pp. 22–26. Describes alleged cruelty to pregnant mares whose urine is used for the estrogen replacement therapy drug Premarin.

Zuzworsky, Rose. "From the Marketplace to the Dinner Place: The Economy, Theology, and Factory Farming." *Journal of Business Ethics*, January 2001, pp. 177 ff. Maintains that examination of whether food animals in the American market system suffer unnecessarily involves consideration of the extent to which economic factors make intensive farming not only profitable but essential under present market conditions and, on the other hand, consideration of spiritual concerns raised by the techniques and effect of factory farming.

WEB DOCUMENTS

"Animal Welfare Kit." American Meat Institute. Available online. URL: http://www.meatami.com/content/PressCenter/FactSheets_InfoKits/FactSheetAnimalWelfareKit.pdf. Posted in 2002. Press kit describes the meat industry's animal welfare practices, including animal handling and stunning, animal welfare in packing plants, ethical and economic reasons to treat animals humanely, ways to improve animal handling, medically and socially useful products derived from animals, and religious (kosher and halal) slaughter.

"The Antibiotics Debate." Animal Health Institute. Available online. URL: http://www.ahi.org/AntibioticsDebate/index.asp. Accessed on January 9, 2004. Fact sheets produced and distributed by the Animal Health Institute, an organization sponsored by the animal farming industry, state that giving antibiotics to farm animals is safe and necessary.

"Bartered Lives: An Animal Aid Investigation." Animal Aid. Available online. URL: http://www.animalaid.org.uk. Posted in 2000. In response to an earlier Animal Aid report called "A Brutal Business," the British government introduced a national strategy intended to make the lives of farm animals less stressful. This report examines how effectively the strategy has been implemented and concludes that, overall, the situation has changed little.

Byrne, David. "Animal Welfare: Higher Standards Show Their Merits." European Commission Press Releases. Available online. URL: http://www.europa.eu.int/rapid/start/cgi/guesten.ksh?p_action.gettxt=gt&doc=SPEECH/01/602101RAPID&lg=EN&display=. Posted on November 30, 2001. Speech by the European Commissioner for Health and Consumer Protection describes the European Union's progress in implementing the high standards that the EU has set for animal welfare, particularly of farmed animals.

Commission of the European Communities. "Communication from the Commission to the Council and the European Parliament on Animal Welfare Legislation on Farmed Animals in Third Countries and the Implications for the EU." European Commission on Food Safety. Available online. URL: http://www.europa.eu.int/comm/food/fs/aw/2002_0626_en.pdf. Posted on November 18, 2002. Describes and compares legislation governing welfare of farm animals in 73 countries. Discusses the cost of higher welfare standards to producers and how these costs may be recovered.

"The Destructive Dairy Industry." Animal Protection Institute. Available online. URL: http://www.api4animals.org/69.htm. Posted in 2001. Recounts alleged abuses in the raising and maintenance of dairy cattle.

Druce, Clare, and Philip Lymbery. "Farm Animal Welfare: Three Decades of Progress in Europe." Animal Rights International. Available online. URL: http://www.ari-online.org/pages/europe1.html. Posted in 2001. Describes new laws in Europe that ban allegedly abusive farm practices such as forced molting in chickens.

D'Silva, Joyce. "Farm Animal Genetic Engineering and Cloning." Compassion in World Farming Trust. Available online. URL: http://www.ciwf.co.uk/Pubs/reports/farm%20animal%20genetic%20engineering%20and%20cloning%20Jan%202002.pdf. Posted in January 2002. An overview of the issues surrounding the genetic engineering of farm animals.

"Facts about the Poultry Industry." Animal Protection Institute. Available online. URL: http://www.api4animals.org/82.htm. Posted in 2001. Fact sheet from animal rights group details alleged abuses of chickens on "factory" farms.

"FMI-NCCR Animal Welfare Program." Food Marketing Institute. Available online. URL: http://fmi.org/animal_welfare/62602finalrpt.pdf. Posted in June 2002. This report details new guidelines established by the Food Marketing Institute and the National Council of Chain Restaurants, working with scientific experts in animal welfare, to improve the care and handling of animals raised for food.

Gellatley, Juliet. "Pig in Hell: A Report into the British Pig Industry." International Vegetarian Union. Available online. URL: http://www.ivu.org/ape/talks/gellatley/gellatley.pdf. Posted on May 17, 1999. Talk presented to Animals, People and the Environment conference describes a typical British pig farm, different ages and genders of pigs, mutilations done as part of the farming process, common diseases encouraged by intensive farming, use of drugs, genetic engineering as an answer to pig farming problems, and British government proposals.

"Gestation Stalls: The Facts." National Pork Producers Council. Available online. URL: http://www.nppc.org/public_policy/gestation_stalls.html. Accessed on April 20, 2003. Industry defense of gestation stalls, which animal rightists have called cruel.

"How Free Is 'Free-Range'?" Compassion Over Killing. Available online. URL: http://www.cok.net/lit/freerange.php. Accessed on April 18, 2003. Maintains that meat and animal products labeled "free range" were not necessarily prepared with any greater regard for animal welfare than products not so labeled. Urges people to become vegetarians or vegans rather than seeking "more humane" animal foods.

Hudson, David L., Jr. "Court Upholds Dismissal of Oprah Lawsuit Without Testing 'Veggie Libel' Law." The Media Institute. Available online. URL: http://www.mediainstitute.org/ONLINE/FAM2001/LPT_C.html. Posted in 2001. Describes the federal appeals court ruling in February 2000 that cleared talk show host Oprah Winfrey and antimeat activist Howard Lyman of libel charges under a Texas food disparagement law.

Linzey, Andrew. "The Ethical Case against Fur Farming." Respect for Animals. Available online. URL: http://www.respectforanimals.org/

respect.html. Accessed on April 20, 2003. Statement signed by international group of ethicists, philosophers, theologians, and other academics opposing fur farming.

Lymbery, Phyllis. "In Too Deep: The Welfare of Intensively Farmed Fish." Compassion in World Farming Trust. Available online. URL: http://www.ciwf.co.uk/Pubs/Reports/itdfull.pdf. Posted in 2002. Fully updated look at the methods, welfare issues, and environmental impact of the fish farming industry.

"Report on the Implications of Cloning on the Welfare of Livestock." Farm Animal Welfare Council. Available online. URL: http://www.fawc.org.uk/reports/clone/clonetoc.htm. Posted in December 1998. Describes potential harms and benefits of cloning for applied biomedical research, fundamental academic research, and livestock breeding.

Stevenson, Peter. "The Economics of Factory Farming." Compassion in World Farming Trust. Available online. URL: http://www.ciwf.co.uk/Pubs/reports/art9857.pdf. Posted in July 2002. This paper examines the real economic costs of improving welfare standards for farmed animals.

———. "Good Agricultural Practices: The Welfare of Farm Animals." Compassion in World Farming Trust. Available online. URL: http://www.ciwf.co.uk/Pubs/Reports/art9673a.pdf. Posted in July 2002. Comprehensive report outlines the principal concerns about industrial farming systems and practices.

"UEP's Animal Care Certified Program." United Egg Producers. Available online. URL: http://www.unitedegg.com/html/welfare/animalhusbandry.pdf. Posted in 2003. New industry guidelines for caring for egg-laying hens.

ANIMALS IN RESEARCH, TESTING, AND EDUCATION

BOOKS

Balcombe, Jonathan. *The Use of Animals in Higher Education: Problems, Alternatives, and Recommendations.* Washington, D.C.: The Humane Society of the United States, 2000. This book covers secondary and elementary as well as higher education. It focuses on the United States but is international in scope. It describes objections, sociological as well as ethical, to the dissection and use of live animals in education, and presents an annotated list of replacements.

Balls, Michael, et al., eds. *Progress in the Reduction, Refinement and Replacement of Animal Experimentation.* New York: Elsevier Health Sciences, 2000. Proceedings of the World Congress on Alternatives and Animal

Use in the Life Sciences in 1999. Discusses development, validation, and regulatory acceptance of alternative methods.

Blum, Deborah. *The Monkey Wars.* New York: Oxford University Press, 1996. Balanced account of the "wars" between animal rights groups and scientists who do research on animals, including the famous "Silver Spring Monkeys" case in the early 1980s, in which PETA cofounder Alex Pacheco exposed alleged abuse in the laboratory of Maryland researcher Edward Taub.

Cothran, Helen, ed. *Opposing Viewpoints: Animal Experimentation.* San Diego, Calif.: Greenhaven Press, 2002. Anthology of pro and con essays that discuss whether animals have rights, whether experimentation on animals is justified, how animal experimentation should be conducted, and whether scientists should pursue new forms of animal testing.

Dolan, Kevin. *Ethics, Animals and Science.* Oxford, U.K.: Blackwell, 1999. Offers an introduction to ethics for those who work with animals in laboratories. Presents and comments on a variety of opinions and looks for common ground that will permit discussion.

———. *Laboratory Animal Law.* Oxford, U.K.: Blackwell, 2001. Describes laws governing the use of animals in science in Britain, chiefly the Animals (Scientific Procedures) Act of 1986; also considers similar laws in other European countries.

Gluck, John P., Tony Dipasquale, and F. Barbara Orlans, eds. *Applied Ethics in Animal Research: Philosophy, Regulation, and Laboratory Applications.* Lafayette, Ind.: Purdue University Press, 2002. Seven essays by scientists and ethicists try to find a middle ground between regarding laboratory animals simply as research supplies and rejecting all research on animals as morally unjustified. They consider the subject from the standpoints of philosophy, ethics in the laboratory, and statutory regulation.

Grayson, Lesley. *Animals in Research: For and Against.* London: British Library Publications, 2000. Summary of papers and reports on animal research from a wide variety of disciplines. Includes political, legal, moral and ethical, historical, scientific, and other aspects, with a focus on Britain and the European Union and on efforts to replace, reduce, and refine animal tests.

Greek, C. Ray, and Jean Swingle Greek. *Specious Science: How Genetics and Evolution Reveal Why Medical Research on Animals Harms Humans.* New York: Continuum Publishing Group, 2002. Claims that medical research done on animals is not sound science because animals differ from humans in important biological ways; recommends clinical research on humans as a substitute.

Grove, Julian McAllister. *Hearts and Minds: The Controversy over Lab Animals.* Philadelphia, Pa.: Temple University Press, 1997. Groves was a participant-observer in a study of the conflict between animal rights activists and animal researchers in a small Southern university town. Focusing on feelings, he concludes that people became more polarized and intransigent than they needed to be because they refused to admit their moral ambivalence to one another.

Guerrini, Anita. *Experimenting with Humans and Animals: From Galen to Animal Rights*. Baltimore, Md.: Johns Hopkins University Press, 2003. History of experimentation on humans and animals from antiquity focuses on debates about ethical issues raised by such experiments.

Haugen, David, ed. *At Issue: Animal Experimentation*. San Diego, Calif.: Greenhaven Press, 2000. This anthology of 18 essays offers opposing views on issues such as medical experimentation on animals, product testing on animals, military research, animal-to-human transplants, and alternatives to research on animals.

Hudson, Vera W., ed. *Alternatives to the Use of Live Vertebrates in Biomedical Research and Testing: A Bibliography with Abstracts*. Bethesda, Md.: National Library of Medicine, 2001. Provides alternatives to numerous animal tests, chiefly for various kinds of toxicity but also including tests for drug action and ability to cause cancer.

Institute for Laboratory Animal Research. *Definition of Pain and Distress and Reporting Requirements for Laboratory Animals*. Washington, D.C.: National Academy Press, 2000. Proceedings from a workshop sponsored by the institute (which is part of the National Academy of Sciences) and the National Institutes of Health.

———. *Guide for the Care and Use of Laboratory Animals*. Washington, D.C.: National Academy Press, 1996. Official guide used by the American Association for the Assessment and Accreditation of Laboratory Animal Care in determining accreditation for institutions using laboratory animals. Covers institutional policies, physical environment, veterinary care, relevant federal laws, and more.

Interagency Coordinating Committee on the Validation of Alternative Methods (ICCVAM). *Validation and Regulatory Acceptance of Toxicological Test Methods*. Research Triangle Park, N.C.: National Institute of Environmental Health Sciences, 1997. Report by a federal agency set up to evaluate tests that offer alternatives to methods that use animals.

Larson, Jean A., Ruth Criscio, and D'Anna J. B. Jensen. *Directory of Resources on Alternatives and Animal Use in the Life Sciences 1998*. Washington, D.C.: U.S. Department of Agriculture, 1998. Covers newsletters, databases, publications, audiovisuals, computer simulations, and miscellaneous. Also provides international list of organizations.

Monamy, Vaughan. *Animal Experimentation: A Guide to the Issues*. New York: Cambridge University Press, 2000. Australian Catholic University professor Monamy introduces life science students to the ethical and moral issues surrounding research on animals, providing a well-balanced review of historical, legal, and other aspects and describing alternatives to animal research.

National Research Council. *Chimpanzees in Research: Strategies for Their Ethical Care, Management, and Use.* Washington, D.C.: National Academy Press, 1997. Discusses value of past and future studies with chimpanzees, long-term care, demography, cost, genetic management, and recommendations for a centralized system to manage chimpanzee research.

———. *The Psychological Well-Being of Nonhuman Primates.* Washington, D.C.: National Academy Press, 1998. A committee of the National Research Council, which in turn is part of the National Academy of Sciences, describes elements of an effective program for fostering the psychological well-being of primates used in scientific research as mandated in a 1985 amendment to the Animal Welfare Act.

Paul, Ellen Frankel, Jeffrey Paul, and Fred Dycus Miller, eds. *Why Animal Experimentation Matters: The Use of Animals in Medical Research.* Bowling Green, Ohio: Social Philosophy Policy Center, 2001. Scientists, philosophers, and historians describe and defend the use of animals in research.

People for the Ethical Treatment of Animals. *Shopping Guide for Caring Consumers.* 7th ed. Summertown, Tenn.: Book Publishing Co., 2002. Provides ways to identify products not tested on animals.

Rollin, Bernard E. *The Unheeded Cry: Animal Consciousness, Animal Pain, and Science.* Rev. ed. Ames: Iowa State University Press, 1998. Considers whether laboratory animals feel pain and suffer, and, if so, what humans should do about it.

Rudacille, Deborah. *The Scalpel and the Butterfly: The Conflict between Animal Research and Animal Protection.* Berkeley: University of California Press, 2001. Provides a neutral history of the conflict between animal research and the animal protection and animal rights movements and considers the issue from both ethical and scientific standpoints.

Salem, Harry, and Sidney A. Katz, eds. *Advances in Animal Alternatives for Safety and Efficacy Testing.* Rev. ed. Washington, D.C.: Taylor & Francis, 1998. Nearly 50 scientists from government, industry, and universities report on the latest alternatives to product testing on animals, covering five types of toxicity.

Shapiro, Kenneth Joel. *Animal Models of Human Psychology: Critique of Science, Ethics, and Policy.* Seattle, Wash.: Hogrefe and Huber, 1998. Executive director of the animal rights group Psychologists for the Ethical Treatment of Animals claims that some psychologists perform inappropriate research on animals in attempts to understand human psychological problems such as eating disorders.

Annotated Bibliography

Smith, Arthur. *House of Lords Select Committee on Animals in Scientific Procedures.* London: Stationery Office, 2002. British government report finds animal experiments necessary for developing human and animal medicine and protecting the environment but agrees that nonanimal experiments should be substituted for animal ones when possible. Recommends methods for balancing the need for effective regulation of animal experimentation with more openness about the use of animals in science.

ARTICLES

"Activists Challenge High Production Volume Testing." *Chemical Market Reporter,* vol. 262, September 23, 2002, p. 9. As discussed in this article, PETA and other animal rights groups have sued to make the Environmental Protection Agency stop proposed new animal toxicity tests of high-production-volume chemicals, which the groups say are unnecessary.

Agres, Ted. "Activists Broaden Efforts; Animal Welfare Groups Lobby for State Legislation." *The Scientist,* vol. 16, November 25, 2002, p. 18. After being blocked from placing rats, mice, and birds under the protection of the federal Animal Welfare Act, animal rights groups are attempting to gain such protection through state laws. Researchers believe, according to this article, that these efforts are both unlikely to succeed and unnecessary.

Aldhous, Peter, Andy Coghlan, and Jon Copley. "Let the People Speak." *New Scientist,* no. 162, May 22, 1999, pp. 31–36. Presents a British survey on the issue of research that uses animals. Most people accept the need for some animal research, but they differ in the types of experiments they accept.

"Animal Research in the Post-Genome Era." *The Lancet,* vol. 357, March 17, 2001, p. 817. This editorial claims that the trend toward using transgenic animals to investigate the human genome may reverse the present decline in the use of animals in research.

"Animal Rights Proponents and Environmental Activists Clash." *Chemical Market Reporter,* vol. 261, June 17, 2002, pp. 9–10. Explains the disagreement between animal rights groups and environmental groups about the necessity and validity of upcoming chemical toxicity tests on animals being required by the Environmental Protection Agency.

Anthes, Gary. "P&G Uses Data Mining to Cut Animal Testing." *Computerworld,* December 6, 1999, p. 44. Describes how Procter & Gamble uses data mining and computerized tests to eliminate most testing of its products on animals.

Barnard, N., and S. Kaufman. "Animal Research Is Wasteful and Misleading." *Scientific American,* February 1997, pp. 80–82. Criticizes the scientific value of research on animals that is designed to shed light on human diseases. Asserts that claims for the importance of animal research to past medical discoveries are greatly exaggerated.

Bogle, Rick. "Primate AnNIHilation." *The Animals' Agenda*, vol. 19, May–June 1999, pp. 20–21. Several animal rights organizations claim that the National Institutes of Health treats animals cruelly in its regional primate centers.

Botting, Jack H., and Adrian R. Morrison. "Animal Research Is Vital to Medicine." *Scientific American*, February 1997, p. 83. Response to article by Barnard and Kaufman in the same issue and listed above; denies the claim that animal research is wasteful and misleading.

Broughton, Zoe. "Seeing Is Believing." *The Ecologist*, vol. 31, March 2001, pp. 31–32. Describes animal abuse that an undercover worker filmed at British animal testing firm Huntingdon Life Sciences in 1996, reaction to the film, and government actions in the wake of subsequent violence.

Cimons, Marlene. "R&D Toxicity Test to Be Eliminated." *Nature Medicine*, vol. 7, October 2001, p. 1077. Animal rights groups and American scientists are joining a worldwide crusade to eliminate the LD50 toxicity test on animals, which many countries are now phasing out.

D'Agnese, Joseph. "An Embarrassment of Chimpanzees." *Discover*, vol. 23, May 2002, pp. 43–48. Laboratories worldwide are phasing out research on chimpanzees, but no one is sure what to do with the animals. Describes a Canadian chimpanzee sanctuary that is taking some of them.

Fishbein, Estelle A. "What Price Mice?" *Journal of the American Medical Association*, vol. 285, February 21, 2001, pp. 939–940. Claims that the U.S. Department of Agriculture's decision to accede to animal rights groups' demands to include mice, rats, and birds under the Animal Welfare Act will cause increases in paperwork that could be "disastrous" for medical research. Urges scientists to pressure Congress to change the situation.

Fox, Michael W. "Tooling with Mother Nature: The Dangers of Genetic Engineering." *The Animals' Agenda*, vol. 21, January–February 2001, pp. 22–26. Explains why animal rightists distrust genetic engineering experiments on animals.

Glickman, Dan. "Regulations for the Use of Laboratory Animals." *Journal of the American Medical Association*, vol. 285, February 21, 2001, pp. 941–942. Secretary of Agriculture Glickman explains why the USDA settled a suit by the Alternatives Research and Development Foundation, a group opposed to the use of animals in research, out of court by agreeing to add regulations covering mice, rats, and birds to the Animal Welfare Act.

Goodall, Jane. "A Question of Ethics." *Newsweek International*, May 7, 2001, p. 62. Renowned primate expert and environmentalist Goodall explains why she feels that research and product testing using animals is usually unethical and unnecessary.

Goodwin, Frederick K., and Adrian R. Morrison. "Science and Self-Doubt." *Reason*, vol. 32, October 2000, pp. 22 ff. Presents arguments against common reasons for demanding that animals not be used in medical research and urges scientists to take a stronger stand against animal rights activists.

"Guidelines for Psychologists Working with Animals." *Quarterly Journal of Experimental Psychology, Part B: Comparative and Physiological Psychology*, vol. 54, February 2001, pp. 81–91. Describes standards, devised by the British Psychological Society, that are mandatory in Britain.

Hague, Cheryl. "Testing Program Gets Underway." *Chemical and Engineering News*, vol. 79, August 20, 2001, pp. 30–33. Describes the Environmental Protection Agency's testing program for high-production-volume chemicals and the claims of animal rights groups that it is unnecessary and will cause the deaths of large numbers of laboratory animals.

Holden, Constance. "Researchers Pained by Effort to Define Distress Precisely." *Science*, vol. 290, November 24, 2000, p. 1474. The U.S. Department of Agriculture's consideration of possible revision of regulations under the Animal Welfare Act, including attempts to define "distress" in animals, is arousing considerable controversy in the research community.

Hunter, Beatrice Trum. "New Alternatives in Safety Testing." *Consumers' Research Magazine*, vol. 83, May 2000, pp. 26 ff. Describes a wide range of existing alternatives to the use of whole animals in product safety testing.

Jones, Trevor. "Reducing Animal Testing." *Manufacturing Chemist*, vol. 73, October 2002, p. 19. Author describes drug industry's efforts to reduce the number of animals used in testing and develop nonanimal alternatives to animal testing but maintains that tests on animals are still necessary under some circumstances.

Koenig, Robert. "European Researchers Grapple with Animal Rights." *Science*, vol. 284, June 4, 1999, pp. 1604 ff. Some scientists feel that the governments of Britain, Germany, and some other European countries have gone too far in trying to compromise with animal rightists on the treatment of animals in research.

Malakoff, David. "Alternatives to Animals Urged for Producing Antibodies." *Science*, vol. 284, April 9, 1999, p. 230. A National Research Council report says that 90 percent of monoclonal antibodies can be made by methods that do not harm mice, but they argue that methods that use mice should not be banned.

Matfield, Mark. "Talk to the People." *Trends in Neuroscience*, vol. 25, March 2002, pp. 166–167. Opinion surveys have shown that the public is willing to accept the use of animals in research provided that regulations enforce high standards of care for them. Author says many people do not know that such regulations already exist. He stresses that the scientific community should communicate to the public its ethics and concern for animal welfare.

Mavany, Salma. "Regulating the Military's Survival Skills Training under the Animal Welfare Act." *Boston College Environmental Affairs Law Review*, vol. 29, Fall 2001, pp. 45–68. Examines alleged animal cruelty involved in military survival training and concludes that such training should be classified as "federal research" and therefore regulated under the Animal Welfare Act.

Morrison, Adrian R. "Ethical Principles Guiding the Use of Animals in Research." *The American Biology Teacher*, vol. 65, February 2003, pp. 105–108. The author, a strong supporter of the use of animals in research, presents the guidelines he employs in such research in a form suitable for use in classroom discussions about the ethics of experimenting on animals.

———. "Personal Reflections on the 'Animal-Rights' Phenomenon." *Perspectives in Biology and Medicine*, vol. 44, Winter 2001, pp. 62 ff. A supporter of the use of animals in biomedical research describes his ill treatment at the hands of animal rights extremists and critiques animal rightists' philosophy and understanding of science.

Plous, Scott, and Harold Herzog. "Reliability of Protocol Reviews for Animal Research." *Science*, vol. 293, July 27, 2001, pp. 608 ff. This study evaluated Institutional Animal Care and Use Committees, mandated by the 1985 revision of the Animal Welfare Act, by having two committees evaluate the same protocol (research plan), and found that the two usually reached different conclusions.

———. "Should the AWA Cover Rats, Mice, and Birds?" *Lab Animal*, vol. 28, 1999, pp. 38–40. Claims that many biomedical researchers support such coverage.

Purchase, Iain. "Experimental Animal Research." *Biological Sciences Review*, vol. 13, January 2001, pp. 26 ff. Describes practical and ethical issues in animal research and stringent British regulations governing such research.

Raloff, Janet. "Of Rats, Mice, and Birds." *Science News*, vol. 158, November 18, 2000, pp. 334–335. Discusses the necessity and possible effects of extending the Animal Welfare Act to cover mice, rats, and birds.

Roberts, Adam M., Grace De Gabriel, and Jill Robinson. "Dying to Heal: The Use of Animals in Traditional Medicine." *The Animals' Agenda*, vol. 19, May–June 1999, pp. 30–31. The use of animal parts such as bear gallbladders and rhinoceros horns in traditional medicine presents a threat to some endangered species and is said to be cruel to animals, whether endangered or not. Animal rights groups, therefore, are trying to have legislation passed to stop or regulate it.

Ruxton, Graeme D. "Experimental Design: Minimizing Suffering May Not Always Mean Minimizing Number of Subjects." *Animal Behaviour,* vol. 56, August 1998, pp. 511–512. Using an "unbalanced" experimental design in experiments that place significant stress on animals reduces the number of animals in high-stress groups without invalidating the experiments, but it requires a higher total number of animals, the author claims.

Sandercock, Peter, and Ian Roberts. "Systematic Reviews of Animal Experiments." *The Lancet,* vol. 360, August 24, 2002, p. 586. Authors recommend conducting systematic reviews of animal studies before beginning human studies of new drugs. They claim that lack of systematic review and sufficiently high scientific standards in animal experiments means that unnecessary studies on both animals and humans are sometimes performed.

Smage, Laurence A., et al. "Advancing Refinement in Laboratory Animal Use." *Laboratory Animals,* vol. 32, 1998, pp. 137–142. Describes ways to refine laboratory experiments on animals to minimize pain and distress in the subjects. Claims that refinement can benefit science as well as the welfare of laboratory animals.

Smith, Richard. "Animal Research: The Need for a Middle Ground." *British Medical Journal,* vol. 322, February 3, 2001, p. 248. Recommends the policy of replacement, reduction, and refinement of animal tests as a middle ground where animal rightists and supporters of research using animals might meet.

Solomon, Gina. "The Lesser Evil." *Earth Island Journal,* vol. 17, Autumn 2002, p. 47. Author, associated with the Natural Resources Defense Council, defends the use of animal tests to detect certain kinds of nonacute but important effects of pesticides and other common chemicals, such as birth defects and endocrine (hormone) disruption.

Trull, Frankie L. "More Regulation of Rodents." *Science,* vol. 284, May 28, 1999, p. 1463. Argues that adding coverage of rats, mice, and birds to the Animal Welfare Act will increase scientists' paperwork and expense without benefiting the animals and that several sets of mandatory guidelines already protect these species in the laboratory.

Wurbel, Hanno. "Better Housing for Better Science." *Chemistry and Industry,* April 16, 2001, p. 237. Argues that improved housing for laboratory animals, including rodents, is necessary for scientific reasons because substandard living conditions can affect the animals' brains, invalidating some tests.

Zahodiakin, Phil. "PETA Submits Strategic Plan Comments." *Pesticide and Toxic Chemical News,* vol. 31, November 25, 2002, p. 11. Commenting on a strategic five-year plan for the Office of Prevention, Pesticides, and

Toxic Substances, part of the Environmental Protection Agency, PETA told the EPA that it should ban or restrict chemicals that present "obvious" dangers to human health or the environment rather than endlessly testing them on animals to prove that they are harmful. The animal rights group also made other recommendations for reducing the use of animals in testing and using animals more efficiently.

WEB DOCUMENTS

"Animal Care and Use Committees: Structural Problems Impair Usefulness." Physicians Committee for Responsible Medicine. Available online. URL: http://www.pcrm.org/resch/anexp/IACUC.html. Accessed on April 20, 2003. Examines and critiques the structure of the institutional animal care and use committees in the United States (where they were mandated by an amendment to the Animal Welfare Act in 1985) and several other countries and offers recommendations for improvement.

"Animals in the Classroom: A Guide for Elementary and Secondary Educators." The Center for Laboratory Animal Welfare. Available online. URL: http://www.labanimalwelfare.org/animals_in_education.html. Accessed on April 18, 2003. Discusses uses of and alternatives to animals as classroom pets and in live animal studies, dissection, and science fair projects, as well as the role of animal care and use committees.

"The Benefits of Biomedical Research." Federation of American Societies for Experimental Biology. Available online. URL: http://www.faseb.org/opar/benefits. Updated on November 4, 1999. Benefits to humans cited include better health, longer lives, and reduced cost of illness.

Budkie, Michael A. "Military Animal Research." Medical Research Modernization Committee. Available online. URL: http://www.mrmcmed.org/mar.html. Accessed on April 20, 2003. Describes animal experiments carried on by the Department of Defense, which author claims are "typically more invasive than projects funded by other sources."

———. "The Rising Tide of Animal Experimentation." Stop Animal Exploitation Now. Available online. URL: http://www.all-creatures.org/saen/articles-rep-rt.html. Accessed on April 20, 2003. Reveals national trends in animal experimentation based on USDA statistics for 2002, including alleged Animal Welfare Act violations.

Capaldo, Theodora. "The State of the Anti-Vivisection Movement: Progress and Challenges." New England Anti-Vivisection Society. Available online. URL: http://www.neavs.org/programs/papers/antivivisection_movement_2001.htm. Posted in June 2001. This speech delivered at a 2001 animal rights conference describes experiences in battling the animal research industry.

Cardello, Nicole. "Analysis of the HPV Challenge: Industry Violations and EPA Negligence." Physicians Committee for Responsible Medicine. Available online. URL: http://www.pcrm.org/resch/anexp/hpv_report0801. html. Accessed on April 20, 2003. Describes and criticizes the EPA's program to encourage chemical companies to conduct new animal toxicity tests on industrial chemicals produced in high volume.

"Chimpanzees in Research." The Center for Laboratory Animal Welfare. Available online. URL: http://www.labanimalwelfare.org/animals_in_research.html. Accessed on April 18, 2003. Group affiliated with the Massachusetts Society for Prevention of Cruelty to Animals discusses welfare and ethical issues involved with the use of chimpanzees in research, as well as the question of what to do with captive chimpanzees no longer needed for research and the development of chimpanzee sanctuaries.

Davis, Karen. "The Experimental Use of Chickens and Other Birds in Biomedical and Agricultural Research." New England Anti-Vivisection Society. Available online. URL: http://www.neavs.org/programs/papers/birdsreasearch_ contents_kdavis.htm. Posted in 2003. Includes a history of birds used in biomedical research, birds used in product testing, birds used in agricultural research, genetic engineering and cloning of domestic fowl, and conclusions. Opposes the use of birds (and other animals) in science.

"Fact vs. Myth about the Essential Need for Animals in Research." Foundation for Biomedical Research. Available online. URL: http://www.fbresearch.org/education/fact-vs-myth.htm. Updated on October 24, 2002. Offers rebuttals to animal rights groups' arguments against animal research. Supports the three Rs but maintains that some research on animals is essential.

Fano, Alix, et al. "Of Pigs, Primates, and Plagues: A Layperson's Guide to the Problems with Animal-to-Human Organ Transplants." Medical Research Modernization Committee. Available online. URL: http://www.mrmcmed.org/pigs.html. Accessed on April 20, 2003. Describes why authors believe that transplanting pig or nonhuman primate organs into humans is dangerous.

"Genetic Engineering: A Look at the Welfare of Animals in Biotechnology Research." The Center for Laboratory Animal Welfare. Available online. URL: http://www.labanimalwelfare.org/genetic_engineering.html. Accessed on April 18, 2003. Describes reasons for thinking that genetic engineering of animals is a threat to their welfare and possibly to that of humans and other animals.

"Genetic Engineering: Animal Welfare and Ethics." The Boyd Group. Available online. URL: http://www.boyd-group.demon.co.uk/genmod. htm. Posted in September 1999. Compiled by the Boyd Group, a U.K.-

based forum whose members discuss issues related to animals in science, this article discusses fundamental moral objections to all use of animals in experimentation and to genetic modification in particular, as well as concerns about the consequences of genetic modification in animals, including threats to the welfare of the animals themselves and threats to human health and the environment.

"1986 Animals Act." Research Defence Society. Available online. URL: http://www.rds-online.org.uk/pages/page.asp?i_ToolbarID=4&i_PageID=47. Accessed on April 20, 2003. Summary of Britain's Animals (Scientific Procedures) Act of 1986, which regulates animal research in Britain, from a group that supports the use of animals in research.

"Insight into the Animals (Scientific Procedures) Act 1986." British Union for the Abolition of Vivisection. Available online. URL: http://www. buav.org/pdfs/insight_into_the_animals.pdf. Accessed on April 19, 2003. Describes this act, which regulates experiments on animals in Britain, and claims that it does not do enough to protect animals.

"Institutional Animal Care and Use Committee Guidebook." Applied Research Ethics National Association. Available online. URL: ftp://ftp. grants.nih.gov/IACUC/GuideBook.pdf. Updated in 2002. Describes the duties of these committees, mandated by a 1985 amendment to the Animal Welfare Act.

"Public Health Service Policy on Humane Care and Use of Laboratory Animals." Office of Laboratory Animal Welfare. Available online. URL: http://grants.nih.gov/grants/olaw/references/phspol.htm. Updated in August 2002. Describes Public Health Service/National Institutes of Health policies regarding care of laboratory animals.

"Regulation of Biomedical Research Using Animals." National Association for Biomedical Research. Available online. URL: http://www.nabr.org/ pdf/green.pdf. Accessed on April 20, 2003. Describes the comprehensive system of federal, state, and local laws and regulations that, authors claim, adequately protects laboratory animals from abuse.

Smith, Jane A., and Kenneth M. Boyd, eds. "The Use of Non-Human Primates in Research and Testing." The Boyd Group. Available online. URL: http://www.boyd-group.demon.co.uk. Posted in June 2002. Published by the British Psychological Society, this group of papers provides background on the subject and discusses empirical evidence on the moral status of nonhuman primates, whether apes are persons, welfare considerations in the use of macaques and marmosets, and the use of nonhuman primates in regulatory toxicology. The authors conclude that research on great apes should be stopped because of their superior mental capabilities, but they do not claim that apes should be considered equivalent to human beings. Use of other nonhuman primates in research might be permissible, they say, but it would require "very strong justification."

Stephens, Martin, and Andrew N. Rowan. "An Overview of Animal Testing Issues." The Humane Society of the United States. Available online. URL: http://files.hsus.org/web-files/PDF/ARIS_An_Overview_Of_Animal_Testing_Issues.pdf. Accessed on April 18, 2003. Covers history of safety testing on animals, types of safety tests, problems with animal tests, obstacles to replacing animal tests, cosmetic and household product testing, the international scene, success stories in replacing tests on animals, and new large-scale animal testing programs.

"Survey of Laureates in Physiology or Medicine." Seriously Ill for Medical Research web site. Available online. URL: http://www.simr.org.uk/pages/nobel/nobel_survey.html. Accessed on July 22, 2003. This group sent a six-question survey about the use of animals in research to all 71 living Nobel laureates in physiology or medicine, and 39 replied. This web page shows a graphic representation of the percentage results for each question.

"Understanding Claims About Animal Experiments." Physicians Committee for Responsible Medicine. Available online. URL: http://www.pcrm.org/resch/anexp/understanding_claims.html. Accessed on April 20, 2003. Animal rights group maintains that experiments on animals cause unnecessary suffering and are scientifically invalid for human medicine.

"The Use of Animals in Testing Household Products." The Boyd Group. Available online. URL: http://www.boyd-group.demon.co.uk/householdproducts.pdf. Posted in December 2002. Published by the Universities Federation for Animal Welfare. Britain banned the testing of cosmetics and cosmetic ingredients on animals in the late 1990s, but some animal testing of household products still continues. This paper discusses the issues involved in such testing and concludes that animal testing of household products should be banned in Britain and, preferably, Europe, because there is neither great need for new versions of these products nor regulatory requirements for testing them on animals.

Worth, Andrew P., and Michael Balls, eds. "Alternative (Non-animal) Methods for Chemicals Testing: Current Status and Future Projects." European Centre for the Validation of Alternative Methods. Available online. URL: http://ecvam.jrc.it/index.htm. Posted in 2002. Originally published as ATLA (Alternatives to Laboratory Animals) Supplement 1. Found through the "publications" link of the site, this article discusses the principles and procedures of validation and the scientific basis of chemical risk assessment, as well as numerous types of toxicity tests, including tests for endocrine disruption.

ANIMALS IN ENTERTAINMENT

BOOKS

Baratay, Eric, and Elisabeth Hardouin-Fugier. *Zoos: A History of Zoological Gardens in the West.* London: Reaktion Books, 2002. Uses scholarly research of unusual depth and 400 illustrations to examine the social history of zoos and related institutions and what that history shows about the way people's view of wild animals has changed over time.

Burt, Jonathan. *Animals in Film.* London: Reaktion Books, 2003. Focuses on the imagery and meaning of animals in film as well as on treatment of actual animals used.

Campion, Lynn. *Rodeo.* Guilford, Conn.: Lyons Press, 2002. Comprehensive, well-illustrated look at rodeos, including backstage views, the different types of events, and how rodeo livestock are raised and selected.

Clubb, Ros, and Georgia Mason. *A Review of the Welfare of Zoo Elephants in Europe.* Southwater, Horsham, West Sussex, U.K.: Royal Society for the Prevention of Cruelty to Animals, 2002. Claims that elephants suffer in captivity and urges that keeping them in zoos be phased out.

Hancocks, David. *A Different Nature: The Paradoxical World of Zoos and Their Uncertain Future.* Berkeley: University of California Press, 2001. Hancocks, director of the Open Range Zoo in Melbourne, Australia, offers criticism of conventional zoos, although he praises certain model institutions such as the Bronx Zoo. He recommends that the zoo be reshaped into "a new type of institution . . . that . . . engenders respect for all animals and . . . interprets a holistic view of nature."

Hanson, Elizabeth. *Animal Attractions: Nature on Display in American Zoos.* Princeton, N.J.: Princeton University Press, 2002. Provides a history of American zoos, focusing on what they reveal about how U.S. culture sees the natural world and humans' place in it and how those ideas have changed over time.

Hediger, Heini. *Wild Animals in Captivity: An Outline of the Biology of Zoological Gardens.* Mineola, N.Y.: Dover Publications, 1964. This seminal book presents the idea of viewing zoo design from the perspective of ethology, the study of animal behavior in the wild. It maintains that zoo habitats should be made to look as natural as possible to the animals that live in them and allow as many of the animals' natural behaviors as possible.

Koebner, Linda. *Zoo Book: The Evolution of Wildlife Conservation Centers.* New York: Forge, 1997. Written with the cooperation of the Association of Zoos and Aquariums and the Wildlife Conservation Society, this book offers a comprehensive, well-illustrated examination of the complex modern zoo and its "natural habitats."

Annotated Bibliography

Margodt, Koen. *The Welfare Ark: Suggestions for a Renewed Policy for Zoos.* Amsterdam: Vrije Universiteit (VU) Press, 2001. Tries to bridge the gap between zoos and organizations working for animal welfare and animal rights. Suggests innovative alternatives to zoos that can help preserve vanishing species while also protecting animal welfare.

Mullan, Bob, and Garry Marvin. *Zoo Culture.* Rev. ed. Champaign: University of Illinois Press, 1998. Considers why people go to zoos, what they learn from them, how those who own or work in them feel about them, and what role they play in modern urban society.

Norton, Bryan G., et al., eds. *Ethics on the Ark: Zoos, Animal Welfare and Wildlife Conservation.* Washington, D.C.: Smithsonian Institution Press, 1996. In papers from a 1992 conference, animal welfare activists, philosophers, conservation biologists, and zoo professionals present different perspectives on the future of aquariums and zoos, how captive animals should be treated, and whether the individual, the species, or the ecosystem should be the most important target of conservation efforts.

O'Barry, Richard. *Behind the Dolphin Smile.* Los Angeles: Renaissance Books, 2000. The trainer of the dolphin that starred in the famous television show *Flipper* describes how he underwent a change of heart and now works to return captive dolphins to the wild.

———. *To Free a Dolphin.* Los Angeles: Renaissance Books, 2000. Describes author's continuing efforts to rehabilitate captive dolphins and release them into their natural habitat.

Rothfels, Nigel. *Savages and Beasts: The Birth of the Modern Zoo.* Baltimore: Johns Hopkins Press, 2002. Profiles Carl Hagenbeck, who initiated the idea of modern, naturalistic zoos in Germany in the mid-19th century.

Ryan, R. J. *Keepers of the Ark.* Philadelphia, Pa.: Xlibris Corp., 1999. Describes the author's experiences as an elephant keeper at the San Diego Wild Animal Park.

Scigliano, Eric. *Love, War, and Circuses: The Age-Old Relationship Between Elephants and Humans.* Boston: Houghton Mifflin, 2002. Shows how humans and elephants, particularly Asian elephants, have interacted in both beneficial and harmful ways throughout history. Includes consideration of modern elephants in zoos and circuses.

Shepherdson, David J., et al., eds. *Second Nature: Environmental Enrichment for Captive Animals.* Washington, D.C.: Smithsonian Institution Press, 1999. An anthology of papers by animal behaviorists presented at a 1993 conference discusses environmental enrichment for captive animals in zoos, marine parks, and laboratories. Covers theoretical bases, conservation and animal welfare, and husbandry and training.

Animal Rights

ARTICLES

Burnside, Mary Wade. "Animal Rights Issues Impacting Fair Biz." *Amusement Business*, vol. 114, July 29, 2002, pp. 3–4. Explains that new state and local laws aimed at protecting animals are likely to have an effect on fairs and rodeos; some members of the industry are concerned.

Ebersole, Rene S. "The New Zoo." *Audubon*, vol. 103, November–December 2001, pp. 64–72. Presents a positive view of the role that the best modern zoos play in conservation and public education.

Eidinger, Joan. "Nowhere to Run: Dog Racing in Decline." *The Animals' Agenda*, vol. 20, September–October 2000, pp. 30–35. Describes alleged mistreatment of greyhounds in the dog racing industry and the decrease in the number of dog racing tracks.

Garrison, Jane, and Amanda Alabaster. "Is It Really Beastly to Keep Animals in Zoos?" *Europe Intelligence Wire*, October 24, 2002. The authors present pro (Garrison) and con (Alabaster) responses to this question, in wake of demands by Britain's Royal Society for the Prevention of Cruelty to Animals that elephants and perhaps other animals no longer be kept in captivity.

Guido, Michelle. "Jury Acquits Ringling Bros. Trainer of Elephant Abuse." *San Jose Mercury News*, December 21, 2001, p. K1505. A jury quickly acquitted Ringling Bros. and Barnum & Bailey animal trainer Mark Gebel of abusing an elephant in his care. Both the circus and animal rights groups say the trial brought out points that they wanted to make.

Hager, Mary. "The Greatest Show on Earth." *Chief Executive*, vol. 183, November 2002, pp. 44–47. Praises Ken Feld, chief executive officer of Ringling Bros. and Barnum & Bailey Circus, for publicly counterattacking PETA after the animal rights group accused the circus of cruelty to its animals.

Hearne, Vicki. "Can an Ape Tell a Joke?" *Harper's Magazine*, vol. 87, November 1993, pp. 58–69. After observing the animal act of entertainer Bobby Berosini, the target of abuse claims by animal rights group PETA, the author, a fellow animal trainer, concludes that Berosini not only does not abuse the orangutans in his act but has a very close relationship with them, in which he and the apes develop their comic routines together.

Merritt, Marianne R. "Tatters in the Big Top: The Crumbling Image of Animal Circuses." *The Animals' Agenda*, vol. 20, September–October 2000, pp. 38–40. Claims that exotic animals in general and elephants in particular are abused in American circuses. Describes moves to have exotic animal circuses legally banned.

Mills, Eric. "The Problem with Rodeo." *Earth Island Journal*, vol. 17, Autumn 2002, p. 48. Describes alleged cruel practices and animal injuries at rodeos.

Rosenberg, Howard. "Real Bull." *The Animals' Agenda*, vol. 21, July–August 2001, p. 35. Describes the plight of bulls in Spanish bull rings and in the streets of Pamplona during the famous "running of the bulls."

Rosenberg, Kirsten. "Eric Mills: Man of Action." *The Animals' Agenda*, vol. 20, September–October 2000, p. 24. Interview with and profile of Mills, an animal rights activist who has crusaded to stop animal suffering produced by such rodeo activities as calf roping.

Satchell, Michael. "Cruel and Usual." *U.S. News & World Report*, August 5, 2002, pp. 28 ff. Even the largest and most respected zoos often sell surplus exotic animals to buyers who may abuse or neglect them, the magazine's investigation shows.

"Setting Free the (Wrong) Bears." *Time International*, vol. 157, April 9, 2001, p. 45. Claims that an animal-rights-supported move by the Indian government to ban performing bears brings hardship to the animals as well as their owners.

Trachtman, Paul. "To the Rescue." *Smithsonian*, vol. 33, March 2003, pp. 91–98. Describes a sanctuary in Nevada for abused or abandoned big cats and other exotic predators.

"When Dolphins Cry." *Swiss News*, March 2001, pp. 10 ff. Swiss animal protection activist Noelle Delaquis describes her attempts to keep parks and shows from exhibiting captive dolphins.

WEB DOCUMENTS

"Animals for Entertainment." The Animals' Voice. Available online. URL: http://www.animal-rights.com/arsec9q.htm. Accessed in December 2002. Gives reasons for claiming that zoos, circuses, rodeos, and dog and horse racing are cruel to animals.

"Animals in Television and Film." Performing Animal Welfare Society. Available online. URL: http://www.pawsweb.org/site/resources/index_factsheets.htm. Accessed on April 20, 2003. Describes alleged abuses by trainers of animals used in these media.

"The Collective Impact of America's Zoos and Aquariums." American Zoo and Aquarium Association. Available online. URL: http://www.aza.org/AboutAZA/CollectiveImpact1. Posted in 1999. Describes the positive impact of AZA-accredited zoos and aquariums on the public, education, conservation, animal care, and other areas.

Creamer, Jan, and Tim Phillips. "The Ugliest Show on Earth: A Report on the Use of Animals in Circuses." Animal Defenders. Available online. URL: http://www.ad-international.org/animals_in_entertainment/circuses/ugliest_show/192398.htm. Accessed in February 2003. This book-length report offers what authors say is conclusive evidence that circus animals endure a life of environmental deprivation and frequent physical and verbal abuse.

Raven, Peter H. "Zoos, Sustainability, and Our Common Future." American Zoo and Aquarium Association. Available online. URL: http://www.aza.org/ForEveryone/RavenPart1. Posted on September 8, 2001. The keynote address to the 2001 annual conference of the American Zoo and Aquarium Association describes the effect of human population growth on habitat destruction, climate change, and extinction rates and presents possibilities for cooperation among aquariums, zoos, botanical gardens, and other conservation organizations.

"Rodeo: Cruelty for a Buck." People for the Ethical Treatment of Animals. Available online. URL: http://www.peta.org/mc/facts/fsent1.html. Accessed on April 20, 2003. This fact sheet describes alleged cruelty to animals in rodeos.

"What the Greyhound Racing Industry Doesn't Want You to Know." Greyhound Protection League. Available online. URL: http://www.greyhounds.org/gpl/contents/racing_industry.html. Accessed on April 18, 2003. A series of short papers explaining why the organization believes greyhound racing should be made illegal provides facts about dog racing, documented cases of abuse, instances of former racing dogs sold to laboratories, and more.

WILDLIFE

BOOKS

Bean, Michael J., and Melanie J. Rowland. *The Evolution of National Wildlife Law.* 3d ed. New York: Praeger, 1998. Provides a comprehensive review of the field, which has expanded greatly in recent years due to litigation and new legislation.

Board of Environmental Toxicology et al. *Science and the Endangered Species Act.* Washington, D.C.: National Academy Press, 1995. Concentrates on the science supporting the Endangered Species Act and describes ways to make the law more effective. Topics covered include extinction of species, conflicts between conservation of different species in the same habitat, and estimating risk of extinction.

Burgess, Bonnie B. *Fate of the Wild: The Endangered Species Act and the Future of Biodiversity.* Athens: University of Georgia Press, 2001. The author, associated with the National Zoo, offers a sophisticated discussion of biodiversity and tries to steer a middle course between the needs of wildlife and the environment and the economic needs of people.

Annotated Bibliography

Cartmill, Matt. *A View to a Death in the Morning: Hunting and Nature Through History.* Cambridge, Mass.: Harvard University Press, 1996. Largely critical of hunting, especially sport hunting, this book shows how hunting has played a part in the Western imagination from ancient times to the present.

Cavalieri, Paola, and Peter Singer, eds. *The Great Ape Project: Equality Beyond Humanity.* New York: St. Martin's Press, 1995. Thirty-four famous figures in wildlife research and other disciplines call for better treatment of chimpanzees, bonobos, gorillas, and orangutans, including possibly granting them moral and legal rights.

Cohn, Priscilla N., ed. *Ethics and Wildlife.* Lewiston, N.Y.: Edwin Mellen Press, 1999. Ten essays offer different, mostly negative ethical perspectives on hunting.

Dizard, Jan E. *Going Wild: Hunting, Animal Rights, and the Contested Meaning of Nature.* Rev. ed. Amherst: University of Massachusetts Press, 1999. Describes the hunting controversy and humans' relationship to nature in terms of a small area in Massachusetts, then places this analysis in the larger context of the history of hunting and white people's relationship to animals, plants, and land in the United States. Favors hunting as a way to control animal overpopulation in some cases but also asserts that hunters cause problems and perpetuate myths.

———. *Mortal Stakes: Hunters and Hunting in Contemporary America.* Amherst: University of Massachusetts Press, 2003. Hunting was once accepted without question as part of American life, but this is no longer the case. Dizard considers why this is so. He examines the role of hunting in the United States today, focusing on hunters' own views, through interviews, opinion surveys, and demographic statistics.

Donahue, Debra L. *Conservation and the Law.* Santa Barbara, Calif.: ABC-CLIO, 1998. An encyclopedia of terms, key court cases, laws, and so on.

Dunlap, Thomas R. *Saving America's Wildlife: Ecology and the American Mind, 1850–1990.* Princeton, N.J.: Princeton University Press, 1988. This history of wildlife preservation in the United States uses attitudes toward wolves and coyotes as examples to describe how and why Americans have felt as they did about wild animals and how these feelings have changed over time.

Goodall, Jane, and Marc Bekoff. *The Ten Trusts: What We Must Do to Protect the Animals We Love.* San Francisco: HarperSanFrancisco, 2002. Famous primatologist Goodall and University of Colorado biology professor Bekoff offer a conservation plan to protect wild animals and their habitats and educate people about the importance of preserving both. Ideas include having rich nations pay "rent" on wild areas in developing countries to preserve them and encouraging children to work with animal protection programs.

Green, Alan. *Animal Underworld: Inside America's Black Market for Rare and Exotic Species.* New York: Public Affairs, 1999. An investigative reporter reveals how zoos dispose of their surplus animals, often causing members of supposedly protected species to be sold and killed for food or medicinal use of their body parts.

Hanmer, Trudy J. *The Hunting Debate: Aiming at the Issues.* Berkeley Heights, N.J.: Enslow Publishers, 1999. Young adult book considers pro and con opinions of hunting, including descriptions of hunting methods, the relationship between hunting and gun violence to humans, and reasons animal rightists oppose hunting.

Irwin, Paul G. *Losing Paradise: The Growing Threat to Our Animals, Our Environment, and Ourselves.* Garden City Park, N.Y.: Square One Publishers, 2000. Irwin, president of the Humane Society of the United States, alleges that humankind is destroying the Earth but also offers solutions and describes steps that must be taken to head off disaster.

Jones, Robert F., ed. *On Killing: Meditations on the Chase.* Guilford, Conn.: Lyons Press, 2001. An anthology of articles and book excerpts on hunting and fishing. Most accept or praise killing for food or to dispose of pests but disapprove of excesses of recreational hunting.

Kruuk, Hans. *Hunter and Hunted: Relationships Between Carnivores and People.* New York: Cambridge University Press, 2002. Discusses human views of carnivores as admired wild animals, threats to human life, livestock-killing pests, hunting trophies, sources of fur and medicine, and beloved pets. Includes carnivores' roles in nature and in art and literature, why humans are drawn to these animals, and issues related to their conservation.

Lauck, Joanne Elizabeth. *The Voice of the Infinite in the Small: Re-Visioning the Insect-Human Connection.* Rev. ed. Boston: Shambhala Publications, 2002. Claims that people in the Western world frequently misunderstand and undervalue insects. Presents both scientific and mythic views of these animals' positive qualities.

Mitman, Gregg. *Reel Nature: America's Romance with Wildlife on Film.* Cambridge, Mass.: Harvard University Press, 1999. Describes the development of the wildlife documentary and the cultural attitudes it reflects and shapes. Concludes that much of what Americans believe about nature has been fabricated by the film industry.

Musgrave, Ruth S., et al. *Federal Wildlife Laws Handbook, with Related Laws.* Rockville, Md.: Government Institutes, 1998. Provides a brief history of wildlife law in the United States and describes federal laws pertaining to wildlife.

Petersen, David. *Heartsblood: Hunting, Spirituality, and Wildness in America.* Washington, D.C.: Island Press, 2000. Sees hunting as a way of expressing a close relationship with nature and claims that hunters fill an ecological role that humans must assume to prevent overpopulation of animals such as deer, whose natural predators have been killed. Criticizes both hunters who abuse the sport and animal rights activists who call it immoral.

Petersen, Shannon C. *Acting for Endangered Species: The Statutory Ark.* Lawrence: University Press of Kansas, 2002. Describes the political and legal history of the Endangered Species Act and shows how the courts expanded and strengthened the original law. Shows how complex interactions among environmentalism, science, government, and natural resource industries have shaped environmental policy in the United States.

Peterson, Dale, and Jane Goodall. *Visions of Caliban: Chimpanzees and People.* Athens: University of Georgia Press, 2000. Goodall and literature professor Peterson examine the place of chimpanzees in popular culture and in what is left of their natural habitat. They picture a grim future for the apes.

Reinke, Danny C., and Lucinda Low Swartz, eds. *Endangered Species: Legal Requirements and Policy Guidance.* Columbus, Ohio: Battelle Press, 2001. Helps students and environmental science professionals understand relevant regulations. Includes excerpts from laws, regulations, and court cases.

Sherry, Clifford J. *Endangered Species: A Reference Handbook.* Santa Barbara, Calif.: ABC-CLIO, 1998. Entries cover biology, biographies of key figures, laws, issues related to the preservation of endangered species, and lists of resources.

Shogren, Jason F., ed. *Private Property and the Endangered Species Act: Saving Habitats, Protecting Homes.* Austin: University of Texas Press, 1999. Provides multidisciplinary perspectives on the conflict between the desire to preserve endangered species, as embodied in the Endangered Species Act (ESA), and the desire to protect private property. Traces the evolution of the ESA and concludes with eight principles that the University of Wyoming's Institute for Environment and Natural Resources Policy Board developed to frame the ongoing debate about whether, and in what form, the ESA should be authorized.

Stange, Mary Zeiss. *Woman the Hunter.* Boston: Beacon Press, 1998. Examines and challenges cultural assumptions about hunting, especially the idea that women play (or should play) no part in it, a belief that some macho men and radical ecofeminists share. Explores ultimate rationales for hunting and claims that appreciating hunting helps one understand the meaning of being human.

Taylor, V. J., and N. Dunstone. *The Exploitation of Mammal Populations.* Boca Raton, Fla.: Chapman and Hall, 1996. Covers animal welfare issues involved in mammal harvesting, hunting, sustainable trade, and eco-tourism worldwide.

University of New Mexico Center for Wildlife Law. *State Laws Handbook.* Rockville, Md.: Government Institutes, Inc., 1993. Summarizes wildlife laws by state.

Watson, Paul. *Seal Wars: Twenty-Five Years on the Front Lines with the Harp Seals.* Toronto, Ontario: Firefly Books, 2003. Captain Watson, founder of the Sea Shepherd Conservation Society, describes confrontations with sealers and others in attempts to save Canadian harp seals from slaughter that began in the late 1970s.

Zimmerman, Michael E., et al., eds. *Environmental Philosophy: From Animal Rights to Radical Ecology.* 3d ed. Upper Saddle River, N.J.: Prentice-Hall, 2000. Twenty-five articles, arranged in five groups according to approach, discuss problems in environmental ethics, focusing on the more extreme views of the environmental movement such as deep ecology. Includes material on the relationship between animal rights and environmental philosophies.

ARTICLES

Andelt, William F., et al. "Trapping Furbearers: An Overview of the Biological and Social Issues Surrounding a Public Policy Controversy." *Wildlife Society Bulletin*, vol. 27, Spring 1999, pp. 53 ff. Trapping has been a controversial issue throughout the 20th century. This article describes biological and social issues related to trapping animals for their fur, especially by means of leghold traps.

Anderson, Gary. "The Clash of the German Hunting Community and the Anti-Hunting Movement." *Germany Politics and Society*, vol. 19, Spring 2001, pp. 37 ff. Movements to oppose hunting have been less successful in Germany than in some other countries, such as Britain. The author feels that this disparity is due both to ideological rifts and organizational difficulties within the antihunting movement and to the presence of a powerful hunting lobby that taps into beliefs about hunting deeply embedded in German culture and myth.

Dowling, Claudia Glenn. "Incident at Big Pine Key." *Smithsonian*, vol. 33, July 2002, pp. 45–51. Controversy over the deaths of a dolphin pod (family and social group) highlights philosophical and personal conflicts between groups involved in dolphin rescue.

"The End of Foxhunting." *The Economist*, vol. 355, June 17, 2000, p. 58. A major report commissioned by the British government finds little reason to ban foxhunting, but the author believes that pressure from animal rights groups and others will persuade the government to do so anyway.

Fraker, Mark A., et al. "Long-Lasting, Single-Dose Immunocontraception of Feral Fallow Deer in British Columbia." *Journal of Wildlife Management*, vol. 66, October 2002, pp. 1141–1147. Evaluates a new form of the PZP (porcine zona pellucida) contraception vaccine for wildlife called SpayVac. SpayVac works with only a single dose, thus solving a major problem of earlier contraceptive vaccines, which required two doses.

Heffer, Simon. "Good People Are Ready to Break the Law." *Spectator*, vol. 290, September 14, 2002, pp. 14–15. Describes how opposing feelings about hunting reveal basic conflicts between rural Britain and the country's government.

Iovino, Shelli Lyn. "Habitat Modification and ESA Takings under *Babbitt v. Sweet Home Chapter of Communities for a Great Oregon*." *Villanova Environmental Law Journal*, vol. 7, issue 2, 1996. Analyzes the Supreme Court's decision in this landmark Endangered Species Act case.

Kerasote, Ted. "Straight Talk on Hunting." *Sports Afield*, vol. 223, August 2000, p. 34. Claims that hunting does less damage to wildlife and the environment than agriculture.

Kluger, Jeffrey. "Hunting Made Easy." *Time*, vol. 159, March 11, 2002, pp. 62 ff. Explains that some hunters as well as animal rights activists question the legitimacy of "canned hunts," where hunting success is often guaranteed.

Kriz, Margaret. "Newfound Restraint at Resources?" *National Journal*, vol. 35, March 22, 2003, pp. 918–919. Interview with Richard Pombo, a Republican representative recently appointed to head the House Resources Committee. Pombo, an advocate of property rights, describes his priorities for natural resource conservation and the Endangered Species Act.

Luoma, Jon R. "The Wild World's Scotland Yard." *Audubon*, vol. 102, November 2000, pp. 72 ff. Describes how the U.S. Fish and Wildlife Service Forensics Laboratory in Ashland, Oregon, investigates the trade in endangered species and other crimes against wildlife.

Markarian, Michael. "The Mean Greens." *The Animals' Agenda*, vol. 19, January–February 1999, pp. 20–21. Claims that some environmentalist groups support legislative changes that animal rights organizations oppose, such as a lifting of the ban on certain tuna fishing techniques that threaten dolphins.

McGrath, Susan. "Shoot-Out at Little Galloo." *Smithsonian*, vol. 33, February 2003, pp. 73–78. An account of a conflict between New York fishers and fish-eating cormorants shows the complexity of ecological and political relationships involved in managing wildlife.

McIntyre, Thomas. "Fishing for Trouble." *Sports Afield*, vol. 224, August 2001, p. 22. Warns that anglers as well as hunters are being targeted by animal rights groups and environmentalists.

———. "Mock the Wildlife Vote." *Sports Afield*, vol. 223, November 2000, p. 24. Criticizes animal rights groups' use of state ballot initiatives to limit hunting, claiming that their successes will ultimately harm wildlife.

Muth, Robert M., and Wesley V. Jamison. "On the Destiny of Deer Camps and Duck Blinds: The Rise of the Animal Rights Movement and the Future of Wildlife Conservation." *Wildlife Society Bulletin*, vol. 28, Winter 2000, pp. 841 ff. Discusses issues arising from the animal rights movement's opposition to hunting and trapping and considers reasons for the increasing influence of the movement.

Ness, Erik. "Oh, Deer." *Discover*, vol. 24, March 2003, pp. 67–71. Excessive populations of deer are destroying ecosystems around the country, but the author says that hunters as well as animal rightists resist state wildlife managers' attempts to reduce deer numbers.

Oborne, Peter. "The Hunting Bill Is Insulting and Appalling—But It Could Be Worse." *Spectator*, vol. 290, December 7, 2002, p. 10. Critiques a recent compromise bill introduced into Parliament that would regulate hunting in Britain rather than banning it entirely, as animal rights groups such as the League Against Cruel Sports have demanded.

Peterson, M. Nils, et al. "Cultural Conflict and the Endangered Florida Key Deer." *Journal of Wildlife Management*, vol. 66, October 2002, pp. 947–968. Arguments about how to preserve Florida Key deer present a recent example of conflict between groups stressing property rights and those stressing the importance of preserving wildlife and the environment.

Rogers, Paul. "Appeals Court Throws Out Part of Law Banning Animal Traps." *San Jose Mercury News*, September 24, 2002, p. K0387. A federal appeals court ruled that a California state law banning leghold traps does not apply to national wildlife refuges because federal laws preempt it. Animal rights groups decry the traps as cruel, but the Audubon Society says that wildlife managers need to use them against predators such as foxes, raccoons, and feral cats to protect ducks, herons, and other waterbirds from attack.

Schrank, Delphine. "Going in for the Kill." *Time International*, vol. 159, April 1, 2002, p. 37. Maintains that motives for banning hunting in Britain are complex, contradictory, and not necessarily related to animal protection.

Spence, Michelle. "The Effect of Age on the Probability of Participation in Wildlife-Related Activities." *American Journal of Agricultural Economics*, vol. 84, December 2002, pp. 1384–1389. Concludes that likelihood of taking part in waterfowl hunting decreases with age, whereas the likelihood of engaging in wildlife viewing increases up to a certain age and then decreases beyond that point.

Van Note, Craig. "Victory at CITES." *Earth Island Journal*, vol. 18, Spring 2003, pp. 34–37. The international treaty to protect endangered species has extended its reach to cover commercial timber and marine fish.

Wheatcroft, Geoffrey. "Great Hatred, Little Room." *New Statesman*, vol. 129, April 3, 2000, pp. 25 ff. Claims that the powerful feelings about hunting in Britain arise from a clash of cultures that extends far beyond different views of animal rights.

Williams, Wendy. "Wildlife in the Balance." *Animals*, November 1998, pp. 14 ff. Urges conservationist and animal rights groups, who sometimes have opposing strategies of wildlife management, to discuss issues thoroughly and look for alternatives that can meet common goals.

WEB DOCUMENTS

"America's Wildlife: The Challenge Ahead." International Association of Fish and Wildlife Agencies. Available online. URL: http://www.iafwa.org/Attachments/America9s%20Wildlife%20Book1.pdf and http://www.iafwa.org/Attachments/America9s%20Wildlife%20Book2.pdf. Posted in 2002. Describes how wildlife is faring in the United States, how it is being conserved, and how it should best be handled in the future. Challenges include obtaining more funding and establishing broad partnerships among stakeholders.

Baldwin, Pamela. "Habitat Modification and the Endangered Species Act: The *Sweet Home* Decision." National Council for Science and the Environment. Available online. URL: http://www.ncseonline.org/NLE/CRS reports/Biodiversity/biodv-9.cfm. Posted on July 6, 1995. A short report to Congress by the Congressional Research Service, a branch of the Library of Congress, summarizes the Supreme Court ruling in this landmark 1995 case involving the Endangered Species Act.

"Committee of Inquiry into Hunting with Dogs in England and Wales." Hunting Policy Unit, Department for Environment, Food and Rural Affairs. Available online. URL: http://www.huntinginquiry.gov.uk. Posted in 2000. Also known as the Burns Report, this influential document commissioned by the British Parliament provides evidence that hunting is an important social activity in the countryside and is no more cruel than other common methods of killing foxes.

"Diary of a Hunt Sab." Hunt Saboteurs Association. Available online. URL: http://hsa.enviroweb.org/diary/index.html. Accessed on April 18, 2003. Describes the experiences of a "hunt saboteur," who carries out direct but nonviolent action in the field to stop hunting, during the 1998–99 fox-hunting season in Britain.

"Economic Importance of Hunting in America." International Association of Fish and Wildlife Agencies. Available online. URL: http://www.iafwa. org/Attachments/Hunting%20Economic%20Impact%202001.pdf. Posted in 2002. Maintains that hunting is economically valuable as well as "good for body and soul." Includes statistics.

"The Endangered Species Act of 1973." U.S. Fish and Wildlife Service. Available online. URL: http://endangered.fws.gov/esasum.html. Updated in October 1996. Describes the principal provisions of the law and the amendments added to it in 1978, 1982, and 1988.

"ESA Basics." U.S. Fish and Wildlife Service. Available online. URL: http://endangered.fws.gov/pubs/esa%20basics.pdf. Posted in October 2002. Defines key terms in the Endangered Species Act and briefly explains how the federal government carries out the mandates of the act.

"Factual Rebuttals to HSUS Non-factual 'Facts About Trapping.'" National Trappers Association. Available online. URL: http://www. nationaltrappers. com/Facts.html. Accessed on February 8, 2002. Contradicts antitrapping statements made by the Humane Society of the United States.

"Federal Wildlife and Related Laws Handbook." University of New Mexico Center for Wildlife Law. Available online. URL: http:// ipl.unm.edu/cwl/fedbook/index.html. Accessed on April 19, 2003. Summarizes statutes and fish and wildlife laws, regulations, and policies.

"Fur Farming in North America." Fur Commission USA. Available online. URL: http://www.furcommission.com/farming/index.html. Accessed on April 18, 2003. A group of short papers describing and supporting the fur farming industry, including statistics and a brief account of animal care.

George, Susan, William J. Snape, and Michael Senatore. "State Endangered Species Acts: Past, Present, and Future." Defenders of Wildlife. Available online. URL: http://www.defenders.org/pubs/sesa00.html. Posted in 1998. The federal government is increasingly counting on the states to help protect endangered species, and state endangered species laws, if carefully crafted, can greatly strengthen national efforts. Authors say that a survey of state endangered species laws shows that many states are not ready for this challenge, however.

Norris, Diane, Norm Phelps, and D. J. Schubert. "Canned Hunts: Unfair at Any Price." The Fund for Animals. Available online. URL: http://

www.fund.org/library/documentViewer.asp?ID=338&table=documents. Posted in February 2000. Criticizes "canned hunts," which are commercial hunts that occur on private land under circumstances that virtually assure the hunter of success.

North, Richard D. "The Hunt at Bay: A Paper on Stag-Hunting." Man in Nature. Available online. URL: http://www.maninnature.com/Deer/Deer1a.html. Posted in October 1999. An article commissioned and first published by the Wildlife Network states that deer hunting brings up many of the same issues as fox or hare hunting and that objections to it lack scientific validity.

"Reasons for Trapping." Coalition to Abolish the Fur Trade. Available online. URL: http://www.caft.org.uk/reasons-for-trapping-main.htm. Accessed on April 19, 2003. In this fact sheet, a British group opposed to the fur trade rebuts arguments frequently given to support trapping of furbearers.

"Report to Congress on the Recovery Program for Threatened and Endangered Species, 1996." U.S. Fish and Wildlife Service. Available online. URL: http://endangered.fws.gov/recovery/report_to_congress.html. Posted in 1996. States that in 1995 and 1996 the U.S. Fish and Wildlife Service "held the line" for endangered and threatened species in spite of a greatly increased workload. Summarizes efforts to preserve and improve the lot of endangered species and develop cooperative programs with landowners. Claims that increased funding will be needed to realize the full potential of the Endangered Species Act.

"Saving Biodiversity: A Status Report on State Laws." University of New Mexico Center for Wildlife Law. Available online. URL: http://ipl.unm.edu/cwl/statbio/intro.html. Posted in 1996. Written by the Center for Wildlife Law and Defenders of Wildlife, this report summarizes state laws, policies, and programs that affect protection of biodiversity. Surveys 10 major categories of state laws and programs.

Senatore, Michael P., and Keiran Suckling. "Safeguarding Citizen Rights under the Endangered Species Act." Center for Biological Diversity. Available online. URL: http://www.sw-center.org/swcbd/Programs/science/ESAreport.pdf. Posted in May 2001. Report by the Defenders of Wildlife, Center for Biological Diversity, and the Endangered Species Coalition describes reasons for opposing a proposed rider to the 2002 Department of the Interior appropriations bill that would greatly limit individual citizens' ability to petition to have species listed as endangered or threatened and thereby protected by the Endangered Species Act.

"Strategic Vision through 2005." Convention on International Trade in Endangered Species of Wild Fauna and Flora. Available online. URL:

http://www.cites.org/eng/news/English%20strategies.pdf. Accessed on April 18, 2003. The plan adopted at the treaty parties' 11th meeting describes what the convention's goals should be between 2000 and 2005.

Wijnstekers, Willem. "The Evolution of CITES." Convention on International Trade in Endangered Species of Wild Fauna and Flora. Available online. URL: http://www.cites.org/common/docs/Evol_2001.pdf. Posted in 2001. Lists and explains the provisions of the convention and relevant later resolutions and decisions, showing how the convention is implemented.

CHAPTER 8

ORGANIZATIONS AND AGENCIES

Many organizations and groups handle various aspects of animal protectionism and uses of animals. The following entries include general-purpose animal welfare and animal rights organizations and also organizations related to animals and animal use in particular areas: companion animals, animals in agriculture, animals in science, animals in entertainment, and wildlife. These latter organizations, which include advocacy groups, trade organizations, and government agencies, may favor or oppose animal use to varying degrees or hold a neutral position on the subject. Most organizations described in this chapter are located in the United States, but some groups in Britain, Canada, and other countries are also listed. In keeping with the widespread use of the Internet and e-mail, the web site address (URL) and e-mail address of each organization are given first (when available), followed by the phone number, postal address, and a brief description of the organization's work or position. When calling an organization in another country, please locate and use the appropriate country code, which is not included. These codes may vary depending on which country one is calling from.

GENERAL-PURPOSE ANIMAL ORGANIZATIONS

Advocates for Animals
URL: http://www.
    advocatesforanimals.org.uk
E-mail: info@
    advocatesforanimals.org
Phone: (0) 131-225-6039
10 Queensferry Street
Edinburgh EH2 4PG, Scotland

Moderate animal rights group that encourages rational discussion by people on both sides of issues such as the use of animals in research.

American Society for the Prevention of Cruelty to Animals
URL: http://www.aspca.org/site/
    PageServer
E-mail: information@aspca.org
Phone: (212) 876-7700
424 East 92nd Street
New York, NY 10128-6804

Exists to promote humane principles, prevent cruelty, and alleviate fear, pain, and suffering in animals. Protests cruelty to animals in entertainment and distributes educational materials on treatment of companion animals.

Animal Aid
URL: http://www.animalaid.
  org.uk
E-mail: info@animalaid.org.uk
Phone: (0) 173-236-4546
The Old Chapel
Bradford Street
Tonbridge, Kent TN9 1AW, UK
Britain's largest animal rights group. Campaigns against all forms of animal abuse, including factory farming, vivisection, and hunting, and promotes a cruelty-free lifestyle.

Animal Alliance of Canada
URL: http://www.
  animalalliance.ca
E-mail: info@animalalliance.ca
Phone: (416) 462-9541
221 Broadview Avenue
Suite 101
Toronto, Ontario
Canada M4M 2G3
Organization of professionals in animal protection. Works on local, national, and international educational and legislative advocacy initiatives to protect animals and the environment. Opposes killing, eating, wearing, experimenting on, and exploiting animals.

Animal Legal Defense Fund
URL: http://www.aldf.org
E-mail: info@aldf.org
Phone: (707) 769-7771
127 Fourth Street
Petaluma, CA 94952-3005
Uses litigation and legal advocacy both to defend the interests of particular animals or groups of animals and to reform the field of animal law. Particular aims are to ensure that anticruelty statutes are enforced and strengthened and to end animals' legal status as property.

Animal Liberation Front
URL: http://www.
  animalliberationfront.com
E-mail: an246614@anon.penet.fi
NAALFSG
P.O. Box 69597
5845 Yonge Street
Willowdale, Ontario
Canada M2M 4K3
Carries out direct action against those it classifies as animal abusers, including rescuing animals and destroying property. Advocates illegal (but nonviolent) actions when necessary to force exploitative companies out of business. Consists of small, autonomous, anonymous groups worldwide.

Animal Protection Institute
URL: http://www.api4animals.org
E-mail: info@api4animals.org
Phone: (916) 447-3085
1122 S Street
Sacramento, CA 95814
P.O. Box 22505
Sacramento, CA 95822
Campaigns for protection of wildlife, companion animals, and ani-

mals in agriculture, entertainment, science, and education.

Animals Australia
URL: http://www.
  animalsaustralia.org/home.htm
E-mail: enquiries@
  animalsaustralia.org
Phone: (613) 9329-6333
37 O'Connell Street
North Melbourne
Melbourne, Victoria, Australia
  3051
The Australian arm of the Australian and New Zealand Federation of Animal Societies, Inc. (ANZFAS). It presents the point of view of approximately 40 animal protection groups in Australia and New Zealand on a variety of animal welfare issues to government, the media, animal users, and the general public.

Animal Welfare Institute
URL: http://www.awionline.org
Phone: (703) 836-4300
E-mail: awi@awionline.org
P.O. Box 3650
Washington, DC 20027
Does not oppose human uses of animals but works to see that those uses are carried out in ways that cause as little pain and fear to the animals as possible. Issues include animals in science, endangered species and trade in wildlife, and animals in agriculture.

Canadian Federation of
  Humane Societies
URL: http://www.cfhs.ca

E-mail: info@cfhs.ca
Phone: (613) 224-8072
102-30 Concourse Gate
Nepean, Ontario
Canada K2E 7V7
National voice on animal welfare issues that represents more than 100 member societies. Works to end suffering of companion animals, wildlife, and animals in entertainment, farming, and research.

Doris Day Animal League
URL: http://www.ddal.org
E-mail: info@ddal.org
Phone: (202) 546-1761
227 Massachusetts Avenue, NE
Suite 100
Washington, DC 20002
Lobbying organization that urges legislators to pass laws that reduce the suffering of animals. Supports legal rights for chimpanzees, spay/neuter pet campaigns, and blocking puppy mills.

Eurogroup for Animal Welfare
URL: http://www.
  eurogroupanimalwelfare.org
E-mail: info@
  eurogroupanimalwelfare.org
Phone: (2) 740-0820
6 rue des Patriotes
1000 Brussels, Belgium
Aims to influence and promote introduction, implementation, and enforcement of animal protection legislation in the European Union.

Friends of Animals
URL: http://www.
  friendsofanimals.org

E-mail: info@
friendsofanimals.org
Phone: (203) 656-1522
777 Post Road
Darien, CT 06820
Works to preserve animals and
their habitats around the world
and protect them from abuse and
institutionalized exploitation. Campaign issues include spay/neuter,
antifur, antihunting, vegetarianism, wildlife protection, and circus
animals.

**Great Ape Project
International**
URL: http://www.
greatapeproject.org
E-mail: gap@greatapeproject.org
Phone: (503) 222-5755
917 SW Oak Street
Suite 412
Portland, OR 97205
Seeks to locate, identify, and tell the
stories of individual nonhuman
great apes. Works to extend legal
rights to great apes.

**The Humane Society
of the United States**
URL: http://www.hsus.org/ace/
352
Phone: (202) 452-1100
2100 L Street, NW
Washington, DC 20037
Encourages a strong human-animal
bond but wants human relationships with animals to be guided by
compassion. Issues of interest include pets, wildlife, animals in research, farm animals, animals in
circuses, the fur trade, and the con-

nection between animal abuse and
human violence.

**Humane USA Political Action
Committee**
URL: http://www.humaneusa.org
E-mail: humaneusa@humaneusa.
org
Phone: (703) 847-0075
P.O. Box 19224
Washington, DC 20036
Nation's first major political action
committee devoted to election of hu-
mane-minded candidates at federal
and state levels. Represents numer-
ous animal protection organizations.
Issues of concern include treatment
of companion animals, farm animals,
and wildlife.

In Defense of Animals
URL: http://www.idausa.org/
index.shtml
E-mail: ida@idausa.org
Phone: (415) 388-9641
131 Camino Alto
Suite E
Mill Valley, CA 94941
Campaign issues include animals in
sport, animals in experimentation,
dissection, circuses, marine mam-
mals, and puppy mills.

**Institute for Animals
and Society**
URL: http://www.
animalsandsociety.org
E-mail: Kim.stallwood@
animalsandsociety.org
Phone: (410) 675-4566
Animal Rights Network, Inc.
3500 Boston Street

Suite 325
Baltimore, MD 21224
Published *The Animals' Agenda*, a bimonthly news magazine of the animal rights movement. The magazine began in 1979 and ended with the March/April 2002 issue. The group is now a "think tank" that focuses on institutional change.

The International Institute for Animal Law
URL: http://www.
  animallawintl.org
E-mail: IIAL@AnimalLawIntl.
  org
Phone: (312) 917-8850
30 North LaSalle Street
Suite 2900
Chicago, IL 60602
Encourages development of legal scholarship and advocacy skills on behalf of animals internationally. Works to enhance development of laws that promote animal welfare, particularly regarding companion animals and animals in laboratories.

Jane Goodall Institute
URL: http://www.janegoodall.org
Phone: (301) 565-0086
8700 Georgia Avenue
Suite 500
Silver Spring, MD 20910-3605
Educates people to improve the environment of all living things. Issues of concern include primate habitat conservation, promoting the welfare of chimpanzees and other primates, and encouragement of noninvasive research programs on primates.

National Animal Interest Alliance
URL: http://www.naiaonline.org
E-mail:
  president@naiaonline.org
Phone: (503) 761-1139
P.O. Box 66579
Portland, OR 97290-6579
Association of business, agricultural, scientific, and recreational interests working to present a moderate alternative to animal rights groups and correct animal rights misinformation.

National Center for Animal Law
URL: http://www.lclark.edu/org/
  ncal
E-mail: ncal@lclark.edu
Phone: (503) 768-6849
Lewis and Clark Law School
10015 Southwest Terwilliger
  Boulevard
Portland, OR 97219
Promotes legal education for animal advocacy, furthers the field of animal law, and promotes animal rights.

People for the Ethical Treatment of Animals
URL: http://www.peta.org
E-mail: info@peta.org
Phone: (757) 622-7382
501 Front Street
Norfolk, VA 23510
Believes that animals are not for humans to eat, wear, experiment on, or use for entertainment. Conducts numerous campaigns to educate policy makers and the public about animal abuse.

Royal Society for the Prevention of Cruelty to Animals
URL: http://www.rspca.org.uk
Phone: 0870-333-5999
Wilberforce Way
Southwater, Horsham
West Sussex RH13 9RS, UK
Animal protection organization devoted to preventing cruelty to animals, promoting kindness, and finding new homes for abandoned animals. Consults on treatment of farm animals, animals in research, pets, and wildlife.

Society for Animal Protective Legislation
URL: http://www.saplonline.org
E-mail: sapl@saplonline.org
Phone: (703) 836-4300
P.O. Box 3719
Washington, DC 20027
Lobbying organization that works for passage of federal laws to protect animals.

Universities Federation for Animal Welfare
URL: http://www.ufaw.org.uk
E-mail: ufaw@ufaw.org.uk
Phone: (0) 158-283-1818
The Old School
Brewhouse Hill
Wheathampstead
Hertfordshire AL4 8AN, UK
Provides scientific and technical expertise to help others improve the welfare of companion animals, wildlife, and animals in zoos, laboratories, and farms.

U.S. Department of Agriculture Agricultural Research Service
URL: http://www.nps.ars.usda.gov
Animal Welfare Information Center (part of ARS)
URL: http://www.nal.usda.gov/awic
E-mail: awic@nal.usda.gov
Phone: (301) 504-6212
Animal Welfare Information Center
U.S. Department of Agriculture
Agricultural Research Service
National Agricultural Library
10301 Baltimore Avenue
Fourth Floor
Beltsville, MD 20705-2351
The Animal Welfare Information Center provides information for improved animal care and use in science, agriculture, and entertainment. The Agricultural Research Service has programs related to food animal health and welfare.

U.S. Department of Agriculture Animal and Plant Health Inspection Service (APHIS)
URL: http://www.aphis.usda.gov/ac
E-mail: ace@ aphis.usda.gov
1400 Independence Avenue, Southwest
Washington, DC 20250
APHIS is the agency of the U.S. Department of Agriculture that administers and enforces the Animal Welfare Act and the Twenty-eight-Hour Law. This is its chief animal care site, which contains numerous resources.

World Animal Foundation
URL: http://www.
worldanimalfoundation.com
E-mail: customerservice@
worldanimalfoundation.com
Phone: (530) 685-6826
P.O. Box 30762
Middleburg Heights, OH 44130
Works for wildlife and habitat preservation and animals rights issues worldwide. Activities include education, research, investigations, animal rescue, legislation, events and media campaigns, and direct action.

World Animal Net
URL: http://www.
worldanimal.net
E-mail: info@worldanimal.net
Phone: (617) 524-3670
19 Chestnut Square
Boston, MA 02130
World's largest network of animal protection societies, with more than 2,000 affiliates in more than 100 countries. Acts as information clearinghouse and coordinator to increase impact of animal protection campaigns and lobbying.

COMPANION ANIMALS

Alley Cat Allies
URL: http://www.alleycat.org
Phone: (202) 667-3630
1801 Belmont Road NW
Suite 201
Washington, DC 20009-5147
Clearinghouse for information on feral and stray cats. Supports reducing feral cat population by trapping, neutering, and then returning feral cats to their colonies.

American Kennel Club
URL: http://www.akc.org
Phone: (212) 696-8200
260 Madison Avenue
New York, NY 10016
Registers purebred dogs and helps people choose a breed and breeder and become responsible dog owners. Opposes legislation that limits dog breeders.

American Partnership for Pets
URL: http://www.
americanpartnershipforpets.org
E-mail: info@
americanpartnershipforpets.org
Prevent-a-Litter Coalition, Inc.
P.O. Box 9294
Reston, VA 20195
Coalition of animal, veterinarian, and fancier organizations that supports spay/neuter programs to prevent unwanted and homeless pets.

American Sanctuary Association
URL: http://www.
asaanimalsanctuaries.org
E-mail: ASARescue@aol.com
Phone: (702) 804-8562
2340 Sterling Heights
Las Vegas, NV 89134
Information center, accreditation establishment, and organizational network for organizations that provide sanctuaries for homeless wild

and domestic animals. Also helps people locate quality facilities in which to place animals.

National Animal Control Association
URL: http://www.nacanet.org
E-mail: naca@interserv.com
Phone: (913) 768-1319
P.O. Box 480851
Kansas City, MO 64148
Professional association for animal control personnel. Provides training programs, a voluntary certification program for animal control facilities, and education to promote responsible animal ownership.

National Council on Pet Population Study and Policy
URL: http://www.
petpopulation.org
E-mail: ncppsp@aol.com
Sally Fekety, Public Information Consultant
P.O. Box 131488
Ann Arbor, MI 48113-1488
Gathers and analyzes reliable data to determine the number, disposition, and origin of pet cats and dogs in the United States and uses this information to encourage responsible stewardship of these animals and recommend methods of reducing the number of unwanted pets.

ANIMALS IN AGRICULTURE

American Meat Institute
URL: http://www.meatami.com
Phone: (703) 841-2400
1700 North Moore Street
Suite 1600
Arlington, VA 22209
Oldest and largest U.S. meat and poultry trade association. Web site includes material on meat animal welfare.

Animal Agriculture Alliance
URL: http://www.
animalagalliance.org
E-mail:
info@animalagalliance.org
Phone: (703) 562-5160
P.O. Box 9522
Arlington, VA 22209
Formerly Animal Industry Foundation. Works to provide positive information about animal agriculture to the media and consumers.

Coalition to Abolish the Fur Trade
URL: http://www.caft.org.uk
E-mail: caft@caft.org.uk
Phone: (0) 845-330-7955
P.O. Box 38
Manchester M60 1NX, UK
Uses investigations, educational and political campaigns, and demonstrations to oppose fur farming and the fur trade in Britain and worldwide.

Compassion in World Farming
URL: http://www.ciwf.co.uk
E-mail: compassion@ciwf.co.uk
Phone: (0) 173-026-4208
Charles House
5A Charles Street
Petersfield
Hampshire GU32 3EH, UK

Campaigns for welfare of animals in intensive farming through peaceful protest, lobbying, and education, including scientific reports.

Compassion over Killing
URL: http://www.cok.net
E-mail: info@cok.net
Phone: (301) 891-2458
P.O. Box 9773
Washington, DC 20016
Focuses primarily on cruelty to animals in agriculture and promotes a vegetarian diet as an alternative to eating animals, but also opposes using animals for fur, circus entertainment, and so on.

Council for Agricultural Science and Technology
URL: http://www.cast-science.org/cast/src/cast_top.htm
E-mail: cast@cast-science.org
Phone: (515) 292-2125
4420 West Lincoln Way
Ames, IA 50014-3447
Assembles, interprets, and communicates science-based information on agricultural and related issues to policy makers, the media, and the public. Composed of scientific societies and individuals.

Farm Animal Welfare Council
URL: http://www.fawc.org.uk
Phone: (0) 207-904-6534
1A Page Street
Fifth Floor
London SW1P 4PQ, UK
Independent advisory body established by the British government in 1979 to keep under review the welfare of farm animals throughout their lives and advise the government of any legislative or other changes that may be necessary.

Farm Animal Welfare Network
URL: www.fawn.me.uk
Fax: 014-846-9408
P.O. Box 40
Holmfirth
HD9 3YY, UK
Opposes cruelty to animals imposed by intensive ("factory") farming.

Farm Sanctuary
URL: http://www.farmsanctuary.org
E-mail: info@farmsanctuary.org
Phone: (607) 583-2225
P.O. Box 150
Watkins Glen, NY 14891
Runs shelters for abused farm animals and campaigns to stop animal cruelty on farms and promote a vegan lifestyle.

Food Marketing Institute
URL: http://www.fmi.org
E-mail: fmi@fmi.org
Phone: (202) 452-8444
655 15th Street, NW
Washington, DC 20005
Conducts programs in research, education, industry relations, and public affairs on behalf of its member companies, which are food retailers and wholesalers throughout the world.

Fur Commission USA
URL: http://www.furcommission.com

E-mail: furfarmers@aol.com
Phone: (619) 575-0139
Teresa Platt, Executive
 Director
PMB 506
826 Orange Avenue
Coronado, CA 92118-2698
Represents fur farmers in the United States. Certifies farmers who follow superior standards of animal husbandry and educates the public about responsible fur farming and the merits of fur.

Humane Farming Association
URL: http://www.hfa.org
E-mail: hfa@hfa.org
P.O. Box 3577
San Rafael, CA 94912
Phone: (415) 771-2253
Aims to protect farm animals from cruelty, humans from dangerous chemicals fed to farm animals, and the environment from pollution by intensive farming. Carries out investigations, exposés, media campaigns, rescues, and lobbying.

Institute for Animal Health
URL: http://www.iah.bbsrc.
 ac.uk
E-mail:
 animal.health@bbsrc.ac.uk
Phone: (0) 163-557-8411
Compton Laboratory
Compton, Newbury
Berkshire RG20 7NN, UK
Government-sponsored group dedicated to improving the health and welfare of farm animals and improving the efficiency and sustainability of livestock farming.

National Cattlemen's
 Beef Association
URL: http://hill.beef.org/
 default.asp
Phone: (202) 347-0228
1301 Pennsylvania Avenue, NW
Suite 300
Washington, DC 20004-1701
Works to preserve and enhance the business and market climate for cattle producers by managing public policy issues, including attacks by animal rightists.

National Dairy Council
URL: http://www.
 nationaldairycouncil.org
E-mail: ndc@dairyinformation.
 com
10255 West Higgins Road
Suite 900
Rosemont, IL 60018
Carries out dairy nutrition research, education, and communication; makes scientifically sound nutrition information available to media, physicians, consumers, children, and others. Promotes dairy products as part of a healthy lifestyle.

National Farmers' Union
URL: http://www.nfu.org.uk
E-mail: NFU@nfuonline.com
Phone: 207-331-7200
Agriculture House
164 Shaftesbury Avenue
London WC2H 8HL, UK
Trade organization representing farmers in England and Wales. Encourages environmentally friendly and welfare-conscious farming practices and works to ensure sur-

vival of rural communities. Works with animal welfare, environmental, and consumer groups.

National Institute for Animal Agriculture
URL: http://www.
animalagriculture.org
E-mail: NIAA@
animalagriculture.org
Phone: (270) 782-9798
1910 Lyda Avenue
Bowling Green, KY 42104
Aims to be the forum for building consensus and advancing solutions for animal agriculture and to provide continuing education to animal agriculture professionals. Works to eradicate disease, promote a safe food supply, and promote good practices in agricultural animal health and environmental stewardship.

National Pork Producers Council
URL: http://www.nppc.org
E-mail: flynnk@nppc.org
Phone: (515) 278-8012
7733 Douglas Avenue
Urbandale, IA 50322
Conducts public policy outreach to aid its members' business interests and build the industry's image. Works for passage and implementation of laws and regulations conducive to production and sale of pork.

United Egg Producers
URL: http://www.unitedegg.
com
E-mail: info@unitedegg.com

Phone: (770) 587-5871
1303 Hightower Trail
Suite 200
Atlanta, GA 30350
Provides services to the egg industry including government relations, market information, and quality assurance programs for animal well-being, environmental protection, and food safety.

United Poultry Concerns, Inc.
URL: http://www.upc-online.
org
E-mail: info@upc-online.org
Phone: (757) 678-7875
P.O. Box 150
Machipongo, VA 23405-0150
Addresses treatment of domestic fowl in all areas of human use, including food production and science. Actively promotes alternatives to use of poultry and educates consumers about abuses. Opposes such practices as forced molting and hatching of chicks in classrooms.

U.S. Department of Agriculture Food Safety and Inspection Service
URL: http://www.fsis.usda.gov
Phone: (202) 720-9113
Washington, DC 20250-3700
The agency of the USDA responsible for inspecting slaughterhouses and enforcing the Humane Methods of Slaughter Act. It also inspects meat, poultry, and egg products to make sure that they are wholesome and packaged as required by law.

ANIMALS IN SCIENCE

**American Anti-Vivisection
  Society**
URL: http://www.aavs.org/home.
  html
E-mail: aavs@aavs.org
Phone: (800) 729-2287
801 Old York Road
#204
Jenkintown, PA 19046-1685
Dedicated to abolition of animal
use in science, which it opposes on
both scientific and ethical grounds.
Includes Alternatives Research and
Development Foundation.

**Americans for Medical
  Advancement**
URL: http://www.curedisease.
  com
E-mail: webmaster@
  curedisease.com
Phone: (310) 678-9076
8391 Beverly Boulevard
#153
Los Angeles, CA 90048
Claims that use of animals as dis-
ease models retards biomedical re-
search and risks human lives.

Americans for Medical Progress
URL: http://www.ampef.org
E-mail: info@amprogress.org
Phone: (703) 836-9595
908 King Street
Suite 301
Alexandria, VA 22314
Provides resources demonstrating
that biomedical research on ani-

mals is necessary and humane; opposes efforts to stop use of animals
in research.

The Boyd Group
URL: http://www.boyd-group.
  demon.co.uk
E-mail: mail@boyd-
  group.demon.co.uk
P.O. Box 423
Southsea P05 1TJ, UK
Forum for exchange of views on issues related to use of animals in science. Aims to promote dialogue
among diverse groups and recommend practical steps toward achieving common goals.

**British Union for the Abolition
  of Vivisection**
URL: http://www.buav.org/f_
  home.html
E-mail: info@buav.org
Phone: (0) 207-700-4888
16a Crane Grove
London N7 8NN, UK
Opposes all experimentation on animals and seeks alternatives to use
of animals in research. European
Coalition to End Animal Experiments is an affiliated organization
at the same address.

**European Biomedical Research
  Association**
URL: http://www.ebra.org
E-mail: secretariat@ebra.org
58 Great Marlborough Street
London W1F 7JY, UK
Association of Europeans in scien-
tific, medical, and veterinary pro-

fessions. Promotes use of animals in medical and veterinary research and safety testing and works to counter the claims of antivivisection groups.

European Centre for the
Validation of Alternative
Methods
URL: http://ecvam.jrc.it/index.htm
Phone: 0332-789111
E.C.-Joint Research Centre
via E. Fermi 1
I-21020 Ispra (VA), Italy
Organization created by the European Union to coordinate information on alternatives to scientific tests that use animals and to validate such tests.

Federation of American Societies
for Experimental Biology
URL: http://www.faseb.org
E-mail: webmaster@faseb.org
Phone: (301) 634-7000
9650 Rockville Pike
Bethesda, MD 20814-3998
Promotes the interests of biomedical scientists and disseminates information on biological research. Supports appropriate use of animals in research.

Fund for the Replacement
of Animals in Medical
Experiments
URL: http://www.frame.org.uk
E-mail: frame@frame.org.uk
Phone: (0) 115-958-4740
Russell & Burch House

96-98 North Sherwood Street
Nottingham NG1 4EE, UK
Works to reduce the use of animals in research and develop and validate alternatives to animal tests but recognizes that immediate and total abolition of all animal experiments is not possible if vital medical research is to continue.

Incurably Ill for Animal
Research
URL: http://www.iifar.org
E-mail: info@iifar.org
Phone: (517) 887-1550
P.O. Box 27454
Lansing, MI 48909
Strongly supports continued use of animals in biomedical research, teaching, and testing.

Institute for Laboratory Animal
Research
URL: http://dels.nas.edu/ilar
E-mail: ilar@nas.edu
Phone: (202) 334-2590
The Keck Center of the
National Academies
500 Fifth Street, NW, Keck 687
Washington, DC 20001
Serves as a clearinghouse for scientific and technical information about the use and care of laboratory animals. Supports the use of animals in research.

Interagency Coordinating
Committee on the Validation
of Alternative Methods
URL: http://iccvam.niehs.nih.gov

E-mail: NICEATM@
niehs.nih.gov
Phone: (919) 541-3398
NICEATM/NIEHS
79 Alexander Drive
Mail Drop EC-17
Research Triangle Park, NC
27709
Agency sponsored by the U.S. federal government to coordinate development, validation, and acceptance of toxicological test methods that do not use animals and are more accurate than present methods.

**Johns Hopkins University
Center for Alternatives
to Animal Testing**
URL: http://caat.jhsph.edu
E-mail: caat@jhsph.edu
Phone: (443) 287-7277
Johns Hopkins University
Bloomberg School of Public
Health
615 North Wolfe Street
Baltimore, MD 21205-2179
Seeks new methods to replace, reduce, and refine use of animals in laboratory experiments.

**National Anti-Vivisection
Society**
URL: http://www.navs.org
E-mail: feedback@navs.org
Phone: (800) 888-6287
53 West Jackson Boulevard,
Suite 1552
Chicago, IL 60604
Dedicated to abolishing use of animals in research, education, and product testing. Believes that such

research is scientifically invalid as well as cruel.

**National Association for
Biomedical Research**
URL: http://www.nabr.org
E-mail: info@nabr.org
Phone: (202) 857-0540
818 Connecticut Avenue, NW
Suite 200
Washington, DC 20006
Advocates public policy that supports humane use of animals in biomedical research, education, and product testing. Connected with the Foundation for Biomedical Research.

**National Institutes of Health
Office of Laboratory Animal
Welfare**
URL: http://grants.nih.gov/
grants/olaw/olaw.htm
E-mail: olaw@od.nih.gov
Phone: (301) 496-7163
National Institutes of Health
RKL1, Suite 360, MSC 7982
6705 Rockledge Drive
Bethesda, MD 20892-7982
Develops, monitors, and enforces compliance with Public Health Service Policy on Humane Care and Use of Laboratory Animals and related regulations in research conducted or supported by any component of the Public Health Service.

**New England Anti-Vivisection
Society**
URL: http://www.neavs.org

E-mail: info@neavs.com
Phone: (617) 523-6020
333 Washington Street
Suite 850
Boston, MA 02108-5100
Opposes use of animals in research, education, and testing and seeks alternative methods. Uses education, lobbying, and litigation to support these aims.

Physicians Committee
for Responsible Medicine
URL: http://www.pcrm.org
E-mail: pcrm@pcrm.org
Phone: (202) 686-2210
5100 Wisconsin Avenue, NW
Suite 400
Washington, DC 20016
Opposes most use of animals in science and promotes nonanimal alternatives in research and education.

Research Defence Society
URL: http://www.rds-online.
  org. uk
E-mail: info@rds-online.org.uk
Phone: (0) 207-287-2818
25 Shaftesbury Avenue
London W1F 7EG, UK
Represents and supports biomedical researchers and appropriate use of animals in science. Provides information about the need for animal research to media, government, and the public and promotes best practice in laboratory animal welfare.

Scientists Center
for Animal Welfare
URL: http://www.scaw.com

E-mail: info@scaw.com
Phone: (301) 345-3500
7833 Walker Drive
Suite 410
Greenbelt, MD 20770
Supports use of animals in science; provides scientific information about and promotes humane treatment and care of laboratory animals through conferences, seminars, and publications.

ANIMALS IN ENTERTAINMENT

American Horse Council
URL: http://www.horsecouncil.
  org/ahc.html
E-mail: ahc@horsecouncil.org
Phone: (202) 296-4031
1616 H Street, NW
Seventh Floor
Washington, DC 20006
National trade association of the horse industry. Represents interests of owners, breeders, and others involved with horses in shows, races, rodeos, and the like to legislators and regulatory agencies.

American Zoo and Aquarium
Association
URL: http://www.aza.org
E-mail: generalinquiry@aza.org
Phone: (301) 562-0777
8403 Colesville Road
Suite 710
Silver Spring, MD 20910-3314
Dedicated to advancement of zoos and aquariums in conservation,

education, science, and recreation. Accredits zoos and aquariums that follow organizational guidelines to maintain high standards. Coordinates members' captive animal and field-based projects.

Equine Protection Network
URL: http://members.tripod.
   com/~EPN/legislation/memo.
   htm
Phone: (570) 345-6440
P.O. Box 232
Friedensburg, PA 17933
Rescues and provides sanctuaries for abused and neglected horses; provides education and information about horse welfare and the equine industry.

Greyhound Protection League
URL: http://www.greyhounds.org
Phone: (800) 446-8637
P.O. Box 669
Penn Valley, CA 95946
Protects greyhounds from the abuses it sees as inherent in the greyhound racing industry and works to help the public see greyhound racing as cruel.

National Greyhound
   Association
URL: http://www.
   ngagreyhounds.com
E-mail: nga@ngagreyhounds.com
Phone: (785) 263-4660
P.O. Box 543
Abilene, KS 67410
Official registry of racing greyhounds and association of greyhound racing.

National Thoroughbred Racing
   Association
URL: http://www.ntra.com
E-mail: ntra@ntra.com
Phone: (212) 907-9280
800 Third Avenue
Suite 1901
New York, NY 10022
Governs and provides information about horse racing. Also provides information about horse ownership and has an adoption referral program for retired racehorses.

Outdoor Amusement Business
   Association Circus Unit
URL: http://www.oaba.org/
   circus.htm
E-mail: oabacircus@aol.com
Phone: (800) 517-6222
1035 South Semoran Boulevard
Suite 1045A
Winter Park, FL 32792
Represents and advances the interests of the outdoor amusement industry. The circus unit represents circuses, animal exhibits, and animal shows. Works toward preservation of endangered species to which many circus animals belong and encourages shows to increase public awareness of these species' plight. Stresses responsible animal care and training methods.

Performing Animal Welfare
   Society
URL: http://www.pawsweb.org
E-mail: info@pawsweb.org
Phone: (209) 745-2606
P.O. Box 849
Galt, CA 95632

Investigates, rescues, and provides sanctuaries for abandoned or abused performing animals and victims of the exotic animal trade. Works for legislation that will ban ownership of wild animals, restrict their breeding, and ban painful discipline techniques.

Professional Rodeo Cowboys Association
URL: http://prorodeo.org
Phone: (719) 528-4747
101 ProRodeo Drive
Colorado Springs, CO 80919
Chief trade organization governing rodeo standards and personnel.

Thoroughbred Adoption and Retirement Association, Inc.
URL: http://www.taragroups. org/tt2_001.htm
Phone: (859) 865-4577
P.O. Box 81
Lawrenceburg, KY 40342
Assists and accredits groups that rehabilitate and place ex-racehorses. Serves as liaison to racing industry to make it easier to donate or sponsor retired thoroughbreds.

World Association of Zoos and Aquariums
URL: http://www.waza.org
E-mail: secretariat@waza.org
P.O. Box 23
CH-3097 Liebefeld-Bern, Switzerland
Umbrella organization for the world zoo and aquarium community. Guides and supports member organizations' animal welfare, environmental education, and global conservation programs.

ANIMALS IN THE WILD

Animals Asia Foundation
URL: http://www.animalsasia. org
E-mail: info@animalsasia.org
Phone: (888) 420-2327
PMB 506
584 Castro Street
San Francisco, CA 94114-2594
Headquartered in Hong Kong, this group works to improve the lives of all animals in Asia. One of their chief concerns is bears farmed for body parts used in Asian medicine.

Audubon Society
URL: http://www.audubon.org
E-mail: education@audubon. org
Phone: (212) 979-3000
700 Broadway
New York, NY 10003
Dedicated to protecting birds and other wildlife and their habitat. Supports nature centers, environmental education programs, and preservation of areas sustaining important bird populations.

Born Free Foundation
URL: http://www.bornfree. org.uk
E-mail: info@bornfree.org.uk

233

Phone: (0) 140-324-0170
3 Grove House
Foundry Lane
Horsham
West Sussex RH13 5PL, UK
International wildlife charity working to phase out traditional zoos and conserve rare species in their natural habitats.

Center for Biological Diversity
URL: http://www.sw-center.org/swcbd
E-mail: center@biologicaldiversity.org
Phone: (520) 623-5252
P.O. Box 710
Tucson, AZ 85702-0710
Combines conservation biology with litigation, political advocacy, and strategic vision to aid plants and animals on the brink of extinction and preserve their habitats.

Center for Wildlife Law
URL: http://ipl.unm.edu/cwl
E-mail: pnathan@unm.edu
Phone: (505) 277-5006
University of New Mexico School of Law
Institute of Public Law
1117 Stanford NE
Albuquerque, NM 87131
Provides research and analysis, education and training, and policy development related to laws affecting wildlife.

Coalition Against Duck Shooting
URL: http://www.duck.org.au
E-mail: info@duck.org.au

Phone: (03) 9826-9715
22c Napier Street
South Melbourne
Victoria 3205, Australia
Opposes duck shooting and rescues and rehabilitates ducks injured by hunters.

Convention on International Trade in Endangered Species of Wild Fauna and Flora
URL: http://www.cites.org
E-mail: cites@unep.ch
Phone: (22) 917-8139
CITES Secretariat
International Environment House
Chemin des Anémones
CH-1219 Châtelaine, Geneva, Switzerland
Organization that implements international treaty limiting trade in endangered species worldwide. Website contains materials describing the convention and how it works, including a database of endangered species and import limits.

Countryside Action Network
URL: http://www.countrysideaction.net
E-mail: info@countrysideaction.net
Phone: (0) 129-165-0962
P.O. Box 22
Usk NP15 1ZA, UK
Coordinates resistance to attempts to ban or restrict country pursuits, including hunting with hounds.

Defenders of Wildlife
URL: http://www.defenders.org

E-mail: info@defenders.org
Phone: (202) 682-9400
1130 17th Street, NW
Washington, DC 20030
Works to slow the accelerating rate of extinction, loss of biological diversity, and habitat alteration and destruction. Includes Endangered Species Coalition, which calls itself the "guardian of the Endangered Species Act."

Ducks Unlimited
URL: http://www.ducks.org
Phone: (800) 453-8257
One Waterfowl Way
Memphis, TN 38120
Duck hunters' organization. Conserves, restores, and manages wetlands and associated waterfowl habitats.

European Federation Against Hunting
URL: http://www.efah.net
E-mail: efah@mclink.it
Phone: (0) 655-286752
Via Angelo Bassini 6
00149 Roma, Italy
Federation of associations and individuals working to abolish hunting in developed countries. Does not oppose subsistence hunting in undeveloped countries.

Federation of Hunters Associations of the European Union
URL: http://bch-cbd.
naturalsciences.be/belgium/
services/face.htm
Phone: (0) 2-627-4343

Belgian National Focal Point to the Convention on Biological Diversity
Royal Belgian Institute of Natural Sciences
Vautier Street 29
1000 Brussels, Belgium
Federation of national hunters' associations in Europe. Works to promote responsible hunting and lobbies against legislation that bans or excessively regulates hunting.

The Fund for Animals
URL: http://www.fund.org/home
E-mail: fundinfo@fund.org
Phone: (212) 246-2096
200 West 57th Street
New York, NY 10019
Works to protect every individual wild animal, whether endangered or not, including members of so-called pest species, from suffering and death.

Hunt Saboteurs Association
URL: http://hsa.enviroweb.
org
E-mail: info@huntsabs.org.uk
Phone: (0) 845-450-0727
P.O. Box 5254
Northampton NN1 3ZA, UK
Works directly but nonviolently in the field to protect wildlife from hunters.

International Association of Fish and Wildlife Agencies
URL: http://www.iafwa.org
E-mail: iafwa@sso.org
Phone: (202) 624-7890

235

444 North Capitol Street, NW
Suite 544
Washington, DC 20001
Quasi-governmental organizaton of public agencies charged with protection and management of North America's fish and wildlife resources. Includes federal and state or province agencies in Canada, the United States, and Mexico. Promotes sound resource management and strengthens cooperation among federal, state, and private entities. Supports sustainable use of natural resources.

International Fund for Animal
Welfare
URL: http://www.ifaw.org
E-mail: info@ifaw.org
Phone: (508) 744-2000
411 Main Street
P.O. Box 193
Yarmouth Port, MA 02675
Mounts rescue and relief operations to help animals in distress; works with local communities to preserve wilderness habitat; promotes economically viable alternatives to commercial exploitation of wildlife; and supports animal sanctuaries worldwide. Advocates strong laws to protect animals.

International Primate
Protection League
URL: http://www.ippl.org
E-mail: info@ippl.org
Phone: (843) 871-2280
P.O. Box 766
Summerville, SC 29484
Works to protect primates in their natural habitats through creation of national parks and sanctuaries, as well as bans on primate hunting and trapping and local and international trade. Supports sanctuaries for primates rescued from poaching, laboratories, and other abusive situations.

International Wildlife Coalition
URL: http://www.iwc.org
E-mail: iwchq@iwc.org
Phone: (508) 548-8328
70 East Falmouth Highway
East Falmouth, MA 02536
Works to save endangered species, protect wild and domestic animals, and preserve habitat worldwide. Projects include rescuing whales and other marine mammals and fighting cruel conditions around the world.

Izaak Walton League
of America
URL: http://www.iwla.org
E-mail: general@iwla.org
Phone: (800) 453-5463
707 Conservation Lane
Gaithersburg, MD 20878
Works to protect wildlife and the environment. Supports hunting and fishing as well as nonconsumptive uses of wildlife such as outdoor photography.

League Against Cruel Sports
Ltd.
URL: http://www.league.uk.com
E-mail: info@league.uk.com
Phone: (0) 207-403-6155
Sparling House
83-87 Union Street
London SE1 1SG, UK

Investigates and exposes the abusive nature of hunting and works to ban it. Purchases land to establish sanctuaries for hunted wildlife.

National Trappers Association
URL: http://www.
nationaltrappers.com
E-mail: ntaheadquarters@
nationaltrappers.com
4111 East Starr Avenue
Nacogdoches, TX 75961
Protects and promotes the interests of trappers and promotes sound conservation and wildlife management to produce a continued annual fur harvest.

National Wildlife Federation
URL: http://www.nwf.org
Phone: (703) 438-6000
11100 Wildlife Center Drive
Reston, VA 20190-5362
Works for wildlife conservation and habitat protection worldwide and educates people about the need to conserve and protect the environment.

SCI (formerly Safari Club
  International)
URL: http://www.
  scifirstforhunters. org
Phone: (520) 620-1220
4800 West Gates Pass Road
Tucson, AZ 85745-9490
Advocate for hunters and wildlife conservation worldwide.

Sea Shepherd Conservation
  Society
URL: http://www.seashepherd.org

E-mail: info@seashepherd. org
Phone: (360) 370-5650
P.O. Box 2616
Friday Harbor, WA 98250
Works to halt illegal fishing activities and killing of marine mammals worldwide and uphold international treaties and laws through investigation and documentation of violations and, where legal, enforcement.

Showing Animals Respect
  and Kindness
URL: http://www.sharkonline.
  org
E-mail: info@sharkonline.org
Phone: (630) 557-0176
P.O. Box 28
Geneva, IL 60134
Works to stop hunting and the use of animals in entertainment; also conducts animal rescues and education projects.

U.S. Fish and Wildlife Service
Endangered Species Program
URL: http://endangered.fws.gov
E-mail: contact@fws.gov
Phone: (800) 344-9453
Website provides information about the program, news, and information about particular species.

U.S. Sportsmen's Alliance
URL: http://www.ussportsmen.
  org
E-mail: info@ussportsmen.org
Phone: (614) 888-4868
801 Kingsmill Parkway
Columbus, OH 43229

Formerly Wildlife Legislative Fund of America. Provides lobbying, legal defense, and grassroots support for hunters, fishers, trappers, and wildlife management professionals. Also sponsors education and research programs.

The Wildlife Society
URL: http://www.wildlife.org
E-mail: TWS@Wildlife.org
Phone: (301) 897-9770
5410 Grosvenor Lane
Suite 200
Bethesda, MD 20814-2144
Promotes continuing education of wildlife professionals and sustainable management and use of wildlife and habitat resources.

World Wildlife Fund
URL: http://www.
worldwildlife.org
Phone: (800) 225-5993
1250 24th Street, NW
P.O. Box 97180
Washington, DC 20090-7180
Works to protect the world's wildlife, especially endangered species such as the panda, and to establish and manage parks and reserves worldwide.

PART III

APPENDICES

APPENDIX A

ANIMAL WELFARE ACT, 1970

As Amended: 7 U.S.C. 2131-2156 [includes amendments passed in 1976, 1985, and 1990]

[Note: Some portions have been omitted.]

Section 1. (a) This Act may be cited as the **"Animal Welfare Act"**.

(b) The Congress finds that animals and activities which are regulated under this Act are either in interstate or foreign commerce or substantially affect such commerce or the free flow thereof, and that regulation of animals and activities as provided in this Act is necessary to prevent and eliminate burdens upon such commerce and to effectively regulate such commerce, in order —

1. to insure that animals intended for use in research facilities or for exhibition purposes or for use as pets are provided humane care and treatment;

2. to assure the humane treatment of animals during transportation in commerce; and

3. to protect the owners of animals from the theft of their animals by preventing the sale or use of animals which have been stolen.

The Congress further finds that it is essential to regulate, as provided in this Act, the transportation, purchase, sale, housing, care, handling, and treatment of animals by carriers or by persons or organizations engaged in using them for research or experimental purposes or for exhibition purposes or holding them for sale as pets or for any such purpose or use. The Congress further finds that —

1. the use of animals is instrumental in certain research and education for advancing knowledge of cures and treatment for diseases and injuries which afflict both humans and animals;

2. methods of testing that do not use animals are being and continue to be developed which are faster, less expensive, and more accurate than traditional animal experiments for some purposes and further opportunities exist for the development of these methods of testing;

3. measures which eliminate or minimize the unnecessary duplication of experiments on animals can result in more productive use of Federal funds; and

4. measures which help meet the public concern for laboratory animal care and treatment are important in assuring that research will continue to progress.

Section 2. When used in this Act —

(a) The term "Person" includes any individual, partnership, firm, joint stock company, corporation, association, trust, estate, or other legal entity;

(b) The term "Secretary" means the Secretary of Agriculture of the United States or his representative who shall be an employee of the United States Department of Agriculture;

(c) The term "commerce" means trade, traffic, transportation, or other commerce

(1) between a place in a State and any place outside of such State, or between points within the same State but through any place outside thereof, or within any territory, possession, or the District of Columbia;

(2) which affects trade, traffic, transportation, or other commerce described in paragraph (1),

(d) The term "State" means a State of the United States, the District of Columbia, the Commonwealth of Puerto Rico, the Virgin Islands, Guam, American Samoa, or any other territory or possession of the United States;

(e) The term "research facility" means any school (except an elementary or secondary school), institution, organization, or person that uses or intends to use live animals in research, tests, or experiments, and that (1) purchases or transports live animals in commerce, or (2) receives funds under a grant, award, loan, or contract from a department, agency, or instrumentality of the United States for the purpose of carrying out research, tests, or experiments: *Provided,* That the Secretary may exempt, by regulation, any such school, institution, organization, or person that does not use or intend to use live dogs or cats, except those schools, institutions, organizations, or persons, which use substantial numbers (as determined by the Secretary) or live animals the principal function of which schools, institutions, organizations, or persons, is biomedical research or testing, when in the judgment of the Secretary, any such exemption does not vitiate the purpose of this Act;

(f) The term "dealer" means any person who, in commerce, for compensation or profit, delivers for transportation, or transports, except as a carrier, buys, or sells, or negotiates the purchase or sale of, (1) any dog or other animal whether alive or dead for research, teaching, exhibition, or use as a pet, or (2) any dog for hunting, security, or breeding purposes, except that this term does not include

(i) a retail pet store except such store which sells any animals to a research facility, an exhibitor, or a dealer; or

(ii) any person who does not sell, or negotiate the purchase or sale or any wild animal, dog, or cat and who derives no more than $500 gross income from the sale of other animals during any calendar year;

(g) The term "animal" means any live or dead dog, cat, monkey (nonhuman primate mammal), guinea pig, hamster, rabbit, or such other warm-blooded animal, as the Secretary may determine is being used, or is intended for use, for research, testing, experimentation, or exhibition purposes or as a pet; but such term excludes horses not used for research purposes and other farm animals, such as, but not limited to livestock or poultry, used or intended for use as food or fiber, or livestock or poultry used or intended for improving animal nutrition, breeding, management or production efficiency, or for improving the quality of food or fiber. With respect to a dog the term means all dogs including those used for hunting, security, or breeding purposes;

(h) The term "exhibitor" means any person (public or private) exhibiting any animals, which were purchased in commerce or the intended distribution of which affects commerce, or will affect commerce, to the public for compensation, as determined by the Secretary, and such term includes carnivals, circuses, and zoos exhibiting such animals whether operated for profit or not; but such term excludes retail pet stores, organizations sponsoring and all persons participating in State and country fairs, livestock shows, rodeos, purebred dog and cat shows, and any other fairs or exhibitions intended to advance agricultural arts and sciences, as may be determined by the Secretary;

(i) The term "intermediate handler" means any person including a department, agency, or instrumentality of the United States or of any State or local government (other than a dealer, research facility, exhibitor, any person excluded from the definition of a dealer, research facility, or exhibitor, an operator of an auction sale, or a carrier) who is engaged in any business in which he receives custody of animals in connection with their transportation in commerce; and

(j) The term "carrier" means the operator of any airline, railroad, motor carrier, shipping line, or other enterprise, which is engaged in the business of transporting any animals for hire.

(k) The term "Federal agency" means an Executive agency as such term is defined in section 105 of Title 5, United States Code, and with respect to any research facility means the agency from which the research facility receives a Federal award for the conduct of research, experimentation, or testing, involving the use of animals;

(l) The term "Federal award for the conduct of research, experimentation, or testing, involving the use of animals" means any mechanism (including a grant, award, loan, contract, or cooperative agreement) under which Federal funds are provided to support the conduct of such research;

(m) The term "quorum" means a majority of the Committee members;

(n) The term "Committee" means the Institutional Animal Committee established under section 13(b); and

(o) The term "Federal research facility" means each department, agency, or instrumentality of the United States which uses live animals for research of experimentation.

Section 3. The Secretary shall issue licenses to dealers and exhibitors upon application therefore in such form and manner as he may prescribe and upon payment of such fee established pursuant to section 23 of this Act: *Provided,* That no such license shall be issued until the dealer or exhibitor shall have demonstrated that his facilities comply with the standards promulgated by the Secretary pursuant to section 13 of this Act: *Provided, however,* That any retail pet store or other person who derives less than a substantial portion of his income (as determined by the Secretary) from the breeding and raising of dogs or cats on his own premises and sells any such dog or cat to a dealer or research facility shall not be required to obtain a license as a dealer or exhibitor under this Act. The Secretary is further authorized to license, as dealers or exhibitors, persons who do not qualify as dealers or exhibitors within the meaning of this Act upon such persons complying with the requirements specified above and agreeing, in writing, to comply with all the requirements of this Act and the regulations promulgated by the Secretary hereunder.

Section 4. No dealer or exhibitor shall sell or offer to sell or transport or offer for transportation, in commerce, to any research facility or for exhibition or for use as a pet any animal, or buy, sell, offer to buy or sell, transport or offer for transportation, in commerce, to or from another dealer or exhibitor under this Act any animal, unless and until such dealer or exhibitor shall have obtained a license from the Secretary and such license shall not have been amended or revoked.

Section 5. No dealer or exhibitor shall sell or dispose of any dog or cat within a period of 5 business days after the acquisition of such animal or within such other period as way be specified by the Secretary: *Provided,* that operators of auction sales subject to section 12 of this Act shall not be required to comply with the provisions of this section.

Section 6. Every research facility, every intermediate handler, every carrier, and every exhibitor not licensed under section 3 of this Act shall register with the Secretary in accordance with such rules and regulations as he may prescribe.

Section 7. It shall be unlawful for any research facility to purchase any dog or cat from any person except an operator of an auction sale subject to section 12 of this Act or a person holding a valid license as a dealer or exhibitor issued by the Secretary pursuant to this Act unless such person is exempted from obtaining such license under section 3 of this Act....

* * *

Section 10. Dealers and exhibitors shall make and retain for such reasonable period of time as the Secretary may prescribe, such records with respect to the purchase, sale, transportation, identification, and previous ownership of animals as the Secretary may prescribe. Research facilities shall make and retain such records only with respect to the purchase, sale, transportation, identification, and previous ownership of live dogs and cats.

* * *

Section 13. (a) Promulgation of standards, rules, regulations, and orders; requirements; research facilities; State authority

(1) The Secretary shall promulgate standards to govern the humane handling, care, treatment, and transportation of animals by dealers, research facilities, and exhibitors.

(2) The standards described in paragraph (1) shall include minimum requirements —

(A) for handling, housing, feeding, watering, sanitation, ventilation, shelter from extremes of weather and temperatures, adequate veterinary care, and separation by species where the Secretary finds necessary for humane handling, care, or treatment of animals; and

(B) for exercise of dogs, as determined by an attending veterinarian in accordance with the general standards promulgated by the Secretary, and for a physical environment adequate to promote the psychological well-being of primates.

(3) In addition to the requirements under paragraph (2), the standards described in paragraph (1) shall, with respect to animals in research facilities, include requirements —

(A) for animal care, treatment, and practices in experimental procedures to ensure that animal pain and distress are minimized, including adequate veterinary care with the appropriate use of anesthetic, analgesic or tranquilizing drugs, or euthanasia;

(B) that the principal investigator considers alternatives to any procedure likely to produce pain or distress in an experimental animal;

(C) in any practice which could cause pain to animals —

(i) that a doctor of veterinary medicine is consulted in the planning of such procedures;

(ii) for the use of tranquilizers, analgesics, and anesthetics;

(iii) for presurgical and postsurgical care by laboratory workers in accordance with established veterinary medical and nursing procedures;

(iv) against the use of paralytics without anesthesia; and

(v) that the withholding of tranquilizers, anesthesia, analgesia, or euthanasia when scientifically necessary shall continue for only the necessary period of time;

(D) that no animal is used in more than one major operative experimenta from which it is allowed to recover except in cases of —

(i) scientific necessity; or

(ii) other special circumstances as determined by the Secretary; and

(E) that exceptions to such standards may be made only when specified by research protocol and that any such exception shall be detailed and explained in a report outlined under paragraph (7) and filed with the Institutional Animal Committee.

(4) The Secretary shall also promulgate standards to govern the transportation in commerce to govern the transportation in commerce, and the handling, care, and treatment in connection therewith, by intermediate handlers, air carriers, or other carriers, of animals consigned by a dealer, research facility, exhibitor, operator of an auction sale, or other person, or any department, agency, or instrumentality of the United States or of any State or local government, for transportation in commerce. The Secretary shall have authority to promulgate such rules and regulations as he determines necessary to assure humane treatment of animals in the course of their transportation in commerce including requirements such as those with respect to containers, feed, water, rest, ventilation, temperature, and handling.

(5) In promulgating and enforcing standards established pursuant to this section, the Secretary is authorized and directed to consult experts, including outside consultants where indicated.

(6) (A) Nothing in this Act —

(i) except as provided in paragraph (7) of this subsection, shall be construed as authorizing the Secretary to promulgate rules, regulations, or orders with regard to design, outlines, guidelines or performance of actual research or experimentation by a research facility as determined by such research facility;

(ii) except as provided in subparagraphs (A) and (C)(ii) through (v) of paragraph (3) and paragraph (7) of this subsection, shall be construed as authorizing the Secretary to promulgate rules, regulations, or orders with regard to the performance of actual research or experimentation by a research facility as determined by such research facility; and

(iii) shall authorize the Secretary, during inspection, to interrupt the conduct of actual research or experimentation.

(B) No rule, regulation, order, or part of this Act shall be construed to require a research facility to disclose publicly or to the Institutional Animal Committee during its inspection, trade secrets or commercial or financial information which is privileged or confidential.

(7) (A) The Secretary shall require each research facility to show upon inspection, and to report at least annually, that the provisions of this Act are being followed and that professionally acceptable standards governing the care, treatment, and use of animals are being followed by the research facility during actual research or experimentation.

(B) In complying with subparagraph (A), such research facilities shall provide —

(i) information on procedures likely to produce pain or distress in any animal and assurances demonstrating that the principal investigator considered alternatives to those procedures;

(ii) assurances satisfactory to the Secretary that such facility is adhering to the standards described in this section; and

(iii) an explanation for any deviation from the standards promulgated under this section.

(8) Paragraph (1) shall not prohibit any State (or a political subdivision of such State) from promulgating standards in addition to those standards promulgated by the Secretary under paragraph (1).

(b)(1) The Secretary shall require that each research facility establish at least one Committee. Each Committee shall be appointed by the chief executive officer of each such research facility and shall be composed of not fewer than three members. Such members shall possess sufficient ability to assess animal care, treatment, and practices in experimental research as determined by the needs of the research facility and shall represent society's concerns regarding the welfare of animal subjects used at such facility. Of the members of the Committee —

(A) at least one member shall be a doctor of veterinary medicine;

(B) at least one member —

(i) shall not be affiliated in any way with such facility other than as a member of the Committee —

(ii) shall not be a member of the immediate family of a person who is affiliated with such facility; and

(iii) is intended to provide representation for general community interests in the proper care and treatment of animals; and

(C) in those cases where the Committee consists of more than three members, not more than three members shall be from the same administrative unit of such facility.

(2) A quorum shall be required for all formal actions of the Committee, including inspections under paragraph (3).

(3) The Committee shall inspect at least semiannually all animal study areas and animal facilities of such research facility and review as part of the inspection —

(A) practices involving pain to animals, and

(B) the condition of animals, to ensure compliance with the provisions of this Act to minimize pain and distress to animals. Exceptions to the requirement of inspection of such study areas may be made by the Secretary if animals are studied in their natural environment and the study area is prohibitive to easy access.

(4) (A) The Committee shall file an inspection certification report of each inspection at the research facility. Such report shall —

(i) be signed by a majority of the Committee members involved in the inspection;

(ii) include reports of any violation of the standards promulgated, or assurances required, by the Secretary, including any deficient conditions of animal care or treatment, any deviations of research practices from originally approved proposals that adversely affect animal welfare, any notification to the facility regarding such conditions and any corrections made thereafter;

(iii) include any minority views of the Committee; and

(iv) include any other information pertinent to the activities of the Committee.

(B) Such report shall remain on file for at least 3 years at the research facility and shall be available for inspection by the Animal and Plant Health Inspection Service and any funding Federal agency.

(C) In order to give the research facility an opportunity to correct any deficiencies or deviations discovered by reason of paragraph (3), the Committee shall notify the administrative representative of the research facility of any deficiencies or deviations from the provisions of this Act. If, after notification and an opportunity for correction, such deficiencies or deviations remain uncorrected, the Committee shall notify (in writing) the Animal and Plant Health Inspection Service and the funding Federal Agency of such deficiencies or deviations.

(5) The inspection results shall be available to Department of Agriculture inspectors for review during inspections. Department of Agriculture inspectors shall forward any Committee inspection records which include reports of uncorrected deficiencies or deviations to the Animal and Plant Health Inspection Service and any funding Federal agency of the project with respect to which such uncorrected deficiencies and deviations occurred.

....

Appendix A

Section 16. (a) The Secretary shall make such investigations or inspections as he deems necessary to determine whether any dealer, exhibitor, intermediate handler, carrier, research facility, or operator of an auction sale subject to section 12 of this Act, has violated or is violating any provision of this Act or any regulation or standard issued thereunder, and for such purposes, the Secretary shall, at all reasonable times, have access to the places of business and the facilities, animals, and those records required to kept pursuant to section 10 of any such dealer, exhibitor, intermediate handler, carrier, research facility, operator of an auction sale. The Secretary shall inspect each research facility at least once each year and, in the case of deficiencies or deviations from the standards promulgated under this Act, shall conduct such follow-up inspections as may be necessary until all deficiencies or deviations from such standards are corrected. The Secretary shall promulgate such rules and regulations as he deems necessary to permit inspectors to confiscate or destroy in a humane manner any animal found to be suffering as a result of a failure to comply with any provision of this Act or any regulation or standard issued thereunder if (1) such animal is held by a dealer, (2) such animal is held by an exhibitor, (3) such animal is held by a research facility and is no longer required by such research facility to carry out the research, test or experiment for which such animal has been utilized, (4) such animal is held by an operator of an auction sale, or (5) such animal is held by an intermediate handler or a carrier.

....

APPENDIX B

ENDANGERED SPECIES ACT, 1973

16 U.S.C. 1531-1554 (1973)

[Note: Some portions have been omitted.]

Section 2.

(a) FINDINGS.—The Congress finds and declares that —

(1) various species of fish, wildlife, and plants in the United States have been rendered extinct as a consequence of economic growth and development untempered by adequate concern and conservation;

(2) other species of fish, wildlife, and plants have been so depleted in numbers that they are in danger of or threatened with extinction;

(3) these species of fish, wildlife, and plants are of aesthetic, ecological, educational, historical, recreational, and scientific value to the Nation and its people;

(4) the United States has pledged itself as a sovereign state in the international community to conserve to the extent practicable the various species of fish or wildlife and plants facing extinction, pursuant to —

(A) migratory bird treaties with Canada and Mexico;

(B) the Migratory and Endangered Bird Treaty with Japan;

(C) the Convention on Nature Protection and Wildlife Preservation in the Western Hemisphere;

(D) the International Convention for the Northwest Atlantic Fisheries;

(E) the International Convention for the High Seas Fisheries of the North Pacific Ocean;

(F) the Convention on International Trade in Endangered Species of Wild Fauna and Flora; and

(G) other international agreements; and

(5) encouraging the States and other interested parties, through Federal financial assistance and a system of incentives, to develop and maintain conservation programs which meet national and international standards is a key to meeting the Nation's international commitments and to better safe-

guarding, for the benefit of all citizens, the Nation's heritage in fish, wildlife, and plants.

(b) PURPOSES.—The purposes of this Act are to provide a means whereby the ecosystems upon which endangered species and threatened species depend may be conserved, to provide a program for the conservation of such endangered species and threatened species, and to take such steps as may be appropriate to achieve the purposes of the treaties and conventions set forth in subsection (a) of this section.

(c) POLICY. —

(1) It is further declared to be the policy of Congress that all Federal departments and agencies shall seek to conserve endangered species and threatened species and shall utilize their authorities in furtherance of the purposes of this Act.

(2) It is further declared to be the policy of Congress that Federal agencies shall cooperate with State and local agencies to resolve water resource issues in concert with conservation of endangered species.

Section 3. For the purposes of this Act — ...

(3) The terms "conserve," "conserving," and "conservation" mean to use and the use of all methods and procedures which are necessary to bring any endangered species or threatened species to the point at which the measures provided pursuant to this Act are no longer necessary. Such methods and procedures include, but are not limited to, all activities associated with scientific resources management such as research, census, law enforcement, habitat acquisition and maintenance, propagation, live trapping, and transplantation, and, in the extraordinary case where population pressures within a given ecosystem cannot be otherwise relieved, may include regulated taking.

(4) The term "Convention" means the Convention on International Trade in Endangered Species of Wild Fauna and Flora, signed on March 3, 1973, and the appendices thereto.

(5) (A) The term "critical habitat" for a threatened or endangered species means —

(i) the specific areas within the geographical area occupied by the species, at the time it is listed in accordance with the provisions of section 4 of this Act, on which are found those physical or biological features (I) essential to the conservation of the species and (II) which may require special management considerations or protection; and

(ii) specific areas outside the geographical area occupied by the species at the time it is listed in accordance with the provisions of section 4 of this Act, upon a determination by the Secretary that such areas are essential for the conservation of the species.

(B) Critical habitat may be established for those species now listed as threatened or endangered species for which no critical habitat has heretofore been established as set forth in subparagraph (A) of this paragraph.

(C) Except in those circumstances determined by the Secretary, critical habitat shall not include the entire geographical area which can be occupied by the threatened or endangered species.

(6) The term "endangered species" means any species which is in danger of extinction throughout all or a significant portion of its range other than a species of the Class Insecta determined by the Secretary to constitute a pest whose protection under the provisions of this Act would present an overwhelming and overriding risk to man…

(8) The term "fish or wildlife" means any member of the animal kingdom, including without limitation any mammal, fish, bird (including any migratory, nonmigratory, or endangered bird for which protection is also afforded by treaty or other international agreement), amphibian, reptile, mollusk, crustacean, arthropod or other invertebrate, and includes any part, product, egg, or offspring thereof, or the dead body or parts thereof…

(15) The term "species" includes any subspecies of fish or wildlife or plants, and any distinct population segment of any species of vertebrate fish or wildlife which interbreeds when mature…

(18) The term "take" means to harass, harm, pursue, hunt, shoot, wound, kill, trap, capture, or collect, or to attempt to engage in any such conduct.

(19) The term "threatened species" means any species which is likely to become an endangered species within the foreseeable future throughout all or a significant portion of its range….

Section 4.
(a) GENERAL. —
(1) The Secretary shall by regulation promulgated in accordance with subsection (b) determine whether any species is an endangered species or a threatened species because of any of the following factors:

(A) the present or threatened destruction, modification, or curtailment of its habitat or range;

(B) overutilization for commercial, recreational, scientific, or educational purposes;

(C) disease or predation;

(D) the inadequacy of existing regulatory mechanisms;

(E) other natural or manmade factors affecting its continued existence….

(3) The Secretary, by regulation promulgated in accordance with subsection (b) and to the maximum extent prudent and determinable —

(A) shall, concurrently with making a determination under paragraph (1) that a species is an endangered species or a threatened species, designate any habitat of such species which is then considered to be critical habitat; and

(B) may, from time-to-time thereafter as appropriate, revise such designation.

(b) BASIS FOR DETERMINATIONS. —

(1) (A) The Secretary shall make determinations required by subsection (a)(1) solely on the basis of the best scientific and commercial data available to him after conducting a review of the status of the species and after taking into account those efforts, if any, being made by any State or foreign nation, or any political subdivision of a State or foreign nation, to protect such species, whether by predator control, protection of habitat and food supply, or other conservation practices, within any area under its jurisdiction, or on the high seas.

(B) In carrying out this section, the Secretary shall give consideration to species which have been —

(i) designated as requiring protection from unrestricted commerce by any foreign nation, or pursuant to any international agreement; or

(ii) identified as in danger of extinction, or likely to become so within the foreseeable future, by any State agency or by any agency of a foreign nation that is responsible for the conservation of fish or wildlife or plants.

(2) The Secretary shall designate critical habitat, and make revisions thereto, under subsection (a)(3) on the basis of the best scientific data available and after taking into consideration the economic impact, and any other relevant impact, of specifying any particular area as critical habitat. The Secretary may exclude any area from critical habitat if he determines that the benefits of such exclusion outweigh the benefits of specifying such area as part of the critical habitat, unless he determines, based on the best scientific and commercial data available, that the failure to designate such area as critical habitat will result in the extinction of the species concerned.

(3) (A) To the maximum extent practicable, within 90 days after receiving the petition of an interested person under section 553(e) of title 5, United States Code, to add a species to, or to remove a species from, either of the lists published under subsection (c), the Secretary shall make a finding as to whether the petition presents substantial scientific or commercial information indicating that the petitioned action may be warranted. If such a petition is found to present such information, the Secretary shall promptly commence a review of the status of the species concerned. The Secretary shall promptly publish each finding made under this subparagraph in the Federal Register.

(B) Within 12 months after receiving a petition that is found under subparagraph (A) to present substantial information indicating that the petitioned action may be warranted, the Secretary shall make one of the following findings:

(i) The petitioned action is not warranted, in which case the Secretary shall promptly publish such finding in the Federal Register.

(ii) The petitioned action is warranted in which case the Secretary shall promptly publish in the Federal Register a general notice and the complete text of a proposed regulation to implement such action in accordance with paragraph (5).

(iii) The petitioned action is warranted but that —

(I) the immediate proposal and timely promulgation of a final regulation implementing the petitioned action in accordance with paragraphs (5) and (6) is precluded by pending proposals to determine whether any species is an endangered species or a threatened species, and

(II) expeditious progress is being made to add qualified species to either of the lists published under subsection (c) and to remove from such lists species for which the protections of the Act are no longer necessary, in which case the Secretary shall promptly publish such finding in the Federal Register, together with a description and evaluation of the reasons and data on which the finding is based.

(C) (i) A petition with respect to which a finding is made under subparagraph (B)(iii) shall be treated as a petition that is resubmitted to the Secretary under subparagraph (A) on the date of such finding and that presents substantial scientific or commercial information that the petitioned action may be warranted.

(ii) Any negative finding described in subparagraph (A) and any finding described in subparagraph (B)(i) or (iii) shall be subject to judicial review.

(iii) The Secretary shall implement a system to monitor effectively the status of all species with respect to which a finding is made under subparagraph (B)(iii) and shall make prompt use of the authority under paragraph 7 to prevent a significant risk to the well being of any such species.

(D) (i) To the maximum extent practicable, within 90 days after receiving the petition of an interested person under section 553(e) of title 5, United States Code, to revise a critical habitat designation, the Secretary shall make a finding as to whether the petition presents substantial scientific information indicating that the revision may be warranted. The Secretary shall promptly publish such finding in the Federal Register.

(ii) Within 12 months after receiving a petition that is found under clause (i) to present substantial information indicating that the requested revision may be warranted, the Secretary shall determine how he intends to proceed with the requested revision, and shall promptly publish notice of such intention in the Federal Register.

(4) Except as provided in paragraphs (5) and (6) of this subsection, the provisions of section 553 of title 5, United States Code (relating to rule-making procedures), shall apply to any regulation promulgated to carry out the purposes of this Act.

(5) With respect to any regulation proposed by the Secretary to implement a determination, designation, or revision referred to in subsection (a) (1) or (3), the Secretary shall —

(A) not less than 90 days before the effective date of the regulation —

(i) publish a general notice and the complete text of the proposed regulation in the Federal Register, and

(ii) give actual notice of the proposed regulation (including the complete text of the regulation) to the State agency in each State in which the species is believed to occur, and to each county or equivalent jurisdiction in which the species is believed to occur, and invite the comment of such agency, and each such jurisdiction, thereon;

(B) insofar as practical, and in cooperation with the Secretary of State, give notice of the proposed regulation to each foreign nation in which the species is believed to occur or whose citizens harvest the species on the high seas, and invite the comment of such nation thereon;

(C) give notice of the proposed regulation to such professional scientific organizations as he deems appropriate;

(D) publish a summary of the proposed regulation in a newspaper of general circulation in each area of the United States in which the species is believed to occur; and

(E) promptly hold one public hearing on the proposed regulation if any person files a request for such a hearing within 45 days after the date of publication of general notice.

(6) (A) Within the one-year period beginning on the date on which general notice is published in accordance with paragraph (5)(A)(i) regarding a proposed regulation, the Secretary shall publish in the Federal Register —

(i) if a determination as to whether a species is an endangered species or a threatened species, or a revision of critical habitat, is involved, either —

(I) a final regulation to implement such determination,

(II) a final regulation to implement such revision or a finding that such revision should not be made,

(III) notice that such one-year period is being extended under subparagraph (B)(i), or

(IV) notice that the proposed regulation is being withdrawn under subparagraph (B)(ii), together with the finding on which such withdrawal is based; or

(ii) subject to subparagraph (C), if a designation of critical habitat is involved, either —

(I) a final regulation to implement such designation, or

(II) notice that such one-year period is being extended under such subparagraph.

(B) (i) If the Secretary finds with respect to a proposed regulation referred to in subparagraph (A)(i) that there is substantial disagreement regarding the sufficiency or accuracy of the available data relevant to the determination or revision concerned the Secretary may extend the one-year period specified in subparagraph (A) for not more than six months for purposes of soliciting additional data...

(C) A final regulation designating critical habitat of an endangered species or a threatened species shall be published concurrently with the final regulation implementing the determination that such species is endangered or threatened, unless the Secretary deems that —

(i) it is essential to the conservation of such species that the regulation implementing such determination be promptly published; or

(ii) critical habitat of such species is not then determinable, in which case the Secretary, with respect to the proposed regulation to designate such habitat, may extend the one-year period specified in subparagraph (A) by not more than one additional year, but not later than the close of such additional year the Secretary must publish a final regulation, based on such data as may be available at that time, designating, to the maximum extent prudent, such habitat....

(8) (c) LISTS. —

(1) The Secretary of the Interior shall publish in the Federal Register a list of all species determined by him or the Secretary of Commerce to be endangered species and a list of all species determined by him or the Secretary of Commerce to be threatened species. Each list shall refer to the species contained therein by scientific and common name or names, if any, specify with respect to such species over what portion of its range it is endangered or threatened, and specify any critical habitat within such range. The Secretary shall from time to time revise each list published under the authority of this subsection to reflect recent determinations, designations, and revisions made in accordance with subsections (a) and (b).

(2) The Secretary shall —

(A) conduct, at least once every five years, a review of all species included in a list which is published pursuant to paragraph (1) and which is in effect at the time of such review; and

(B) determine on the basis of such review whether any such species should —

(i) be removed from such list;

(ii) be changed in status from an endangered species to a threatened species; or

(iii) be changed in status from a threatened species to an endangered species. Each determination under subparagraph (B) shall be made in accordance with the provisions of subsection (a) and (b).

(d) PROTECTIVE REGULATIONS.—Whenever any species is listed as a threatened species pursuant to subsection (c) of this section, the Secretary shall issue such regulations as he deems necessary and advisable to provide for the conservation of such species. The Secretary may by regulation prohibit with respect to any threatened species any act prohibited under section 9(a)(1), in the case of fish or wildlife, or section 9(a)(2), in the case of plants, with respect to endangered species; except that with respect to the taking of resident species of fish or wildlife, such regulations shall apply in any State which has entered into a cooperative agreement pursuant to section 6(c) of this Act only to the extent that such regulations have also been adopted by such State.

(e) SIMILARITY OF APPEARANCE CASES.—The Secretary may, by regulation of commerce or taking, and to the extent he deems advisable, treat any species as an endangered species or threatened species even though it is not listed pursuant to section 4 of this Act if he finds that —

(A) such species so closely resembles in appearance, at the point in question, a species which has been listed pursuant to such section that enforcement personnel would have substantial difficulty in attempting to differentiate between the listed and unlisted species;

(B) the effect of this substantial difficulty is an additional threat to an endangered or threatened species; and

(C) such treatment of an unlisted species will substantially facilitate the enforcement and further the policy of this Act.

(f) RECOVERY PLANS. —

(1) The Secretary shall develop and implement plans (hereinafter in this subsection referred to as "recovery plans") for the conservation and survival of endangered species and threatened species listed pursuant to this section, unless he finds that such a plan will not promote the conservation of the species. The Secretary, in development and implementing recovery plans, shall, to the maximum extent practicable —

(A) give priority to those endangered species or threatened species, without regard to taxonomic classification, that are most likely to benefit from such plans, particularly those species that are, or may be, in conflict with construction or other development projects or other forms of economic activity;

(B) incorporate in each plan —

(i) a description of such site-specific management actions as may be necessary to achieve the plan's goal for the conservation and survival of the species;

(ii) objective, measurable criteria which, when met, would result in a determination, in accordance with the provisions of this section, that the species be removed from the list; and

(iii) estimates of the time required and the cost to carry out those measures needed to achieve the plan's goal and to achieve intermediate steps toward that goal.

(2) The Secretary, in developing and implementing recovery plans, may procure the services of appropriate public and private agencies and institutions, and other qualified persons. Recovery teams appointed pursuant to this subsection shall not be subject to the Federal Advisory Committee Act.

(3) The Secretary shall report every two years to the Committee on Environment and Public Works of the Senate and the Committee on Merchant Marine and Fisheries of the House of Representatives on the status of efforts to develop and implement recovery plans for all species listed pursuant to this section and on the status of all species for which such plans have been developed.

(4) The Secretary shall, prior to final approval of a new or revised recovery plan, provide public notice and an opportunity for public review and comment on such plan. The Secretary shall consider all information presented during the public comment period prior to approval of the plan.

(5) Each Federal agency shall, prior to implementation of a new or revised recovery plan, consider all information presented during the public comment period under paragraph (4).

(g) MONITORING. —

(1) The Secretary shall implement a system in cooperation with the States to monitor effectively for not less than five years the status of all species which have recovered to the point at which the measures provided pursuant to this Act are no longer necessary and which, in accordance with the provisions of this section, have been removed from either of the lists published under subsection (c).

(2) The Secretary shall make prompt use of the authority under paragraph 7 of subsection (b) of this section to prevent a significant risk to the well being of any such recovered species....

Section 9. PROHIBITED ACTS

(a) GENERAL. —

(1) Except as provided in sections 6(g)(2) and 10 of this Act, with respect to any endangered species of fish or wildlife listed pursuant to section 4 of this Act it is unlawful for any person subject to the jurisdiction of the United States to —

(A) import any such species into, or export any such species from the United States;

(B) take any such species within the United States or the territorial sea of the United States;

(C) take any such species upon the high seas;

(D) possess, sell, deliver, carry, transport, or ship, by any means whatsoever, any such species taken in violation of subparagraphs (B) and (C);

(E) deliver, receive, carry, transport, or ship in interstate or foreign commerce, by any means whatsoever and in the course of a commercial activity, any such species;

(F) sell or offer for sale in interstate or foreign commerce any such species; or

(G) violate any regulation pertaining to such species or to any threatened species of fish or wildlife listed pursuant to section 4 of this Act and promulgated by the Secretary pursuant to authority provided by this Act....

[(2) makes similar stipulations for plants]

Section 11. Penalties and Enforcement...

(g) CITIZEN SUITS. —

(1) Except as provided in paragraph (2) of this subsection any person may commence a civil suit on his own behalf —

(A) to enjoin any person, including the United States and any other governmental instrumentality or agency (to the extent permitted by the eleventh amendment to the Constitution), who is alleged to be in violation of any provision of this Act or regulation issued under the authority thereof; or

(B) to compel the Secretary to apply, pursuant to section 6(g)(2)(B)(ii) of this Act, the prohibitions set forth in or authorized pursuant to section 4(d) or section 9(a)(1)(B) of this Act with respect to the taking of any resident endangered species or threatened species within any State; or

(C) against the Secretary where there is alleged a failure of the Secretary to perform any act or duty under section 4 which is not discretionary with the Secretary.

The district courts shall have jurisdiction, without regard to the amount in controversy or the citizenship of the parties, to enforce any such provision or regulation or to order the Secretary to perform such act or duty, as the case may be. In any civil suit commenced under subparagraph (B) the district court shall compel the Secretary to apply the prohibition sought if the court finds that the allegation that an emergency exists is supported by substantial evidence....

APPENDIX C

———

ANIMAL LEGAL DEFENSE FUND V. GLICKMAN I, 154 F.3D 426, 1998

U.S. COURT OF APPEALS, DISTRICT OF COLUMBIA CIRCUIT, FILED SEPTEMBER 1, 1998

ANIMAL LEGAL DEFENSE FUND, INC., ET AL., APPELLEES, V. DANIEL R. GLICKMAN, SECRETARY OF AGRICULTURE, ET AL., AND NATIONAL ASSOCIATION FOR BIOMEDICAL RESEARCH, APPELLANTS

(Note: Excerpted. Footnotes, most citations, dissent, and some other matter have been omitted.)

Appeals from the United States District Court for the District of Columbia (No. 96cv00408)

Before: Edwards, Chief Judge, Wald, Silberman, Williams, Ginsburg, Sentelle, Henderson, Randolph, Rogers, Tatel and Garland, Circuit Judges.

Argued in banc May 13, 1998

The opinion of the court was delivered by: Circuit Judge Wald.
Dissenting Opinion filed by Circuit Judge Sentelle, with whom Silberman, Ginsburg and Henderson, Circuit Judges, join.

Appendix C

Wald, Circuit Judge:

The 1985 amendments to the Animal Welfare Act ("AWA") direct the Secretary of Agriculture to "promulgate standards to govern the humane handling, care, treatment, and transportation of animals by dealers, research facilities, and exhibitors." (1985) (codified at 7 U.S.C. § 2143(a) (1994)). They further provide that such standards "shall include minimum requirements" for, inter alia, "a physical environment adequate to promote the psychological well-being of primates." Id. Pursuant to this authority, the United States Department of Agriculture ("USDA") issued regulations for primate dealers, exhibitors, and research facilities that included a small number of mandatory requirements and also required the regulated parties to "develop, document, and follow an appropriate plan for environment enhancement adequate to promote the psychological well-being of nonhuman primates. The plan must be in accordance with the currently accepted professional standards as cited in appropriate professional journals or reference guides, and as directed by the attending veterinarian." 9 C.F.R. § 3.81 (1997). Although these plans must be made available to the USDA, the regulated parties are not obligated to make them available to members of the public. See id.

The individual plaintiffs, Roseann Circelli, Mary Eagan, and Marc Jurnove, challenge these regulations on the ground that they violate the USDA's statutory mandate under the AWA and permit dealers, exhibitors, and research facilities to keep primates under inhumane conditions. The individual plaintiffs allege that they suffered aesthetic injury during their regular visits to animal exhibitions when they observed primates living under such conditions. A divided panel of this court held that all of the plaintiffs lacked constitutional standing to pursue their claims. See *Animal Legal Defense Fund, Inc. v. Glickman*, 130 F.3d 464, 466 (D.C. Cir. 1997).

This court subsequently vacated that judgment and granted rehearing in banc.

We hold that Mr. Jurnove, one of the individual plaintiffs, has standing to sue. Accordingly, we need not pass on the standing of the other individual plaintiffs. . . .

I. BACKGROUND

A. Marc Jurnove's Affidavit

Mr. Jurnove's affidavit is an uncontested statement of the injuries that he has suffered to his aesthetic interest in observing animals living under humane conditions.

For his entire adult life, Mr. Jurnove has "been employed and/or worked as a volunteer for various human and animal relief and rescue organizations."

261

Jurnove Affidavit ¶ 3. "By virtue of [his] training in wildlife rehabilitation and [his] experience in investigating complaints about the treatment of wildlife, [he is] very familiar with the needs of and proper treatment of wildlife." Id. ¶ 6. "Because of [his] familiarity with and love of exotic animals, as well as for recreational and educational purposes and because [he] appreciate[s] these animals' beauty, [he] enjoy[s] seeing them in various zoos and other parks near [his] home." Id. ¶ 7.

Between May 1995 and June 1996, when he filed his affidavit, Mr. Jurnove visited the Long Island Game Farm Park and Zoo ("Game Farm") at least nine times. Throughout this period, and since as far back as 1992, the USDA has not questioned the adequacy of this facility's plan for the psychological well-being of primates.

Mr. Jurnove's first visit to the Game Farm, in May 1995, lasted approximately six hours. While there, Mr. Jurnove saw many animals living under inhumane conditions. For instance, the Game Farm housed one primate, a Japanese Snow Macaque, in a cage "that was a distance from and not in view of the other primate cages." Id. ¶ 14. "The only cage enrichment device this animal had was an unused swing." Id. Similarly, Mr. Jurnove "saw a large male chimpanzee named Barney in a holding area by himself. He could not see or hear any other primate." Id. ¶ 8. Mr. Jurnove "kn[e]w that chimpanzees are very social animals and it upset [him] very much to see [Barney] in isolation from other primates." Id. The Game Farm also placed adult bears next to squirrel monkeys, although Jurnove saw evidence that the arrangement made the monkeys frightened and extremely agitated.

The day after this visit, Mr. Jurnove began to contact government agencies, including the USDA, in order to secure help for these animals. Based on Mr. Jurnove's complaint, the USDA inspected the Game Farm on May 3, 1995. According to Mr. Jurnove's uncontested affidavit, however, the agency's resulting inspection report "states that [the USDA inspectors] found the facility in compliance with all the standards." Id. ¶ 18. Mr. Jurnove returned to the Game Farm on eight more occasions to observe these officially legal conditions.

On July 17, 18, and 19, 1995, he found "virtually the same conditions" that allegedly caused him aesthetic injury during his first visit to the Game Farm in May. Id. ¶ 20. For instance, Barney, the chimpanzee, and Samantha, the Japanese Snow Macaque, were still alone in their cages. This time, Mr. Jurnove documented these conditions with photographs and sent them to the USDA. See id. WW19–20. Nevertheless, the responding USDA inspectors found only a few violations at the Game Farm; they reported "nothing" about many of the conditions that concerned Mr. Jurnove and that he had told the agency about, such as "the fact that numerous primates were being housed alone" and the lack of adequate stimulation in their cages. Id. ¶ 21.

Mr. Jurnove devoted two trips in August and one in September to "videotaping the conditions that the inspection missed," and on each trip he found that the inhumane conditions persisted. Id. WW 22-28. At the end of September, the USDA sent three inspectors to the Game Farm in response to Mr. Jurnove's continued complaints and reportage; they found violations, however, only with regard to the facility's fencing.

Mr. Jurnove returned to the Game Farm once more on October 1, 1995. Indeed, he only stopped his frequent visits when he became ill and required major surgery. After his health returned, Mr. Jurnove visited the Game Farm in April 1996, hoping to see improvements in the conditions that he had repeatedly brought to the USDA's attention. He was disappointed again; "the animals [were] in literally the same conditions as [he] had seen them over the summer of 1995." Id. ¶ 33. Mr. Jurnove's resulting complaints prompted the USDA to inspect the Game Farm in late May 1996. For the fourth time, the agency found the facility largely in compliance, with a few exceptions not relevant to the plaintiffs' main challenge in this case. In June 1996, Mr. Jurnove filed the affidavit that is the basis of his claim here. He concluded this affidavit by stating his intent to "return to the Farm in the next several weeks" and to "continue visiting the Farm to see the animals there." Id. ¶ 43.

B. THE PLAINTIFFS' COMPLAINT

The plaintiffs' complaint elaborates a two-part legal theory based on the factual allegations in the individual plaintiffs' affidavits. First, the plaintiffs allege that the AWA requires the USDA to adopt specific, minimum standards to protect primates' psychological well-being, and the agency has failed to do so. . . . ("Instead of issuing the standards on this topic, USDA's regulation [at 9 C.F.R. § 3.81] simply states that the 'plans' must be in accordance with currently accepted professional standards."); id. ¶ 107 ("By providing that animal exhibitors and other regulated entities shall develop their own 'plans' for a physical environment adequate to promote the psychological well-being of non-human primates, USDA has failed to satisfy the statutory requirement that it set the 'minimum' standards.").

Second, the plaintiffs contend that the conditions that caused Mr. Jurnove aesthetic injury complied with current USDA regulations, but that lawful regulations would have prohibited those conditions and protected Mr. Jurnove from the injuries that he describes in his affidavit. See id. ¶ 53 ("Marc Jurnove has been and continues to be injured by USDA's failure to issue and implement standards for a physical environment adequate to promote the psychological wellbeing of primates because this harms the nonhuman primates he sees at the Long Island Game Farm and Zoo which in turn caused and causes him extreme aesthetic harm and emotional and physical distress."); id. ("[B]ecause USDA regulations permit the nonhuman primates in zoos, such as the Long Island Game Farm and Zoological Park to be housed in isolation, Marc Jurnove was exposed to and will be exposed in the future to behaviors exhibited by these animals which indicate the psychological debilitation caused by social deprivation. Observing these behaviors caused and will cause Marc Jurnove personal distress and aesthetic and emotional injury."); id. ¶ 58 ("Marc Jurnove experienced and continues to experience physical and mental distress when he realizes that he, by himself, is powerless to help the animals he witnesses suffering when such suffering derives from or is traceable to the improper implementation and enforcement of the Animal Welfare Act by USDA.").

C. PROCEDURAL HISTORY

The United States District Court, Judge Charles R. Richey, held that the individual plaintiffs had standing to sue, finding in their favor on a motion for summary judgment. See 943 F. Supp. at 54-57. On the merits, the district court held that 9 C.F.R. § 3.81 violates the Administrative Procedure Act ("APA") because it fails to set standards, including minimum requirements, as mandated by the AWA; that the USDA's failure to promulgate standards for a physical environment adequate to promote the psychological well-being of primates constitutes agency action unlawfully withheld and unreasonably delayed in violation of the APA; and that the USDA's failure to issue a regulation promoting the social grouping of nonhuman primates is arbitrary, capricious, and an abuse of discretion in violation of the APA.

A split panel of this court held that none of the plaintiffs had standing to sue and accordingly did not reach the merits of their complaint. See 130 F.3d at 466. This court granted rehearing in banc, limited to the question of Marc Jurnove's standing.

II. ANALYSIS

"The question of standing involves both constitutional limitations on federal-court jurisdiction and prudential limitations on its exercise." Bennett v. Spear, 117 S. Ct. 1154, 1161 (1997). To meet the "case or controversy" requirement of Article III, a plaintiff must demonstrate: (1) that she has suffered "injury in fact;" (2) that the injury is "fairly traceable" to the defendant's actions; and (3) that a favorable judicial ruling will "likely" redress the plaintiff's injury. Id.; see also *Lujan v. Defenders of Wildlife*, 504 U.S. 555, 560-61 (1992). In addition, the Supreme Court has recognized prudential requirements for standing, including "that a plaintiff's grievance must arguably fall within the zone of interests protected or regulated by the statutory provision or constitutional guarantee invoked in the suit." Bennett, 117 S. Ct. at 1161.

We find that Mr. Jurnove's allegations fall well within these requirements.

A. INJURY IN FACT

Mr. Jurnove's allegations solidly establish injury in fact. As his affidavit indicates, Mr. Jurnove "enjoy[s] seeing [animals] in various zoos and other parks near [his] home" "[b]ecause of [his] familiarity with and love of exotic animals, as well as for recreational and educational purposes and because [he] appreciate[s] these animals' beauty." Jurnove Affidavit ¶ 7. He decided to tour the primate cages at the Game Farm "in furtherance of [his] appreciation for exotic animals and [his] desire to observe and enjoy them." Id. During this tour and the ones that followed, Mr. Jurnove suffered direct, concrete, and particularized injury to this aesthetic interest in observing animals living under humane conditions. At this particular zoo, which he has regularly visited and plans to keep visiting, he saw particular animals enduring inhumane treatment. He developed an interest, moreover, in seeing these particular animals living under humane treatment. As he explained, "[w]hat I observed [at the Game Farm] was an assault on my senses and greatly impaired my ability to observe and enjoy these captive animals." Id. ¶ 17. "I want to observe, study, and enjoy these animals in humane conditions." Id. ¶ 43.

Simply put, Mr. Jurnove has alleged far more than an abstract, and uncognizable, interest in seeing the law enforced. See *Allen v. Wright*, 468 U.S. 737, 754 (1984) ("This Court has repeatedly held that an asserted right to have the Government act in accordance with law is not sufficient, standing alone, to confer jurisdiction on a federal court."). . . . To the contrary, Mr. Jurnove has made clear that he has an aesthetic interest in seeing exotic animals living in a nurturing habitat, and that he has attempted to exercise this interest by repeatedly visiting a particular animal exhibition to observe particular animals there. This interest was allegedly injured, however, when Mr. Jurnove witnessed the actual living conditions of the primates described and named in his affidavit. . . .

The Supreme Court has repeatedly made clear that injury to an aesthetic interest in the observation of animals is sufficient to satisfy the demands of Article III standing. . . .

The key requirement, one that Mr. Jurnove clearly satisfies, is that the plaintiff have suffered his injury in a personal and individual way—for instance, by seeing with his own eyes the particular animals whose condition caused him aesthetic injury. . . .

[Court cases proving these points are cited and described.]

Myriad cases recognizing individual plaintiffs' injury in fact based on affronts to their aesthetic interests in observing animals living in humane habitats, or in using pristine environmental areas that have not been despoiled, articulate a second principle of standing. It has never been the law, and is not so today, that injury in fact requires the elimination (or threatened elimination) of either the animal species or environmental feature in question. . . .

[T]he Animal Welfare Act, with which we deal here, is explicitly concerned with the quality of animal life, rather than the number of animals in existence. . . . Quite naturally, suits alleging violations of this statute will focus on the conditions under which animals live. . . . Along these lines, this court has already noted in *Animal Welfare Institute*, which recognized injury in fact based on an aesthetic interest in seeing animals living under humane conditions, that "[w]here an act is expressly motivated by considerations of humaneness toward animals, who are uniquely incapable of defending their own interests in court, it strikes us as eminently logical to allow groups specifically concerned with animal welfare to invoke the aid of the courts in enforcing the statute." 561 F.2d at 1007. Moreover, and perhaps more importantly, it does not make sense, as a matter of logic, to suppose that people suffer aesthetic injury from government action that threatens to wipe out an animal species altogether, and not from government action that leaves some animals in a persistent state of suffering. To the contrary, the latter seems capable of causing more serious aesthetic injury than the former.

Mr. Jurnove has adequately alleged injury to an aesthetic interest in observing animals living under humane conditions. His affidavit describes both the animal exhibition that he regularly visits, and the specific animals there whose condition caused Mr. Jurnove injury. It requires no expansion of existing standing doctrine to find that he has established a cognizable injury in fact.

B. CAUSATION

Plaintiffs allege that the AWA, 7 U.S.C. § 2143, requires the USDA to adopt explicit minimum standards to govern the humane treatment of primates, and that the agency did not do so. They further contend that the conditions that caused Mr. Jurnove injury complied with current USDA regulations, but that lawful regulations would have prohibited those conditions and protected Mr. Jurnove from the injuries that his affidavit describes. We find that these allegations satisfy the causation prong of Article III standing.

As Mr. Jurnove's affidavit elaborates, he allegedly suffered aesthetic injury upon observing conditions that the present USDA regulations permit. Mr. Jurnove, for instance, "saw a large male chimpanzee named Barney in a holding area by himself. He could not see or hear any other primate." Jurnove Affidavit ¶ 8. Mr. Jurnove also "viewed a monkey cage [containing one Japanese Snow Macaque] that was a distance from and not in view of the other primate cages." Id. ¶ 14. As the plaintiffs observe, see First Amended Complaint WW 84, 95, 114-17, the housing of these two primates appears to be compatible with current regulations, which state only that "[t]he environment enhancement plan must include specific provisions to address the social needs of nonhuman primates of species known to exist in social groups in nature. Such specific provisions must be in accordance with currently accepted professional standards, as cited in appropriate professional journals or reference guides, and as directed by the attending veterinarian." 9 C.F.R. § 3.81(a). Thus, an exhibition may apparently comply with the procedural requirement that this standard creates—by establishing a plan that "address[es]" the social needs of primates—and still leave a primate caged singly. Similarly, 9 C.F.R. § 3.81(a)(3) provides that "[i]ndividually housed nonhuman primates must be able to see and hear nonhuman primates of their own or compatible species unless the attending veterinarian determines that it would endanger their health, safety, or well-being." Here again, the regulation is structured so that an exhibitor that secured the approval of the veterinarian in its employ could comply with the regulation without actually housing nonhuman primates within the sight or sound of other primates. . . . Whatever the ultimate merits of the plaintiffs' case, they most definitely assert that the AWA requires minimum standards to prohibit or more rigidly restrict the occasions on which such allegedly inhumane treatment can occur.

Mr. Jurnove's affidavit also states that "[t]he pen next to the adult bears housed the squirrel monkeys. . . . I observed the monkeys repeatedly walking over to the door and sniffing and acting very upset when the bears came near." Jurnove Affidavit ¶ 11. Plaintiffs allege that the current regulations permit the housing of incompatible species next to each other. See First Amended Complaint WW 46-47. Specifically, these regulations state that "[n]onhuman primates may not be housed with other species of primates or animals unless they are compatible." 9 C.F.R. § 3.81(a)(3). This provision does not expressly regulate animals housed next to each other, but in separate cages. But even if section 3.81(a)(3) does apply to the situation that Mr. Jurnove observed, it includes the caveat that "[c]ompatibility of nonhuman primates must be determined in accordance with generally accepted professional practices and actual observations, as directed by the attending veterinarian," thus again permitting wide discretion on the part of the local veterinarian.

Similarly, Mr. Jurnove's affidavit observes that "[t]he only cage enrichment device [a Japanese Snow Macaque] had was an unused swing." Jurnove Affidavit ¶ 14. The plaintiffs allege that such a situation is perfectly legal under the present regulations, see First Amended Complaint ¶ 84, which provide only that "[t]he physical environment in the primary enclosures must be enriched by providing means of expressing noninjurious species-typical activities." 9 C.F.R. § 3.81(b). The regulations do not include any specific requirements governing the particular kind or number of enrichment devices. According to the plaintiffs, providing only a single swing, and one that the primate appears to shun, offends the AWA's mandate for minimum standards, although it is perfectly compatible with 9 C.F.R. § 3.81(b).

The USDA's own actions in this case further support the plaintiffs' allegation that the agency's current regulations allow the conditions that allegedly caused Mr. Jurnove injury. As Mr. Jurnove's affidavit makes clear, the Game Farm has repeatedly submitted to inspection by the USDA. The allegedly inhumane conditions at the Game Farm have persisted precisely because the USDA inspectors have concluded on the basis of these visits that in every important aspect the conditions at the Game Farm comply with the USDA regulations. If the USDA had found the Game Farm out of compliance with current regulations, or if the governing regulations had themselves been more stringent, the Game Farm's owners would have been forced (in order to remain in accord with the law) to either alter their practices or go out of business and transfer their animals to exhibitors willing to operate legally; either scenario would protect Mr. Jurnove's aesthetic interest in observing animals living under humane conditions. Instead, however, the USDA has not questioned the legality of the Game Farm's plan since 1992. Since May 1995, when Mr. Jurnove began visiting the Game Farm and complaining to the agency, the USDA inspectors have examined, and largely approved, the actual conditions at the facility at least four times. The USDA's first inspection report "states that [the USDA inspectors] found the facility in compliance with all the standards." Jurnove Affidavit ¶ 18. Although subsequent inspection reports identify a few conditions that Mr. Jurnove agrees violate the USDA regulations, the USDA continued—in at least three more inspection reports—to conclude that the Game Farm was in compliance with existing USDA regulations in all other respects, including presumably the existence of a plan that met the regulations' standards.

Supreme Court precedent establishes that the causation requirement for constitutional standing is met when a plaintiff demonstrates that the challenged agency action authorizes the conduct that allegedly caused the plaintiff's injuries, if that conduct would allegedly be illegal otherwise. . . . [Citation of cases establishing this point have been omitted.]

A question was raised at oral argument about whether Mr. Jurnove has nonetheless failed to satisfy the causation prong of constitutional standing, on the ground that the governing law simply permits the conditions that allegedly injured him, rather than requiring animal exhibitors to follow the allegedly inhumane practices. The background condition governing animal exhibitors, this argument proceeds, is that anything the exhibitors do is legal unless statutes and regulations make specific conduct illegal. Because neither the AWA nor the USDA's implementing regulations have changed this status quo—i.e., in no way have they affected the conditions that allegedly injured Mr. Jurnove—there is no causal link between any government action and Mr. Jurnove's injury.

This argument, however, is founded on a false premise. The proper comparison for determining causation is not between what the agency did and the status quo before the agency acted. Rather, the proper comparison is between what the agency did and what the plaintiffs allege the agency should have done under the statute. The plaintiffs' legal theory of this case, which we accept for purposes of determining Mr. Jurnove's standing, is grounded on their view that animal exhibitors are in fact governed by a mandatory legal regime. Specifically, the plaintiffs allege that the AWA requires the USDA to establish specific, mandatory requirements that establish humane living conditions for animals. . . . According to this view, the AWA itself prohibits the conditions that allegedly injured Mr. Jurnove, and the USDA regulations misinterpret the statute by permitting these conditions. Both the Supreme Court and this circuit have repeatedly found causation where a challenged government action permitted the third party conduct that allegedly caused a plaintiff injury, when that conduct would have otherwise been illegal. Neither court has ever stated that the challenged law must compel the third party to act in the allegedly injurious way. . . . [Citations of cases establishing this point have been omitted.]

Mr. Jurnove's affidavit accordingly falls well within our established causation requirement for constitutional standing. He alleges that the USDA failed to adopt the specific, minimum standards that the AWA requires. He further describes how the conditions that caused him injury complied with current USDA regulations, and alleges that regulations complying with the AWA would have prohibited those conditions and protected him from the injuries that his affidavit recounts.

C. Redressibility

We also find that Mr. Jurnove has satisfied the redressibility element of constitutional standing. Mr. Jurnove's affidavit alleges that he has a current routine of regularly visiting the Game Farm and provides a finite time period within which he will make his next visit, stating that he plans to "return to the Farm in the next several weeks" and to "continue visiting the Farm to see the animals there." Jurnove Affidavit ¶ 43. As the plaintiffs' complaint argues, more stringent regulations, which prohibit the inhumane conditions that have consistently caused Mr. Jurnove aesthetic injury in the past, would necessarily alleviate Mr. Jurnove's aesthetic injury during his planned, future trips to the Game Farm. See First Amended Complaint WW 53, 58. Tougher regulations would either allow Mr. Jurnove to visit a more humane Game Farm or, if the Game Farm's owners decide to close rather than comply with higher legal standards, to possibly visit the animals he has come to know in their new homes within exhibitions that comply with the more exacting regulations.

The Supreme Court's recent decision in *FEC v. Akins*, moreover, rejects the possible counterargument that the redressibility element of constitutional standing requires a plaintiff to establish that the defendant agency will actually enforce any new binding regulations against the regulated third party. . . . [Description of this case has been omitted.]

Mr. Jurnove, accordingly, has met all three of the constitutional requirements for standing.

D. PRUDENTIAL STANDING/ZONE OF INTERESTS

Mr. Jurnove also falls within the zone of interests protected under the AWA's provisions on animal exhibitions. As the Supreme Court has recently reaffirmed, the zone of interests test is generous and relatively undemanding. "[T]here need be no indication of congressional purpose to benefit the would-be plaintiff." *National Credit Union Admin. v. First National Bank & Trust Co.*, 118 S. Ct. 927, 934 (1998). Instead, the test, a gloss on APA § 10(a), 5 U.S.C. § 702 (1994), asks only "whether the interest sought to be protected by the complainant is arguably within the zone of interests to be protected by the statute," *National Credit Union Admin.*, 118 S. Ct. at 935 [76]. . . . [Citations of further cases to prove this point have been omitted.]

In this case, logic, legislative history, and the structure of the AWA, all indicate that Mr. Jurnove's injury satisfies the zone of interests test. The very purpose of animal exhibitions is, necessarily, to entertain and educate people; exhibitions make no sense unless one takes the interests of their human visitors into account. The legislative history of both the 1985 amendments to the Animal Welfare Act and the 1970 act that first included animal exhibitions within the AWA confirms that Congress acted with the public's interests in mind.

In introducing the 1985 amendments, Senator Robert Dole explained "that we need to ensure the public that adequate safeguards are in place to prevent unnecessary abuses to animals, and that everything possible is being done to decrease the pain of animals during experimentation and testing." 131 Cong. Rec. 29,155 (1985). The Congressmen who went on the House floor to introduce the act that first extended the AWA to cover animal exhibitions recognized that their bill "ha[d] been a focal point of concern among animal lovers throughout the Nation for some time" and spoke of the "great pleasure" that animals bring to the people who see them. 116 Cong. Rec. 40,159 (1970) (statement of Rep. Mizell); see also H.R. Rep. No. 91-1651, at 1 (1970) ("Beginning with the legislation passed in 1966 (Public Law 89-544), the United States Government has implemented a statutory mandate that small helpless creatures deserve the care and protection of a strong and enlightened public.") Indeed, Congress had placed animal exhibitions within the scope of the AWA after hearings documenting how inhumane conditions at these exhibitions affected the people who came and watched the animals there....

Throughout, the Congressmen responsible for including animal exhibitions within the AWA encouraged the continued monitoring of humane societies and their members. They spoke, for instance, of how America had long depended on humane societies to bring the mistreatment of animals to light. See, e.g., 116 Cong. Rec. 40,305 (1970) (statement of Rep. Whitehurst). The Congressmen further acknowledged that humane societies were the moving force behind the legislation to include animal exhibitions within the AWA. See, e.g., 116 Cong. Rec. 40,156 (1970) (statement of Rep. Foley).

The structure of the AWA also makes clear that Mr. Jurnove falls within the statute's zone of interests. While the AWA establishes oversight committees with private citizen members for research facilities, see 7 U.S.C. § 2143(b)(1) (1994), it created no counterpart for animal exhibitions. But, as the legislative history shows, the AWA anticipated the continued monitoring of concerned animal lovers to ensure that the purposes of the Act were honored. Mr. Jurnove, a regular viewer of animal exhibitions regulated under the AWA, clearly falls within the zone of interests the statute protects. His interests are among those that Congress sought to benefit through the AWA, and he certainly is one of the individuals "who in practice can be expected to police the interests that the statute protects." *Mova Pharmaceutical Corp.*, 140 F.3d at 1075.

III. CONCLUSION

Mr. Jurnove has standing to sue. He satisfies the injury, causation, and redressibility elements of constitutional standing, and also falls within the zone of interests for the Animal Welfare Act. We accordingly have no need to consider the standing of the other individual plaintiffs. We leave a determination of the merits of the plaintiffs' claim to a future panel of this court.

So ordered.

APPENDIX D

ANIMAL LEGAL DEFENSE FUND V. GLICKMAN II, 204 F.3D 229, 2000

[Some case citations and other material are omitted.]
United States Court of Appeals, District of Columbia Circuit. Judge WILLIAMS, Circuit Judge delivered the opinion of the court.

In *Animal Legal Defense Fund, Inc. v. Glickman,* 154 F.3d 426 (D.C.Cir.1998) (en banc), we held that plaintiff Marc Jurnove has standing to challenge regulations promulgated by the Secretary of Agriculture in 1991 that purport to set "minimum requirements ... for a physical environment adequate to promote the psychological well-being of primates." 7 U.S.C. § 2143(a)(1)-(2). The en banc court left untouched the panel's decision that Animal Legal Defense Fund lacked standing. The court referred the merits—the question whether the Secretary's regulations satisfy that statutory mandate and the Administrative Procedure Act—to a future panel. Finding that the regulations do meet the statutory and APA tests, we reverse the district court's decision to the contrary.

* * *

In 1985 Congress passed the Improved Standards for Laboratory Animals Act, Pub.L. No. 99-198, 99 Stat. 1645, amending the Animal Welfare Act of 1966. See 7 U.S.C. § 2131 et seq. The 1985 amendments directed the Secretary of Agriculture to promulgate "standards to govern the humane handling, care, treatment, and transportation of animals by dealers, research facilities, and exhibitors." Id. § 2143(a)(1). The Act specified that among these must be "minimum requirements ... for a physical environment adequate to promote the psychological well-being of primates." Id. § 2143(a)(1)-(2).

There are over 240 species of non-human primates, ranging from marmosets of South America that are a foot tall and weigh less than half a pound to gorillas of western Africa standing six feet tall and weighing up to 500 pounds. It proved no simple task to design regulations to promote the psy-

272

chological well-being of such varied species as they are kept and handled for exhibition and research. Notice of intent to issue regulations was first published in the Federal Register in 1986, 51 Fed.Reg. 7950 (1986), but the Secretary did not publish proposed regulations until 1989. 54 Fed.Reg. 10897 (1989). After receiving a flood of comments (10,686 timely ones, to be precise), the Secretary reconsidered the regulations and published new proposed regulations in 1990. 55 Fed.Reg. 33448 (1990). After receiving another 11,392 comments, he adopted final regulations in 1991. 56 Fed.Reg. 6426 (1991); 9 C.F.R. § 3.81.

The final regulations consist of two separate modes of regulation, typically known as engineering standards and performance standards. The former dictate the required means to achieve a result; the latter state the desired outcomes, leaving to the facility the choice of means. The Secretary identifies five guidelines that he considers engineering standards, which in substance require as follows: (1) restraints are generally prohibited subject to certain exceptions as determined by the attending veterinarian or the research proposal, 9 C.F.R. § 3.81(d); (2) primary enclosures must be "enriched" so that primates may exhibit their typical behavior, such as swinging or foraging, id. § 3.81(b); (3) certain types of primates must be given special attention, including infants, young juveniles, individually housed primates, and great apes over 110 pounds, again in accord with "the instructions of the attending veterinarian," id. § 3.81(c); (4) facilities must "address the social needs of nonhuman primates … in accordance with currently accepted professional standards … and as directed by the attending veterinarian," but they may individually house primates under conditions further specified in the regulations, id. § 3.81(a); and (5) minimum cage sizes are set according to the typical weight of different species, id. § 3.80(b)(2)(i).

To implement these guidelines and to promote the psychological well-being of the primates, facilities must develop performance plans:

Dealers, exhibitors, and research facilities must develop, document, and follow an appropriate plan for environment enhancement adequate to promote the psychological well-being of nonhuman primates. The plan must be in accordance with the currently accepted professional standards as cited in appropriate professional journals or reference guides, and as directed by the attending veterinarian. This plan must be made available to APHIS [Animal and Plant Health Inspection Service] upon request, and, in the case of research facilities, to officials of any pertinent funding agency. Id. § 3.81.

Jurnove primarily maintains that nothing about these regulations establishes "minimum requirements … for a physical environment adequate to promote the psychological well-being of primates," and that the Secretary's use of performance plans and his apparent deference to on-site veterinarians amount to an impermissible delegation of his legal responsibility.

The district court agreed. *Animal Legal Defense Fund v. Glickman* (*"ALDF"*), 943 F.Supp. 44 (D.D.C.1996). It held that the regulation "fails to set standards," by which the district court meant engineering standards, and that "the regulation completely delegates the establishment of such standards to the regulated entities" because "[a]t best, the regulation refers these entities to the direction of their attending veterinarians—who are not under the control of the agency." Id. at 59. The district court also concluded that the Secretary had a duty to require social housing of primates given a finding by the Secretary that "[i]n general, housing in groups promotes psychological well-being more assuredly than does individual housing." Id. at 60 (quoting 56 Fed.Reg. at 6473). As the court read the regulation "the agency delineates only when social grouping might not be provided," and therefore "the regulation does not contain any minimum requirement on a point recognized by the agency itself as critical to the psychological well-being of primates." Id.

* * *

Jurnove argues that the plain language of the statute—the Secretary shall establish "minimum requirements ... for a physical environment adequate to promote the psychological well-being of primates"—requires that the Secretary spell out exactly how primates may and may not be housed and handled (i.e., engineering standards), or at least spell out the "minimum requirements" in this manner. The Secretary's emphatic first response is: we did.

Jurnove consistently reads the regulations, as did the district court, as if the only "requirement" of the facilities is the production of a performance plan and that, basically, anything goes—provided the facilities honor what he views as the empty formality of finding some sort of support from "currently accepted professional standards as cited in appropriate professional journals or reference guides" and from "the attending veterinarian." 9 CFR § 3.81. This reading yields an obvious parade of horribles. Facilities will find unscrupulous veterinarians to rubber-stamp outrageous practices, and fringe periodicals will be the coin of the animal realm. This, argues Jurnove, is not the setting of "standards" or "minimum requirements" that the statute plainly commands.

We need not decide when performance standards alone could satisfy a congressional mandate for minimum requirements, or whether the sort of agency deference depicted by Jurnove could ever do so. The regulations here include specific engineering standards. The most obvious example is the regulation of cage sizes, id. § 3.80, which even Jurnove grants is an engineering standard. Jurnove attempts to discount the "primary enclosure" requirements because they appear in a different section of the regulations, and the Animal Welfare Act had previously mandated standards for "housing." But the Secretary stated that the cage requirements were set as part of the standards for promoting psychological well-being, 56 Fed.Reg. at 6468, and it is perfectly permissible to implement congressional commands through complementary regulations, some of which serve multiple goals.

The Secretary's requirement bases cage size on the weight of the primate, with special provisions for great apes, whereas the previous regulations merely required "sufficient space to allow each nonhuman primate to make normal postural adjustments with adequate freedom of movement." 56 Fed.Reg. at 6469. By hiking the requirements, the Secretary addressed an issue that Congress considered one of the central elements of a primate's psychological well-being. The statutory language speaks of minimum requirements for the "physical environment" of the primate, 7 U.S.C. § 2143(a)(2)(B), and the Conference Committee noted that "[t]he intent of standards with regard to promoting the psychological well-being of primates is to provide adequate space equipped with devices for exercise consistent with the primate's natural instincts and habits." H.R. Conf. Rep. No. 99-447, at 594 (1985).

Similarly, the regulations on environmental enrichment, special consideration of certain primates (infants, juveniles, etc.), and restraint devices all plainly provide engineering standards. 9 C.F.R. § 3.81(b)-(d). The facilities "must" provide environmental enrichment and special consideration for certain primates, id. § 3.81(b), (c), and they "must not" maintain primates in restraint devices "unless required for health reasons as determined by the attending veterinarian or by a research proposal approved by the Committee at research facilities," id. § 3.81(d). The regulation on restraints then makes clear that even where a veterinarian approves of restraints, there are still limits:

> *Maintenance under such restraint must be for the shortest period possible. In instances where long-term (more than 12 hours) restraint is required, the nonhuman primate must be provided the opportunity daily for unrestrained activity for at least one continuous hour during the period of restraint, unless continuous restraint is required by the research proposal approved by the Committee at research facilities. Id.*

Although research facilities may be allowed to restrain primates continuously, this limited exception is not offered to non-research handlers and is in keeping with the statute's bar on the Secretary from interfering with research. See 7 U.S.C. § 2143(a)(6)(A)(i)-(iii).

These "requirements" may be minimal but they are clearly mandatory. Jurnove argued, and the district court agreed, that this case begins and ends with the fact that the Secretary provided no engineering standards. ALDF, 943 F.Supp. at 59. But in fact he did.

It of course remains possible that the engineering and performance standards chosen by the Secretary are not enough to meet the mandate of "minimum requirements." We assess this issue under the familiar doctrine that if Congress has spoken to the precise question at issue, we must "give effect to the unambiguously expressed intent of Congress," but if Congress has not, we defer to a permissible agency construction of the statute. *Chevron U.S.A. Inc. v. NRDC*, 467 U.S. 837, 842-43, 104 S.Ct. 2778, 81 L.Ed.2d 694 (1984).

Here Jurnove's Exhibit A (and indeed his only serious example) is the Secretary's handling of primates' "social grouping." In 1989 the Secretary proposed to include a requirement of group housing for primates, saying that he intended to emphasize that

> *nonhuman primates must be grouped in a primary enclosure with compatible members of their species or with other nonhuman primate species, either in pairs, family groups, or other compatible social groupings, whenever possible and consistent with providing for the nonhuman primates' health, safety, and well-being, unless social grouping is prohibited by an animal care and use procedure and approved by the facility's Committee. 54 Fed.Reg. 10822, 10917 (1989).*

This proposal was based on evidence that "nonhuman primates are social beings in nature and require contact with other nonhuman primates for their psychological well-being," and that "[s]ocial deprivation is regarded by the scientific community as psychologically debilitating to social animals." Id.

The final rule, of course, refrained from imposing such a general group housing requirement. Jurnove (stating his case in the best light) would tie the agency to its 1989 proposal on two theories: He argues first under *Chevron* that because of this finding any interpretation of the statute not recognizing social grouping as one of the "minimum requirements" could not be a reasonable interpretation of the statute. And second he claims that the Secretary's decision was arbitrary and capricious because he failed to explain it adequately, in violation of the Administrative Procedure Act....

The Secretary's 1989 proposal was at odds with comments already in the record. For example, comments of the American Psychological Association had noted the wide disparities in social behavior among primates, with some forming large troops of 50 to 100 or more, others living in small groups of 10 to 20, and still others spending their lives in almost solitary isolation or as pairs in the wild. The 1989 proposal itself then generated new opposing comments, most notably from the University of Chicago, which pointed out that group housing "can significantly increase the incidence of trauma, the spread of upper respiratory and gastrointestinal diseases and more recently has been responsible for the outbreak of Simian Acquired Immune Deficiency Syndrome." Moreover, according to these comments, an image of nonhuman primates blissfully coexisting in groups is a substantially incomplete depiction of species-typical behavior. Again, as the University of Chicago informed the Secretary: "Even in compatible groups in no specific distress, species typical activities include threatening, chasing, fighting, wounding, hair-pulling, food competition, dominance challenges and reversals, and displacement of subordinate animals from food, water and shelter. Such activity can threaten the animals' health and well-being."

The Secretary took account of such comments, just as the designers of "notice and comment" rulemaking intended. He pointed to expressions of concern that "social grouping would endanger the animal's [sic] welfare by increasing noise and fighting," 55 Fed.Reg. at 33491, and to contentions that differences among species (there are, recall, over 240) required "discretion be used in deciding whether to employ group housing," id. Although it is true (as the district court noted and Jurnove here argues) that even in the final rulemaking the Secretary observed that "[i]n general, housing in groups promotes psychological well-being more assuredly than does individual housing," 943 F.Supp. at 60 (quoting 56 Fed.Reg. at 6472-73), that generality was obviously qualified by the remarks just quoted.

Thus the Secretary proposed a new regulation on social grouping:

> *The environment enhancement plan must include specific provisions to address the social needs of nonhuman primates of species known to exist in social groups in nature. Such specific provisions must be in accordance with currently accepted professional standards, as cited in appropriate professional journals or reference guides, and as directed by the attending veterinarian. 55 Fed.Reg. at 33525; 9 C.F.R. § 3.81(a) (final rule same).*

The regulation then offers "exceptions" to the social needs provision if the primate is vicious or debilitated, if it carries contagious diseases, or if its potential companions are not compatible. Id. § 3.81(a)(1)-(3). Even though social grouping is no longer formally mandated (facilities must only produce a "specific" plan for action that addresses "social needs"), the Secretary rightly argues that the enumeration of the "exceptions" makes social grouping the "norm."

Contrary to the view of the district court, the statute did not force the Secretary to require social grouping and then specify exceptions. See 943 F.Supp. at 60. To the contrary, we accord agencies broad deference in choosing the level of generality at which to articulate rules. . . . [Citations proving this point have been omitted.] Nothing in the statutory mandate required greater specificity. ... [Citations omitted.] [B]ecause the Secretary was reasonably concerned that more precise specification might cause harm, it was entirely reasonable under the statute for him to choose a relatively flexible standard.

The explanation that renders the Secretary's interpretation of the statute reasonable also serves to establish that the final rule was not arbitrary and capricious. Where "Congress delegates power to an agency to regulate on the borders of the unknown, courts cannot interfere with reasonable interpretations of equivocal evidence"; courts are most deferential of agency readings of scientific evidence. There is little question that the Secretary was forced to regulate "on the borders of the unknown" in setting the baseline of rights to "psychological well-being" for nonhuman primates, or at least how to "promote" their psychological well-being. In changing the design of the regulations, the Secretary pointed to substantial conflicting evidence on whether a stringent social grouping requirement was a good idea, 55 Fed.Reg. at 33491, and thus his final policy judgment on social grouping was reasonable.

Jurnove may well be correct that some of the Secretary's regulations may prove difficult to enforce, or even difficult to augment through subsequent "interpretation." But the requirements such as the ones on cage size and restraints are eminently enforceable, and the Secretary has begun to offer interpretations likely to assist both regulatees and enforcers. See Draft Policy on Environment Enhancement for Nonhuman Primates, 64 Fed.Reg. 38145 (1999).

[Discussion of two additional minor issues omitted.]

* * *

The decision of the district court is
Reversed.

APPENDIX E

TABLES AND GRAPHS

HUNTERS, BY CENSUS DIVISION, 1955–1985

Year	Number of Hunters (Millions)	Total U.S. Population (Millions)	Percent
1955	11.8	118.4	10.0%
1960	14.6	131.2	11.2%
1965	13.6	142.0	9.6%
1970	14.3	155.2	9.2%
1975	17.1	171.9	9.9%
1980	16.7	184.7	9.1%
1985	16.3	195.7	8.4%
1990	14.1	190	7%
1995	14.0	201	7%
2000	13.0	212	6%

U.S. population includes people twelve years and older.

Note: 1955 was the first year that the survey was conducted. The information is based on data from surveys conducted every five years, from 1955 to 2000. Those figures for 1990 and on were compiled differently and so should not be compared directly.

Source: 1991 National Survey of Fishing, Hunting, and Wildlife-Associated Recreation, U.S. Fish and Wildlife Service.

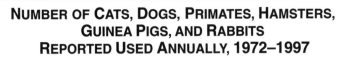

NUMBER OF CATS, DOGS, PRIMATES, HAMSTERS, GUINEA PIGS, AND RABBITS REPORTED USED ANNUALLY, 1972–1997

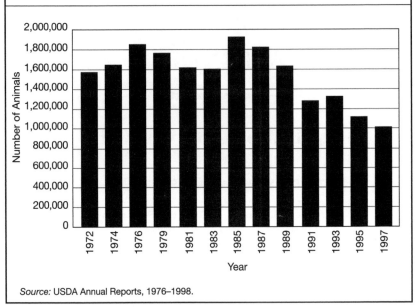

Source: USDA Annual Reports, 1976–1998.

NUMBER OF STATE FELONY CRUELTY LAWS, 1800–2001

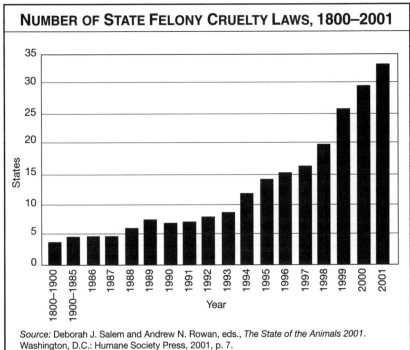

Source: Deborah J. Salem and Andrew N. Rowan, eds., *The State of the Animals 2001.* Washington, D.C.: Humane Society Press, 2001, p. 7.

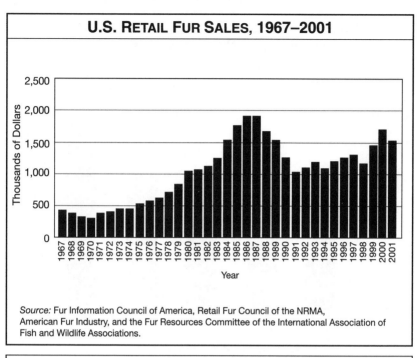

U.S. RETAIL FUR SALES, 1967–2001

Source: Fur Information Council of America, Retail Fur Council of the NRMA, American Fur Industry, and the Fur Resources Committee of the International Association of Fish and Wildlife Associations.

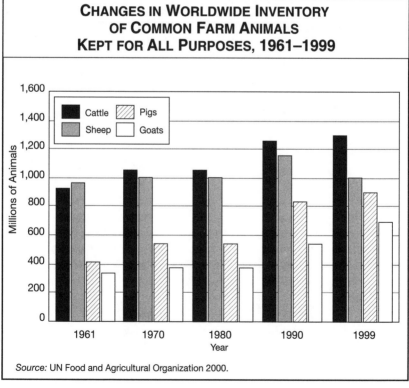

CHANGES IN WORLDWIDE INVENTORY OF COMMON FARM ANIMALS KEPT FOR ALL PURPOSES, 1961–1999

Source: UN Food and Agricultural Organization 2000.

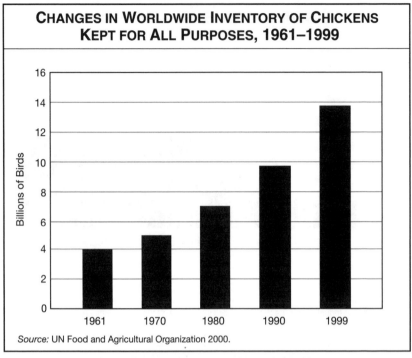

CHANGES IN WORLDWIDE INVENTORY OF CHICKENS KEPT FOR ALL PURPOSES, 1961–1999

Source: UN Food and Agricultural Organization 2000.

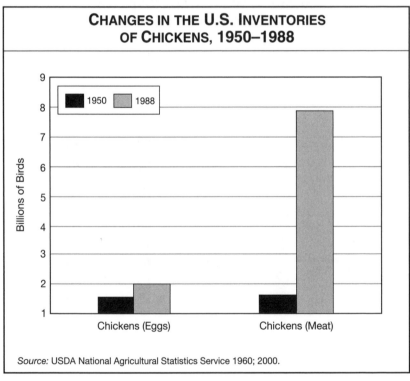

CHANGES IN THE U.S. INVENTORIES OF CHICKENS, 1950–1988

Source: USDA National Agricultural Statistics Service 1960; 2000.

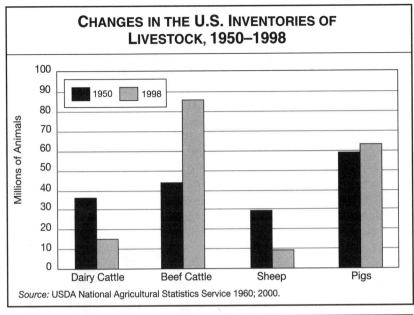

CHANGES IN THE U.S. INVENTORIES OF LIVESTOCK, 1950–1998

Source: USDA National Agricultural Statistics Service 1960; 2000.

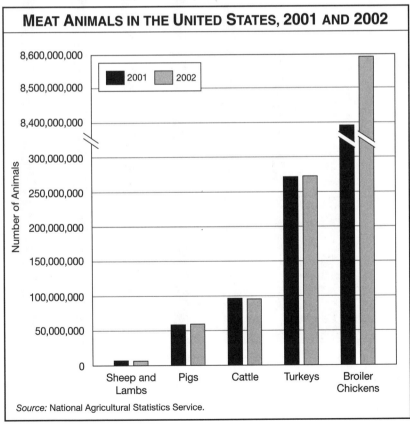

MEAT ANIMALS IN THE UNITED STATES, 2001 AND 2002

Source: National Agricultural Statistics Service.

283

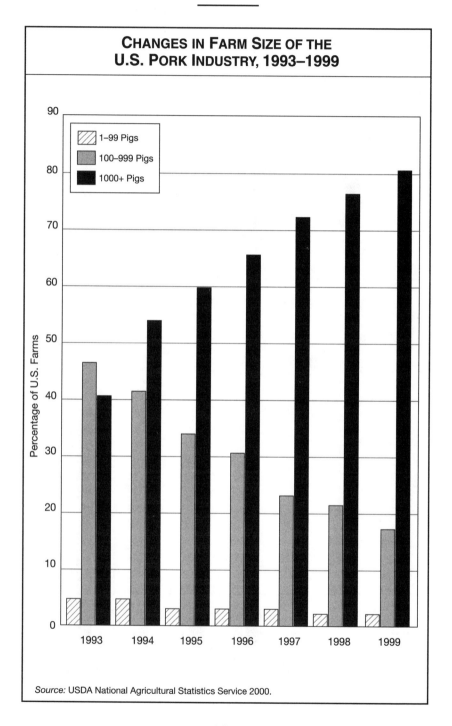

CHANGES IN FARM SIZE OF THE
U.S. PORK INDUSTRY, 1993–1999

1–99 Pigs
100–999 Pigs
1000+ Pigs

Percentage of U.S. Farms

Source: USDA National Agricultural Statistics Service 2000.

INDEX

Locators in **boldface** indicate main topics. Locators followed by *g* indicate glossary entries. Locators followed by *b* indicate biographical entries. Locators followed by *c* indicate chronology entries.

A

About.com 143–144

Administrative Procedures Act 82, 99

Advocates for Animals 217

Agricultural Research Service 34, 140, 222

agriculture, animals in **26–37**. *See also* intensive farming; specific kinds of animals

bibliography 182–189

diseases and disabilities 28–31, 36–37

laws and regulations affecting 26, 35–37, 74, 81

numbers 281–283

organizations 224–227

protests concerning 15, 32–34, 116*c*, 123

slaughtering 32, 36–37, **79–80**, 109*c*, 112*c*, 124, 131

transportation 35–37, 116*c*, 134

treatment and raising 16, 19, 22, **26–32**, 33–34, 68, 74

web sites 140

working animals, protection of 3, 20–21, 81, 107*c*, 124, 132

Agriculture, Department of (U.S.). *See* U.S. Department of Agriculture

Agriculture (Miscellaneous Provisions) Act 33, 110*c*

AIDS 42, 43, 102

Alaska 57–58

Alcmeon of Croton 106*c*, 121*b*

ALDF. *See* Animal Legal Defense Fund

ALF. *See* Animal Liberation Front

Alley Cat Allies 223

Alternatives to Animal Testing on the Web 140

American Animal Hospital Association 67

American Anti-Vivisection Society 25, 127, 228

American Demographics 68

American Horse Council 231

American Humane Association (AHA) 35, 38, 109*c*

American Kennel Club 22, 223

American Meat Institute 31, 224

American Medical Association 42

American Partnership for Pets 223

American Sanctuary Association 223–224

Americans for Medical Advancement 228

Americans for Medical Progress 140, 228

American Society for the Prevention of Cruelty to Animals (ASPCA) 14, 17, 21, 107*c*, 115*c*, 121, 128, 217–218

American Veterinary Medical Association 31, 67

American Zoo and Aquarium Association 56, 231–232

Animal Agriculture Alliance 224

Animal Aid 15, 218

Animal Alliance of Canada 218

Animal and Plant Health Inspection Service (APHIS) 36, 38, 39, 53, 75, 128*g*, 222

Animal Enterprise Protection Act 16, **80**, 115*c*, 128*g*

Animal Experiments Directive (EU) 42

Animal Fighting Venture Prohibition Act 51, 112*c*

285

Index

Index

289

Index

Hunt Saboteurs Association
65, 110*c*, 111*c*, 235
Hunt v. United States 58,
109*c*

I

IACUC. *See* Institutional
Animal Care and Use
Committees
ICCVAM. *See* Interagency
Coordinating Committee
on the Validation of
Alternative Methods
Ill Treatment of Horses
and Cattle Bill 20, 132
Improved Standards for
Laboratory Animals Act
40, 75–76
Incurably Ill for Animal
Research 229
In Defense of Animals 220
Indonesia 133
InfoTrac 148
Institute for Animal Health
226
Institute for Animals and
Society 220–221
Institute for Behavioral
Research 39, 89–90,
126
Institute for Laboratory
Animal Research 229
Institute of Laboratory
Animal Sciences (Zurich)
49
Institute of Medicine 42
Institutional Animal Care
and Use Committees
(IACUCs) 40, 48, 76, 91,
113*c*, 131*g*
intensive farming **26–34**,
64, 68, 109*c*, 110*c*, 123,
131–132*g*
    advantages 27, 31
    antibiotic use in 29
    defense of 19, 31, 33
    hormone use in 29, 30
    human health, effects
        on 29–31, 33

protests against 32–34
regulation 32–33, 110*c*
Interagency Coordinating
Committee on the
Validation of Alternative
Methods (ICCVAM) 48,
115*c*, 118*c*, 229–230
Interior, Department of
(U.S.). *See* U.S.
Department of Interior
International Association of
Fish and Wildlife
Agencies 235–236
International Fund for
Animal Welfare 126, 236
International Institute for
Animal Law 151, 221
International Primate
Protection League
90–91, 236
*International Primate
Protection League v.
Institute for Behavioral
Research* **89–92**
International Society for
Animal Rights 139
International Wildlife
Coalition 236
In the Company of Animals
(James Serpell) 19
Iovino, Shelli Lyn 96–97
Irwin, Paul G. 66
Izaak Walton League 236

J

Jane Goodall Institute 221
Japan 58, 108*c*
Jarboe, James 16
Jasper, James 13
Jensen, Patricia 25
Jewish Defense League 16
Johns Hopkins University
    Alternatives to Animal
        Testing on the Web
        140
    Center for Alternatives
        to Animal Testing 230
Johnson, Lyndon 110*c*
Jones, Edith L. 103

Jones, Grant 55, 111*c*,
124*b*, 132
Jones v. Butz 80, 112*c*
*Journal of the American
Medical Association* 41
Judeo-Christian tradition,
attitude to animals 4
Jurnove, Marc 11, 55,
97–100, 117–118*c*, 124*b*
Justice Department (animal
rights group) 16, 117*c*

K

Kent, University of 7
Kerasote, Ted 62
Kleppe v. New Mexico 58,
112*c*
kosher slaughter 36, 80,
112*c*, 131, 132*g*
Kraft, Jonathan 54

L

Laboratory Animal Welfare
Act (LAWA) 38, 75, 76,
110*c*, 111*c*
Lacey Act 58, 59, 108*c*,
132*g*
landscape immersion 55,
111*c*, 124, 132*g*
LAWA. *See* Laboratory
Animal Welfare Act
laws and regulations
affecting animals 12,
74–81, 149–150. *See also*
cruelty to animals, laws
against; *names of specific
laws*.
LD50 test 44–46, 48, 109*c*,
132*g*
League Against Cruel
Sports 65, 109*c*, 110*c*,
236–237
Leahy, Michael P. T. 7
Legal Information Institute
151
legal personhood 11–12,
84, 127, 132*g*
legal research **149–152**
legal rights of animals
9–12, 68, 121, 123

Index

legal standing 9, 132*g*
legislation, pending, finding 150
Lewis and Clark College 11
Lexis 151
Library of Congress 147, 150
Life 38, 110*c*
Little Tennessee River 85, 110*c*, 112*c*
Liverpool Society for Preventing Wanton Cruelty to Brute Animals 21, 107*c*
Long Island Game Park Farm and Zoo 96–98, 100
Lujan v. Defenders of Wildlife 10, 98, 115*c*, 134
Lyman, Howard 30, 102–104, 117*c*, 124*b*, 127

M
"mad cow disease." *See* bovine spongiform encephalopathy
Mallalieu, Anne 61
Man in Nature 139
Mann, Keith 17
Marine Mammal Protection Act 59, 76
Martin Act 20–21, 26, 107*c*, 132*g*
Martin, Richard 20, 124*b*
Mary Kay Cosmetics 45, 117*c*
Massachusetts Bay Colony 81, 107*c*, 127
Massachusetts Society for Prevention of Cruelty to Animals 35
mastitis 29, 30, 132*g*. *See also* cattle, dairy
Matfield, Mark 19
McBurnett, Sara 104–105, 125*b*
McDonald's 32, 34, 36, 104, 116*c*, 118–119*c*

"McLibel case" 34, 104, 116*c*
meat animals in the United States, 2001 and 2002 (graph) 283
meat eating 109*c*. *See also* agriculture, animals in; *names of specific meat animals*
and hunting 62, 64
campaigns against 15, 33–35
health risks of 14, 30–31, 102
moral objections to 6, 14–15
Meat Inspection Act 112*c*
media web sites 141–142
medical experimentation on animals. *See* scientific experiments on animals
Michigan State University 17
Migratory Bird Hunting Stamp. *See* duck stamp
Migratory Bird Treaty Act 58, 59, 108*c*, 132*g*
milk industry 15, 118*c*. *See also* cattle, dairy
Mineral King Valley 82–85
Misplaced Compassion (Ward Clark) 94
molting, forced 27, 32, 33, 131*g*. *See also* chickens, egg-laying
Monash University 13
Morrison, Adrian 40, 43, 47, 91, 125*b*
Morton, Rogers 10, 82, 84
Mothers Against Drunk Driving 15, 118*c*
Munro, Lyle 13–15, 18, 20, 37
Murphy, Kevin 105

N
National Animal Control Association 224

National Animal Interest Alliance 139, 221
National Anti-Vivisection Society 230
National Association for Biomedical Research 18, 25, 41, 48, 126, 230
National Association of Biology Teachers 47
National Cattlemen's Beef Association 36, 226
National Center for Animal Law 221
National Council of Chain Restaurants 34, 119*c*
National Council on Pet Population Study and Policy 139, 224
National Dairy Council 226
National Environmental Policy Act 85
National Farmers' Union 226–227
National Geographic 57
National Greyhound Association 232
National Institute for Animal Agriculture 227
National Institutes of Health (NIH) 41, 48, 89–91, 115*c*, 123
National Institute of Mental Health 42, 123
Office of Laboratory Animal Welfare 140, 230
National Institutes of Health Revitalization Act 48, 115*c*
National Marine Fisheries Service 78
National Pork Producers Council 227
National Research Council 29
National Science Teachers Association 47
National Society for Medical Research 38

293

Index

Index